THE LAST HERO

A Biography
of Gary Cooper

Books by Larry Swindell

THE LAST HERO: A BIOGRAPHY OF GARY COOPER

SCREWBALL: THE LIFE OF CAROLE LOMBARD

BODY AND SOUL: THE STORY OF JOHN GARFIELD

SPENCER TRACY: A BIOGRAPHY

THE LAST HERO

A Biography of Gary Cooper

LARRY SWINDELL

B
C 78 ℛ

Doubleday & Company, Inc.
GARDEN CITY, NEW YORK
1980

mc

PICTURE ACKNOWLEDGMENTS

In the insert of personal photographs:

The picture of Gary Cooper with his brother is from United Press International, Inc.

The photo of Cooper with his parents, Charles and Alice, is from Penguin Photo.

The photo of Cooper with Ernest Hemingway is from Bettmann Archives.

Pictures of Cooper with the chimpanzee Tolucca, with Mary Pickford, and with Patrick Hepburn are from Down Memory Lane in Santa Monica, California.

Pictures of Cooper with his dog, and working on a rifle at his home are from Larry Edmunds Book Store in Hollywood, California.

The production shot of *The Wedding Night* is from the collection of the Museum of Modern Art Film Library in New York City.

All other personal photographs are used through the courtesy of the Philadelphia *Inquirer* or are from private collections, including the author's.

In the insert of film stills:

All representations are from the stills collection of the Museum of Modern Art Film Library in New York City, with two exceptions: the still for *Souls at Sea* is from the Philadelphia *Inquirer*, and the still for *The Cowboy and the Lady* is from the author's collection.

ISBN: 0-385-14316-8
Library of Congress Catalog Card Number 78-22800

This book is dedicated with love to my mother,
Lucille Howard Swindell
. . . she was always ready to see one of his pictures

AUTHOR'S NOTE

Ostensibly this biography of Gary Cooper is a three-year project but it incorporates "research" conducted sometimes innocently over a period of more than thirty years. For example, I had the privilege of watching and listening to Ernst Lubitsch as he held court following a 1946 screening of *Design for Living*. I was an impressionable teen-ager then, and remembered vividly things Lubitsch said about Gary Cooper as a great screen actor.

This endeavor has also been nourished by research accomplished for my earlier biographies of Spencer Tracy, John Garfield, and Carole Lombard. Because all valid biography is also history, I came to appreciate Gary Cooper as an ideal subject for a professional biography because of the extraordinary time span of his career in films. He became an important player when the movies were still silent. He developed into one of the dominant stars during the Golden Age of the great studios. Later he retained his high standing during an era of predominantly independent production, when like other leading stars he was sometimes his own producer.

As it synthesizes the depositions of many of Gary Cooper's professional co-workers, such a book also becomes a work of criticism to some uncertain degree. Most individual contributions will be apparent, and I am grateful to everyone who helped, including those few who have requested anonymity. I was fortunate to have the benefit of persons more immediately deceased than Ernst Lubitsch, including Jack Oakie, William Wellman, and Nunnally Johnson. I should also indicate that Frank Capra has been more vital in defining Gary Cooper's screen substance for me than might be apparent here, or than he might realize.

I must thank others whose contributions could never be apparent: Charlotte and Morris Green; Joan and Vince LaCorte; Richard Altman; Richard DeNeut; James Wasson; Joseph DiMarino; and Frank Glackin. I am grateful once again to Paul Myers's staff of the Theatre Collection of the New York Public Library and particularly to Rod Bladel, who is a great encourager. Thanks, too, to the staff of the Margaret Herrick Library of the Academy of Motion Picture Arts and Sciences; to the Library of Congress, the best resource for viewing old Gary Cooper films; the Museum of Modern Art and particularly Mary Corliss, keeper of the film stills; the Montana State Historical Society; William Deminoff and the office of college relations at Grinnell College; and to my discerning editor Lisa Drew and her very able assistant Mary Trone.

I must thank my daughters Julie, Susan, and Wendy and sons Tod and Mark for their help or just for their patience; and most of all I am grateful once again for the needling encouragement of my wife Ellie, who has become a magnificent research associate.

Richboro, Pennsylvania
October 15, 1979

CONTENTS

On April 17, 1961, just about everyone in America suddenly realized that Gary Cooper was dying.

It wasn't planned, for only a few knew of Cooper's terminal cancer, and James Stewart was ashamed of himself for giving it away by breaking down.

Accepting a special Academy Award for Cooper for his over-all contribution to the movies, Stewart said, "We're all very proud of you, Coop . . ."

He was shaking, tears forming, voice breaking.

". . . all of us are . . . terribly proud."

When Gary Cooper died less than four weeks later, few persons in the world of films or in any avenue of public life had been so deeply, so genuinely mourned. Many screen stars have been idolized, and many others have been admired. Gary Cooper was idolized and admired but he was also beloved, as perhaps no other contemporary screen figure was beloved.

He was beloved by many for the person they knew or believed him to be, but he was beloved by many others for whom Gary Cooper was entirely defined by his screen projection. He was an encouragingly heroic image in an optimistic era of hero worship. He belongs to a very recent yet thoroughly bygone American era, such as many of our citizens yearn for.

Thought of Gary Cooper conjures a great era of the movies when they were part of a national unity that now somehow eludes us. He had a great career; and some would say, a great life. Like Gary Cooper himself, it was a life remarkably ordinary and spectacular.

This is a story of the movies, and it is Gary Cooper's story.

THE LAST HERO

A Biography of Gary Cooper

1

☆ ☆ ☆

☆ ☆ ☆

BORN TO THE WEST

IT ALWAYS SEEMED just right that he had been christened Frank James Cooper—a name solidly American, seducing the imagination with flickering visions of the old, wild West. Yet the parents who named him intended no honor to the lore of outlaws; nor were Charles and Alice Cooper quite the people you expected to find in turn-of-the-century Montana. Both were English, and obtained American citizenship only months before their younger son was born. When Gary Cooper began to make his first distinct impression in motion pictures, his studio publicists promoted "a personality that combines Western affability with British reserve." Later, when he was more knowingly marketed as an all-American hero, the British heritage was played down. Yet the Gary Cooper personality was the curious resolution of a conflict between heredity and environment, and he also embodied the contradictions of his parents' relationship.

To the casual observer, Charles and Alice Cooper were a couple ideally matched, who in a later era could have been brought together by a computerized dating service. Yet they could hardly have been more different in their personal drives, and although they talked lightly about their own proof that "opposites attract," they were natural antagonists. This was not easily seen, for a high diplomacy was exercised even in their private relationship. Gary Cooper meant it when he said, often, that "I look to my parents as the supreme example of wedded happiness." It was more easily seen that Charles and Alice Cooper loved each other very much.

His birthplace, too, was certainly appropriate: Helena, the capital city of Montana but a small town after all, alternately proud and ashamed of its raucous heritage as Last Chance Gulch. Gary Cooper personified the contradictions that shaped the character of the town in which he spent most of his childhood and youth. The screen would frequently reveal him as a shy cowpoke hungering for a young lady as beautiful as she was aristocratic, and on such occasions he was a human metaphor for Helena, Montana— once a brawler and still not quite tame, but coveting grace and decorum.

He was born there during an unseasonable heat wave on May 7, 1901. The Coopers' older son, Arthur, was then six. Alice Cooper, risking a pregnancy that doctors feared might kill her, had hoped desperately that her second and surely her last child would be a girl. She rationalized her disappointment by telling her husband that "It's better to have another boy if we must go on living in this dreadful place. It would be tragic to have to raise a little girl in Montana."

Charles always loved Montana and his wife always hated it. That was the principal conflict that lay beneath their outwardly placid marriage. Both sons, but the younger one especially, became pawns in a marital struggle over where the family should live. That Charles Cooper and Alice Brazier could have found one another in Helena was hardly logical; and when they met for the first time, Alice was anxious to get out of Helena as soon as it could be arranged. Charles, though, was quietly determined from the start to keep her there.

Helena was still a very young town then, but a lot of high adventure had been crammed into its brief history. And gold started it all.

In 1848 a carpenter named James Marshall discovered gold in a stream beneath a sawmill he was building at the California settlement of Coloma, near Sutter's Fort and what is now the city of Sacramento. Marshall's find incited the nation's first great gold rush, and the saga of the Forty-niners became a staple of American folklore. Gold was a powerful impetus for the winning and building of the West. Prospecting scenes shifted often, and for every San Francisco that flourished, scores of once-optimistic settlements became ghost towns. Not even the tragic resolution of the 1859 Pikes Peak gold rush could dissuade many prospectors, and the great Northwest absorbed new hordes of them while the Civil War raged far to the east. When word spread of a strike at the little town of Bannack, the gold-seekers converged on the previously virgin Montana territory. The yield at Bannack was less prodigious than expected, and southern Montana soon was pockmarked by scores of ragged, unproductive mining camps. In 1864 four discouraged prospectors moved northward from the Bannack area toward the Missouri River, to work the previously untested Prickly Pear Valley. They were near starvation in July when they took their "last chance" and hit pay dirt.

When news of their find circulated, other mining towns were abandoned and the town of Last Chance Gulch sprang up almost overnight. It was an all-male enterprise for only a matter of days, and what happened to the new settlement could have provided the story line for a Gary Cooper Western. Soon the whores drifted in from other mining towns that had run their course. Some of the opportunistic merchants brought their wives. A wagon train bound for Idaho, and transporting a score of women seeking husbands, made its terminal stop at Helena instead. With the women came the churches and the schools; and before the first chill of autumn, the town had been renamed Helena and had acquired a civilized veneer. Helena survived despite—or because of—its customary application of lynch law. The town was notorious for its imposing "hanging tree," until an enraged parson cut it down in 1870. He was a member of the English clique whose influence was beginning to be felt.

Helena's first inhabitants were mostly itinerant Americans who tended to move on. A clutch of German immigrants took root there, but remained rather apart during the early years. Then a party of English adventurers came in, and their more righteous members banded with the Germans to clean up the wicked, violence-prone town. The English in particular advocated government by formal law, and succeeded somewhat shakily in attaining it. A distinct English community began to thrive in Helena, and more Britons were coaxed to emigrate to the land of the Big Sky. When Helena was incorporated as a city in 1881, its culture favorably reflected both the English and German influences; and when Montana achieved statehood in 1889, Helena was selected as its capital, despite not being centrally located, because it was considered the most genteel small city in the Northwest. The Helena dialect, strikingly dissimilar from most Montana speech, was slow, deliberate, musical. The English influence produced an accent that was unflinty but western nonetheless, and that would distinguish many a Gary Cooper movie in a later period.

In that same year of Montana statehood, Charles Cooper arrived in Helena. He had been born in Bedfordshire, in the south Midlands of England, where the Coopers, of the rising middle class, had been farmers through many generations. The gradual attainment of wheat-growing prosperity had made it possible for Charles Cooper's parents also to maintain a town house in the borough of Dunstable. There Charles attended the prestigious public school. As an exemplary scholar, he was encouraged to aim for the legal profession. Charles, though, was distracted by the idea of America, as many young Englishmen were. His older brother, Walter Cooper, planned a trip to America in hope of establishing himself in a business there. Charles prevailed upon his parents to permit him to accompany Walter. The brothers arrived in Boston harbor in 1885, when Charles was nineteen. Very soon afterward, he bade farewell to brother Walter and struck out on his own, for the Far West was the America that owned his imagination.

Charles Cooper was inclined toward solitude. His passion was the open land. He worked on a wheat farm in Nebraska and made application to homestead there. Then he decided that what he truly wanted to do was raise cattle, and he moved farther west. His family implored him to return to England and did not suspect the extent to which Charles was captivated by the American West. He loved its mountains and streams and its festival of wild life, and above all its sweet air. A true romantic, he was prepared to fail and be happy. But he was destined to succeed.

During the railroad boom of the eighties, the Northern Pacific had routed through Helena. Charles had taken a clerical job with the railroad and was sent to Helena. Immediately assimilated by the town's substantial English community, he began to sense that a legal practice could thrive within it. So while working nights in the Northern Pacific roundhouse, he "read for the law" by day in the office of a Helena attorney. By 1893 he was regarded as a local expert on the vagaries of the law, and that was when Alice Brazier came to him, seeking his legal advice.

She was a frightened twenty-year-old who wanted to go home to England. She was from Gillingham, in the graceful meadow-lands of Kent, southeast of London. The Braziers, transplanted from France a few generations earlier, were a modestly prosperous family, merchants by tradition. Alice was everyone's pet: a vivacious beauty who delighted in being pampered. She was especially close to her brother Alfred, whose own adventurous streak sent him to America in 1891. In the summer of the following year, Alfred offered to pay his sister's passage to America and her rail fare across almost the entire continental width if she would visit him in Montana, where he was employed. So Alice sailed the Atlantic and then toured the eastern seaboard before making the five-day train trip to Helena.

America disappointed her even before she arrived in Montana. In England she had listened vaguely to tales of quickly attained wealth, so she anticipated cities of new splendor. But she found the landscapes glimpsed from her train less beguiling than those of her homeland. She also regarded New York as a poor substitute for London, which she had visited often; and on its own scale, she rated Helena as inferior to Gillingham. Despite her characteristic exuberance, Alice Brazier nurtured all the appointments of an earnest snob. She was acutely conscious of breeding, and harbored fixed Victorian notions of propriety. While the raffish miners and cowboys captivated many damsels of the local English colony as exotics, Alice viewed them as barbarians.

Alfred Brazier satisfied his sister's innate coquetry by introducing her to bachelors of his acquaintance who were sufficiently courtly, and certified English. At an Episcopalian social, he introduced her to Charles Cooper. He was somewhat more mature than the youths who served rather stiffly as her Montana escorts. She continued to notice Charles at functions they attended; and while they seldom exchanged words, she was confident of his interest in her. What brought them together at last was the Panic of '93.

In the late 1870s silver had supplanted gold as the principal mining concern of the Northwest. It was silver, not gold, on which Helena's economic foundation was built. It was silver that built Helena's fabled Millionaire's Row. But the crash of 1893, coming in the wake of decreased production in the mines, brought about the repeal of the Sherman Silver Purchase Act. The silver boom collapsed completely—the sure oracle of a depression for such mining centers as Helena. Some local millionaires were wiped out instantly. In a bid for survival, the four Helena banks froze their assets. Alice Brazier had deposited all of her capital into one of the banks to cover the expense of her return to England. Painfully homesick and bored by Helena after almost a year there, she was preparing for her departure when the panic struck. The bank's actions left her without funds and fearful of a total loss. Someone told her to get advice from Charles Cooper, who knew all about banking laws.

Gratified to meet Alice for something more than an awkward nod, Charles put her at ease with a promise to retrieve all her money; but meanwhile, they could get to know one another better. There was a brief, intense courtship, followed by an even shorter period of formal engagement; and they were married in Helena toward the end of 1893. The advent of romance altered Alice's disposition toward Montana, if only briefly, and she was a merry bride. She began her new life in an unnecessarily large frame house that Charles obtained during the panic, when the bottom fell out of Helena real estate values. He expected his wife to adjust and live contentedly in the American West. Alice, on the other hand, relied on her ability to charm and coax her bridegroom into returning eventually to England, perhaps to become a barrister there someday. Although Charles still worked for the railroad, he had initiated a small legal practice before their marriage, and later he liked to say that he had married his first client.

Charles was twenty-seven when they married, and Alice had just turned twenty-one. Earlier she had dallied with a succession of ardent suitors, including a young medical student in Kent who had expected her to return and marry him. Charles, however, was not known to have revealed an interest in any woman prior to Alice, and was a rumored celibate. Certainly he was believed never to have patronized Helena's lively whorehouse. Yet other young women had sought his favor, and found him most attractive: a quiet, steady sort whose firm jaw seemed to imply strength of character. He was stockily built and of only average height; Alice was very nearly as tall as he. She was an animated contrast to her husband, and her beauty was enhanced by a feature Gary Cooper would inherit from her: eyes of soft azure—the very color, Charles said, of Montana's big blue sky.

Their first son was born in 1895. Arthur was a healthy baby but Alice experienced a difficult delivery, and was told that future childbearing would be hazardous for her. Yet she continued to hope for a daughter—a child that would truly be hers, as Arthur surely belonged to Charles. The Coopers were both products of an England that still honored the ancient family law of primogeniture. The custom did not begin and end with the royal family but was practiced by all the responsible classes; or if not practiced, was obeyed more subtly, in the reverence bestowed upon first-born sons. If the eldest son did not inherit the title and all claims to inheritance (plus the implied responsibility to provide for, or administer to, his siblings), he could expect to be the one given the best education, or perhaps a partnership in the family firm. Even when such advantages were denied the oldest male heir, the custom of many generations assured an extraordinary closeness between an English father and his first son. That a special relationship must exist between them was accepted by all members of the family.

In the Cooper household, Alice neither doubted nor objected to her husband's parental priority. Charles was an affectionate father, although not given to smothering Arthur with attention. But he assumed responsibilities toward his son that would usually be assigned to the mother—in America, anyway, and certainly in a later generation. He selected the clothing that was purchased for Arthur to wear, as Alice expected him to. So perhaps it was fitting that Arthur bore a remarkable physical resemblance to his father, appearing to have inherited none of Alice's features.

In 1896 Charles Cooper quit the railroad to become clerk of Helena's municipal court. A few years later he was the choice of a retiring judge to be his successor on the bench. Then it came to light that Charles was still a British subject, so he did not become a candidate. That disappointed Alice, who savored the prestige and the likelihood of improved fortune a judgeship could give to their family. Sensing that political opportunity would come to her husband with U.S. citizenship, she urged him to seek papers; and finally, they made application together. Yet the knowledge that England was slipping away from her, perhaps forever, reawakened her dissatisfaction. Now she feared that in Helena, Arthur would be vulnerable to such unsavory influences as she did not believe existed in England. Long before Arthur was ready to begin his schooling, Alice insinuated the need to have him educated in England. Charles's preference was that Arthur be as American as possible. He vetoed the idea of a "nanny," and told Alice that in any event, they could not afford to have Arthur educated abroad.

At Helena's Fourth of July celebration in 1900, Alice had her fortune told by an old Indian woman, who said that Alice would bear a second child before another year passed. When Alice complained that she could have no more children, the woman assured her that there would be no difficulty with the birth, and that the baby would be healthy. Furthermore, it would be a beautiful girl. Later Alice joked about the soothsaying in chatter with friends over tea. But soon afterward her pregnancy was confirmed, and Alice was certain that she would bear a daughter in the spring. The thought kept her cheerful throughout the coldest winter of her Montana experience, and her optimism eased her husband's concern over her condition.

Alice came through nicely when the baby arrived on schedule. Charles was supremely amused by the advent of a second son, against his wife's certainty of a daughter, and Arthur was delighted to have a brother. Alice's nagging disappointment was that she had made and collected a lot of baby clothes that ideally would advertise a little girl. She decided that Frank James Cooper would look just fine in them anyway.

His first five years passed without memorable incident. Frank was an infant of especially pleasant disposition, and he was easily amused. He cried with cunning when his doting mother was endeavoring to give him every satisfaction, but was not inclined to cry in the presence of his stern father. He adored the older brother whose attention he sought, but who generally ignored him. When Frank could no longer be displayed in dresses, he wore frilly boy's clothes selected not by Charles, but by Alice. Frank Cooper was Little Lord Fauntleroy in black velvet and lace collar, although his light brown curls were shorn just after his third birthday.

He would have no lasting recollection of the first house he lived in, or the names of any of his earliest playmates. Usually they were the children of Alice's genteel friends, which meant they were *clean* children, though surely not so clean as Frank. Twice daily he was scrubbed thoroughly, although he seldom had opportunity to become really dirty. Frank's cleanliness became a mild obsession with his mother, who may have supposed that her son was covered by a quality of Montana that soap and water perhaps could purge. Whatever he thought of this, he would grow up with a revulsion toward filth.

Surely he was a mama's boy during his earliest years, and he returned Alice's undue attention with demonstrative affection. He worshiped his mother despite her apparent general refusal to let him play with other boys. Gary Cooper would recall that all of his first friends seemed to be girls, and that dolls were the dominant properties of their activity. He doubted that he had dolls of his own, and remembered that his favorite toy had been a horse-drawn milk wagon, cast in iron. His first ambition was to become a milkman, and he played at delivering milk to the little girls, who then fed their dollies.

Contrary to a rumor likely of fan-magazine origin that circulated long afterward, a little girl named Myrna Williams was not one of his childhood playmates. She, too, would become a famous and well-liked movie star, by name of Myrna Loy. The Coopers were acquainted with the Williams family, and Myrna indeed was born in Helena and lived there for several years. But Frank Cooper was four years older than Myrna Williams, and in their later parallel fame each would claim not to remember the other from their days in Helena.

Gary Cooper said his first vivid memory was the move to the ranch in the summer of 1906, after he had turned five.

For several years Charles Cooper had coveted a large cattle ranch located about fifty miles north of Helena. The Northern Pacific had acquired the six-hundred-acre spread by a grant in 1889, the year of Montana statehood. The ranch, called the Seven-Bar-Nine, had flourished for a time but had fallen into disarray—its buildings deteriorating, its beef production erratic, and its general decline attributed to the absence of concerned management. Cattle rustlers were a chronic problem. Charles Cooper believed he could put the ranch on a paying basis once more. By agreeing to assume all its debts, he persuaded the railroad directors to give him full title to the ranch for less than four thousand dollars.

Dealing with the railroad may have been easier than convincing Alice that she wanted to be a ranch wife. She respected Charles's long-held wish to be a cattleman, and she viewed the property as a wise long-term investment. But she fretted about taxes that would amount annually to about thirty cents an acre—applied, though, only to land under cultivation. About a hundred acres were planted in wheat, oats, and hay, and there was a large potato field. Otherwise the ranch was a vast sloping meadow framed by imposing mountains, and the Missouri River was its northern boundary. Some modest foothills were part of the ranch proper, and the flat-faced Eagle Rock Mountain provided a picturesque backdrop. There was more than enough lush grassland for a cattle population that had dwindled to two hundred head, and Charles Cooper's first objective was to increase the ranch's beef production. Alice's attention would be to the ranch house itself, which she knew was in desperate need of a woman's touch.

When the Coopers left Helena for the ranch, Arthur rode with his father and a couple of ranch hands in a wagon loaded with the family furnishings and driven by a team of horses. Alice and little Frank watched them leave before dawn. In the afternoon, mother and son boarded a northbound train that rode a single track from Helena to Great Falls. The line was routed over a corner of Seven-Bar-Nine land, and the train made a stop to discharge Alice and Frank within a mile of the ranch house. They were met by one of the cowboys, who was driving a single-seated buckboard. Gary Cooper would retain memory of riding to the ranch house for the first time, seated on the flat bed behind the driver and Alice. There were more cowboys on hand to greet them when they arrived at the house. There was also a scattering of small, curious children, most of whom appeared to be Indians.

"My mother was received as a queen," Gary Cooper recalled, "and I was probably treated like a little prince. We were taken inside a mostly empty house, and had to wait several hours for my father to arrive with the furniture, bedding, and just about everything we had. That would have been in the summertime when the days were long, but it was after dark when the wagon and horses finally pulled in. By then I'd probably decided I liked living out in the country."

For one who had been guarded so closely by his mother for five years, Frank James Cooper was now almost inexplicably free, as if suddenly weaned. His mother was busily painting and redecorating the house, or conferring with his father about the priorities of ranch management. Arthur went wherever his father went; and Frank, left alone, began to form friendships with the scruffy small children who lived in shacks scattered around the ranch lands. Not all of the people who lived at the Seven-Bar-Nine seemed to belong there. A woman with several small children and no apparent income had wandered onto the ranch after her husband deserted or disappeared, and occupied an abandoned cabin there. The Coopers gave the woman employment as a housemaid, with the added responsibility to clean the bunkhouse occupied by the untidy bachelor cowboys. Charles also gave paying jobs to some of the Indian men who had been only docile observers of the ranch activity.

Alice wanted the house to have a name, so she called it Sunnyside because it was on the sunny side of the river. She never called the ranch the Seven-Bar-Nine, but the cowboys never called it anything else. They were a grimy lot, although Alice's presence in the main house had the effect of transforming some of them, who now found new excuses to come to the house. Ostensibly they had business to discuss with Mr. Cooper, but they were lured by the beauty of the ranch mistress in whose presence they were uncharacteristically well spruced.

The Coopers had been at the ranch less than a month when disaster struck. The Hauser Dam, located about forty miles upstream, collapsed without warning, sending a torrent of river water into the ranch grounds. The Coopers were roused from their sleep by the cowboys, who expected the flood to carry the ranch house with it. Gary Cooper would recall being bundled into a buggy and driven to the safety of a shack in the foothills. In the morning the Coopers were relieved to know their house was spared: the flood waters had stopped practically at the doorstep. New crops and much good grazing land were destroyed, and millions of pebbles from the river bed were washed onto the turf. This was only the first of many setbacks in Charles Cooper's long, failing effort to make the Seven-Bar-Nine sufficiently profitable to erase its debts. Most new owners would have been devastated, but both Charles and Alice revealed typical British resiliency toward bad luck. Determined to give it another try, they were put to a cruel test. In September and October hard rains fell for thirty-eight successive days. The entire ranch became a quagmire. It was counted a miracle that no cattle were lost. Alice struggled to manage meals from dwindling supplies, and Charles often was pressed to wallow in a muck of mud and gravel and water to fetch food from the nearest store, several miles away.

There was no school within ten miles, so Charles decided to establish a school right on his ranch. The daughter of a friend from his railroad days in Helena came up to live at Sunnyside and to teach the elementary grades in a log cabin by the ruined potato field. Arthur Cooper was the oldest of perhaps a dozen pupils, some of whom were Indians. The five-year-old Frank was not enrolled, but during school term he spent most of his time at the schoolhouse, anyway. Later, when he was expected to attend, he was much less reliable.

In the spring Charles managed to clear most of his land of flood debris. New crops were planted, and optimism for the Seven-Bar-Nine again seemed in order. Gary Cooper would say in later years that "My father poured his heart and all his money into his ranch, but never got much of it back because he had no business sense." But Charles had a talent for organizing the ranch labor, so that activities of the Seven-Bar-Nine could proceed smoothly despite his increased absence. He was in growing de-

mand as an attorney in Helena and throughout southwestern
Montana, and his legal fees enabled him to continue improving
the ranch.

As the mistress of Sunnyside, Alice exhibited more fortitude
than patience. Gary Cooper would often invoke the image of his
mother "out chopping wood at twenty below zero." If his memories of the Montana ranch were reliable, it was *always* twenty
below zero. The winters, though, truly were vivid and mean, and
finally Alice could take no more of it. At the height of a blizzard
during their second winter at the ranch, she trudged through the
snow with Arthur and Frank to the railroad tracks to flag the
southbound train. They stayed with friends in Helena until
Charles joined them; and after deciding that henceforth they
would spend the winter months in Helena, they occupied a small
house in town that Charles already owned.

Frank Cooper was regarded as an agreeable, emotionally tran-
quil child by all who knew him. Yet he was miserable whenever
the family returned to Helena to pass the winter. Having started
his schooling on his parents' own land had given him special status among his handful of schoolmates. Attending classes in Helena among several hundred pupils was a more formal obligation
and much less enjoyable for him. There was also more homework,
to which his response certified that he was no scholar. If he made
new friends, he would only be saying good-by to them soon afterward when the Coopers returned to the ranch. In Helena he also
felt himself encumbered by supervision. His mother, perhaps reacting to a social pressure she overrated, would restrict his activities and watch him closely. So he was exhilarated whenever spring
sent him back to the Seven-Bar-Nine.

Already he was a committed outdoorsman. He liked the sheer
spaciousness of the ranch, and the little animals that were everywhere scampering into the wild. He liked his scruffy Indian
friends, and the cowboys whose mascot he had become. It was his
nature to want to mix with people, and to be alone at other times;
and the freedom provided by the ranch life encouraged his independence. Arthur Cooper defaulted on his responsibility to look
after his little brother. Arthur's friends regarded Frank as a nui-

sance, which did not bother Frank since he did not find them an interesting lot.

"Arthur and his pals were content just to stay on the low ground and chase after rabbits," Gary Cooper recalled. "But the higher I went up into the hills, the higher I wanted to go, and felt I had to go. I knew there were eagles nesting up there, because eagles were always flying high above us. So I'd set out to find an eagle's nest and never get there, but I'd see every other kind of critter in the brush."

Sometimes he explored with little Indian companions who bore such interesting names as Black Fish, White Face, Spotted Feather . . . and his first girl friend, a tiny thing named Mary Three-feet, although she had only the normal ration of two feet. The Indian children were curious, but characteristically silent and solemn. Even when they spoke among themselves, Frank could make no sense of their language. They got along well enough, but he was hardly dependent on their companionship. Frank amused himself by making solo expeditions into the small mountains, despite the inevitable scoldings for having wandered too far off. There were bears in the vicinity, and poisonous snakes, and mountain lions that occasionally ventured down near the ranch to terrorize the livestock. Once, following a severe lecture on safety precautions, Frank disappeared from the ranch for several hours. The cowboys were forming a search party when he returned home. He'd simply heard so much talk about bears that he went off exploring in hopes of spotting one. He hadn't, but he'd seen a white-tailed deer. His reputation for fearlessness was established early.

It was probably in the spring of 1909 that he met Zeb, the grizzled, long-haired plainsman who would be a powerful influence on his young life.

"If Zeb had a last name, I never knew it, nor did anyone seem to recall it," Gary Cooper once reflected. "His name may have been Zebulon or some such, but Zeb was all I ever heard. I thought of him as very old, but he may have been no more than fifty or so. He had lived what to me seemed like an exciting life, and he was a great storyteller. He'd been married to a squaw once, and had children but didn't know where they were. He'd been in the buffalo wars, and had fought both with the Indians and against them. He may even have been a liar, but I loved him."

Zeb was a journeyman ranch hand, a blacksmith who could also tend the chuck wagon. He had his own horse, an aged sorrel mare, and he taught Frank Cooper to ride. He also gave him his first instruction in handling firearms, and in shooting at a moving target. When Zeb and Frank made forays into the hills to hunt, the Coopers were assured that their young son was well protected. They soon recognized another problem, however. Zeb regularly employed an incomparably crude vocabulary that little Frank naturally sought to imitate. Once, in retaliation for a classroom reprimand, Frank called the schoolmarm a son of a bitch. Alice Cooper decided that Frank must be permanently separated from Zeb, but her effort to accomplish that was not successful. Before the summer was over Zeb had also taught Frank to swim.

The swimming hole was in Andy's Creek, a broad, sluggish stream that snaked through the Seven-Bar-Nine and emptied into the Missouri. Frank swam there sometimes with Zeb, and sometimes with the Indian boys. It became a point of pride for Frank that he learned to swim before Arthur did, and indeed before either of his parents could. Alice, however, was more worried than impressed by his precociousness. She feared that he was becoming something of a savage—the word she usually applied to his Indian friends. She was particularly horrified to learn that he customarily swam naked, sometimes in the presence of little Mary Three-feet.

The novelty of being the queen bee of Sunnyside had long worn off for Alice. Satisfied that she had proved her mettle, she was now in a discreetly managed conflict with her husband over whether they must continue to live at the ranch. Charles could make a financial gain by selling to any of several potential buyers. Alice wanted him to sell, feeling marooned at the ranch and often lonely there, with Charles off in Helena or somewhere on legal business. When Alice became severely ill, her doctor reasoned that an advanced state of nervousness had caused her to be afflicted with shingles.

Charles would not consider selling; but to placate his wife, he enrolled the boys in schools at Helena for the 1909–10 winter, and deferred their return to the ranch until the following summer.

This plan left Frank devastated, although it pleased his older brother. Soon the adolescent Arthur was mixing with some boys who Alice thought were of dubious character, and that revived her plea to have the boys educated in England.

The new problem with Frank was his truancy. He had a penchant for wandering from the school ground during recess and not returning to the classroom. One morning he left the house and did not go to school at all, but headed straight for the railroad depot. Intending a surprise visit to the ranch, he climbed into a box car on a freight train that he knew would be going there. His presence was detected before the train pulled out of the station. He was taken home, and Alice became hysterical over the thought that her son, who was not yet nine, had tried to run away from home. Frank only protested that he had intended to come right back after getting in a little hunting at the ranch.

Then Frank had to consider the awful thought that he might never live at the ranch again.

Early in 1910 the forty-four-year-old Charles Cooper was appointed to the Montana Supreme Court. He was a lifetime Republican, selected for the bench by a Democratic governor who may have only sought to reduce Cooper's role in party politics, wherein he had been quite effective. In any event, being a judge in the State Court would require Charles to reside full time in Helena, so returning to the ranch was now out of the question. He would continue its management from a distance, while entrusting its everyday supervision to his foreman. Now the main house would be unoccupied except as a "summer place" for the Cooper family. The security of his permanent appointment to the Montana Court prodded Charles to purchase what would be the family's permanent home in Helena—a large brick house on a quiet, tree-lined street only a block removed from the main Helena thoroughfare, which was still named Last Chance Gulch. Alice gave the house such appointments of furnishings and decor that seemed appropriate for the family of a judge. But soon after the family moved in, Judge Cooper found himself occupying the house alone.

Frank's erratic behavior had given Alice more ammunition for her English cause, and Charles decided the time had come for the long-promised visit to her homeland. Alice's shingles appeared to vanish as soon as the trip to England became a firm plan, and her excitement was only barely diminished by the thought that Charles could not accompany her. His responsibility to the bench as its newest member made him cancel his own vacation plans.

So Alice went to England with only her sons.

Arthur and Frank Cooper had been hearing about England for all of their young lives. Dutifully they had sent greetings at Christmas and on birthday occasions to relatives whom they had never expected to meet. Yet the trip to England in the late spring of 1910, designed as a great adventure for only a few months, would carry into several years.

First there was the train ride across the country—a full week of Pullman sleepers. The voyage by ocean liner took nine days, during which Frank never became seasick although both his mother and brother did. They docked at Southampton where they were met by one of Alice's relatives, who drove them to the family home in Kent in his new automobile.

Alice's family had made elaborate plans that included a sightseeing trip to London. The Coopers arrived in that august city only to find it deep in mourning. It was entirely by chance that nine-year-old Frank witnessed the funeral procession of Edward VII. The following year, by more conscious design, he would also observe the coronation procession of George V.

Alice and her sons traveled by rail from Gillingham to Bedfordshire, to be swamped by an entirely new set of adoring relatives. Both of Charles's parents were still living, and Alice came particularly under the spell of her aged mother-in-law. Alice was newly determined to arrange English educations for her sons, knowing that she had powerful allies in her husband's family. The elder Mrs. Cooper believed that Arthur and Frank should be going to the Dunstable School, which had been attended by their father, and by his father before him.

The Coopers of Bedfordshire clearly were more prosperous than Charles had ever hinted, or else had risen to unaccustomed affluence during the Edwardian years. His parents had come to regard Charles as their black sheep, who had forfeited certain success in a civilized land for the lottery of a barbaric one. Nor were Charles's relatives very impressed by his new judgeship, which, like all things American, rated lower in their estimation than any British equivalent. The elder Coopers still believed that with Alice's help they might persuade Charles to return to England and take over administration of the family estate; he might also consider raising cattle there. But besides knowing that Charles was irretrievably Americanized, Alice was anticipating the life of a Montana judge's wife with excitement of her own. She was determined, though, to enroll her sons in the Dunstable School and return to America without them, and conveyed her intention in a letter to Charles.

His response surprised her. He thought that having Arthur and Frank attend the Dunstable School was a grand idea, now that they could afford it. However, he wanted to attend to the matter personally, and would have the boys return to America with Alice until the following summer, when the entire family could vacation together. So in 1911 the four Coopers made the journey to England.

They were in London for the coronation celebration, and to do what was expected of American tourists in that city. They visited the Tower of London and ogled the Crown Jewels. They went to the theater, and Frank fidgeted through a production of Shakespeare's *Cymbeline* with Sybil Thorndike and Lewis Casson. He much preferred the Punch and Judy show they also saw, and what impressed him most of all were the waxwork figures at Madame Tussaud's.

In Bedfordshire for the first time in more than a quarter-century, Charles Cooper found the scene essentially unchanged yet had a stranger's unease. His kinfolk lamented that he no longer talked like an Englishman, and he reckoned that he had long since stopped thinking like one. He was anxious to get back to *his* country.

When the Coopers sailed for America without their sons, Alice was the tearful one but Charles had the deeper sadness. The prospect of Arthur and Frank being turned into perfect English gentlemen was hoped for by their mother, and feared by their father.

Over the years Gary Cooper fielded questions from scores of interviewers about the time he spent in England. His standard account was of having not fit in, of being unable to adjust to formal regimen both at school and at home with his grandparents. Yet he always adapted easily to new people and new situations, and England was no exception.

He did get off to a bumpy start in school, rather in contrast to his older brother, who was a smashing success at Dunstable and in Bedfordshire society.

On his first day, Frank fought after school with boys who taunted him mainly for his speech. He held his own against the English adversaries who, in a most gentlemanly manner, challenged him one at a time. Frank was merely being subjected to the ordeal of the "new boy," and he met the test. On the second day he was accepted as a friend by the boys who had sent him home with a torn collar and scuffed shirt. Ridiculed only briefly for his American ways, he was soon valued by schoolmates as an exotic. They were spellbound by tales of cowboys and Indians he had actually known. The accounts also made him a hit with little girls who made his formal acquaintance.

Accomplishment as a horseman gave him added stature, especially when he outraced a "champion" older boy named Harry Trent, who became one of his chums. Another one was Patrick Hepburn, who would grow up to become a Member of Parliament and would visit Gary Cooper in Hollywood. Most of the Dunstable boys could ride, and in a few years would be expected to ride to the foxes. But they couldn't whoop, cowboy-style, and whooping was easy and natural for Frank Cooper. Otherwise he was a disappointing athletic prospect, showing no real interest in football or in any other team sport promoted at Dunstable. His success in the English public school was mostly social; he was no scholastic prodigy.

The headmaster was appalled that Frank had received no instruction in Latin during his American education. At the Dunstable School he studied both Latin and French, while also enduring several courses in English history that made hardly any mention of America. Frank's poor scholarship was consistent with his performances at Helena and in the one-room school cabin on the ranch. He seemed always to be distracted. Nor was he the silent, basically reserved boy that might have been expected of a very young Gary Cooper. The Dunstable tutors considered him overly spirited, noisy, often disruptive; and they tolerated him mainly because his brother Arthur was an exemplary upper classman.

During his second year at Dunstable, Frank was almost expelled from the school for conduct unbecoming a young gentleman. He had not kept his "place" if he had even known it. In an apparent attempt to make friendly small talk with a newsboy, he overstepped his way into a fist fight. The raffish newsboy, thinking he was being ridiculed by a dandy, knocked the Dunstable cap from Frank's head and loosened the Old School Tie, as preface to a light jostling. In retaliation, Frank struck back with his fists, they scuffled, and soon he had taken the measure of the newsboy, who was larger and probably older than he. The fracas attracted a modest crowd, mostly of laborers who cheered the newsboy to no avail.

Although the fight had not occurred on the school ground, Frank was brought before the headmaster and asked to explain the incident.

"Well, I finished it," the boy offered, "but *he* started it!"

In the headmaster's view, it did not matter who started or finished the fight, who won or lost, or even who might have been right or wrong. Frank Cooper had made the mistake of pursuing first an association, and then fisticuffs, with someone beneath him in class. Such behavior would not be tolerated. The expulsion order might have been enforced but for an appeal by Arthur Cooper, who assured the headmaster that he would supervise his brother and keep him out of further mischief.

The Cooper brothers' stay in England stretched to more than three years. It was probably the only time they were ever really close. On at least one occasion Frank even succeeded in getting proper, cautious Arthur into trouble.

"My grandfather's spread was adjacent to the Duke of Bedfordshire's estate," Gary Cooper would recall, "or at least to part of it, for it was sort of vast. One thing Arthur and I both liked to do was hunt. In Montana he'd done a lot of hunting with his own friends, and some with our dad, at about the same time I was learning to hunt with old Zeb. Arthur even got in on a couple of fox hunts in England that made me pretty jealous. There wasn't any real hunting over there, though, not of the kind we were used to. That is, there wasn't until I spotted some unusual birds on the duke's estate.

"I liked to peep through our privet hedge into his lordship's grounds. There were many fine trees, and squirrels were everywhere. I tempted Arthur into some squirrel hunting, and no sooner had he shot one than we were arrested for poaching. Well, not arrested. But they filed a report, and my grandfather had to pay a fine, and Arthur was pretty embarrassed about it at home—especially when our uncle tanned Arthur's britches, even though Arthur was about seventeen at the time. I didn't get whipped and felt guilty about it, because any time Arthur got into trouble it was my own doing."

Yet Gary Cooper reflected that the effort to transform him into a little gentleman was very nearly successful, even though he never adjusted to the Eton collars, or the high hats they were made to wear on Sundays. He learned the social graces, and his speech acquired a distinctly English inflection—as his mother was aware during subsequent vacation trips to England that she made without Judge Cooper's escort.

Arthur, upon completing his Dunstable schooling, was certified as ready for Oxford, which presumably was also a distant prospect for Frank. That he no longer pestered his parents with the wish to go home to Montana was taken as proof that he had adjusted to his new life. Both Cooper sons might have stayed in England for several more years, but for the intervention of the World War.

Upon England's entry into the great conflict in 1914, the Coopers whisked their sons back to Montana. Over the next few years, while they were being reassimilated by the very different life of the American Northwest, all notions of Oxford for either Arthur or Frank would evaporate.

Frank Cooper's reception upon re-entering the Helena middle school was similar to his rude welcome at Dunstable, and even more discomfiting. Against his own fierce protest, he was made to wear suit, tie, and hat to school. "Just for the first day," Alice Cooper had insisted. "Everyone dresses well on the first day."

But no one dressed nearly so well as Frank. His appearance in the classroom provoked uproarious laughter, especially from the

young ladies, which made his return to coeducational classes a dubious pleasure at best. Some boys whom Frank remembered as his
friends from earlier years now chose not to recognize him.

When the school day ended, he was loudly hooted. He responded, characteristically, with his fists. The Helena youths
obeyed no gentleman's code. They ganged up on him, ripping his
English suit while generally mauling him. When Frank returned
to the house on Eleventh Street to confront his astonished
mother, he was crying more from the indignity than from his
freely bleeding nose. Thereafter he wore only the clothes of his
own choosing to school. Yet he continued to be razzed, for the
English glaze on his speech made him seem foppish to the Helena
pupils. In making a conscious effort to purge the accent, he
resorted mainly to silence.

Eventually he won the social aspect of his battle at school, but
not the scholastic part. His training in Latin now went for
naught. He was behind in the Montana curriculum, so he was not
promoted. As a repeater in sixth grade, he would be with classmates who generally were at least a year younger than he.

Still, Frank decided he was happy to be back in Montana. The
Cooper family now owned its first automobile, and the drive from
Helena to the Seven-Bar-Nine could be made in less than three
hours over the bumpy dirt road. Frank could not contain his excitement on returning to the ranch, even though it was manned
mostly by new cowhands.

Zeb was long gone; no one seemed to know where. There were
still Indians on the premises, but not the ones Frank remembered.
The ranch itself seemed more magnificent than before, as surely it
was. The cattle population had more than doubled under Charles
Cooper's administration, and now stood at almost five hundred
head. The big house still contained the furnishings the Coopers
had first brought to it, but there were some striking new appointments, of which the most imposing was an original oil painting
that was displayed prominently in the large parlor. It depicted an
Indian scene in Montana, and was signed by Charles M. Russell.
At about the same time that Charles Cooper arrived in Helena,
Charles Russell had come to Montana from St. Louis, and the
two men were friends even before Russell began to gain recogni-

tion as an artist. Only later was Russell's wife revealed to be a distant cousin to Charles Cooper.

The painting that fascinated young Frank was a gift to Judge Cooper from the artist. Russell paid occasional visits to the ranch to observe the cowboys, whose workaday lives he would celebrate on canvas. It was right there in the house on the sunny side of the Missouri River that Frank Cooper met Charles M. Russell in the flesh, and acquired the ambition that would be nurtured in his adolescence: to become himself a painter of western scenes.

His parents encouraged Frank's announced goal of becoming an artist, possibly because his undistinguished scholastic performance had suggested no special aptitudes other than a modest talent for drawing. Alice Cooper sought Charles Russell's advice on an art school which Frank could eventually attend; but Russell, who was entirely self-trained, said that if the boy wanted to paint he should just start painting. So Frank received oils, watercolors, brushes, and canvases as presents on his fifteenth birthday. Showing enthusiasm for a novelty pastime, he hurriedly painted several scenes at the Seven-Bar-Nine, including a study of Eagle Rock Mountain. Then he put away his brushes for the less sedate activities that would characterize his teen years.

Adolescence reached him somewhat belatedly, and transformed his appearance remarkably. As a child Frank Cooper was only an average specimen for both height and weight, and was unspectacularly normal in every measurement—a child of pleasant appearance but without suggestion of physical grandeur. A rather rounded face gave a false hint of stockiness. His teeth seemed too large for his mouth, and his sandy hair was unruly. A slightly ruddy complexion completed the all-American boy image that was belied only by his customary careful dress. But in 1916 his appearance began to change markedly, and even more drastically the following year.

Between his fifteenth and sixteenth birthdays, Frank Cooper gained fourteen inches in height, shooting up from less than five feet to more than six. Because he was a late grower, he had been shorter than many boys in his class although older than most of them; but the rapid spurt made him very nearly the tallest youth in the Helena schools. To support his astonishing elongation, he became a suddenly powerful eater. As a child he had been selective about food if not finicky, but now he had a taste for every edible thing and an almost unlimited capacity. Those are undoubtedly the eating traits of many adolescent boys, but in his case it was not merely a phase. The mature Gary Cooper would earn an added measure of intramural movieland fame for his enormous appetite.

Now he was gaunt-faced, with prominent tapered cheekbones. His eyes, rather than taking on a deeper hue, became an even softer blue in adolescence. That he was on the threshold of exceptional handsomeness was largely obscured by his gangling awkwardness. A lengthening slender neck was a feature outdone only by Frank's legs, which were truly bizarre—two supremely narrow stilts, attached to only an average torso. Height would become one of the particulars of his incomparably attractive manliness, but at age fifteen his height only made Frank Cooper an object of ridicule.

Growth proved a painfully embarrassing ordeal. By nature Frank had been a talkative child; now he became almost sullen, responding to conversation but seldom initiating it. He developed a stammer that seemed to certify his loss of confidence. To his neighbors he was a "strange, aloof kid" who was often seen riding box cars out of Helena toward the family ranch. There he might be glimpsed riding his colt all over the Seven-Bar-Nine terrain. He stayed to himself, seldom socializing with the ranch hands. An exception was a spindly, taciturn cowboy named Jay Talbot. Their relationship would deepen over many years ahead, and "Slim" Talbot eventually would become a Hollywood fixture as Gary Cooper's stand-in, sharing with him an essentially silent close relationship.

In 1917 the United States finally entered the World War, and Frank Cooper began to emerge from his shell. He was now the only son living at home. Arthur enlisted in the Army and soon was shipped to France, after which Charles Cooper made an effort to give Frank such attention as he had previously bestowed on Arthur. In a failed effort to turn his son into a baseball fan, Charles provided him with an entirely new set of friends.

Charles Cooper and his fellow judges were baseball fans although far removed from the scenes of major league play. They followed the sport's professional life in the Northwest League that

had teams nearby at Butte and Great Falls. The judges had a particular friend in Joe McGinnity, who in his younger days had
been the invincible "Iron Man" pitcher for the New York Giants.
McGinnity, a sometime visitor to the Cooper ranch, was manager
of the Butte team and still took his regular turn as a pitcher although in his mid-forties. During their summer court recess, the
judges often made excursions to Butte or Great Falls when
McGinnity was scheduled to pitch there. Sometimes the judges
took their sons along on the trips, treating them to overnight residence in nice hotels. Frank Cooper had only disdain for the game
of baseball—which, owing largely to his time spent in England,
he had not even played. But he liked the adventurous junkets to
towns that were somewhat larger than Helena, and he became
quite friendly with the teen-aged sons of his father's associates.

Jim Galen and Jim Calloway were both about Frank's age.
They all became great pals even though the two Jims did not immediately know what to make of Frank, who shunned even simple games of catch. It seemed they preferred playing ball to just
about anything, but Frank said he would much rather be off in
the woods hunting. His new friends had no experience as hunters,
but Frank would take care of that. He invited both Galen and
Calloway to the ranch for some hunting and fishing. They became
frequent guests there, riding the range with Frank and adopting
his outdoor pastimes.

Charles Cooper hunted or fished only rarely but encouraged his
son's interests. Alice fretted over Frank's passion for firearms but
was pacified by his having taken up with "respectable" youths.

"My friends were mostly sons of lawyers," Gary Cooper once
told Jim Tully in an interview, "and that seemed to make everything all right, no matter what we did Actually they were about
as wild a bunch as you'd find anywhere, though no more so than
myself. They surely didn't corrupt me. We sort of inspired each
other in every kind of devilry. It's a wonder we didn't get into any
real trouble, and we almost did—many times."

Jim Galen, whose fixed broad grin betrayed a taste for mischief,
became Frank's most frequent companion. They formed what
would be recalled as a Tom Sawyer-Huckleberry Finn relationship, although which party was the more disreputable Huck
was never made clear. They roamed into the wooded hills that

surrounded the Seven-Bar-Nine, stalking deer and elk and usually
settling for smaller game. Or they hunted in the wilds around
Helena, often illegally. Frank yielded to Jim Galen for inven-
tiveness, and Jim was always up to the kind of mischief that tests
a school teacher's spirit.

On a crisp fall morning after their sophomore term had commenced, Jim and Frank held a rendezvous on the school ground
before dawn. Frank had obtained a skeleton key for entry into the
school building, and Jim had brought limburger cheese—many
pounds of it. They stole into the building and proceeded to smear
cheese on all the radiators. Then they returned to their respective
homes. Frank appeared for breakfast at the usual time, pretending
to be rousing from a sound sleep but reeking of a mysterious odor
that he attributed to some strange soap he'd been using. On the
walk to school he intercepted Jim Galen, who was also drenched
with the telltale perfume. On the school ground they loitered at a
distance from the crowd of pupils gathered outside the building.
Finally everyone was sent home for the day, as the classrooms
were temporarily uninhabitable. Frank and Jim hopped a freight
train to the ranch and went hunting in the low mountains. Deer
were everywhere, and each bagged a buck.

On another trek in the hills, the boys stole some dynamite from
the cabin of an old prospector whom Frank knew. Curious to see
what kind of blast they could make, they set off the dynamite on
a grass knoll where some cattle were grazing nearby. The explosion incited a mild stampede, from which several head of cattle
were never recovered.

Before taking up with Jim Galen, Frank had enjoyed few close
friendships, and those only for brief durations. That promised to
change, for Galen was a gregarious youth into whose "gang"
Frank was comfortably absorbed. Its inner sanctum included Jim
Calloway, who could ride any horse as well as Frank could; Hugh
Potter, whose knowledge of sex assured his popularity in a circle
of restless innocents; Tommy Miller, a "brain" whose assistance
sometimes enabled Frank to pass examinations he might have
flunked; and Weldon Hinton, who kept them all supplied with
tobacco from his father's shop. Their main activity was tinkering
with automobiles, although no one in Frank's circle was permitted
to drive one. The automobile made a somewhat tardy conquest of

Montana and still rated as a novelty. The boys decided to build a car of their own from such parts as they could collect, and Frank Cooper was caught in the act of appropriating some equipment from the automobile of a Helena minister.

The gang association deepened his identity as "Judge Cooper's wild kid." Perhaps there were other such happenings that would not be sustained by legend. Frank's tenure as a member of the gang came to a sudden end, however, with his removal from the Helena high school. In later years he would say he had flunked out, or at other times would say he had dropped out, which might better explain his mid-semester departure. What really happened probably cannot be verified, but it seems more likely that he was expelled. It would not have been characteristic of his parents, who persistently encouraged his education, to have permitted him to leave school on his own volition. But in the spring of 1918, before the end of the school term, both Frank and his mother returned to the ranch because someone had to do the work there.

Most of the younger ranch hands had left the scene, answering the call to military service. At the same time, the business of the ranch became more vital because the armed services needed beef, and Judge Cooper's livestock could be sold at higher prices. Over the coming summer Frank attained his full height of six feet, three inches, while building fences and making other repairs on all the ranch structures that had again started to deteriorate. Alice, too, did man's work, and during this period believed that her bond with her second son grew even stronger. Charles would generally be at the ranch only on weekends.

Frank returned to school in the fall of 1918, a sophomore still, and at seventeen older by two years than most of his classmates. One of his new friends was very nearly his own age, because Harvey Markham had also been delayed in the pursuit of his education.

A poor little rich boy, Harvey Markham had been permanently crippled by polio some years earlier. He was a fan of every competitive sport that denied his participation, and he always wanted to go on hunting trips with Frank and his companions, who probably regarded him as an impediment. Still, everyone wanted to be Harvey Markham's friend, because Harvey had his own car.

Frank Cooper went on his first "date" in Harvey's 1916 Model

T Ford, which was specially equipped with hand controls for its driver. The two youths escorted a pair of girls who were visitors from the East to a box supper at the Episcopalian church. There was some proper square dancing, and Frank alternately partnered each girl as Harvey watched. But there was an agreed-on romantic pairing, and Frank's date was a plump blonde named Alma, who fancied herself a singer and continually warbled Victor Herbert's "Kiss Me Again." If her song offered an invitation, Frank didn't accept it.

Later Frank and Harvey began squiring young ladies to the motion picture programs. As a child Frank had seen few photoplays, making first acquaintance with them during his stay in England. His mother did not consider the movies a sufficiently dignified entertainment, with a few exceptions—as when the Cooper family reveled in D. W. Griffith's *The Birth of a Nation* at the Marlow. A huge old opera house that had been one of Helena's proudest cultural appointments, the Marlow still functioned occasionally as a legitimate theater but had a new primary identity as a movie palace. The Marlow was a favorite hang-around place for Frank's pals, who liked to observe the young ladies attending the picture shows, invariably chaperoned. But Harvey Markham was captivated by that fairly new thing, the feature film, and he attended every new program at the Marlow. One of the first pictures Frank saw in Harvey's company was called *The Woman God Forgot*; and it was directed by the same Cecil B. De Mille who, in a later era, would shape many expensive projects as vehicles for Gary Cooper. *The Woman God Forgot* was a picture to thrill Harvey, but Frank Cooper was bored by it and not enamored of its portly star, who was the diva Geraldine Farrar—silent on film, although the piano accompaniment sometimes featured arias associated with her. The pictures made by the De Milles and Griffiths always played the Marlow, but Frank was more easily pleased by visits to the little Antlers Theatre, which was built especially for the movies, but was accustomed to less pretentious fare. Most of the Westerns were screened at the Antlers, and those were the pictures that held no appeal for Harvey but that Frank enjoyed without exception. So he began attending the shows at the Antlers by himself, often imagining that he was the hero in the saddle, whether the image on the screen was the fading G. M. (Broncho

Billy) Anderson or someone like Ed (Hoot) Gibson, who was just starting out.

The most prestigious Western star of the day was the veteran William S. Hart, although Tom Mix had surpassed him in popularity. Frank Cooper's own idol was neither Hart nor Mix but the stoic Harry Carey, who revealed little emotion whenever he cleaned up a frontier town; and who, unlike both Hart and Mix, never seemed distracted by pretty women. Harry Carey reminded Frank of the two ranch hands who had most impressed him—old Zeb; and Jay Talbot, who was always leaving the Seven-Bar-Nine, to chase Pancho Villa or to fight the Hun, or simply to ride on the rodeo circuit.

At about the time that Frank was becoming addicted to the flickering Westerns, he took a spill not from a horse but from Harvey Markham's automobile. He had taken to riding to school regularly in Harvey's car, and one morning Harvey lost control when the hand brakes failed as he attempted to negotiate a curve. Both boys were thrown from the car just before it turned over. The Model T was ruined and the boys were "lucky to be alive." Frank was immediately attentive toward Harvey, and only when he established that Harvey was not badly hurt did he acknowledge a painfully aching hip. Judge Cooper was summoned to the scene, and took Frank home believing him only to be shaken up. But on the following morning the hip was hot and Frank could get out of bed only with difficulty. He was taken to the family doctor, who put the Coopers at ease. The doctor said that Frank would probably be nursing a sore hip for several days. He may have torn some muscles in his left hip, but it was not serious. After all, the boy was walking, wasn't he?

In a later period, taking X rays would have been a common precaution. Instead, a friendly doctor failed to diagnose a broken hipbone. Perhaps he was caught up in the euphoria of the Armistice that had been signed in France, which meant that America had saved the world for democracy. The doctor advised Frank not to favor the hip, but to exercise it. Frank tried to shake it off, but the pain sent him back to bed. He missed some exams that again slowed his progress in school. The principal said they could be made up, thereby showing more consideration than the doctor— who, on one of Frank's return visits after the ailment failed to go away, prescribed horseback riding as the best exercise for ironing out the muscular kinks.

So Frank went back to the Seven-Bar-Nine, not as the scion of the big house, but as one of the cowboys. It was something he had dreamed about as a small child, and it had been discussed as a possibility throughout his growing years: to experience the workaday life of the ranch, asking no special favors. Arthur Cooper had worked grueling summers at the ranch, and although the cowboy life had not been to his liking, it had put him in top physical shape. Hard work would be Frank's therapy for the aches and pains that were persistent reminders of the car accident. Not until many years later would it be revealed that he had sustained a broken hip, for which riding and other ranch labor were dubious recommendations. Still, the hip healed, although the bone re-formed unnaturally and the pain never disappeared entirely. To reduce the stabbing sensation, Frank changed his posture in the saddle and rode on the bias. He thought it made riding somehow easier than it had been before, once he'd mastered his new style. But even in simple walking, he was often twinged with a little needling pain, and learned to "walk around it." That his physical impairment generally escaped notice could only be attributed to the silence he kept about it. He was a cowboy now, and cowboys were not known to complain about physical ailments.

At eighteen he was a strapper too long for the primitive bed that was given to him in the bunkhouse. The chronic hip ailment made it impossible for him to attain a comfortable sleeping posture, and he curled snakelike in his bunk. Finally he learned to sleep in almost any position, but found that sleep came easiest when he was sitting. Sleep would always be an indulgence for him, but it was sweetest after the hard ordeal of working 450 cattle.

He did not enjoy the labor. Years later he would reflect that "The work was just too damn hard. Not that I wasn't capable of doing the work, because I was and I did it. But having to work hard never had any real appeal for me, and that may have some connection with me being in the movies. The hardest work I ever did was on my father's ranch. I'd been admiring Dad's cowboys since I was six years old, and I thought I wanted to be like them and do what they did. Well, I changed my mind over the summers and winters I worked there, but that doesn't mean I stopped respecting the cowhands. If anything, that respect increased, and they never ceased to fascinate me."

He learned that being a cowboy was more than just riding on a horse amid scores of white-faced cattle. He soon knew that the grim activity of bull-wrestling was not the exclusive concern of rodeos. The chores he detested most were branding the animals and castrating them, although he became proficient at both. He was amazed that almost every cowboy he knew really loved the work.

Most of the cowboys were itinerant. Few of the ones who had gone off to war returned to the Seven-Bar-Nine, but others came. Frank never knew where most of them came from, and the protocol of range life seemed to be never to ask. If they wanted you to know something, they'd tell you. Frank could only wonder about someone like Roy Smith, who chewed tobacco and spat through his teeth and always packed a Luger. He was expert at hitting a swiftly moving target. Roy Smith almost never spoke; but according to Ashburton Carter, Roy might learn to appreciate talk if it were taken entirely away from him.

Frank's new surrogate father at the ranch was the leathery-faced Ashburton Carter, who was something of a legend. Once he had survived six months of being snowbound in the Colorado Rockies, without seeing a human being in all that time. Ash Carter told Frank that the only way he'd kept his sanity was by holding long conversations with his horse. Back among humanity, Ash simply could not stop talking, and he regaled Frank with many a tale of frontier resourcefulness.

Walter Seton was also resourceful in his way, and Ashburton Carter's warning, which Frank failed to heed, was not to become overly friendly with him. In one of his first Hollywood interviews, the newly named Gary Cooper told of his infamous association with Walter Seton, and was reprimanded by his studio for his indiscretion.

This Seton was a charming fellow with a sinister trimming. He went to work at the Seven-Bar-Nine as most did, with no questions asked. He probably would not have provided the correct answers, anyway. Much later it was revealed that Seton was a member of the notorious Carlisle gang, which had a habit of rob-bing mail trains throughout the Northwest. Carlisle and some of the gang were captured, tried, and put in prison for killing the guards during one of their robberies. When Carlisle himself escaped while under sentence of death, Seton vanished suddenly from the Seven-Bar-Nine, and speculation was that he had been an informer on Carlisle and now feared for his life. But before any of that, Frank Cooper had been under Seton's spell, even to the point of helping him steal sheep.

"He was quite a hero to me. What appealed to me was the money he talked about making someday—fabulous sums of it. I don't know why he thought a rangy, scrawny kid could be of help to him, but he told me about his different plans, and not all of them were nefarious. But one of his schemes was to round up a couple of hundred head of cattle and drive south with them. I was about to do it, too, before I realized it was Dad's cattle we'd be rustling. But then he used to steal sheep when he had a craving for fresh meat, and I was with him one night on one of his forays. The moon was full, and as we went over the crest of a hill the sheepherder saw us and took some shots at us. Believe me, we burned leather riding back to the ranch. I didn't try stealing sheep after that."

Most of the cowboys moved on and were never seen again. Some, like Jay Talbot, returned time and again after getting adventure out of their systems. It was commonplace for a ranch to lose a cowboy or two on a trip to market, and replacements frequently checked in on the return swing.

Cattle no longer were trail-driven to market. The cowboys periodically herded beef on the hoof right into the cattle cars for rail shipment, often to Chicago but to other beef-trading centers as well. A team of cowboys would accompany the cattle on the slow freights, with one of them empowered to make the transactions with the beef merchants. Frank Cooper's most memorable adventure as a cowboy was to go on a few hauls to market when Ashburton Carter had the trading responsibility.

It was customary for the cowboys to engage in some spirited carousing after unloading the cattle and taking them to market and making the transaction with the merchant. Frank Cooper went on his first bender in Omaha. The trip also provided his sexual initiation, although he was too drunk to recall later much of what had happened. He was a sick boy when Ash Carter carried him aboard the train that would take them back to Montana. By the time they were safely returned to the ranch, Frank had recovered his health and sobriety, and was a little bit pleased with himself.

There was unaccustomed screaming in the Cooper household when Frank announced absolutely that he would not return to high school. He had failed to advance to the junior class, although well into his nineteenth year. A lot of his friends were not finishing high school but expected to do all right for themselves, and so did he. At what? his father asked him. Frank really had no idea. Alice blamed his lack of direction on Montana.

Finally Judge Cooper used his prestige to obtain a special accommodation for his son. He arranged for his son to re-enter high school not at Helena but at the neighboring town of Bozeman; and not as a sophomore or even a junior, but as a senior for whom a unique curriculum would be designed. This would enable him to accomplish the work of three school years in one, and would give him a diploma. Frank eventually agreed to the proposition. It would mean a lot of hard work—but not so hard, he reasoned, as punching cattle.

The Armistice had touched off a celebration that continued long afterward in some places; and according to the Gary Cooper version, the people of Bozeman never stopped celebrating in all the time he was there.

"Bozeman was a smaller town than Helena, and more intimate, without the pretense of a capital city. Everyone in town knew everyone else. Maybe every little town in the country became hysterical after the Armistice, and maybe that helped bring on Prohibition. Well, Bozeman was no exception. I got to running around in one of the school sets. The boy who looked the most adult would buy a couple of quarts of hard liquor and we'd start in to drink it. It was harder on our stomachs than on our morals. Everyone goes through that kind of liberating period, and I took it big."

He also took Bozeman, and rather by storm. He was still remarkably thin, but the vigorous labor of the ranch had hardened him. The sun had also bronzed him, and surely the girls of Bozeman High thought him the handsomest thing that ever zoomed into town on a motorcycle.

Although he helped pay for it with his own earnings, the motor-

cycle was a concession from his parents for his agreeing to finish
high school in Bozeman. He burned up the dirt road between
Helena and Bozeman, pushing the engine for maximum speed
while impressing observers as being both a daredevil and a show-
off. Of course the local girls were captivated, and pleaded for an
invitation to ride with him on his motorcycle—which required
them to sit behind him and cling to him for dear life. Driving
with a passenger may have made him more cautious, but Judge
Cooper's wild kid was not likely to win the trust of a girl's parents.

He fell in love, or said he did.

"Looking back now, I'd hardly call it love. It was more a symbol of my maturity. We danced, skated, and drank together, the
whole crowd. I don't believe I ever saw the girl alone, except to escort her home. But the girl and I were separated, after long lec-
tures, before we'd even thought about going too far. Her folks
may have thought I was a bad influence, but the school board
acted as if it wanted to save *me*, as a brand from the burning. I
was a boy from another town, who needed protection and guid-
ance."

What the school board may have failed to accomplish was
nicely managed for Frank by an English teacher named Ida Davis.
He had other teachers but she was the one who paid attention to
him. As a spinster about twice his age, she logically could have
been secretly in love with him. Nothing about his scholastic performance indicated a genius that only needed encouragement, but
Ida Davis persuaded Frank's teachers, his parents, and Frank Cooper himself that he was a diamond in the rough, whose only need
was to find himself. The Coopers credited Miss Davis with getting Frank to hit the books in a concentrated effort to graduate.

Miss Davis seemed most effective in pulling strings, pushing
levers, and generally persuading the authorities that the young
man should be graduated from high school on general principles,
not the least of them being that he was Judge Cooper's son. He
gained his diploma in a little over one school term by attending
the 1920 summer session. With that battle won, Ida Davis did
not stop. She wanted Frank to go on to college, where his "great
potential" could be put to honest test. It was not too late for a
nineteen-year-old to decide on becoming a lawyer or doctor, and
Bozeman had a college . . .

Few persons have had such difficulty as Frank Cooper in getting squared away with college. He delayed entering Montana State College at Bozeman in order to help his father run the state Republican campaign for the national ticket led by Senator Harding. Judge Cooper was resolutely opposed to the League of Nations as advocated by the departing and disabled Woodrow Wilson.

Frank enrolled in the spring of 1921 and dropped out without completing a semester. Taking a job at Yellowstone National Park, he became a tour guide for the first of three consecutive summers. In the fall he entered a junior college in Helena, then called Wesleyan, primarily because Harvey Markham was enrolled there. In the following spring on the eve of his twenty-first birthday, he again dropped out without having earned any credits.

He seemed lost, but then he bought a large sketch pad for his second Yellowstone summer, and began to draw everything he saw in the park. Ida Davis was the first person he had heard use the term "commercial art," and she had suggested it as a vocational objective for him. So the idea again formed in his mind: he would be an artist—surely not so fine a painter as Charles M. Russell, but possibly able to earn a living by doing something he enjoyed.

Arthur Cooper, long returned from military service and earning his own handsome living, offered to help his skinny brother in finding his way. Arthur urged Frank to investigate the small liberal arts colleges that were mostly in the East, whose curricula included commercial art. He helped Frank write letters of inquiry to several such colleges around the country, one of which was Grinnell in Iowa. The tuition there was reasonable, the dormitory living economical, and the college had a good academic reputation without being considered especially difficult. Frank applied to several colleges, but his first acceptance was from Grinnell.

Toward the end of August in 1922 he returned to Helena from Yellowstone, having saved most of the money he'd earned there. He spent it on two new, conservative suits that would form his collegiate wardrobe. A few days later he left Montana to enter the college named for its little Iowa town of Grinnell. The mark of the West was on him indelibly.

2

☆ ☆ ☆

☆ ☆ ☆

PORTRAIT OF
THE ARTIST

UNDERGRADUATES OF GRINNELL College still fan the
flame of a legend that Gary Cooper once brought a horse into
Rawson Towers and rode it up the stairs to his room. Then, according to the story, the frightened animal could not be budged,
and had to be destroyed after all efforts to coax it downstairs had
failed. This was often cited as the reason for Cooper's expulsion
from Grinnell.

Probably no part of the story was true; and if there was any substance to it at all, Frank Cooper was not expelled. He left Grinnell as a high sophomore, in acceptable academic standing and in
the good graces of the college administrators. The story may have
been invented by a Paramount publicist who was being paid to
make Gary Cooper's past sound interesting. The incident was
noted in a Cooper biography prepared in the studio in 1930; and
Hollywood publicists often reveal extraordinary resourcefulness
for building tales out of scant information, or none at all. As
recently as 1979 the story was disputed by the Grinnell *Scarlet
and Black*, which knew that in any event, Gary Cooper never lived
in Rawson.

The story logically raises other questions. Would a dead horse

be more easily transported downstairs than a live one? This particular horse's tale points up the natural tendency to embellish the
lives of the famous in those dark areas where little is known. Gary
Cooper's twenty months in Iowa are not exactly lost to history,
but it is the least accessible period of his life. He had become
fairly well established in films under his modified name before the
people at Grinnell realized he was the same Frank Cooper who
had gone there. By then all who had been his college mates had
left Grinnell to do their own grappling with the world, and it was
difficult for those on campus to reconstruct a chapter in the academic prehistory of their own movie star.

He had nothing to hide. Indeed, he spoke of his Grinnell days
only with fondness, implying rather subtly that they formed one
of his happiest periods. He once wrote, "Josiah Grinnell thought
he had discovered the West when he went to Iowa, but I went
there and thought I had discovered the East."

Josiah Grinnell was a feisty Congregationalist minister who
after being dismissed from his Washington, D.C., church for
delivering a ringing sermon against slavery, struck out for the
western frontier and in 1854 established the Iowa town that bears
his name. Five years later Iowa College was moved to Grinnell
from Davenport, where it had been founded in 1846. It was a
coeducational institution long before the name was changed to
Grinnell College in 1909, to avoid confusion with Iowa State University and the University of Iowa. The college, like the town,
started small and stayed that way.

When Frank Cooper arrived there, Grinnell was inhabited by
about four thousand permanent residents as well as the students,
who numbered around eight hundred, of whom nearly five hundred were men. Like most small college towns, Grinnell was clean
and genteel. Commercially it served a farming community of
modest prosperity. The town was not a county seat so there was
no graceful courthouse square; but it was neatly manicured and
had a nice park, and the college campus set a standard of physical
dignity that the town fairly matched.

Without accreditation from either of his Montana colleges,
Frank Cooper entered as a twenty-one-year-old freshman, older by
three years than most of those in his class. He was a general academic major, not yet eligible for the upper division classes in com-

mercial advertising that were part of the lure to Grinnell. He enrolled in a basic drawing class, but most of his first semester was committed to required courses that would give him some difficulty. He dreaded foreign languages but faced a requirement to take both a classical language and a modern one. Recalling his disdain for both Latin and French at the Dunstable School, he chose as alternatives Greek and Spanish, and decided to be done with both requirements in his first year. A capricious counselor assigned him to a class in Greek at 9 A.M. and to a Spanish class that followed immediately at 10; and this would have the result of keeping him forever "all mixed up in the lexicons of those two languages."

He was billeted on the second floor of Langan Hall, one of the male dormitories. He had a small, private upstairs room—number 226—that became one of the likeliest spots for dorm mates to congregate. It is no conjecture that he quickly achieved an easygoing popularity. That other undergraduates were drawn to him as a campus "character" was indicated by the affectionate nickname he carried throughout his stay at Grinnell. He was Cowboy Cooper.

A few Grinnellians came from Iowa farms where the tall corn grew. More were from the multitude of hamlets encircling the town, and from cities larger than Grinnell, such as Newton, Oskaloosa, and Marshalltown. There was only a light scattering of pupils from other states, and fewer still came from such a distance as Montana. Immaculately decked out in his best Three-G suit, Frank Cooper still looked like a cowboy, or else fulfilled an Iowan's notion of what a westerner eternally should be. He was probably the oldest new freshman, and very nearly the tallest as well; and both of those traits imparted a substance of character to his appealing western presence. He was seldom called Frank. Addressed directly, he might be either Cowboy or Cooper; but when referred to in the third person, he was Cowboy Cooper, completely and alliteratively, to all the Grinnellians. He liked the tag, and endeavored to become what his friends would make of him. He had brought with him a Stetson hat of the ten-gallon variety that was an off-to-college gift from Jim Galen's parents. He wore it more often than he had expected he would; and although he arrived in Grinnell without cowboy boots, he ordered a pair through the Montgomery Ward catalogue soon after he started college.

Charles Cooper paid Frank's tuition and board and also sent a small monthly allowance to cover his incidental needs. It didn't. Like so many other collegians, Frank would write home that he needed extra cash, the money just went regardless of how careful he was about spending it. The Coopers usually would respond by sending him small amounts, but he was still always broke. So he took work in Grinnell to help pay his way, although finding a job wasn't easy as he had to compete with scores of other hard-pressed students. He went to work at a local shoe factory but hated the monotony of it, and it was a Saturday-only job that removed him from the campus scene on a day when there were no classes but everything was happening. Then Morgan Taylor, an upper classman who was his match for height and also lived in Langan, got Frank a job at the Poweshiek Café. That was more to Frank's liking because the Poweshiek, named for the Iowa county where Grinnell is located, was a popular gathering place for students. Most who worked there were also students, and they had some latitude in determining their own hours. Frank was waiter, bus boy, and sometime short-order cook, preparing hamburgers that sold at ten cents. He was particularly gratified to be working alongside Morgan Taylor, who as football star and all-around athlete was a magnet for the pretty coeds. If Frank required assistance in making their acquaintance, the personable Morgan Taylor provided it.

Frank's first girl friend was a starkly thin blonde named Edna Lundegard, from the town of Winterset, which would later acquire some fame as the birthplace of John Wayne. Edna was almost six feet tall, and they were briefly a spectacular couple; then she left school because of family obligations, and Morgan Taylor introduced Frank to the brown-haired Doris Anna Smith from Marshalltown, northwest of Grinnell. Doris was also a first-year student but already had many close friends on the campus, most of them from her home town. Frank was smitten, but his original information that Doris had given her heart to a boy who was waiting for her in Marshalltown proved accurate. They had only a few dates and could hardly have been said to "go together"; but through Doris Smith and Morgan Taylor, Frank soon knew virtually every student on a personal basis.

Everyone at Grinnell knew almost everyone else, but there was a rigid social organization by academic classes that would erode in subsequent generations. The hundred or so students who had persevered to become seniors formed their own aristocracy and maintained a haughty disregard of the lower classmen. There was spirited interclass rivalry among juniors and sophomores, and the larger freshman class kept to itself more or less involuntarily. His comparative maturity made an exception of Cowboy Cooper, who rode over such barriers to associate mainly with a crowd of juniors that polarized around Morgan Taylor. But he obeyed every custom, which meant that he sat with the freshmen in the huge room where all of the boarding male students dined together. Seniors sat nearest the heads of the long tables that ran the length of the room, followed by the other classes in their normal sequence. Each class also had its own seating area in the chapel where evening vesper services were attended daily.

Initially endowed by the Congregationalist sect, Grinnell College enforced high moral standards that were adhered to by most of the students despite the perils of the Jazz Age that had been launched by the Prohibition amendment. That the Grinnell coeds were resolutely chaste was accepted by the male students, whose oat-sowing more often was accomplished away from the scene. Frank often would ride with a mash of junior men in a clanking Reo driven by Foxy Miller to the nearby town of Montezuma, where they would find bootleg liquor and perhaps some girls of more liberal inclination. This may have helped him acquire some reputation as a "rakehell," which is part of the lingering legend, most of it probably undeserved.

His deportment on campus and in the town of Grinnell was exemplary—at least in his first year when, as he would recall, "I seldom had a spare dime, and that reduced the chance of my getting into trouble." Grinnell had two movie houses and Doris Smith was devoted to their entertainment. She was usually in a better financial position than Frank to attend the picture shows at the Colonial and Strand, and he would go with her only when he was capable of paying her admission. That meant that Doris Smith usually went without him, although they saw Valentino in *Blood and Sand* on what may have been their first date. Later they saw the new Ramon Novarro play Rupert of Hentzau in *The Prisoner*

of Zenda and steal the show from its stars; and Frank thought
Novarro was a better actor than Valentino, whom he particularly
disliked. Doris' own idol, though, was Wallace Reid, and she
thought Frank resembled him. Not long after his screen appearance locally as Booth Tarkington's *Clarence*, Wallace Reid's
shocking death had the Grinnell girls weeping in unison.

Despite being victimized by foreign languages, Frank fared well
in his freshman studies. He was not a diligent scholar, and never
developed good study habits. Yet he found college courses easier
to handle than any of his lower education had been. He seemed
to have a knack for literate composition, and since papers were
required for most of his classes, it held him in good stead. He decided that "whether what I wrote was right or wrong wasn't as important as whether it made basic sense." Short and to the point,
he made sense. His favorite course, though, was drawing, for
which the homework was simply to draw the things around him.
He attempted to sketch the fellows living in Langan realistically,
with indifferent results. Then, by exaggerating their more prominent features, he soon found himself achieving minor campus celebrity as a caricaturist, and his cartoons and other drawings began
to appear in the local publications—including the Grinnell *Scarlet
and Black*, the "oldest college newspaper west of the Mississippi
River."

He did not seem to approximate an actor of promise. He had
been attending classes at Grinnell for only a week or so when he
tried out for the college dramatic society for the first time. It was
also the first indication of his giving any thought to acting, and he
was undone by an obvious case of stage fright. The stammer that
had marked his speech during early adolescence suddenly returned, beyond which "I not only stuttered but spoke my lines so
softly that no one could hear me two feet away." The lines he had
memorized were Ferdinand's in *The Tempest*, and no doubt it
mattered very little if they heard him or not. Homer Abegglen,
the senior student who was president of the dramatic club and the
principal assessor of its aspirants, would say about a decade later
that "Gary was only a freshman, tall and lanky, and we naturally
thought he'd have another chance to make our club." There
would be other chances, and he would always try, but only to be
rejected again.

He was not rejected by Chrestomathia Lit, the literary fellowship calling itself a "society that develops man." Those who
would defend Gary Cooper's general disposition at Grinnell have
often cited his acceptance by the "distinguished" literary group
that had begun back in 1852 on the old Davenport campus. Anyone could wonder to what sort of screening his application may
have been subjected. It would seem unlikely that he had to pass a
literary equivalent of his dramatic audition. Some years later he
would reveal a flair for prose expression that easily surpassed his
frequent ghostwriters, but by 1922 he may have had an aptitude
for composition but showed no real interest in it. He was not a
voluntary reader or a willing student of literature, and Chrestomathia paid homage to the great writers. Yet he was one of its
more active members over three semesters, and may have
stretched a definition of literature to include his own drawings.

So he was an agreeable "joiner" who was also active in a natural
science club, and became sufficiently afflicted with school spirit.
The Iowa writer Ruth Suckow, a Grinnell alumna, noted that the
college was artlessly representative of the small coeducational colleges of the Middle West that were alike in spirit although each
spirit was unique. Frank's inoculation with the Grinnell spirit was
so effective that he wouldn't miss any of its football games, even
though he had no interest in participating in the sport and had
rejected an overture by the coach of the Grinnell Pioneers, who
thought he saw the makings of a pass-catching end in Cowboy
Cooper. There were no athletic scholarships to Grinnell, and the
football program operated on a shoestring as the Pioneers com-
peted with other colleges of similar scope. Frank knew all of Grinnell's players, whether they lived in Langan or one of the other
dorms, and he was remembered for his raucous cheerleading from
the stands. Before a homecoming game, he once led the Pioneers'
torchlight parade. Doffing his Stetson while exhibiting full cowboy regalia, he pranced on horseback and issued a shrill succession
of Indian whoops.

In the spring of 1923 he was briefly on the track team as a pro-
spective hurler of the javelin, but soon resumed the status of a
mere spectator. He would watch "that big blond galoot of a super-
man, Morgan Taylor, run the 100-yard dash, the 440, the 220, and
the 220 high hurdles all in the same day, and win every one."

After completing an unspectacular but generally promising freshman term, Frank went home to Montana for a brief visit, and then put in a final summer as a Yellowstone guide.

His passion for hunting sent him to Yellowstone in the first place. Hunting in the national park was strictly illegal, but on occasions of serious overpopulation in certain species, exceptions were made—as in 1921 when there were too many elk. Frank joined the National Park Service as a rifleman and helped reduce the herd. Then he stayed on as a tour guide over pedestrian trails. When he returned for the 1922 summer, he became a driver of the jitney buses that chugged up the steep inclines and made harrowing descents on roads built over ancient Indian trails through the rustic mountain paradise. Every junket was a grim adventure. The buses designed to transport about a dozen passengers were difficult to control under normal conditions, and were downright heart-stopping when going down a curving steep hill.

Frank's most memorable experience occurred when the brakes in his bus failed completely just as he began the descent from a sightseeing pinnacle. The road curved radically and often during its straight downward trajectory, and only his rapid jerking turns could check the vehicle's speed. His passengers squealed in horror as they were rudely jostled by the sudden twists.

"I knew it was all over. The road was narrow and there were no more turns, so it meant hurtling straight down and no way to stop it. What happened next has to be credited to pure instinct, for I know it wasn't presence of mind. Another steep road was about to meet the one I was about to die on, to junction into a single road still heading down. There wasn't much room for it, but somehow I yanked the old bus clean around and headed uphill on the other trail. The tourists were all black and blue when they finally were able to get out. They gave me every dirty look they could devise, and felt obliged to report my daredevil ways to the park authorities, not any of them ever knowing, I suppose, that somehow I'd saved all of their lives. The brakes on the old bus were shot completely, and right after that they junked it."

He was a good driver. As an informant for the tourists, he was something else.

"Ladies and gentlemen, this is . . . uh . . . it's called Inspiration Point, it's . . . pretty inspiring. Off over there you see the falls . . . they're the Yellowstone Falls. And across the way is Artists Point. Well . . . a lot of people like to paint there."

His chore was to drive the paying tourists to the park's major points of interest and deliver an informative pitch. He had no assurance in delivering a prepared spiel for a bunch of strangers. Another guide said Frank should take a course in public speaking, and that may have had a connection with his effort to join the dramatic club at Grinnell. When he returned to Yellowstone during the 1923 college recess, he may not have been a more accomplished orator, but he was given the choice driving assignment—around the network of geysers dominated by Old Faithful. He was also given free lodging in the log palace that was the Old Faithful Inn, where wealthy tourists were an abundance. Frank's salary was meager, but he collected over two hundred dollars in tips and saved all of it in anticipation of sophomore affluence back at Iowa.

There have been hints that the services he provided the tourists sometimes went beyond their immediate need to see all the sights. The man who was Cowboy Cooper to the Grinnellians became "The Sheik" to his fellow guides in his last Yellowstone summer.

Doris Smith had not answered the letters he'd mailed from the national park, although he had heard from Edna Lundegard—except that was no longer her name. She had married a Winterset boy and now they were living in Des Moines. Frank returned to Grinnell entirely unattached, then proceeded to fall painfully in love, not with a coed but with a "town girl" also named Doris.

She was a vibrant young woman who had her own car. Doris Virden had always lived in Grinnell and had watched the young men come and go, but had never seen anyone quite like Cowboy Cooper. Yet his version was that he was the pursuer in a one-sided relationship. Whatever, she destroyed his equilibrium, and from the time of their meeting was the only romantic object of Frank Cooper's remaining tenure in Iowa.

Someone else had snapped up his job at the Poweshiek Café, but Frank secured an unusual job pressing apples for sweet cider. The apples belonged to a Grinnell professor named Tatlock, who gave him a token payment to collect the windfall from his orchard and operate the cider press. Professor Tatlock invited him to press an occasional gallon of cider for the boys in Langan Hall.

At a Halloween party given by Professor Tatlock in 1923 for other faculty members, Cowboy Cooper ostensibly led a student raid on the five-gallon vat of cider he had pressed himself. More definitive and celebrated was another of the cowboy's capers involving the same substance.

By his own accounting, "I cut the professor in for about three gallons out of every four I pressed. I was secretly reserving the 'spillage' for a chemistry major in my dorm who had a book explaining the process of distilling. Now when he followed the book the stuff was terrible, but once I suppose he was guided by inspiration alone and must have split a cider atom. I'll never forget the impact of that applejack as it went down."

Sure enough, the applejack created a sensation on campus, and Professor Tatlock wanted no further business with young Cooper. Ultimately Frank and his chemist friend were made to give an explanation to Grinnell's President Main, who firmly reprimanded them for violating the Eighteenth Amendment. Their experiments continued nevertheless, although the magic formula was not found again, and finally the cider ran out. Stealing the Tatlock apples could be done easily, but what could they do for a cider press?

So Frank forsook applejack for Arthur Child's bathtub gin.

It was probably through Doris Virden that he met Arthur Child, who was not affiliated with the college in any way but exercised considerable influence over the impressionable collegians. Child was Grinnell's most sophisticated businessman. With his stunning red-haired wife he operated the town's principal photography studio and also maintained their home as a salon for students to discuss art and music and drama and literature, and occasionally even the movies. Frank was a visitor in their house when the Childs entertained the Chrestomathia Lit over tea. When Arthur Child decided he liked the fellow they called Cowboy Cooper, he invited him into his regular "set" for social congress enlightened by stronger stuff than tea.

Bathtub gin was a hardy fad for persons determined to transcend the oppression of the Volstead Act. At their functions the

Childs served gin that had literally been distilled in the upstairs bathroom, sometimes with Frank's participation. Their gatherings, though, were really quite innocent. Often they were musicales in which the participants all warbled the new songs of Mr. Jerome Kern and lesser composers.

It was during one of their Sunday afternoon sociables that Mrs. Child told Frank his looks belonged only in pictures . . . so why didn't he go out to Hollywood? He snickered at the thought and said he could never be any kind of actor; why, he couldn't even get into the dramatic club at Grinnell. Mrs. Child only hooted that being in the movies had almost no connection with real acting.

Rejected on his third audition for the club in as many semesters, Frank nevertheless was encouraged to try out for the college production of Eugene O'Neill's *Beyond the Horizon.* He was almost cast in the leading role of a young man with a wanderlust who gets marooned on the farm. He believed he missed getting the part not because another actor was better, but because he would have appeared too ludicrously tall and skinny beside the preponderance of short and plump pupils who had been otherwise cast.

More encouraging was his progress along artistic lines. His drawings and watercolors were exhibited in the dormitory club rooms. He was named art editor of the college yearbook, which rated as an exceptional plum for a sophomore. He was taking courses in history and economics as well as art subjects, and doing nicely in all of them. He was also a roaring social success, and because of his imposing height was blacked up to resemble a guard of a Numidian tribe and stand in garish costume at the entrance of the senior banquet decorated in a North African motif. In a balloting restricted to the coeds, he lost by only one vote to Cole van Gordon, one of his closest friends, as "winter sweetheart" of the soph class.

He had been almost certain of remaining at Grinnell to graduate, expecting then to pursue one of the good "leads" into advertising that Arthur Child knew about. His outlook changed suddenly upon receiving a letter from his father that was a serious contrast to the frivolous notes Alice usually sent.

The Coopers were in serious financial difficulty. Charles had made some speculative investments with disastrous results, at about the same time that the Seven-Bar-Nine appeared, finally, to have failed completely as a business venture—despite the judge's having continually poured money into its operation over a seventeen-year period. The letter was a secret, or its contents were: Alice was not aware of the Coopers' near ruin, which carried a very real possibility of their losing the ranch. Charles wanted his son to understand that he would be unable to send his regular allowance for an indefinite period. If things improved, tuition for Frank's junior term at Grinnell would of course have priority consideration, but it might be advisable to consider as an alternative taking his upper division work in Montana, perhaps at the state university in Missoula. In the meantime, he urged Frank to economize and make every effort to get by until the present crunch eased.

Frank made every effort. He had been without even a part-time income of his own since the debacle of Professor Tatlock's cider, and had been drawing from his Yellowstone earnings to savor a bit of college high life. Now he got another café job at a place called The Antlers and began to hoard his money. Experimentally he proved that with his room and board paid in advance, he could exist from week to week on practically nothing. But nothing was what he got from it. He had observed the poorer students who struggled through the term with no spending money and had pitied them. His family's allowance had spelled the difference for him, and now the fun had gone out of Grinnell.

Possibly he was advised by someone such as Arthur Child, or he may only have obeyed a sudden impulse; but Frank left Grinnell in February of 1924 with hardly any warning. It was the beginning of the spring semester and he withdrew from the classes that had been assigned him, but left most of his belongings in his room at 226 Langan and caught a bus to Chicago. He took a room at a YMCA hotel and began making the rounds of the professional advertising agencies in Chicago. He had brought samples of work accomplished at what he supposed was his best level, but it failed to generate any excitement in the offices he visited. He was looking for a job and there were no offers, but he suspected it was not his lack of professional experience that counted against him. No doubt the people in Grinnell had overpraised him; the Chicago pros really didn't think his work was any good.

One person who rejected his services advised Frank to seek training, not in college but at an authentic art school. There was one in Chicago that he could recommend without reservation. Frank investigated the school and evaluated it as a likely steppingstone to becoming a professional artist. But the school would cost money and he was running out of that.

He was in Chicago almost a month. Then he returned to Grinnell, packed his belongings, cleared out of Langan Hall, and bought the cheapest train passage back to Helena. He said few good-bys, and the main one was to Doris Virden, who drove him to the depot. He told her he was going to save the money he would earn at whatever work he got in Montana, and that as soon as he could afford it he'd go to art school in Chicago. Then he would get settled in the advertising business, and after that, well, he was going to marry her.

Sitting in a westbound train, he tried to fathom Doris Virden's reaction to his proposal. Had she even returned his kiss? She certainly hadn't said anything. For once, Cowboy Cooper had done all the talking.

Charles Cooper did not lose the ranch. He found that to solve his financial dilemma he had only to retire from the bench. He had become an expert on corporate law, and saw clearly that he could have a lucrative private legal practice merely by giving himself to it full time. He had all the necessary contacts.

Father and son were disappointed, though, one with the other. Charles's decision to resign from the state court had been made partly, he said, to guarantee Frank's four-year tenure at Grinnell. Now Frank had pulled out of school, and was disappointed that his father was no longer a judge and seemed for the first time to be an old, broken man. Alice, too, had aged rapidly during Frank's exile to Iowa. Now she was almost completely gray, and more nervous than he'd ever seen her.

He told his parents he would be heading back to Chicago after he could build up a nest egg. From now on he was going to pay his own way; he was almost twenty-three and it was time he was on his own. He would accept their offer of his old room and some good home-cooked meals, and that was all.

Another summer as a Yellowstone guide was not even considered. Frank went to work at one of Helena's new filling stations and briefly entertained a notion to become an auto mechanic. Then he concluded that driving a car was more enjoyable than working on one, and figured he'd better stick to advertising.

In the summer his father took a business trip to California and was gone several months. Living alone with her younger son, Alice proceeded to spoil him all over again. He startled her by revealing his hope of getting married soon, and told his mother everything about Doris Virden that he thought she would like to hear. He wrote to Doris and to several recent friends. He heard regularly from Arthur Child or his wife, or from both. From Doris he received a friendly, warm letter that covered all of the doings around town but did not explore their future. He also received a letter from Jim Galen, from a place in California called Burbank where Galen and also Jim Calloway were riding on horseback for the movies . . . and why didn't Frank come join them?

After Charles Cooper returned to Montana, he called on a friend of his who was editor of the Helena *Independent*, representing his son as a fairly talented artist. Frank was invited to submit some editorial cartoons to the paper, which could be considered for purchase on an individual basis. Over a period of several months he sent about thirty drawings, of which only seven were accepted for publication. For those he received five dollars each. He suspected he was receiving an unofficial tryout for a regular job as editorial cartoonist for the *Independent*, and that he was flunking it.

His drawings were adequate, strong enough in line if weak in perspective; but they lacked a distinctive style and he knew they resembled everyone else's all-right drawings. Getting ideas for cartoons was yet another matter. It was sheer murder for him, as wit and a clever "angle" forever eluded him. He sensed he would enjoy the atmosphere of a working newspaper, and he began spending a lot of his free time in the *Independent* office. He may have speculated on getting a job on charm alone if talent failed him. He quickly shattered the heart of a girl reporter whose name, of all things, was Doris. Once when he was despairing over his future, she said he ought to take his good looks down to Hollywood and try to get into pictures. He'd heard that before.

He was also finding it difficult to build his capital on fitful income. Chicago seemed farther off in the future, so he applied for a correspondence course in commercial art that guaranteed to return his money if he was not completely satisfied. Chicago became a less certain thing.

November came, and an early snow blanketed Helena. He trudged downtown in the snow, and in a brand-new store on Last Chance Gulch he listened for the first time to a radio. A phantom voice was talking about the national weather, and noted that the people of Chicago were bracing themselves for another mean winter such as they'd become accustomed to.

He thought it over. He had heard that it was always sunny and warm in southern California. And he had received another letter from Doris Virden—probably the last one. She said she had enjoyed knowing him. Suddenly he had no wish ever to return to the Midwest.

He had been prepared to starve in Chicago, and he supposed it was possible that he could starve in Hollywood just as easily.

But he figured he wouldn't freeze there.

3

☆ ☆ ☆

☆ ☆ ☆

LIFE ON POVERTY ROW

HE ARRIVED IN Los Angeles on Thanksgiving Day, 1924. He got off the train, collected his luggage, and simply asked the people at the depot to point him toward Hollywood.

Stories of Gary Cooper's early days in filmland are standard Hollywood lore, and typically apocryphal. He did not really go to California because his father was already there, trying to settle a client's estate. He did not meet old friends from Montana entirely by accident on the street, to be coaxed into joining them as horseback extras for the movies. Nor did he seek a career as a commercial artist.

He went to Hollywood to break into the movies.

Not long after he arrived in California, Frank Cooper was joined there by his parents, because his father was involved in the tangled legal disposition of a millionaire's estate down in San Diego. Frank knew that his parents would not encourage his effort to get into the movies they held in such low regard, so he told them he was going to Los Angeles because prospects were good there for a commercial artist. He extended the charade by taking with him a kit of drawing equipment and such samples of his art as could approximate a professional portfolio. Otherwise his suitcase was distinguished only by his one good dress suit, with an extra pair of pants.

When he finally informed his parents in a letter that he had gone to work in pictures, they were not pleased. Alice, whose notion of Hollywood amounted to all the sins of Araby, was horrified. The filmland had been scandalized by the rape-and-murder trial of Fatty Arbuckle, then the posthumous revelation that the great Wallace Reid was a drug addict, and later by the mysterious murder of director William Desmond Taylor. Knowing that his parents would oppose his speculation on the movies, Frank was determined to pursue success in Hollywood without their financial assistance. It was necessary that he take other jobs to have an income, but he made no real attempt to market himself as a professional artist.

He knew that Jim Galen and Jim Calloway were in Hollywood, earning money just for riding horses. An exchange of correspondence with Galen had helped form his own plan to try the movies, and he had hoped to see Galen as soon as he hit Hollywood. But he lost Jim's address shortly after he arrived, and was unable to trace him. When they finally met, Frank had run into many dead ends trying to earn a living, and was grateful for such help as Galen could give him toward getting a foothold in picture work.

From downtown Los Angeles he rode a trolley into Hollywood for a dime. He was already watching his expenses carefully. The rail fare to California had reduced his cash reserve to little more than a hundred dollars. Thanksgiving was an inopportune day to look for a place to live, but Frank found a dollar-a-day room on Mansfield Avenue. He soon realized that eating in restaurants would quickly exhaust his capital, so he watched the newspaper ads for rooms offering board. For twelve dollars a week he obtained a small but clean room on Romaine Avenue near Cahuenga Boulevard. Boarders were accommodated with two meals a day "and chicken every Sunday." Frank could only blink in disbelief, though, when told that the breakfast call was for five-thirty, in the morning dark. That was because most of the boarders were employed by the movie companies or hoped to be, and a day of shooting began early. A spirit of high adventure seemed to hover over the fairly new activity of making motion pictures.

Much of Hollywood had once been a ranch very unlike the one Frank Cooper knew so well. A pioneer named H. H. Wilcox had developed a 320-acre tract for citrus and walnut orchards and garden vegetables. Mrs. Wilcox chanced to visit friends in the East who called their estate Hollywood, and the word was so appealing to her that she made it the name of a California ranch that bore no holly bushes at the time. Hollywood became a real estate word when the ranch was subdivided, only a few years before Hobart Bosworth made *The Roman*—probably the first motion picture shot in Hollywood, entirely in the open air. That was 1908, the same year in which Colonel William Selig established the first movie studio in California, at Eighth and Olive Streets in downtown Los Angeles. Over the next few years most of the companies dominant in the new enterprise made exploratory visits to California. In 1911 D. W. Griffith filmed *Ramona* there for authentic locale, and stayed on for a dozen other two-reelers before returning to New York. Adolph Zukor delivered Mary Pickford to the West Coast for *Tess of the Storm Country* in 1912, but his Famous Players Company still shot most of its pictures in the East.

David Horsley, whose quickly forgotten Nestor company was soon absorbed by Universal, opened the first Hollywood studio in 1911, at Sunset and Gower. Only a block away, *The Squaw Man* in 1913 became the first feature-length picture shot in Hollywood —produced by an illustrious new team consisting of Jesse Lasky, Cecil B. De Mille, and Samuel Goldwyn. Their venture became an oracle for the moviemakers. In 1914 Charlie Chaplin moved to California, and both Hal Roach and Mack Sennett began filming their short comedies in and around Hollywood In 1915 William Fox took over and expanded the short-lived Dixon studio in Hollywood, and Thomas Ince built the studio that would evolve into M-G-M in Culver City. Within the following two years, studios were constructed in Hollywood by Metro, Pathé, and First National; and the audacious merging of the Zukor and Lasky companies made their Paramount studio the most imposing one in Hollywood, or anywhere else. By 1919, when Griffith,

Chaplin, Pickford, and Douglas Fairbanks became the original United Artists, Hollywood was a factory town unlike any other.

During those years that recorded the triumph of the feature-length film, perhaps half of America's movies continued to be shot in the East. The companies attaining major industrial status tended to maintain physical operations of about equal scope on both coasts. But the eastern studios were scattered, with no visible nucleus. In contrast, an authentic film colony materialized in southern California, and Hollywood was its vortex. It was a part of Los Angeles and it wasn't: a city within a city, almost entirely new and mostly stucco, with young palm trees lining the paved streets. Soon there were imposing banks and hotels with elegance to rival those in San Francisco; but the sophisticated business community of Hollywood was built entirely around the rapidly expanding motion picture industry and primarily sustained by it. Hollywood became more than a place. Mainly it was an idea that cajoled the collective imagination of the American people, and then of those around the world. This was the dawn of the Age of the Movies, when Hollywood and its celluloid product came to dominate American life and thought, for better or worse.

The movie colony was anathema to the settled, basically conservative Los Angeles community. They viewed the Hollywood folk as rootless, for they came from all parts of the country and seemed to have left their moral scruples wherever they came from. The people who colonized Hollywood were adventurers, and they were all young. At the beginning of the Jazz Age twenties, most of the industrial founding fathers were in their forties, but the people who made the movies—the directors and writers, the cameramen, technicians, and artisans—were mostly in their twenties. Movie players were more youthful still; and the most famous heroines—Pickford, Swanson, and the sisters Gish and Talmadge—all attained stardom while in their teens. Now they were as rich as they were famous, for doing something they all enjoyed. Making movies wasn't really work; it was fun. That it was an exciting, youthful activity was conveyed from the screen. The girls and boys who acted out the naïve romances of the silent screen became the envy of their counterparts in cities and towns and on the farms throughout America. The youthful American dream was to make good in Hollywood.

The girls arrived in town by the annual hundreds, then by untold thousands. They came alone or in pairs and groups, and sometimes they were marshaled by the pushy mothers who accompanied them. Young men also arrived with hope of conquering the movies, but they were in less plentiful number and generally were less vulnerable to exploitation. Even when sociologists began painting lurid pictures of hedonistic Hollywood as the land of broken dreams, that only magnified its appeal for new cycles of youthful adventurers. They had heard all of the stories, but they came anyway.

Frank Cooper was one who hadn't heard all the stories. He was astonishingly naïve about the movie business and he knew it, or would soon suspect that almost everyone in Hollywood was more knowledgeable than he. He enjoyed the movies for their entertainment but was not versed in their special mythology, having never been "interested" in them. He said he had not known that Paramount, say, was a more prestigious company than Hodkinson, some of whose Harry Carey Westerns he had enjoyed; or that Harry Carey was a less "important" screen star than Douglas Fairbanks.

He would learn all of these things, and would say that it was an advantage after all that he had arrived in Hollywood with no fixed notions about the place or its magical product.

Across the street from his apartment building was an abandoned studio where mingled the ghosts of movies past. Until quite recently, it had been a vibrant, active lot. The Metro studio on Romaine Avenue had been considered one of Hollywood's finest. But after Louis B. Mayer negotiated the merger of the Metro and Goldwyn companies that barely preceded Frank Cooper's arrival in filmland, production activity was consolidated at the Goldwyn studio in Culver City. The Metro studio was for sale and its gate was padlocked, but Frank could scale a short wall that was obscured from the general view and roam among the fading papier-mâché sets, communing with inspiration.

Soon he knew where all the studios were located, but had no success at obtaining an interview at any of them. He was less than certain about what he really wanted to *do*. Having never acted, he felt ill at ease when nodding that yes, he wanted to "act"—even

though he supposed that standing before a movie camera had little connection with what he thought of as real acting.

One of the boarders played small roles in pictures but had
worked as a cook at Universal before starting to act. He suggested
that since Frank was experienced in restaurant work, he might be
able to get work in one of the studio lunch rooms, or "commis-
saries" as they were called. The first objective was to get inside the
studio gates. So Frank applied for work as a bus boy at Jesse
Lasky's Paramount studio on Marathon Avenue, and at the Fox
studio on Western Avenue toward Los Angeles. There were long
waiting lists at both places. Eventually they would call him for
work, but only after he had become a mounted extra, earning
slightly more money than a bus boy.

He hadn't known that such a thing as Central Casting existed.
When asked there if he was represented by an agent, he said he
didn't know that actors had them. He registered with Central
Casting for work as an extra but never heard from them. He
earned his first three dollars as an extra by getting the work on the
spot—a crowd scene for a comedy short filmed outside Al Christie's studio, which was Hollywood's oldest, originally the Nestor
concern at Sunset and Gower. Frank Cooper concluded that even
if he could obtain such work often, there was no future in it. But
if he was generally discouraged by his prospects, what he had said
about not freezing in Hollywood stayed with him. His first California Christmas was sunny and warm, but his mother had written that Montana was already enveloped in snow. And Frank decided that he preferred California for some other distinct
advantages. Hollywood, he discovered, was a wilderness of girls.
They may not have been out to take his money, but he was inclined to want to give it to them.

He sympathized with a pretty girl from South Dakota who
sought a room in his boarding house but was turned away because
it accepted only men. Frank offered to buy dinner for her, and
they ate at a humble café called Barney's Beanery that would become a movieland institution but was then quite new and very in-
expensive. After dining they walked the considerable distance
back to his boarding house; and as they passed the Metro studio,
Frank asked if she'd like to look inside. He helped her scale the
wall, and soon they were walking among the still-standing sets of

In England with relatives. Brothers Arthur and Gary (age 13) Cooper wear their Dunstable beanies.

With his parents, Charles and Alice Cooper, in Hollywood in 1929.

Right,
a bleary-eyed international
pleasure cruiser in 1932.

Below,
the bachelor squire of
Beverly Hills, with friend Peter.

Left,
*back from Africa
with Tolucca.*

Below,
*the white hunter with
some trophies taken on safari.*

Clara Bow in the obligatory scene from Red Hair *in 1928, at the height of her love affair with Cooper.*

Left, the Countess di Frasso, nee Dorothy Taylor, in 1931. Right, Anderson Lawler and Tallulah Bankhead in 1932.

Left, Cooper squires Mary Pickford to the Brown Derby in early 1933 following her separation from Douglas Fairbanks.

Below, Cooper bids fiancée "Sandra Shaw" farewell as she flies to New York in November 1933.

The newlyweds depart following their Park Avenue ceremony on December 15, 1933.

Joel McCrea and Frances Dee, with the Coopers at a Hollywood ball in 1934 when they all were newlyweds.

The Coopers manage smiles with Lupe Velez and her new husband, Johnny Weissmuller, at a Little Club event in 1934.

*Right,
Cooper at the Paramount studio
with Patrick Hepburn,
young British Member of Parliament
and a friend.from Cooper's days
at the Dunstable School in England.*

*Below,
filming a scene with Anna Sten
for* The Wedding Night *in late 1934.
The director with the scarf is King Vidor.*

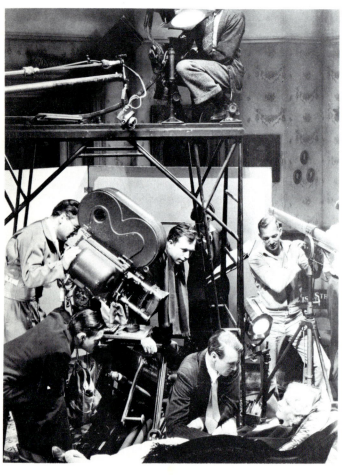

bygone Metro pictures. Even with darkness coming on, the girl could identify the properties of movies she'd seen. She shrieked with the joyous discovery of a set from Valentino's *The Four Horsemen of the Apocalypse,* and had a sudden urge to make love on the spot. Afterward she talked about someday being a movie queen and showing all those people back in Sioux Falls.

Later Frank would bring many a star-struck girl onto the deserted lot and show them where Valentino danced the tango. It worked every time. He may have felt a sense of loss when the studio finally was torn down. Years later he might have wondered if the first girl ever knew he became Gary Cooper, and if she got her own start in pictures, and if she ever found a room to rent.

The thing he hated most was looking for work, so he concentrated on the help wanted listings in the newspapers. His first regular job was as door-to-door salesman for a photographer whose studio was on Vermont Avenue. Working the Hollywood territory, Frank would book appointments for portrait sittings, taking a one-dollar deposit. If the party kept the appointment, Frank received a small commission; and if the appointment was broken, he kept the deposit. Most of the commissions were from girls who needed professional photographs to enforce their efforts at crashing the movies.

Frank earned fourteen dollars the first week, eleven the second, six the third. There was no fourth week, even though he was meeting a lot of girls. Told by the photographer that a certain girl had failed to show for her sitting, Frank paid her another visit to return the dollar deposit, since she seemed to be living close to the margin and he'd liked her. She was surprised by his offer, for she had kept the appointment and had made a large order for prints.

Frank knew he had been taken. He did not confront the photographer to demand his cut, but simply called a halt on his door-to-door hustle and sought other work. That was his way, and he would be taken again. He would say that "The papers were full of ads that were come-ons for suckers, and I was a sucker because I tended to believe the things I was told."

He tried selling advertising on theater curtains for a promised 50 per cent commission on each sale; but there were no sales. He got a more promising start as a real estate salesman but quit when he learned it was phony real estate he was selling. He truly despised any kind of selling, but those were the only jobs available through the newspaper listings. His nest egg was dwindling, then gone. Whether true or not, it was a minor Hollywood legend that Gary Cooper had once spent his last dime on a loaf of bread. He knew he needed steady work with a guaranteed income. When he heard that the young man who delivered milk to his boarding house was getting a movie contract and quitting his route, he applied as his replacement even before the man had given notice.

So Frank Cooper became a milkman for the Adohr dairy firm, several of whose early morning carriers seemed to be would-be movie actors. The hours were ideal for them. A milkman's work was done mostly before dawn, affording a lot of daylight time for making the rounds of the casting offices. Frank was a milkman for five months in 1925. He would rise at midnight, drive his truck to the dairy, and load up for the deliveries that were supposed to be completed by 6 A.M. His custom, though, was to work at a rushed pace and finish his rounds an hour early, so he could make the early breakfast at the boarding house. Then he would return to the dairy on schedule and unload the empty bottles he'd collected. He liked the early morning work but soon began to give in to fatigue. He could not make himself go to bed early and often felt that he was functioning numbly without sleep. He also wouldn't go to bed by day, but was likely to fall asleep anywhere he might be seated.

What he liked most about the Adohr milk run was having the little Dodge truck in his custody. Even after he started getting the Hollywood work he supposedly came for, Frank wanted to keep the milk run rather than surrender his means of transportation. The matter was solved for him the first time he slept through the morning. He was fired.

By then, he was a rider for the movie cameras.

One evening a supper guest at the boarding house was George O'Brien, who had lived there earlier but had lately made a name for himself as a leading man in Fox pictures. Frank told O'Brien that he had tried to get into pictures but had given it up because he didn't know how to go about it. When he mentioned that his friend Jim Galen had put the idea in his head, O'Brien responded to the name.

"Galen? From Montana? Why, I know that boy. We rode together for Al Neitz before I got my break. If you want to find Galen, Al Neitz will know where he is."

But how could Frank find Al Neitz?

George O'Brien said, "Ask anyone on Poverty Row. They all know Al."

Frank had never heard of Neitz or of Poverty Row, but O'Brien believed that Neitz had probably directed more Western pictures than anyone in Hollywood, and they were the very stuff of Poverty Row. That was a collective term for all the independent movie-making operations that were a tattered contrast to the likes of Paramount and Fox and First National. They ground out the cheapest grade of Hollywood sausage, but there was a market for it. Their specialty was Westerns that could be shot in only four or five days, or perhaps three days for a two-reeler. Primitive in their dramatic content, those formula photoplays were supplied to the smaller exchanges. Some of the companies folded, only to be supplanted by others of similar substance.

Frank Cooper learned that Poverty Row was also an actual place name, applied to several threadbare companies strung out along Hollywood's Gower Street. But the term embraced every nickel-and-dime entry in the movie commerce, of which there were hundreds during the early Hollywood history. They bore such interchangeable names as Majestic and Mascot, Realart and Rayart, Crescent and Capitol, Beacon and Signal. In later years groups of them would merge into more substantial concerns such as Republic and Monogram. Of all the Poverty Row entities, only Columbia would graduate to respectability and industrial eminence; and the row was certainly no breeding ground for players courting prestige. Even John Wayne, who endured a long apprenticeship in pulp Westerns, got started first with Fox and then with Warner Brothers. Of all the screen heroes whose professional lives actually began on Poverty Row's lowest stratum, only Gary Cooper would achieve important stardom.

But before he was Gary Cooper, Frank found Al Neitz working for a company called Chesterfield. Neitz even knew who he was, for Jim Galen had talked about his tall friend who was supposed to have come down from Montana but hadn't been heard from. Al Neitz brought them together at last, and Galen was startled by Frank's appearance. He'd never seen even Frank Cooper looking that skinny, and lack of sleep had left dark circles under Frank's eyes to give him an incomparably gaunt appearance. Frank explained that he was on a morning milk run, but hoped to line up some work in pictures.

"You still ride, don't you?" Jim Galen nudged him. "They can never find enough people here who can ride horses. Hell, sometimes it isn't even ten bucks a day, but you can ride almost every day and it adds up. *You* can do it, too."

Jim Galen could count on three or four days of work for Al Neitz in a month but was on regular call to all the companies, including the "majors," which paid ten dollars for the same things you did on Poverty Row for five or maybe seven-fifty. Galen suggested that Frank could earn even more if he wanted to get into stunt riding.

"Stunt riding? What's that?"

"It's just taking a fall from a horse, like when you're supposed to be shot. A studio like Fox will pay five extra dollars for a fall."

If Jim Galen couldn't clear Frank's entry as a movie rider, Al Neitz could. He knew every assistant director in Hollywood, and they were the ones responsible for such mundane matters. But Frank wanted to be an actor, where Jim Galen held no such notion. Al Neitz explained that there were two altogether different levels of living and working in Hollywood. He wasn't a man who needed the high style and he could manage a comfortable living on thirty to fifty dollars a week, the variance depending on which Poverty Row outfit had him on hire—he'd worked for all of them. Maybe Frank Cooper could expect the same sort of steady living but not much more than that. Al Neitz said that while some people "might fall from the big time and end up on Poverty Row, nobody on the row makes it to the big time, or should even try." Then, more considerately, Neitz appraised his subject and added, "On the other hand, Mr. Cooper, there's nobody on Poverty Row as good looking as you are, and looks are what really count in the picture business."

Often during his first year in Hollywood, Frank Cooper resolved to banish his pipe dream and pursue a more reasonable career field. Yet he never considered returning to Montana, which was what Jim Galen did shortly after their reunion in the filmland. Frank was serenaded by the steady warmth of the southland, and he knew that whatever he did with his life, he was in the place where he wanted to do it.

Then something would spur him to persevere for a movie career. One such occasion was his first experience as an extra. After filming a group scene on horseback in the San Fernando Valley for a Tom Mix picture, Frank and some others were invited to serve as pedestrian extras in scenes to be shot in Fox's Hollywood studio. By his own recollection, it was a dream sequence in which Tom Mix appeared as Robin Hood, and all the extras were archers in green tights. That may have been some other picture. The Mix opus was called *Lucky Horseshoe* and the dream-within-the-story had Tom Mix appearing as Don Juan and eluding his captors, one of whom was extra man Frank Cooper. After his scene had been shot, Frank lingered on the set to watch Tom Mix enact a love scene with the very beautiful Billie Dove. He confided to another onlooker that he didn't think Mix was a very good actor.

"He's good enough to make seventeen thousand dollars a week for what he's doing," came the rejoinder.

Frank decided he could summon plenty of patience for eventually earning that kind of money.

His income as an extra on horseback was indeed meager. Ten dollars a day was standard, whether the "day" amounted to two hours or six. His stints for Al Neitz and other Poverty Row elements always paid less. But it was as Jim Galen had said: Frank could always count on five dollars extra for a fall. Many riders shunned falling because it was a dangerous business, with other horses always charging by. Frank wanted the money; he would always *ask* them to let him take a fall.

Later he would say he had been one of the last riding extras. After the stock footage companies came into prominence, a producer could buy a ready-made scene much cheaper than he could shoot one, and for an almost identical result. Gary Cooper once reasoned that he had "appeared" in hundreds of pictures, because many scenes in which he was a riding extra became staples of the stock footage inventory and were incorporated into untold scores of minor Westerns.

He also said that "Riding was tough and cruel. Not enough was known about trick shots then. Sometimes horses would run into a nest of ankle-deep wires, tripping them and hurling their riders with great realism. Too great, you might say. Often the riders were hurt or the horses had to be destroyed, or both. Later the riders could control a wire-and-strap lash-up."

Injuries were commonplace, and fatalities were not exactly rare. Frank Cooper absorbed his share of physical abuse as a riding extra. During one of his falls, his left arm was sliced open by a wire. When he sought first-aid assistance, the director hollered, "Don't wipe off the blood yet, let me get it in a close-up."

At other times Frank said merely that riding for the movie cameras beat working. The regular riders—"the posse," as they called themselves—were a jovial fraternity of misfits. Most had been cowboys. Frank Cooper believed he understood them, and knew he enjoyed their company.

There can be no accurate accounting of the pictures he made as a mounted extra. He seldom knew the name of the picture in whose group scenes he was appearing. Sometimes the scenes never got used. He estimated that he answered about two dozen calls in 1925 from the companies of Poverty Row. He said he rode often for Al Neitz, which would have put him in such illustrious titles as *Warrior Gap, Thundering Speed, Bad Man's Bluff,* and *A Six-Shootin' Romance.*

He could not recall the name of the minor company for whom he appeared in several scenes of a Western called *North Star,* whose leading player was a dog by that name. But he did remember a conversation he had with one of the actors playing support to the canine. The actor resembled nobody's candidate for stardom, for he was jug-eared and had bad teeth. He, too, was disappointed not to be making any kind of dent in pictures, and was thinking of trying the New York stage; and he was Clark Gable.

Frank had better memory of his assignments for the major companies. Paramount had purchased all the Zane Grey books but for the few already owned by Fox, and Zane Grey kept the riders in business. For Paramount Frank appeared in *The Thundering Herd* and *Wild Horse Mesa,* both featuring Jack Holt, and also in the more prestigious *The Vanishing American,* who was the rising

Richard Dix in one of the first pictures to depict the American Indian sympathetically. Frank was one of the *Riders of the Purple Sage* in another Tom Mix epic for Fox, and in *The Trail Rider* he had a nice scene riding side by side with another popular Fox cowboy, Buck Jones.

The best-known silent picture of his extra participation was probably *The Eagle*, which was not Rudolph Valentino's final screen appearance but was the last picture released before his death. Cooper was a Cossack in that one, and is recognizable in one scene with Valentino in prints that have survived.

He remembered that in a picture about the Boer War he fought on both sides. One day he was on horseback, firing a pistol at soldiers on a moving train; and on the following day he was one of the extras on the train, firing at the riders on horseback—trying to kill himself, at least theoretically.

Occasionally he was an extra in films that required no riders on horseback but needed throngs of people anyway. He was in one of the *Ben-Hur* crowd scenes, along with almost everyone else; and at Fox he was in another spectacle, *The Johnstown Flood*, renewing acquaintance with its star, George O'Brien. Frank also joked that he appeared both as a victim of the flood and as a survivor.

All of this activity would seem to have been worthless toward advancing him professionally. He believed otherwise. He was making a lot of friends at the studios, and reasoned that some of them might be beneficial to him at a later stage. Two young assistant directors at Paramount were his early good friends; and indeed, both John Waters and Henry Hathaway would be vital to him in only a few years.

Fitfully he would try to line up some movie acting that went beyond extra work. He thought he might have succeeded when he was told he was being given "a part" in a Franklyn Farnum picture for a Poverty Row mainstay called, simply, Independent. The fading Franklyn Farnum was brother to both Dustin (the movies' original *Squaw Man*) and William, and *Drug Store Cowboy* proved to be one of his last pictures. Frank Cooper's "big scene" found him holding the hoof of a horse that was being shod by the star. Still, the chore brought him twenty dollars and that was more money than he had pocketed for one day's work, anywhere. Another significance of *Drug Store Cowboy* logically eluded him at the time. Franklyn Farnum's teen-aged leading lady, who watched the horse get shod, was the winsome Jean Arthur, destined to become one of Gary Cooper's more memorable co-stars.

When Frank Cooper finally began to obtain movie work that suggested real "parts," his main indebtedness was to his father.

While his parents were in Montana, Frank wrote to them dutifully without revealing the ulterior motives of his workaday existence as a milkman or door-to-door salesman. When Charles Cooper's business obligations sent him and Alice to San Diego, Frank knew they would shortly be paying him a visit, so he prepared them for the news that he was working in the movie game they thought they despised. Indeed, the news hastened their visit.

Alice Cooper was properly shocked, but Charles was calm and of a mind to have serious discussion about his son's prospects. That pleased Frank, who knew he could charm his mother into wanting anything that *he* wanted, but was less confident of winning his father's support. When Charles and Alice arrived in Los Angeles in the late summer of 1925 intending only a brief visit, the retired judge and his errant son had one of their rare heart-to-heart talks. Frank said he knew he had been a disappointment to them, in contrast to Arthur, who had married well and was now admirably employed in Montana by the federal reserve. Frank was twenty-four with little to show for it, but asked his parents' patience because his instincts told him his future was in motion pictures, and he knew he would like the work, which really wasn't like work at all, once he got established. Besides, he was entirely on his own, having rejected his parents' frequent offers of financial assistance. Nor did he seek it now; but he wanted their encouragement, or at least their blessing.

The ever-placid Charles Cooper said, "Well, son, I'll see what I can do to help you."

It had not occurred to Frank Cooper that his father could assist him in any way that was not financial. But on the day immediately following his talk with Judge Cooper, Frank and his parents were invited to dinner at the home of Colonel Starret Ford, whose wife Frances was from Helena and a friend to Alice, and for whom Judge Cooper had become an investment counselor.

Colonel Ford had worked in pictures, most notably as production manager for such elaborate Rex Ingram productions as *The Four Horsemen of the Apocalypse*, which made Valentino famous, and *The Prisoner of Zenda*, which similarly boosted Ramon Novarro. Now Colonel Ford was removed from the scene of production but was deriving a fancy income as a background figure—ironically, as a financier for the tawdry product of Poverty Row. His primary investment was in two-reel featurettes. Colonel Ford said he would arrange for Frank Cooper to be assigned a leading role in one of the forthcoming Westerns. A few days later Colonel Ford telephoned instructions for Frank to report to a man named Albert J. Neitz, who would direct the picture.

Al Neitz was amused that one of his favorite riding extras was being pushed on him as a leading man, but cautioned Frank against expecting something bigger to come of it. The two-reeler in question was called *Lightnin' Wins* and would be shot in just two days on a budget of only eight hundred dollars, of which fifty represented Frank Cooper's own salary. A fourth of the budget was allotted to the "star," who was Eileen Sedgwick, and who also played leading roles in very minor feature films. Frank was tickled that his salary was the equal of Al Neitz's.

Lightnin' Wins was shot painlessly, the film was processed and edited in only a matter of days, and it got a few bookings to fill out a program dominated by a full-length Western; then it disappeared from view. Other than recording a rare overacting Cooper, its main accomplishment was to win over Alice Cooper completely to the idea that her son should become a movie star. She thought him the most beautiful thing she had seen on a screen.

More might have come of it, for Starret Ford had implied that there might be other leads in two-reelers, with features in the offing, but Charles Cooper continued to function as a phantom agent for his son, and helped arrange something that appeared more substantial. He befriended a man named Hubert Bruning, who was an immigrant from the Netherlands and was manager of the largest bakery in Los Angeles, and whose daughter was billed as "the beautiful Marilyn Mills" when she appeared in pictures.

Mary Bruning was a trick rider who toured the vaudeville circuit as a teen-ager with her amazingly responsive horses, Beverly and Star. A dark-eyed brunette raised in Hollywood from childhood, she sometimes doubled for Mary Pickford or Norma Talmadge as a horseback rider, and later on would do so for Pola Negri and Greta Garbo. She was married to a minor producer named J. Charles Davis, who sought to promote her as a Western star in a series of features made for a Poverty Row company called Arrow. The Davises had formed their own company for the purpose of showcasing Marilyn Mills and her wonder horses in a feature-length Western called *Tricks*. And Charles Cooper had talked Hubert Bruning into talking Marilyn Mills into persuading her husband to cast Frank Cooper in *Tricks*—not as the leading man, since the picture already had one, but as an antagonist, the "heavy."

The director was Bruce Mitchell, for whom Frank had often been a riding extra—sometimes in pictures featuring Frank Glendon, who now was cast as Marilyn Mills's leading man, and who measured about five-six.

Marilyn Mills, who along with many other persons would take pride in having "discovered" Gary Cooper, gave her own version:

"I didn't want to be bothered, but here was this boy Frank Cooper, and my father had never asked a favor, and it wasn't so important anyway. So we put him in the picture and he did just fine, even though Bruce Mitchell wouldn't let him appear in a full shot with Frank Glendon because Frank was so short—that is, Frank Glendon was short, not Frank Cooper! As for Frank Cooper, well, he didn't look very mean, but he looked interesting. That's why I put him in touch with Nan Collins."

Nan Collins was a Hollywood agent, only briefly and without particular accomplishment on behalf of the actors she represented. She was certainly not successful in securing work for Frank Cooper during the brief period that he was her client. But she earned her own footnote in the chronicle of movie stardom by changing his name.

The Los Angeles newspapers at that time were offering running accounts of the trial of another Frank Cooper who was accused of murder, and eventually convicted. So Nan Collins thought Frank should modify his name, which she considered a mite too common in any event. She thought about it and suggested Gary Cooper because Gary, Indiana, was her home town.

Frank decided in an instant that he liked it. He would be Gary Cooper. If he changed his mind, he could always drop it.

A Davis company press release listed Gary Cooper among the players in *Tricks*, but not by any name did he appear in the credits when prints were released toward the end of 1925. It would be almost a full year before his new name began to accrue recognition. Nan Collins did circulate a fact sheet on her new client, whose name was printed on the white frame of the first glossy photos that advertised him as a would-be actor. *Tricks*, meanwhile, did nothing to identify him, and it obtained few bookings —nor did the next Marilyn Mills picture, which was called *Three Pals*. It gave Gary Cooper a slightly larger role but he was still uncredited nominally . . . and still on Poverty Row.

Three Pals was shot in a week, just before the Thanksgiving holiday marked Cooper's first year in Hollywood. It hardly mattered that his name was omitted from the credits; he knew he could appear in throwaway Westerns indefinitely and not gain an identity. He might have made even more pictures with Marilyn Mills, who was at least as considerate toward him as she was beautiful; but there were no more Marilyn Mills pictures. All he remembered of *Three Pals* was that he wore three extra shirts in an effort to look less skinny.

The best Nan Collins could do for Gary Cooper was get him a walk-on at Universal in *Watch Your Wife*, a supposed comedy. It was little more than dress extra stuff, and he did not make the credits. Cooper became acquainted with one of the extras, new to Hollywood, and at thirty-one already wizened and balding, and hoping to carve a career as a character player. He was Walter Brennan, and he would become one of Cooper's closest friends in a later and splendid professional association.

After Nan Collins dropped him or he dropped her, he scouted his own jobs. He did some more riding for slightly better pay, and did some stunting for a Jack Holt Western at Paramount, *The Enchanted Hill*. His friend John Waters was the assistant director, and he introduced him around as Frank Cooper. Frank said the name was Gary Cooper now, and wouldn't that look fine on a marquee for a Paramount picture? Cooper met the young, sandy-haired Richard Arlen, whose career was just beginning in a small role, with a new Paramount contract tucked under his arm. Arlen called him "Coop" and John Waters picked it up. Soon they were all calling him Coop, and he didn't mind.

With his legal matters in California resolved, Judge Cooper was ready to return to Montana but his wife was not. Alice said their son needed them now, more than ever. She deplored his boarding-house existence and wanted to make life easier for him. She coaxed her husband into renting a fine house at 7511 Franklin Avenue, in the heart of Hollywood, and following the fad for Spanish architecture. Then she preached economy to her son until he agreed to move in with them. The Coopers purchased the house only a few months later. Property in southern California, after all, was a smart investment. It was a "temporary" arrangement, but Charles Cooper may have sensed it would be permanent. The Coopers would continue to own the Seven-Bar-Nine ranch for many years, but would not live in Montana again. Alice had found a home in America at last: it was clear that she was caught up in the excitement that was Hollywood.

Charles may also have realized that Alice could only be content if Frank were somewhere nearby. She seemed increasingly foolish over him, and did not appear bothered that his fledgling career came near to foundering on the shoals of her protection. For a while he appeared to have lost his motivation and to have taken on the ways of a playboy, having almost exclusive use of the family Buick. He was probably squiring an assortment of girls, but he didn't bring them home to introduce them to his parents. Yet he found himself being drawn closer to both parents and especially to Charles, who taught him to play bridge and became his favorite partner in games they played at home when he wasn't out raising hell. Charles persisted in calling him Frank and could not get accustomed to the name of Gary, which Alice adjusted to immediately. In time he solved the matter simply by calling him "Son."

Gary Cooper suspected that his father was still trying to be helpful when Colonel Starret Ford called with an offer of a part in a Western feature. He tried not to appear ungrateful when he rejected the offer. He remembered Al Neitz's warning that people who became too easily identified with Poverty Row could not expect better things.

"I'm done with Poverty Row," he told John Waters. "And I'm done with riding for five dollars a fall. I may never make another picture, but if I do it'll be for a major company. Or for somebody like Samuel Goldwyn."

Waters got Cooper an interview at Paramount with the famous Jesse Lasky, who was friendly but offered no contract and said, "Let's stay in touch." Cooper, in fact, stayed in touch with persons of some authority at all the important studios. He knew now who all of them were, and knew how to arrange an interview, but always came away empty-handed. A girl who worked as a secretary at M-G-M conspired to introduce Cooper to Irving Thalberg at the Hollywood première of the Lillian Gish-John Gilbert *La Bohème*, and he found himself chatting amiably with someone slightly older than himself but appearing much younger—an authentic "boy wonder." Thalberg told Gary Cooper to make an appointment to see him at the M-G-M studio and Cooper did; then he waited outside Thalberg's office for several hours without being summoned and finally left in dejection. When they became friends some years later, Thalberg said, "You should have waited a bit longer. That's just my way of testing people. But I suppose I'm properly punished for having missed out on a future star."

There was still the matter of "somebody like Samuel Goldwyn," except that there was no one quite like Sam, so Gary Cooper decided he would just go after the great man personally.

Goldwyn wasn't really his name at all. But as Samuel Goldfish, he inspired much joking in the early days of Hollywood enterprise. A Polish-born Jew who arrived in America at age thirteen, he was already beginning to go bald when he became a U.S. citizen at twenty. Aggressiveness made him a successful glove salesman; but he was coaxed into joining his brother-in-law, Jesse Lasky, as a business partner in the highly speculative new game of the movies. The famous *Squaw Man* was their first production, in 1913. Four years later Lasky merged his operation with that of Adolph Zukor, whom Sam Goldfish loathed; so Sam went off on his own, forming a producing partnership with a theatrical figure, Edgar Selwyn, who he could easily dominate. The company combining parts of both their names became Goldwyn, and Sam liked the sound of it so much that he adopted it as his own surname.

He bought and.expanded one of the Ince studios in Culver City, and built the Goldwyn company into near-giant status. Then he was eased out in an industrial power play, and it was after Sam's departure that the financial collapse of the Goldwyn organization set up the merger with Metro. Sam was in no way ever associated with the colossus known as Metro-Goldwyn-Mayer, but was not displeased that it gave him a lot of free advertising over the years.

Shunning further involvement with a major producing corporation, he became the best-known independent producer. His mania was for that elusive thing called quality, and there was general acknowledgment that his pictures attained it. If they varied in their merits, they all had an aura of "importance." So did Samuel Goldwyn, who, by the Hollywood standard of age, was already a senior citizen. He was in his mid-forties when he made *The Winning of Barbara Worth* in 1926.

Based on a best-selling novel by Harold Bell Wright, it augured a commercially volatile exposure for Goldwyn's illustrious romantic team, Mr. Ronald Colman and Miss Vilma Banky. The adaptation was by the prolific Frances Marion, and top professional hands were in every department: a major director in Henry King, an ace photographer in George Barnes, and technicians who would accomplish a breakthrough in special effects with a spectacular flood caused by a dam burst. *The Winning of Barbara Worth* was, in fact, very nearly a smash hit. Yet it is forgotten today, except for having been the picture that launched Gary Cooper.

Both the size and importance of his role have been exaggerated by the historians, although there is no doubt that he was the surprise hit of the picture. There are several versions of how he came to get the part of Abe Lee, and not all of them can be reconciled.

Cooper probably had not read the novel, for reading was not one of his pastimes and the reading of fiction almost never occupied him. But he had heard that the newest Goldwyn project was a Western of sorts, and he believed that kind of picture offered his own best opportunity. Westerns produced on a grand scale by "name" producers were rare enough, but Cooper also heard that *The Winning of Barbara Worth* had a good secondary part for a young cowboy type.

Cooper sought an appointment with Samuel Goldwyn, and pre-

dictably was shunted to Bob McIntyre, who was Goldwyn's casting director and production manager. McIntyre took credit for
hiring Gary Cooper, but so did Henry King; and years later Sam
Goldwyn became convinced that he had discovered Cooper personally. What is certain is that they cast another actor as Abe Lee,
and that Gary Cooper was a "temporary" fill-in when the other
actor was late in reporting.

For his meeting with McIntyre, Cooper brought along a can of
film containing a "screen test" of himself, made under his own direction. He had hired a cameraman to film him riding a horse,
mounting and dismounting, taking a daring spill, and then looking somber in close-up before breaking into a wide grin. The strip
ran just over a minute and had cost him sixty-five dollars, including the processing fee. It was a primitive exhibition that might
have served him well on Poverty Row, but McIntyre was un-
impressed and dismissed him politely. Cooper then managed to
see Henry King, who said he might be given one of the very small
roles; there would be a kind of "cowboy chorus." He could count
on fifty dollars a week.

As Abe Lee they had cast Harold Goodwin, a juvenile of distinctly modest promise who had appeared in many humdrum
Westerns. After Goodwin was featured in a spy drama called *Secret Orders*, which became a "sleeper" hit, McIntyre signed him
for *The Winning of Barbara Worth*, with the further promise
that if he did well, he would be put on the Goldwyn contract list.
But when *Barbara Worth* went into production, Goodwin was
still filming *The Honeymoon Express* for Warner Brothers. It was
not unusual to "shoot around" an absentee performer, so work
commenced on *Barbara Worth* and Henry King asked Gary Cooper to stand in for Goodwin because Cooper "just seemed to be
hanging around the set."

Frances Marion in her autobiography suggested that Gary Cooper was hanging around because he was romancing one of the
Goldwyn secretaries. Miss Marion recalled that she was working
on the scenario at the Goldwyn office when the secretary asked
her to come to a window and gaze upon her lanky young man,
who was lingering outside. Wouldn't he be just perfect for the
Abe Lee role in the picture? Frances Marion thought he would be
just perfect, and said so to Sam Goldwyn himself. She was certain

that Cooper was eventually tested for the part. Furthermore, Sam Goldwyn blamed *her* when he believed the inexperienced Cooper was ruining his picture.

The Winning of Barbara Worth was shot primarily on location —in the Utah Rockies, the Black Rock Desert of Nevada, and in California's Imperial Valley. Before the company departed, some scenes involving the principals were shot at the United Artists studio on Formosa Avenue. That was when Henry King decided to test Cooper as Abe Lee, seriously but secretly. He had liked his appearance in the rough footage from a couple of takes, but was concerned about the young man's nervousness. In a scene at a water hole, Abe was supposed to dipper the water in his hands to drink. King was fascinated that Cooper, as if by nature, appeared to be blowing dust from the top of the water before starting to drink it. King decided then that the "test" footage would be in the completed film.

King asked Gary Cooper how badly he wanted to play Abe Lee, and Cooper said he'd give his left ball for the part. King said, "You won't have to, it's yours."

A few years later Harold Goodwin would fail to make the transition to the talkies, and would be best remembered only for a role he very nearly played.

Movie buffs respond to the name of Abe Lee, but who remembers Willard Holmes? That was the mining engineer Ronald Colman played, who won Barbara Worth. Abe Lee was a bashful young cowboy lingering in the near background, mooning after pretty Barbara, who wouldn't give him a tumble. Abe would be fatally injured while accomplishing some super heroics with Holmes during the flood; and Gary Cooper would die in Ronald Colman's arms in the only film they made together. Some have said it was that death scene that really put Gary Cooper over. Many takes of it were filmed, as the director kept thinking that Cooper "wasn't giving enough"; but from the screen Gary Cooper almost always would reveal a sufficiency, and seldom too much.

Henry King was the first of many directors who would misgauge Cooper's talent—or better, his substance—while shooting a picture. King soon believed he had made a grave mistake by casting someone obviously unsure of himself, and almost pathetically nervous. Later he came to believe that the condition imparted to any Cooper performance a valuable edge of tension. It illuminated a special quality, expressing a purity reminiscent of the young Richard Barthelmess in King's earlier, classic *Tol'able David*.

At a point in the early shooting when King felt Cooper should be replaced, he wouldn't suggest it because he really liked the boy. If Goldwyn wanted him removed, it would be done; but Sam never ordered it, although he monitored many complaints about Cooper's shortcomings. Goldwyn did not go on location with the picture, but screened the new footage regularly in his Hollywood office.

Cooper sensed that the other players felt he was not meeting their own performance standard. He believed that Ronald Colman shunned him more pointedly as the shooting progressed, and he supposed the gorgeous Vilma Banky offered a gentle friendship mainly out of sympathy. She had her own insecurity, groping with a language still fairly new to her. Together in some *Barbara Worth* stills, Vilma Banky and Gary Cooper are the beauty of youth itself. He was smitten by her, but could only emulate Abe Lee's silent adoration for Barbara Worth. Cooper was older than Miss Banky by two years, and she had not yet become Mrs. Rod La Rocque in the fabulous Hollywood wedding financed entirely by Samuel Goldwyn. But in the protocol of that era, an unproven supporting player did not court the favor of a star. Vilma Banky would be a casualty of the talkies in her mid-twenties, done in by a thick Hungarian accent. In her retirement she would win filmland golf tournaments as Mrs. Rod La Rocque, still happily married to a silent screen idol who would sell real estate to Gary Cooper.

After the company's return from the location shooting, Goldwyn ordered retakes at the studio of some scenes involving Cooper, who was made doubly uncomfortable by Sam's scowling presence on the set. His chore as Abe Lee completed, Cooper was embarrassed by his apparent failure and inclined to want to give up acting. Word of his inadequacy had filtered into the other studios, which discouraged him from investigating new prospects. And no one in the Goldwyn company asked him to attend the Los Angeles première of *The Winning of Barbara Worth*.

Following that event in the United Artists Theatre on October

14, Gary Cooper probably could have obtained a player contract with any major company. Had he realized that, he doubtless would not have been so hasty in signing with Paramount surely for less money than he could have bargained. But a hundred and fifty dollars a week seemed an enormous amount to someone who had fallen dangerously from running horses for five dollars; and it seemed generous by comparison with his financial treatment at the hands of the Goldwyn organization. Sam was to have paid Harold Goodwin two hundred dollars a week to play Abe Lee, but was delighted to learn that Henry King had hired Gary Cooper for only fifty. King protested that he'd offered fifty for Cooper to play a walk-on, but to Goldwyn an agreement was an agreement and there was no further obligation. For fifty dollars he'd hired an actor who was lucky to have an important exposure in a big picture. It was a sore spot with Cooper until he began to feel he was a flop and probably not worth even the fifty. He supposed he *knew* he was a flop when he failed to hear anything more from the Goldwyn company, even after reviewers of *The Winning of Barbara Worth* praised him as a likely future star.

So he called on his friend John Waters at Paramount. Waters had made several vain efforts to sponsor Gary Cooper as a likely hero for the Zane Grey Westerns. Now the Paramount executives were interested; and B. P. Schulberg, the production supervisor, invited Cooper to come to his office to talk about a possible screen test. Cooper wore a new vested suit purchased with some of his *Barbara Worth* earnings, and was ushered into Schulberg's office where the two men proceeded to talk about horses and Montana, and Hollywood and Sam Goldwyn. Schulberg was informally congenial, and Cooper felt relaxed enough to talk freely. For all his celebrated long silences, he could always lead a conversation whenever he was relaxed. As time passed without mention of a screen test or possible contract, several Paramount officials entered Schulberg's office for an introduction to Gary Cooper, then took other chairs and silently audited the two-way conversation. Cooper met Albert Kaufman, who was Jesse Lasky's special assistant; and Sam Jaffe, general manager of the studio; and a few others whose names he would not recall. Finally there seemed to be nothing more to say, and a long pause was broken by Schulberg asking if Cooper was ready to become a contract player for Paramount.

Cooper said, "Well, yes, but what about the screen test?"

"This *was* your screen test, Gary. These gentlemen merely wanted to look you over, and they have indicated to me that they approve of you. Our offer is a hundred and fifty a week, with escalations of course, provided you . . . ah, do well."

Cooper signed the contract in early November, marking the end of his second year in Hollywood. Before making brief mention of his signing in her gossip column, Louella Parsons telephoned Sam Goldwyn to ask why he hadn't signed Gary Cooper for his own company. The easily flustered Goldwyn sputtered assurance that he had, he had. Immediately he got in touch with Henry King and Bob McIntyre, certain that one of them must have seen to the matter of putting the young actor who was such a hit in his new picture under an exclusive Goldwyn contract. Neither had been instructed to do so, and McIntyre had heard Sam say at the *Barbara Worth* première that Gary Cooper was a no-talent. Now Sam's disposition was to want to sue somebody, although he clearly had no case. He also wanted to discuss the matter with Gary Cooper, and they had a cordial meeting at Goldwyn's home, with Cooper as dinner guest. Sam expressed his intention of someday getting Cooper back—provided, of course, the young man didn't fall flat on his face in his Paramount pictures.

Alice was bursting with pride for her beautiful boy, who she was certain would flutter many a tender heart from the silver screen. Her stoic husband was telling people that *The Winning of Barbara Worth* was the first picture he had truly enjoyed since *The Birth of a Nation*. The least celebrative of the Coopers was Gary himself, who now worried that his success had been a fluke and that he *would* fall flat on his face. The new contract with its escalation clauses also contained an option clause which meant that Paramount could cut him adrift after only one year. He was somewhat reassured by information that his first Paramount assignment would be a Western opus that John Waters would direct, with shooting to commence right after the New Year's holiday.

In the meantime he would report daily to the studio for photographs and costume fittings, and to be biographically profiled by the Paramount publicists. By the time he went to work before the cameras, he would know most of the regular faces at the studio.

Early in December he attended his first Hollywood party, at the home of a Paramount executive and dominated by studio folk. Many of the younger contract players were there, of whom he was acquainted only with Richard Arlen and James Hall. He sensed that other partygoers were staring at him, assessing a newcomer. He was miserable enough to want to leave, but would not risk offending anyone associated with his new employer. Then there was a mirthful explosion in the form of a girl arriving to put him out of his misery.

It was Clara Bow.

4

GLORIOUS YOUNG LOVER

OLD-TIMERS AROUND Hollywood will tell you that when the young Gary Cooper was securing his foothold in pictures, he became calculating to the point of obliging anyone who could help advance his career.

His early associations reveal a pattern to support that premise. He was a "name" ahead of Paramount's timetable for building him into one, and soon was a far more substantial name than the studio had hoped to build. His amorous activity provided better copy than a publicist could fabricate, and a combustible liaison with Clara Bow started it all. Surely their lively affair boosted his career, but that was no scheme of his. As she had done to so many other men, Clara simply wound him like a top and then set him spinning. He lost his balance over the little Brooklyn bombshell, and some thought he may have lost his marbles as well.

Until she accosted him at the Paramount party, he had never met a girl so frank or so direct. Here was a fellow of unbelievable good looks that she hadn't seen before, and she thought they should be acquainted. So she took him to the house in Beverly Hills that had just been built for her, and they stayed the night there—just the two of them. By the next day they were well acquainted indeed, and Clara wanted Gary to be in her new picture. And at about that time, she was getting everything she wanted.

Clara Bow's life is recalled as tawdry and pitiful, perhaps genuinely tragic. Scandal ruined her career and she was seldom a stable person afterward. But Gary Cooper met her at the very moment of her gaudy pinnacle in the filmland. In November of 1926 she was absolutely the hottest thing in pictures.

She was also the most promiscuous girl in town and almost everyone knew it. Asked in 1979 to name Hollywood's all-time tramp, Anita Loos considered the candidates she had observed over seven decades and said "Clara Bow." Only with reluctance did Paramount grant her stardom, for Clara was the antithesis of the Pickford and Gish images that had idealized movie queendom. She was slangy and a gum-chewer, but infectiously merry and incredibly animated.

Up to a point, her life was an authentic Cinderella story. Her poverty-bound Brooklyn heritage included a mentally disturbed mother and pathetic father who rarely had work and then couldn't keep it. Still, she bloomed in squalor. At sixteen she won a beauty contest and got her picture in the newspapers. It put her in the movies. In 1922 she was a hit in *Down to the Sea in Ships* and worked steadily thereafter. B. P. Schulberg, then producing independently in the East, put her under contract and began to exploit her, lending her to other companies for ever-higher fees although Clara herself remained underpaid. In 1925 alone she was seen in fifteen pictures—mostly sleazy fare, but she was becoming a well-known player with her own popularity. With her mother dead, she took her father to Hollywood where she was always considerate of him, and she showed no inclination to marry. She had a more-the-merrier attitude toward men and an apparently insatiable appetite for sex.

In 1926 Paramount made Schulberg a producer as a means of acquiring the fast-rising Miss Bow. At about the same time, a ludicrous Englishwoman named Elinor Glyn was all afuss about It. When asked what "It" was, she gave no definition, except that It was a quality so magical, so elusive as to be indefinable. Elinor Glyn was a popular novelist of romantic pulp and the Jacqueline Susann of her day for effective self-promotion; and when she proclaimed that Clara Bow had It, suddenly everyone seemed to know just what It was.

In the wake of a sensational showing as a Sinclair Lewis heroine in *Mantrap*, Clara Bow was exploited by Paramount as the "It Girl." It was believed that her subsequent appearance in Eddie Cantor's *Kid Boots* turned that farcical film into a box-office winner. (It also very nearly destroyed the fabled marriage of Cantor and his beloved Ida.) Clara was herself a mantrap, whose tempestuous private life emulated the jittery jazz-baby she enacted on film but without the Hays Office restrictions. And now that she was Paramount's biggest draw, she would be accommodated with specially prepared starring vehicles. To capitalize further on their potent publicity gimmick, the Paramount people devised a picture called *It*.

She had just finished shooting *It* when she met Gary Cooper. Finished or not, she breezed into the office of her old sponsor and said she wanted Gary in the picture. Holding the studio production reins, Schulberg first protested, then relented—logically because exposure in a Clara Bow picture could only benefit their new contract player. So Louis (Bud) Lighton wrote an additional scene that could be shot on the only *It* set not already dismantled. The director, Clarence Badger, had gone off to New York, but Josef von Sternberg was on hand to supervise the brief scene involving only Clara Bow and Gary Cooper, who played a newspaper reporter.

Cooper's parents saw little of him during the waning days of 1926. His time that wasn't owned by the studio was given to Clara, in her Beverly Hills mini-palace or wherever they went. They took long drives and made love on the beaches above Malibu, in the mountains above San Bernardino, in walnut groves of the San Fernando Valley . . .

She was the veteran trouper but was four years younger than he, and theirs was a stupendous case of mutual physical attraction. He was simply the most beautiful thing she'd seen in Hollywood, and there was much about Clara Bow to dazzle anyone. She had huge dark eyes, a bee-sting mouth that was pouty and sensuous, and her hair bob was a new vogue. And she was irrepressibly high-spirited, so that even her detractors said it was not hard to enjoy her presence. Her presence could only have been enormously stimulating for Gary Cooper, but she had a particular failing that would give him an ever-growing displeasure. She talked too much.

Clara Bow would kiss and tell, and then tell of her adventures beyond kissing. She'd had scores of lovers and often juggled them simultaneously. The incumbent was Victor Fleming, her *Mantrap* director, who was filming *The Rough Riders* in Texas when Clara took up with Gary Cooper. Clara rated her lovers for proficiency and gave Cooper rave reviews; it was her original information that made Cooper an intramural legend for being magnificently endowed in the masculine appointments. He was already a celebrity when he reported to Paramount after the New Year holiday for his first leading role. John Waters called him "Studs" until he sensed that Cooper didn't accept it in good humor.

Arizona Bound was only a minor Western, a "B"; otherwise he would not have been entrusted with a lead. From start to finish it was shot in two weeks, partly in Utah's majestic Bryce Canyon where Cooper did his own stunts. For another scene shot beyond the rural reaches of Hollywood, he was joined by the posse of Hollywood extras that had once enlisted him. He later reflected that only his familiarity with pictures of the type and scope of *Arizona Bound* enabled him to get through the chore without becoming a nervous wreck. He counted it a blessing that John Waters went about his business methodically, directing with little attention to acting. Featured with Cooper was a "wonder horse" named Flash, a hoped-for equine equivalent to Rin-Tin-Tin; they were to be regular teammates and Cooper already knew that Flash would also be in his next picture. In *Arizona Bound* there were bad guys and Cooper licked 'em; and there was a girl played by Betty Jewel. Cooper got the girl but didn't kiss her.

He expected to have a brief vacation from work upon completing *Arizona Bound*. Although he reported daily to the studio for the incidentals of being a movie contract player, that wasn't really work—especially with Clara Bow on the scene, getting ready for her new picture. Clara was having costume fittings for a very dramatic venture to be called *Children of Divorce*. Her dressing room became their trysting place, and it was evident that Cooper was still so smitten that he forgave her indiscretions. And now

Clara's sudden inspiration was that Gary should be her leading man in *Children of Divorce.*

James Hall, also getting fitted, was set for the playboy role. Clara said, "Find something else for Jimmy, I've got my mind set on Gary now and ain't gonna change it." When told that Cooper was scheduled for *The Last Outlaw,* she said it could wait. Getting her way was not going to be easy. *Children of Divorce* rated as an "important" picture, for which a leading director—Frank Lloyd—was being specially borrowed from First National. It was also a sophisticated contemporary story, and the reckoning was that Cooper was strictly a cowboy type. But Clara got her way.

The talk around the studios was that Clara Bow was paying off her gigolo. From Louella Parsons on down, all the filmland reporters made the casting a top item, with primary reference to Cooper's "memorable" debut in *The Winning of Barbara Worth* —still the only picture in which nominally he had been seen. When *Children of Divorce* was put before the cameras in February, *It* had a fussed-over New York opening. The critics were not impressed but the picture would be the smash hit to confirm Clara's commanding position in the firmament, even though Gary Cooper's participation was barely noted.

During the filming of *The Winning of Barbara Worth,* a woman journalist had interviewed Cooper and then submitted her story about him to *Photoplay* on speculation. The piece was not purchased, but editor James Quirk retained it "just in case he turns out to be somebody." Cooper's assignment to *Children of Divorce* prompted Quirk to buy the article and run it more or less as it had been written. Most of the facts were right, including partial education in England, living on a Montana ranch, and going to college in Iowa. But it escaped editorial notice that the author spelled his new name incorrectly; and the first story to feature him in a fan magazine introduced Gary Cooper to the readers.

Frank Lloyd, a movie pioneer long in America but still the polished Briton, had accrued reputation as a director capable of extracting solidly dramatic performances from players of dubious ability. He was an autonomous producer-director for First National when Paramount borrowed him for the express purpose of turning Clara Bow into a serious actress. Then Lloyd became distracted from his primary mission by his attempt to make an adequate actor of Gary Cooper, and he thought it was a losing effort.

Children of Divorce was a jazz-age triangle story, adapted from a popular new Owen Johnson novel. Clara Bow would be that staple of the movies called the vamp. She would take Gary Cooper away from the nice girl that Esther Ralston would play; but eventually she would feel pretty rotten about what she'd done, and her suicide would reunite the kids who of course were meant for each other. The "children of divorce" were Cooper and Miss Ralston, a lovely blonde who had made steady progress up the ladder and usually had leading lady status in films of consequence.

On the first day of shooting, Gary Cooper was in a couple of mundane scenes and felt he got through them quite smoothly; his confidence began to build. On the second day he muffed an elaborate party scene by losing control of a tray filled with cocktails and dousing Hedda Hopper in particular. He explained that he was nervous; his confidence was imperiled. On the third day he was supposed to make love to Esther Ralston and his confidence was completely shattered. He felt awkward and embarrassed, and explained to his director that he hardly knew the girl. Frank Lloyd said, "Then I'll expect you to be better tomorrow, when you have to kiss Clara."

He was no better kissing Clara. From day to day it only got worse. Cooper's worry was reflected in his face. He was unable to smile and was approximating the most woebegone playboy of the age. Whenever he was in a standing position for a take, his legs shook visibly. After a week of shooting, Lloyd asked Schulberg to replace Cooper with another actor, and Schulberg ordered a shutdown until one could be assigned. Lloyd left the studio to avoid a confrontation with Cooper, who got the word from Schulberg. Rather than crushed, Cooper seemed relieved; and Clara didn't protest his being fired, for she sensed he would rather be making a picture with Flash the wonder horse.

The *Children of Divorce* company reassembled for another go at the cocktail party scene, with William Boyd summoned as Cooper's replacement. While the cameras were being set up, Hedda Hopper said, "We won't hear any more talk about Frank Lloyd being able to get a good performance from just *anybody!*" Lloyd overheard the remark, which may have been what Miss

Hopper intended, for long after she traded movie acting for movie gossip she boasted of having "saved" Gary Cooper's career at an early stage. Lloyd told William Boyd to go home, and told Schulberg to get hold of Cooper.

Not until firmly ordered to do so would Gary Cooper consent to resume filming *Children of Divorce*. Then Frank Lloyd said, "I'll make an actor out of you or I'll eat the print!" Shooting proceeded without immediate further incident, but Lloyd put Cooper in a chair and kept him there, shooting him in a sitting position so his legs wouldn't shake. Cooper remained gloomy and was cold toward Lloyd, who he knew had wanted him fired in the first place.

The strain on Cooper also briefly cooled his ardor for Clara, and she was accommodating the recently returned Victor Fleming on the side. Not even Clara had any idea where Gary could be when he disappeared without explanation, a few days before the scheduled completion of shooting. Cooper's parents hadn't heard from him for more than a week, and had supposed he was somewhere with the well-known It Girl. Entirely by chance, Frank Lloyd found Cooper, weary and unshaven, in Henri's restaurant in Hollywood three days after he disappeared.

Cooper was almost tearfully apologetic. After an especially hectic day of shooting, he had left the studio to go off hunting, down toward San Diego, and to be alone with his thoughts. The whole acting thing was a mistake, he said. He was going to give it up before it drove him crazy, but he had returned to finish the picture.

Children of Divorce ran over schedule but was finally in the can. Frank Lloyd didn't eat the print, but no one accused him of having made a satisfactory dramatic performer of Gary Cooper, or even of Clara Bow. The studio folk conceded that *Children of Divorce* was a mess, and put it into release immediately without fanfare. Its reception did not alter their judgment, and Esther Ralston received the best notices.

Cooper was summoned for his first meeting with the great Jesse Lasky, who said that everyone knew his assignment to *Children of Divorce* had been a mistake. But it wasn't a fatal mistake. There was nothing the matter with that little *Arizona Bound* picture that was just going into release; and the wonder horse was already on location for *The Last Outlaw*, just waiting for its rider. Having learned their lesson, they would cast Cooper only in Westerns; and as a show of good faith, his Paramount salary would be doubled to three hundred a week.

Gary Cooper went right out and bought a fire-engine-red Chrysler roadster, with red upholstery. And he didn't quit the movies.

Sometime in the late spring of 1927, Gary Cooper probably proposed marriage to Clara Bow. He never made public admission of it, and in later years would vigorously deny that they had a serious relationship. Clara, though, said it was only when Gary started talking marriage that their relationship began to sour. She believed the only reason anyone should get married was to have kids—and she believed she couldn't anyway, since "some of my parts are missing." Besides, Gary would probably want some kids and be disappointed, "but he doesn't have to worry about knocking me up."

Both Hedda and Louella would go on record that Gary wanted to marry but Clara wouldn't say yes. He objected to sharing her with other men and wanted an exclusive contract. He knew that not only Victor Fleming was contending for her generosity, and studio chatter had Clara roughhousing with actor Reed Howes behind the set of her *Rough House Rosie* picture, which followed *Children of Divorce*.

Their romance, far from dead, was on again, off again. It percolated anew with a famous picture called *Wings* that both were in. In a roundabout way it was also Clara's doing that he was assigned to *Wings*, which certainly was no Western.

King Vidor's historic *The Big Parade* had placed the fairly new M-G-M company in position to challenge Paramount's long-acknowledged supremacy. Jesse Lasky's idea was to meet the challenge with his own epic of the Great War, but one about flyers rather than foot soldiers. Ex-flyer John Monk Saunders produced a scenario to accommodate Lasky's own title of *Wings*. The young William Wellman, who had been a pilot in the Lafayette Escadrille and had been chafing to make an aerial picture, was invited to direct. The picture went into production with very nearly an all-male cast until someone panicked. *The Big Parade* had a fabulous aching love story between a doughboy and a French girl, and *Wings* had no such embellishment. So one of the small female roles in *Wings* was built up, only slightly and rather awkwardly, but perhaps all it needed was the right star. The picture had only lower-case male leads in Buddy Rogers and Richard Arlen, and a more formidable star became desirable both for prestige and box-office insurance. The best bet was Clara Bow.

She liked the idea of playing queen to a hive of men, but didn't like what the part offered, or didn't: she scanned the scenario and couldn't find the obligatory scene where she appeared in her stepins. No, she wouldn't do the picture; and according to the new contract that had been worked out for her, she didn't *have* to if she didn't want to. But she might want to, if Gary Cooper had a part in the picture.

So Cooper made fast work of *The Last Outlaw,* for which Betty Jewel again was his leading lady before vanishing from pictures; then he took off with Clara to join the *Wings* company at Kelly Field near San Antonio. The brief role of Cadet White, a cowboy-type flyer, was a late addition to the worked-over script.

Clara was confident that her affair with Cooper would be restored to full flame if they could get away from Hollywood where Victor Fleming was lingering somewhere nearby. Then some retakes were ordered for Fleming's *Rough Riders* film, which had been pulled from distribution when found wanting. And there was Fleming with his crew, shooting adjacent to the *Wings* encampment in Texas, with a common chuck wagon. Clara had made a game effort to keep them from meeting one another, and now Fleming and Cooper were lunching together, and becoming fast friends.

Clara endeavored to do double duty until Fleming took his Rough Riders back to Hollywood. Then she and Cooper had a lot of time together because her role wasn't large and his was small, and often neither was on call. They went into San Antonio because Gary wanted to see the Alamo, and it was anybody's guess where else they went. If one of them was absent from the location roll call, so was the other. But when Cooper's role was completed before hers and he went back to Hollywood, Clara became very friendly with an actor whose provocative name was Gunboat Smith.

Some chroniclers have reported that Gary Cooper's appearance in *Wings* was limited to one brief scene, which, however, had the effect of securing for him a large national following. Neither is exactly true. He appeared around the edges of the frame throughout the first part of the picture when the cadets played by Arlen and Rogers were in training. He was showcased in one fairly large scene that surely won him some new adherents, but only after his popularity had been clearly established. For the film's initial exposure in the fall of 1927, *Wings* played only roadshow engagements in large cities, and did not have national distribution until 1929—by which time it was already the Best Picture winner in the first year of the Academy Awards, and was a near-talkie with a grafted musical score and sound effects.

The scene in question finds experienced flyer Cooper visiting Arlen and Rogers in their tent. He munches on a chocolate bar while philosophizing about the inevitability of death in the sky. Then he gives them a smile and a salute, and moments later is killed in a test flight.

The camera fixes on the half-eaten chocolate bar he has left behind in the tent. Gary Cooper liked to say that "Some people think I gave my best performance as a piece of candy."

Frank Lloyd was said to have ordered one setting for *Children of Divorce* shot eighteen times before Gary Cooper got his movement right. For a contrast, Wild Bill Wellman shot Cooper's big scene only once.

"It was perfect," Wellman wrote in his autobiography. "I yelled cut it, print it, and Coop's face dropped. I thought it was because he knew this was his finish in *Wings*." Later, though, Cooper was begging him to reshoot the scene "because I just, just think I could do it better . . . well, you know, right in the middle of the scene I, I picked my nose, and . . ."

Wellman said, "Coop, you keep right on picking your nose and you'll pick yourself into a fortune."

The director would not minimize Cooper's achievement in the tent scene:

"To be remembered, Coop not only must salute and smile, he must have something unusual about him, that indescribable something called motion picture personality, to make it that effective that quickly. Don't ask me what it is or how you get it, because I don't think you can get it. If you have it, it came with you, and you're lucky as hell. Gable had it, Cagney, Tracy, Bogart despite his lisp had it, but there are a lot of fine actors that haven't got it and never will . . . but Cooper did."

In other words, like Clara Bow, Gary Cooper had It.

They all got to calling him Coop in Texas. Dick Arlen was the first permanent friend he found in Hollywood, and Arlen never called him anything else. Buddy Rogers became Arlen's inseparable pal during the *Wings* filming, and when Cooper was around they were a trio. Although Arlen was married soon afterward, he and Cooper and Rogers were briefly limned in the fan magazines as a junior version of Hollywood's fabled Three Musketeers—the older bachelors who were Ronald Colman, Richard Barthelmess, and William Powell.

Young Charles Rogers became news when Mary Pickford chose him for her leading man in *My Best Girl*, which led to the Paramount contract initiated with his *Wings* lead. Some years later he would become Miss Pickford's second husband when she divorced Douglas Fairbanks. Opposite America's Sweetheart in *My Best Girl*, he became "America's Boy Friend." His nickname of Buddy was awkwardly but permanently incorporated into his billing with *Wings*. In the tragic climax of *Wings* he shoots down his best friend, who is piloting a German plane he has captured. The doomed friend, shaping into Paramount's perennial second lead, was the well-born-and-sounding-it Richard van Mattemore, who became Arlen for an easier fit on the marquee.

Wings brought Buddy Rogers an immense but fleeting popularity and it solidified Arlen's status. Gary Cooper's fame would far outstrip them both, and soon; but not just yet.

He left them in Texas when summoned to the studio for *Nevada*, which was actually filmed there in part. As his first Zane Grey Western, *Nevada* had a larger budget than *Arizona Bound* and *The Last Outlaw*, and was more carefully produced. It was clearly a promotion for him, for having drawn a fan reaction that was distinctly positive if not emphatic. Even his showing in the desperately sophisticated *Children of Divorce* had been palatable to the audience, especially its distaff members. To the end of his career, Cooper would always feel more at home in a Western; and in making *Nevada* he was no longer nervous, he was merely tense.

He doubted that *Nevada*, which John Waters directed, was better in any way than the earlier, cheaper Westerns, but it did better business in response to more extensive promotion. He did have an interesting new leading lady in the blond Thelma Todd, whose reference to the movie camera as "the enemy" amused him. He seemed to know it was Gary Cooper's friend.

With his three Westerns and the two Clara Bow pictures, plus the climactic *Wings* in whose scenes Gary and Clara were never together, he was in six pictures that were shot and also exhibited in 1927. In the fall he also started and finished *Beau Sabreur*, for issue early in the following year. He would make six more silent features in 1928. It was a favorable sign. His featured player's contract did not specify a quota of screen appearances. Soon afterward the new Screen Actors Guild would apply pressure on the studios that would result in a contractual guarantee of an annual vacation; but Gary Cooper's obligation to the studio was for fifty-two weeks of the year, with vacations tendered at his employers' discretion. Some contract players seemed almost never to be actually shooting a picture, or they would be filming for another company that had borrowed their services. If other companies were requesting Gary Cooper, Paramount wasn't lending him. He took it as a favorable sign that he was always working, suggesting that they liked him. His option was renewed during the *Beau Sabreur* filming, with another salary increase.

Percival Christopher Wren's *Beau Geste* was the internationally best-selling novel of 1925, and a year later it became a historic Paramount film with Ronald Colman in the title role, borrowed from Sam Goldwyn immediately before he won Barbara Worth. In time to come Gary Cooper would have his own turn as Beau Geste, but Wren's and Paramount's sequel gave him his first title role. It was more business about the French Foreign Legion, and as with most sequels it would suffer in comparison with the exemplary original. When John Waters' direction was found deficient, Paramount returned him to its quickie mill.

At least it rated as an occasion for Cooper to be billed above respected veteran players. William Powell and Noah Beery had character roles similar to the ones they essayed in *Beau Geste*. The picture was also a modest commercial success, indicating that Gary Cooper perhaps was becoming a draw.

Another thing about *Beau Sabreur*: it delivered a new girl friend.

There was hardly any doubt that Gary Cooper had "gone Hollywood." The Chrysler that suggested a streak of blood when he raced through the filmland arteries was matched by the gaudy clothes he wore. He seemed bent on matching Clara Bow for dazzle in the time they were "living together."

Officially he was still living with his parents but now they saw little of him. He also kept Clara at a distance from them; and on possibly the only occasion of their meeting, Alice was polite to Clara but could not conceal her displeasure. On the other hand, Alice became quite friendly with Evelyn Brent. Gary Cooper's fling with her was a form of going Hollywood that was in sharp contrast to his affair with the It Girl.

His leading lady in *Beau Sabreur* became the leading lady in his private life while his adventures with Clara were winding down. Victor Fleming had jockeyed his way back to the rail position in the Clara Bow sweepstakes, just when the fan magazines were beginning to exploit Bow and Cooper as an item. Clara and Gary could still generate steam together, but they saw less of each other. Then Cooper went off on location again, in an Arizona desert whose oasis was the darkly sharp-featured Evelyn Brent.

Born just before the century's turn, she was nearly two years older than Cooper and was something of a pioneer. Back in Fort Lee, New Jersey, she had appeared in a picture as the mother of two small children when she was only fourteen. She had an early remarkable aura of maturity.

Before coming to Hollywood she did some stage work on Broadway and in stock, and she rated as an accomplished movie actress, reliably professional although lacking an individual popularity. She had been playing leading roles in films of little consequence when Paramount took her on, only months before Gary Cooper checked into the studio. Then, while filming *Beau Sabreur*, she became suddenly famous as that cherished Hollywood thing, a "hot property" . . . which may have enhanced her appeal for Cooper. The picture she had completed a few months earlier went into release and captured all the critical superlatives. It was the gangster melodrama *Underworld*, which established Josef von

Sternberg's reputation; and besides boosting Evelyn Brent, whose portrayal of "Feathers" won the highest praise, it made stars of its two leading men—the burly George Bancroft and that most dour of Englishmen, Clive Brook.

Evelyn Brent, whom everyone called Betty, came back to Hollywood with Paramount at her feet and Gary Cooper on her arm. Then they started doing the town.

His romance with Clara Bow had been vividly public but deceptively private. They attended a few parties together, but more often were in seclusion doing whatever it was they did. Evelyn Brent may have been as sexually adventurous as Clara, but she was certainly discreet. She moved in respectable filmland society, and Cooper became her escort at formal dinners and elegant industrial parties. He took her to meet his folks, and they all played bridge together.

Alice Cooper would later tell a magazine writer that "I like Betty and shall always appreciate the good influence that she was on Gary." But it is doubtful that Alice would have endorsed any notion her son may have had of marrying Miss Brent, and he probably had no such notion. He was not the aggressor in their relationship.

In her interviews of the time, Evelyn Brent encouraged speculation that she and Cooper would marry. A failed marriage lay in her past, and she had come close to marrying Harry Edwards, who was a comedy director for Mack Sennett. Edwards was known to be pining as Evelyn and Gary retained high visibility as a couple throughout 1928. Then something happened, and it may have been only that Evelyn grew impatient and decided to do her own proposing, and got turned down. For she surprised Cooper and everyone else by suddenly marrying the patient Harry Edwards.

Gary Cooper could count on Clara Bow for consolation. Miss Bow's biographers, Joe Morella and Edward Epstein, noted that they continued to meet intermittently whenever Clara really wanted "a great lay."

His Paramount employers were no longer worried over his ability. They may have undervalued it, but there was a general feeling around the studio that Cooper was on his way up, and might even be developed into a star whose name would go above the title—

although, surely, not an "important" star. There was no more talk of confining him to Westerns.

Florence Vidor had been an important silent star throughout the twenties but her popularity had waned and her name no longer preceded the titles of the films she appeared in. In *Doomsday* she was merely featured over her leading man, who was Gary Cooper. *Doomsday* was released while *Beau Sabreur* was still in general distribution, and its comparatively poor take at the box office carried the suggestion that Gary Cooper's pull had been overstated, and that Florence Vidor was washed up. It was all very unfortunate, for Florence Vidor was splendid in the ways of acting for the silent screen. She had married her fellow Texan, King Vidor, and retained his name professionally after their divorce. She was still a stunning beauty. Perhaps the trouble with *Doomsday* was its gloomy title. It was no gay thing, certainly, but Doomsday was merely the name of an English manorial estate. Warwick Deeping's novel had been fairly popular, so the title wasn't changed; and the film derived from it was an intelligent, sedate drama with a happy ending. Miss Vidor was helpful in bringing out Cooper's "naturalness," which reviewers were just beginning to emphasize. It was evident, however, that at thirty-two Florence was rather too mature for her leading man.

The order came from Jesse Lasky: Gary Cooper's build-up must have an emphasis on youthfulness, and he must no longer be cast opposite such ladies of advanced years as Evelyn Brent and Florence Vidor. Furthermore, matching him with an attractive girl and building them as a team should be considered.

The contract girls for whom "starlet" was Arch Reeve's newly coined word all wanted to be cast opposite Gary Cooper in *Legion of the Condemned*, for whoever drew the role would become with him Paramount's "Glorious Young Lovers." Esther Ralston, who had been tentatively cast, was withdrawn for being already sufficiently "built." Louise Brooks, Mary Brian, and June Collyer were all considered, and Paramount had just taken on that other refugee from the Hollywood sagebrush, Jean Arthur. Then John Monk Saunders, who was writing the scenario, insinuated his own pretty girl friend into the reckoning. So Paramount signed the little-known Fay Wray to a contract and launched her as an entry with Cooper.

They did not exactly become the hoped-for equivalent of Fox's fast-rising team of Janet Gaynor and Charles Farrell, and the firm notion of them as a team was abandoned after only two pictures. Yet with four eventual appearances opposite him, Fay Wray would become Gary Cooper's most frequent leading lady almost by default. The "glorious young lovers" designation surely helped them both at the time, so perhaps it seemed odd that she was one of the few leading ladies of his bachelorhood with whom he did not become romantically involved. They worked together while he was heavily committed to Evelyn Brent, and in 1928 Fay Wray also became the bride of John Monk Saunders, who wrote *Legion of the Condemned* because he had been the writer of *Wings*. Saunders was also a playwright who would be even more successful as a screenwriter in the sound era—particularly for two of the finest early talkies, *The Dawn Patrol* and *The Last Flight*, both with Richard Barthelmess.

Legion of the Condemned was an afterthought, a cinematic postscript to *Wings*. In the fashion of half a century later, it could have been called *Wings II*. The idea was to make use of the excess aerial footage that had not been used in *Wings*, and Saunders designed a new story of wartime flyers to accommodate it. William Wellman again was the director and it was routine but proficient stuff. Whether for the aerial dogfights or the charms of the glorious young lovers, it was a box-office winner.

A jazz-age problem play called *Half a Bride* was projected as the new team's encore, but Erich von Stroheim became enamored of Fay Wray's luminous beauty and wanted to borrow her for *The Wedding March*. Calculating that exposure in a Stroheim film might hasten prestige for Miss Wray, Paramount was happy to lend her. She was replaced by Esther Ralston, whose second experience with Cooper was more pleasant than the ordeal of *Children of Divorce*. Gregory LaCava directed them in a picture that was efficient and thoroughly forgettable. In a scene cut from the release print of *Half a Bride*, Cooper had a flirtation with a young blond actress he'd observed around town; and while Evelyn Brent's back was turned, he sneaked a date with the teen-aged Carole Lombard.

Fay Wray returned to Paramount to share *The First Kiss* with Cooper, entirely appropriately for lovers so glorious. While filming a scene in the Chesapeake Bay, Miss Wray fell out of a small boat and Cooper dived in fully clothed to save her. It was remarked that it made for good publicity, even though true. Obviously the well-publicized teaming was successful, and *The First Kiss* was a presold hit. Gary Cooper was receiving a thousand fan letters a week at the studio, and all the magazine writers were doing stories on Fay Wray.

Now he was cranking them out, and not even the love scenes bothered him, regardless of who or how many were looking on. Yet some fans of the Westerns lamented the recent loss of the likable young cowboy, so Cooper was slotted for another Zane Grey Western that would also be an interesting change of pace for Fay Wray. The projected picture was probably *Stairs of Sand*, which was eventually made without either of them. That was because another company wished to borrow Gary Cooper, and it looked like something that could only be refused unwisely. So Paramount loaned him to First National and Colleen Moore, for the heady scented fragrance of *Lilac Time*.

The mythology of silent screen stardom has been abused by the historians, and by obituary writers who by now have commemorated hundreds of "silent stars." There were few silent stars, and at no time were there more than three dozen. But they were *real* stars.

The movies adopted the stage definition of stardom and then refined it. In that era a player achieved stardom when his or her very presence became a more important consideration than the story in which the player appeared. A star's name preceded the dramatic title, and stardom was the exacting proof of a player's magnetism or ability, and usually of both. Screen stardom was formulated in the studios in the immediate aftermath of the Great War, after the Francis X. Bushmans and Florence Lawrences of the feature film's prehistory had had their day.

Mary Pickford, Lillian Gish, Gloria Swanson, and the sisters Norma and Constance Talmadge were undisputed stars who spanned the essential era, and their counterparts were Douglas Fairbanks, Richard Barthelmess, Thomas Meighan, and the brothers John and Lionel Barrymore. When early death took Wallace Reid and Rudolph Valentino, they were supplanted by

John Gilbert and Ramon Novarro. Charles Chaplin, Harold
Lloyd, and Buster Keaton were stars of a special order, and Lon
Chaney became an authentic character star. William Randolph
Hearst insisted that Marion Davies was the biggest star of all, as
her billing suggested; and Pola Negri exuded the essence of star-
dom even though the American public was seldom responsive.
Corinne Griffith, Rod La Rocque, Leatrice Joy, Milton Sills, Mae
Murray—several players briefly suggested the unalloyed substance.
Toward the end of the era there were new stars: Ronald Colman,
Norma Shearer, Richard Dix, Clara Bow, Charles Farrell, Janet
Gaynor . . . and Greta Garbo, who would succeed in a crucial
transition where Vilma Banky and Germany's Emil Jannings
failed.

That the era was coming to an end was grasped only belatedly
by the persons and the industry involved. Even after the minor
Warner Brothers company gambled boldly on sound experi-
mentation and scored the historic singing hit with Al Jolson as
The Jazz Singer, the power brokers of the omnipotent studios
dismissed the talkies as a novelty that would soon fade. Warner
began to produce all-talking pictures and no one else fretted, because those first Warner talkies weren't really very good and the
silent feature remained stable at the box office . . . until about
the middle of 1928. Then there were stirrings of discontent
among the paying movie-goers, who began to prefer the most ludicrous talkie to even the most admirable silent film.

And then there was panic. It simmered in the second half of
1928 and bubbled over in the early months of 1929. It was Hollywood's most hectic, zany, troubled, and adventurous chapter, pro-
viding industrial comedy and melodrama in about equal measure.
There was never anything quite like it, anywhere; and soon the
movies would be a brand-new ball game.

While Gary Cooper and Fay Wray were giving the silent
screen its last glow of youthful romance, there was hardly any
workaday chatter at the studio about what the gentlemen Warner
had wrought. And when Cooper reported to the First National
studio in May of 1928 to begin *Lilac Time*, everything was bliss-
ful, the silence before the storm. He knew only that he was getting his biggest break in pictures, for Colleen Moore was the star,
and now every picture of hers was an Event. She had been in the

hierarchy of silent players for several years, but in recent steady ascent had overtaken them all in popularity. In a poll conducted nationally toward the end of 1928, Colleen Moore was the most popular female player of the movies. Clara Bow was runner-up.

They were also the screen's definitive flappers—naughty Clara and wholesome but uninhibited Colleen. In many ways Colleen Moore was only typical of scores of spunky girls who got a toehold in the movie business and started up its ladder. Born Kathleen Morrison in 1900, she crashed pictures in 1917 playing tiny parts for D. W. Griffith. She learned a new craft and as she got better, her parts got bigger until she was no longer typical. She was a refreshing, original personality and with a mirthful innocence she defined the newly emancipated young American woman of the twenties. Scott Fitzgerald said, "I was the spark that lit up Flaming Youth, Colleen Moore was its torch." In 1923 *Flaming Youth* became her representative film. Then she was *Ella Cinders* and *Irene* and *Twinkletoes* and *Sally*. She sowed *Her Wild Oat* and preened in *Orchids and Ermine*. She was *Naughty but Nice* and that made her *The Perfect Flapper*. Like Norma Shearer at M-G-M only a little bit later, she was married to a powerful producer and surely that did her no harm; but John McCormick also owed his position as production head of First National at least partly to being Colleen Moore's husband.

In the spring of 1928 Colleen Moore and her director, Mervyn LeRoy, were on Catalina Island for a few days to shoot some comical rum-running scenes for *Oh, Kay!* The Gershwin musical romp was just getting started as a silent picture, but Miss Moore was already looking ahead to her next and most ambitious picture; and that was Jane Cowl's stage hit, *Lilac Time*. At the end of a long day of shooting the tired star and crew settled into the tiny movie theater in the island village to watch whatever was playing. It wasn't the newest picture or the biggest one, but a little Western, something called *The Last Outlaw*, which wasn't about an outlaw at all, but an amiable cowpoke played by an ingenuous Gary Cooper she didn't believe she'd seen before. It is likely that she would at least have seen *The Winning of Barbara Worth* as well as *Wings*, which was playing a roadshow engagement in Hollywood. But she watched him on the screen with a sense of discovery and decided on the spot that he would play opposite her in *Lilac Time*.

Nor would Gary Cooper have sensed that *Lilac Time* would be of significance in the transition from silence to sound. It began shooting as a conventional silent feature, and was even completed as such.

The production was bathed in difficulty, especially for Cooper in a personal way. The director was the effete George Fitzmaurice, who had an accomplished pictorial style but in the overall sense was a consistently overrated director, although he wouldn't have thought so. Over his entire career Cooper would have trouble with a director only rarely, but he knew that Fitzmaurice beheld him as a nonactor. And on a day when Fitzmaurice was home ill, Cooper's old nemesis Frank Lloyd stepped in to direct a scene involving Cooper and several other young men, all supposed to be English flyers; and Cooper felt all of his old insecurities returning to plague his performance. He was also uneasy whenever he was engaged in an emotional love scene with Colleen Moore, whose husband invariably was standing nearby and watching intently.

Lilac Time was part *Big Parade*, part *Wings*, but with a decidedly stronger emphasis on florid romance. Colleen Moore played the French girl, Jeannine, and Cooper was an English aviator. They would fall in love, war would separate them, he would be presumed dead, and she would honor his memory with lilacs— a design to jerk many a tear before the crescendo of the happy ending.

In mid-production there was a rumbling of concern about the exhibitors' demand for more talking pictures, and it grew louder. Like the production chiefs of other studios, First National's John McCormick was faced with a decision to abandon silent features and submit to expensive studio conversion for talkie production, or to stand by the traditional product and hope for the best. Most companies were modifying some of their pictures in a way that would enable their exploitation as talkies. Sometimes a whistle would blow, production on a silent feature would stop, a writer could come in and start hatching dialogue, and after the "wiring" was accomplished the rest of the picture would be shot as a talkie. Sometimes a silent project would be scrapped and started all over with sound, or sometimes simply scrapped in favor of something else for which sound was more appropriate. But that mostly occurred toward the beginning of 1929. McCormick ordered revisions for certain First National pictures but ultimately decided to leave *Lilac Time* in the silent state for which it had been thoroughly planned. There was a strong foreboding, though, that every silent picture in production was some kind of lame duck.

Cooper returned to Paramount to encounter a spirit of panic that even exceeded the scene at First National. Some weird alterations had been made on a few unreleased Paramount pictures that had initially been shot without sound, but now had some of it. In a hobo picture called *Beggars of Life*, a road song was warbled by none other than Wallace Beery. Those often embattled titans, Jesse Lasky and Adolph Zukor, were said to be at cross-purposes over which course subsequent production should take. Lasky appeared to be winning the struggle, and his plan was to continue the production of silent features but to begin also a steady production of talking pictures that were entirely preplanned as that. Gary Cooper said he never heard the term "silent picture" in all the time he was making them. He said talking pictures defined the silents "just like the second war created World War I."

Cooper told Evelyn Brent that *Lilac Time* was sure to be a disaster anyway. Then he heard that the edited film had been screened at First National and nobody liked it. If that were not worry enough for him, he could entertain the possibility that Paramount might just drop his option. The most startling rumor circulating throughout the studio was that most of the contract players who weren't stars would be dropped in favor of stage actors. All of the studios were sending their gadflies to New York to sign up the best Broadway talent. Cooper felt relieved when he was finally cast in *Shopworn Angel*, but not very. Evelyn Brent was going into a melodrama whose actual shooting script was the text of a recent Broadway play. The movie was *Interference* and its four leading players—Miss Brent, Clive Brook, William Powell, and Doris Kenyon—drew their assignments because all were sufficiently experienced as stage actors. They could Talk.

The situation might change radically from one day to the next, then change again. Cooper heard that First National had decided to affix a synchronized musical score to *Lilac Time*, and some sound effects as well to simulate noises of the Great War. He went to work in *Shopworn Angel* amid recurring rumors that it would be switched to a talkie and a stage actor would replace him. Nancy Carroll, who was the angel of the title, apparently had no such worry because she had come to Paramount from Broadway; but the fact that Gary Cooper had never been on stage was something absolutely everyone seemed to know.

He received an invitation to attend the première of *Lilac Time*. That it would be held in the new, serene Carthay Circle Theatre was in itself a hint that the picture might have been salvaged. It would be a "gala" requiring formal dress. He had never attended a première except as a paying customer just to watch the movie. Of his own pictures only *The Winning of Barbara Worth* and *Wings* had been accorded splashy premières, and he was uninvited to the first one and out of town for the other. He thought of going, then of not going. He had no tuxedo, but his mother told him to buy one and just go. He didn't buy a tuxedo, figuring that if his movie career was about to end, there would be no further need of one. But he rented a tux, and attended the *Lilac Time* première. His appearance with Evelyn Brent had been anticipated, but he surprised everyone by squiring Clara Bow.

Lilac Time, in 1928 as when viewed more than half a century later, was a maudlin, unbelievably corny picture that just worked, and worked beautifully. It was a smoothly professional silent picture, with satisfactory performances by its petite star and her lanky leading man. The immediate suggestion was that for the first time, the normally reticent Gary Cooper had made overmuch of his emoting. That was because of the manner in which the musical score emphasized and underlined all of the emotion packed into the photoplay. After all was said and done, *Lilac Time* owed its success to the eleventh hour decision to give it a musical score and, perhaps more important, a theme song. The dawn of the talkie revolution was the golden age of the movie theme song. First National took its lead from Fox's *Seventh Heaven* ("Diane") and *What Price Glory?* ("Charmaine") with yet another musical salute to a French girl; and Wolfe Gilbert's "Jeannine, I Dream of Lilac Time" became the most popular new song in the land. It helped build *Lilac Time* into a smash hit, surpassed only by Al Jolson's *The Singing Fool* as the most commercially successful American movie released in 1928.

Gary Cooper also believed at length that *Lilac Time* probably saved his Paramount career. He was not replaced by anybody's stage actor, although players with Broadway calling cards were increasingly a part of the studio scene. *Shopworn Angel* was completed as a silent feature, and looked for a time like a foundling child when preplanned talkies became the exclusive concern of the studio. His next assignment was to a Western drama called *Wolf Song*, and that meant they still weren't willing to gamble on Gary Cooper in a talkie. *Wolf Song* and three other pictures were started at the same time, accompanied by a studio announcement that they would be the *last* Paramount silents. Cooper checked in at the location site in the California Sierras for *Wolf Song*, but a phone call ordered him right back to the studio before a scene had been shot. In the aftermath of First National's *Lilac Time* fairy tale, B. P. Schulberg decided there would have to be a *Shopworn Angel* theme song for Nancy Carroll to sing. A few scenes could be reshot with sound, and with one reel of song and dialogue it could be sold as a part-talkie. And Gary Cooper would talk.

Shopworn Angel is, in fact, a picture fondly recalled by many who saw it. It became one of the more popular attractions of the transitional period. It made a star of Nancy Carroll, who had been at Paramount less than a year; and the kewpie-cute Nancy Carroll is usually cited as the first star created by the talkies. She was an appealing actress in the new vogue, but her presence as a silent performer in *Shopworn Angel* is memorable. The song she sang, "A Precious Little Thing Called Love," became quite popular. Miss Carroll enacted a kept woman who befriends a naïve soldier and marries him out of sympathy, before he goes off to get killed in the war. The appended talkie reel was undistinguished, but the makeshift script for the wedding scene gave Cooper seven lines of dialogue. Movie patrons heard a nicely modulated voice that was pleasantly drawled and perfectly attuned to his personality. It was just enough to persuade the nail-biters at Paramount that Cooper would not be one of their worries.

Richard Wallace directed *Shopworn Angel* and Cooper, who believed Wallace was always underrated, took a tip from him that made him a more effective actor. Wallace detected a tendency in Cooper to turn away from other players, just a slight twist of the head but sufficient to lose eye contact. He advised Cooper to watch Paul Lukas closely. Lukas, a shy Hungarian, was rated one of the best "eye actors"; and in *Shopworn Angel* he had the third leading role as Nancy Carroll's hard-boiled regular man. Cooper watched Lukas' eyes while filming scenes with Nancy; and in his own confrontation with Lukas "we just stared at each other with neither of us making a facial expression, and people said it was great acting." It was good enough to be recalled by people at M-G-M some years later when James Stewart was being developed there as a "new Gary Cooper." The property was purchased from Paramount and remade with Stewart, Margaret Sullavan, and Walter Pidgeon.

Several takes were made of a scene in which Cooper and Miss Carroll fall asleep on the Coney Island beach. When Wallace was satisfied with a take and yelled, "Cut it and print it!" the soldier kept his slumber. Cooper really *was* sound asleep, and would sleep often during the coming years while waiting for the setups.

Shopworn Angel opened nationally in the first week of 1929, while Cooper was in the Sierras filming *Wolf Song* and falling in love with Lupe Velez. *Wolf Song*, too, would finally be modified for release as a part-talkie, along with every other Paramount silent then in production. A young, unknown Italian crooner named Russ Columbo joined the cast to sing a couple of pseudo-Mexican love ballads. A scene filmed back in the Hollywood studio was stretched to fill a reel. *Wolf Song*, about old New Mexico and adapted from a Harvey Fergusson novel with literary substance, emerged as an unsatisfactory patchwork although it had strong atmosphere. That it achieved fair box-office success owed to the public knowledge that its leading players were steaming into their own off-screen love affair.

Irony underscored the assignment to *Wolf Song* of Lupe Velez, who was not a Paramount player. The role of the Mexican heroine was expected to go to Mona Maris, a new Argentinian actress. Then Universal's Lupe Velez was strongly sponsored by her boy friend of the moment, who was that ubiquitous rogue Victor Fleming, and the *Wolf Song* director. Cooper and Fleming had become close friends since Clara Bow abandoned Fleming, apparently in favor of the entire University of Southern California football team—the "Thundering Herd" Trojans, who participated in filmdom's most famous gang-bang.

Had Fleming not persuaded Paramount to borrow Lupe for a one-shot visit, the three-year Cooper-Velez rocky love affair might never have ignited. But it became chilly of an evening up there in the Sierras, and Lupe was nothing if not warm.

Guadeloupe Velez de Villalobos was a delightful little liar. She told everyone she had come to Hollywood in poverty and had only been fourteen when Douglas Fairbanks picked her to play the mountain girl in *The Gaucho*. She was nineteen then and had never been poor.

Lupe was born in a village near Mexico City in 1908. Her father was a colonel in the Mexican Army and her mother was an opera singer. After her education in a San Antonio convent, Lupe took a sight-seeing trip to California. In the courtyard of Hollywood's Egyptian Theatre she was noticed by Ted Reed, who sent her to his boss, Doug Fairbanks, on a hunch. She was a demure thing when Fairbanks got her in front of a movie camera, but the klieg lights seemed to transform her instantly into the vibrant girl they would call the Mexican Spitfire. She spoke English better on the day she arrived in Hollywood than after she'd been there a decade. The Mexican accent became an exaggerated affectation but an engaging one, and she was always beautiful.

After the Fairbanks film she was D. W. Griffith's *Lady of the Pavements*. The talkies made her difficult to cast. De Mille's early talkie remake of *The Squaw Man* with Warner Baxter suggested that Lupe Velez might have been a splendid actress. Eventually she was sentenced to the strictly B *Mexican Spitfire* series, produced by RKO and teaming her with Leon Errol and the fading Buddy Rogers. She was a suicide at thirty-six, unmarried at the time and pregnant by her latest lover. Until its grim denouement, her life had never seemed tragic. She was popular with the picture people, and writers and reporters loved her. She was a buoyant, earthy spirit with a piercing cackling laugh, and she made a studied effort to be hilarious and succeeded.

She was helplessly in love with Gary Cooper from the moment she saw him. Victor Fleming sensed the situation and stepped politely aside. Lupe was the aggressive, irresistible force and Cooper capitulated. When the *Wolf Song* company returned from the Sierras, Cooper packed his bags, kissed his mother good-by, and moved into Lupe's Beverly Hills mansion on Rodeo Drive, which a discarded sugar daddy had bought for her. Its décor was futuristic, and her boudoir was a dazzle of gold, black, and silver. Its centerpiece was an enormous bed puffed with huge silver pillows.

"Theez eez where Lupe makes loff," she would tell anyone she was showing around her place. But she was no Clara Bow for promiscuity. She only made "loff" when she fell really hard for a man, and she fell for only one man at a time.

For almost three years there was recurring speculation that Lupe and Gary had secretly married. The rumor could hardly die, with Lupe often implying that it was true. Then they would become "engaged"—once with a ring Cooper never admitted buying. Or it would appear to be all over between them, and then Lupe would make a trip to New York especially to buy her trousseau. They split; they made up. They fought constantly—or Lupe scratched and clawed and Cooper only defended himself. His passiveness easily provoked her. She said, "I theenk I keel my Garree because he does not get angry when Lupe eez angry weeth heem."

The way she talked, she was always about to kill somebody. She kept a loaded revolver in her bedroom to dissuade possible assailants. When she was out doing the town, she had a stiletto concealed beneath her dress, attached to a leg by a garter. She never killed anyone but herself, but she kept everyone off balance. Cooper usually could stand it for about two weeks and then would stalk out of her house, not to return for days or weeks, sometimes even months. But he would return, because being with Lupe offered him a level of enjoyment and unbridled excitement he couldn't find elsewhere.

They were fairly visible as a couple. They went night-clubbing, and never missed the fights at Hollywood Legion Stadium. If the boxing didn't regale Cooper he could always watch Lupe, the loudest and most animated girl in the throng. No one doubted his genuine devotion to her, and many of Cooper's close friends believed his ultimate refusal to marry Lupe lay in his reluctance to break his mother's heart.

It may only have been Lupe that kept the elder Coopers in Hollywood on a full-time basis. Alice was basking in her son's movieland glory, making it her own fulfillment, and Charles knew they were there more or less permanently. But he had almost succeeded in getting Alice to agree to year-round residence divided equally between Montana and Hollywood when the advent of Lupe changed everything. Alice made a show of diplomacy, but her intense dislike for Lupe and even her fear of her were easily seen. She would not abandon her boy while the Mexican Spitfire was mesmerizing him. For a few years the Coopers paid extended fall visits to Montana because it was Alice's favorite season there, with such autumn colors as Hollywood could never match. Charles, though, had sold the house near Last Chance Gulch a few years earlier; and eventually the tie to Montana would be severed when he finally sold the ranch.

Lupe became increasingly outspoken about "Garree's mama" long after the affair with Cooper was over. Yet she probably could understand Gary's deference to his mother. On the other hand, she may not have known what to make of his relationship with Anderson Lawler.

In 1929 they trickled into the movie colony by the dozens, and then in the hundreds they formed a steady stream. They were the stage players signed for the talkies—Broadway luminaries and players of more youthful promise, some plucked from obscure stock companies. Those signed by Paramount in the East didn't usually come for a while, and did their first filming in the large Long Island studio where many of the company's films were still being shot. Eventually, though, they all made Paramount's Hollywood scene—Claudette Colbert, Fredric March, Miriam Hopkins, Walter Huston, Kay Francis, Hal Skelly, Ruth Chatterton, Stuart Erwin, Helen Kane . . . even the great Maurice Chevalier, not to ignore Groucho, Harpo, Chico, and Zeppo or their sublime Madame Dumont.

Scores of others, however, never made a dent on the public consciousness but were there for a spell, taking tiny picture parts with hopes of larger parts in the future, until their options were dropped and there were no parts at all. One of Paramount's young actors destined for such disappointment was Anderson Lawler, the refined scion of one of the first families of Virginia.

Cooper met Anderson Lawler early in 1929, probably when they were working on adjacent sets in the Hollywood studio. Lawler was making his debut in the ensemble of *River of Romance,* a Booth Tarkington story with Buddy Rogers heading the cast. Rogers may have introduced them. Cooper was involved in *Betrayal,* an Emil Jannings vehicle that became a frustrating project for everyone connected with it, and was his assignment immediately following *Wolf Song.* It may be only conjecture that Cooper took Lawler onto the *Betrayal* set to meet Jannings. But it seems that Lawler saw some charcoal sketches of Jannings and Esther Ralston that Cooper had made on the set. He exclaimed over the drawings and wanted to see some of Gary's other work. Before much conversation had passed between them, Lawler had revealed his own interest in hunting.

Cooper was spending most of his nights on Rodeo Drive, and he took Anderson Lawler there to meet Lupe. She found him quite amusing, for Lawler could be sarcastically witty in a careful way. They double-dated at least once, with Lawler squiring June Collyer to the fights. Little is known of the interim, but Lupe and Gary had a real squabble a few months later, and he walked out on her for a spell and went back to the house on Franklin Avenue. This was when his parents were paying their last long visit to Montana, but Cooper was not alone in the house, for Anderson Lawler had also taken up residence in it.

"Coop queer? Are you kidding?"

Jack Oakie said Gary Cooper was about the un-queerest of all the Paramount fellows that raised hell together in the good old days. He also discredited a story about a "rich fairy," while conceding that such types abounded in Hollywood, especially in that era.

For five decades a rumor has endured that Gary Cooper accepted the favors of a wealthy homosexual early in his career. Choose your version: the man was a shipbuilder, or he was a tobacco heir; he had influence in the movie colony, or nobody in Hollywood knew him; they met only by assignation, usually in San Diego, or they lived together briefly in Santa Monica; the man dumped Cooper, or Cooper took a powder when the man was of no further use to him. In any account, Cooper is not defined as a homosexual, merely as a co-operative fellow. A tangent rumor was that this particular relationship soured Clara Bow on Cooper because even Clara, like the well-remembered Fanny Hill, had her own ideas about what was immoral.

Most of Cooper's vintage pals have insisted there was no truth to the rumor, which has been sustained by reference in certain scabrous books about filmland morality or the lack of it. In the matter of Anderson Lawler, they recall the name only with hesitation. Jack Oakie said, "Oh yeah, Andy Lawler, real nice kid . . . later produced some plays. Well, for a while there Coop and him were real good friends."

Cooper's friendship with Lawler ran directly parallel to his erratic love affair with the Mexican Spitfire. It eroded over a three-year period during which Lawler was often absent from Hollywood for stage work. He shared Cooper's house until his parents returned from Montana, and afterward was often a dinner guest with the family. Alice was fonder of Lawler by far than of Lupe, yet Lupe was always somewhere in the picture. Lupe got her live-in lover back for a time, but later Cooper took a place of his own on Argyle Avenue and Lawler sometimes lived there with him.

They had pet nicknames. Lawler called him not Coop but Jamey, possibly for his middle name. Everyone called Lawler Andy, but to Cooper he was Nin, after Lawler's favorite stage role of Ninian in St. John Ervine's *The First Mrs. Fraser*. Jamey Cooper and Nin Lawler went on hunting trips together, and did a bit of sailing. They saw plays in Los Angeles and attended the Hollywood Bowl concerts. Lawler gave Cooper some things Lupe couldn't. Three years Cooper's junior, he was conversant in art, music, and literature. He often disparaged motion pictures—pointedly so as his own career foundered. His glibness was envied by Cooper, who deplored his own lack of natural wit. Lawler was a polished success in filmland society and was on most invitation lists, although he and Cooper never attended the same functions. He moved within Hollywood's insulated homosexual community. Reliable for one-liners, he amused everyone in the film colony (except Jean Harlow) when a remark he made at one of Edmund

Lowe's parties got printed. He called the blondest blonde "the white Stepin Fetchit."

Lawler was an archer, a fine swimmer, an experienced mountaineer. He prepared kitchen delicacies and Cooper praised his spongecake and pudding. As a stage actor he usually received good notices. He may not have had the right breaks in pictures, or perhaps his natural personality couldn't penetrate the screen. He was handsome, but possibly not enough: sandy, wavy hair that was thinning early; a strong cleft chin; and glinty eyes that, when opened wide, gleamed brilliant blue like Gary Cooper's.

Although Paramount was more liberally disposed toward its players' behavior than, say, M-G-M, there may have been some concern in the front office over the Cooper-Lawler friendship. This may have had something to do with Lawler's option being dropped. He made only three Paramount pictures and one on loan to M-G-M, then left. Before that, while Cooper was filming *The Virginian*, Lawler went on location and became a shorter shadow figure for the tall star. Lawler was a Virginian, so publicists devised a story that he was instructing Cooper for an authentic accent. If Cooper wanted coaching, he could have obtained it from Virginia native Richard Arlen, who was also in the picture, and whose accent suited a cowboy better than Lawler's cultured one.

Dick Arlen, although married, was ringleader for the stag parties that were a magnet for Paramount's bachelor actors, on the beach or at Lake Arrowhead, and more often on Catalina Island. Lawler became a regular participant for these outings that were weekend bacchanals during Prohibition's tertiary stage. There was free-flowing bootleg stuff, a lot of blaring phonograph music, and ample allegiance to sun and surf. Arlen and Jack Oakie were fixtures, Buddy Rogers was usually along, and so were such newcomers as Stuart Erwin, Harry Green, and Chico Marx, and now and then Fredric March. Women were strictly forbidden. These were he-man occasions, but some known or suspected homosexuals often attended, such as young actors Stanley Smith and Phillips Holmes. The studio made an effort to discourage such activity, especially after a photographer sneaked onto a Catalina scene and snapped the actors all swimming in their birthday suits. The pictures still were being sold in the back alleys of Los Angeles many years later.

Probably no other studio had the kind of fellowship that matched Paramount's in that era. But the atmosphere favored those who were on top or getting there, and Anderson Lawler eventually was very bitter over his treatment at the studio. He was promised an important role in *The Devil's Holiday*, a Nancy Carroll picture that became a big hit. But suddenly he was out, Phillips Holmes was given the part, and Lawler had his walking papers. Later George Cukor brought him back to Paramount to play the husband of Kay Francis in *Girls About Town*, a good comedy and his most encouraging screen opportunity; but nothing came of it.

He returned to Broadway and for a time was Tallulah Bankhead's coat-holder and protégé. After World War II he became a producer, sometimes in association with Cheryl Crawford, and was a presenter of Tennessee Williams' *Camino Real*. In 1959 he died. He never married.

In contrast to *Shopworn Angel* and *Wolf Song*, which began as silents and emerged as part-talkies, *Betrayal* was planned as an all-talkie and became the last silent film of the long Paramount history. Its star was Emil Jannings, the great German tragedian. Esther Ralston and Gary Cooper were featured below the title in a triangle tale that aimed for high tragedy. Some said it was a tragedy in diverse ways.

Emil Jannings was considered the greatest screen actor in the world during the last decade of silent pictures, and no doubt deserves that rating still although there is an aroma of ham when his old pictures are screened today. It is now seen that his best work owed much to intelligent direction, particularly F. W. Murnau's use of the camera for *The Last Laugh*. That one and several others, especially *Variety*, were great international hits and did sturdy American business, so it was only a matter of time until the financial resources of a big company lured him to Hollywood. He arrived at Paramount in 1927 and made *The Way of All Flesh*, which had nothing to do with Samuel Butler's famous novel, but which was a strong enough picture to give Jannings the first Academy Award any actor would win. For Josef von Sternberg he made an even better film—*The Last Command*—but thereafter his Paramount vehicles deteriorated in quality and began to sag at the box office. *Betrayal* was filmed as his talkie debut. Lewis Milestone directed, or attempted to: he found Jannings impossible to work with. Beyond a language barrier, there was about Jannings a distinct egomania. He loathed working in Hollywood, and much preferred filming at the Astoria studio. He sized up Gary Cooper as a pretty-faced nonactor and would have nothing to do with him except when they filmed together. *Betrayal* had a production set as gloomy as its story, but they got the picture shot as a talkie. It was previewed and test-released but quickly withdrawn, because no one could understand Jannings. At that time all talking pictures were being made as silents simultaneously to serve the mostly rural theaters not yet wired for sound. So Paramount put the silent version into saturative national issue and it was a box-office disaster; critically, too. It was Jannings's sixth American film and his last one. Oddly enough, he is best known for a talking picture made in his native language—*The Blue Angel*, the Sternberg classic that made Marlene Dietrich world-famous. And Paramount distributed it in America.

After finishing *Betrayal*, Cooper was given a well-earned vacation while his first all-talking picture was being shaped. He did some traveling with Lupe Velez, then returned to find himself assigned to *Darkened Rooms*, as leading man to Evelyn Brent. He considered it an awkward situation. In the little he had seen of the now-married Betty Brent when their paths crossed at the studio, she had been cordial to him but unmistakably cool. He knew he didn't want to make the picture, and wondered that nothing more was being done about his supposed "regular" partnership with Fay Wray, who had already proved herself an actress for the talkies. He had never refused to do a picture. He had always done what was asked of him, even when he supposed he knew better than they did. Yet when he told Schulberg he wouldn't make *Darkened Rooms*, he was informed his salary would be suspended. So Cooper reported for work in a dreadful state of mind. The situation with Evelyn Brent was of less importance to him than the fact that he hardly knew the director, Louis Gasnier, who wasn't very friendly toward him. Furthermore, Cooper was frankly quite worried about making an all-talking picture.

At the same time Cooper was having trouble with the people at Paramount, the people at Paramount were having trouble with Richard Dix. He had been in pictures for nearly a decade, rising professionally all the while, until he had become Paramount's leading male star, Emil Jannings perhaps apart. Now he was more solid than ever on the strength of two talkies that had done well, and Paramount was rewarding him with a really important assignment—a talkie version of Owen Wister's *The Virginian*. Occasionally Dix would break the rhythm of his melodramas and sophisticated comedies with a "class" Western, and *The Virginian* would have all the classy appointments, with the redoubtable Walter Huston cast as that extraordinary villain Trampas. The director was Victor Fleming. Richard Dix was excited about the whole thing—so excited, in fact, that he thought he should be making a lot more money. His contract had another year to run, but he knew how much Paramount had paid Maurice Chevalier to come aboard; and he believed his talkie success entitled him to renegotiate his contract. He had done some investigating, and knew he could improve himself financially by moving to RKO.

Paramount offered more but not enough and they reached a stalemate. Finally it was a matter of take the money or leave it, and Dix left. If the story is true, Victor Fleming was summoned to the front office to receive a new assignment, since they'd decided to scrap *The Virginian* because they had no actor good enough and big enough to do it with Dix gone. Whereupon Fleming said he'd sure as hell like to give it a try with Gary Cooper.

Neil Hamilton replaced Cooper in *Darkened Rooms*, and *The Virginian* commenced on schedule with Cooper leading a cast that included Mary Brian as the schoolteacher Molly Wood and Richard Arlen as the hero's errant friend Steve, besides the illustrious Huston. *The Virginian* is one of the few 1929 pictures that will get an occasional screening on TV half a century later, and viewers may wonder what all the fuss is about. The scene in which the Virginian stands by while Steve is hanged for helping Trampas rustle some cattle offers possibly the most ludicrous moment in Cooper's career as an actor. At the time, though, it was an exemplary photoplay, with passages that caught the eloquence of Wister's novel. Using his own natural Montana speech, Cooper was an agreeable talking actor giving a performance of unargued sincerity and sensitivity—especially in the scenes where the schoolmarm is begging him to give up work with guns and he's struggling with his conscience to do what's right. The most famous scene, though, emulated the classic moment in the novel, during the poker game in the Medicine Bow saloon. When Trampas says, "Your bet, you long-legged son of a . . . ," the Virginian purses his lips and says, after an eloquent pause, "When you call me that . . . *smile!*"

It was a line that cried out for Cooper's intonation and inflection. It is clearly seen that in his first fully talking picture, he had a role to formulate a standard screen image that would be refined over three decades. It also made him a star. He was listed below the title in *The Virginian,* but the picture to follow would be a "vehicle" prepared just for him, with more hand-picked stories to come. His name alone would appear in large letters above the words, *Seven Days Leave.*

Cooper's salary was raised incrementally by figures that exceeded the escalations promised when he signed his contract in 1926. Doubled in 1927, his salary was redoubled in 1928, and an offer came in 1929 to double it yet again, while he was filming *The Virginian.* He thought $1,250 sounded like a nice weekly pay check, until he considered what others were earning. Lupe Velez, with status shakier than his, was making twice that amount at a less affluent studio. Compared to Cooper, Chevalier and some of the other new people were in an economic stratosphere.

"Dick Arlen and I called him 'Mr. Chandelier.' We were furious that a Frenchman could come to America and get so much more money than we were collecting."

He was less gullible than before. He knew his own progress had exceeded the company's expectation of it, both as a performer and a ticket seller. He did not intend, though, to battle the front office and lose, like Richard Dix. He would accept their offer, but just before signing he would ask for a little more money, after they saw he wasn't being difficult.

Then he attended a studio luncheon honoring some visiting exhibitors, and got into a chat with the owner of a theater chain in Wisconsin, who was a Gary Cooper fan. The fellow showed him a formal document establishing certain guarantees, one of which was that four new Cooper pictures would be available in theaters in 1930. Cooper asked what would happen if the theaters didn't get those pictures. The exhibitor said something about forfeiture and indemnities, and Cooper decided in an instant that he would not sign a contract for $1,250 a week. He would ask a nice round figure—$5,000, or four times that amount. He got a brand-new contract, seven years without options, starting at $3,750 and with a substantial percentile increase every year. Then he got back to the business of making movies and soon realized that once again he'd been taken. The four Gary Cooper pictures the theater owners could expect were guaranteed as a *minimum*; and there was no stipulation in his contract for four pictures or even five. In an eighteen-month period he would make eleven pictures.

Seven Days Leave was a maudlin but charming little comedy-drama that reprised his *Shopworn Angel* role of a naïve young soldier who'll meet death on the battlefield in the last reel. This time, though, he was befriended not by a cute little shopworn angel like Nancy Carroll but by such a fussy old character actress as Beryl Mercer. The film was a stretched-out version of James M. Barrie's short play *The Old Lady Shows Her Medals*. Cooper was the exception to an all-English cast. He would never hold the picture or his callow performance in high regard, but critics of the day generally raved over both. Yet *Seven Days Leave*, without a youthful love story, did poor business during its early 1930 release, while *The Virginian* was still packing the houses. It confirmed the studio thinking that the Western was Cooper's forte. He was more or less rushed into two of them, with the shooting of the second one following the first without a break.

Only the Brave was about the cavalry and some spies, and teamed Cooper with his schoolmarm from *The Virginian*, Mary Brian. A better film in every way was *The Texan* and it got Gary Cooper on the cover of *The Saturday Evening Post* in a famous Norman Rockwell painting—a movie cowboy in full regalia, being made up for his role. *The Texan* was from an O. Henry story about the Llano Kid. When Warner Baxter played the Cisco Kid, also from the O. Henry legacy, he won the Academy Award. There was no talk of any kind of award for Cooper's performance, which, however, fairly oozed with personality at no sacrifice of naturalness. *The Texan* was also probably a better all-around picture than *The Virginian* although, curiously, it was directed by a man whose entire career had been on the stage as actor and director. John Cromwell, like George Cukor, came to Hollywood with the talkies and earned a reputation for drawing excellent performances from his players. Yet Cromwell's first and only Western had a lovely visual quality with no suggestion of the confinements of a stage. The girl was Fay Wray, but the "glorious young lovers" tag was not revived for them, and her billing was no longer equal to Cooper's. *The Texan* did not approach *The Virginian* at the box office, but it smartly surpassed the take for *Only the Brave*, possibly because it more immediately sounded like a Gary Cooper picture.

A Man from Wyoming sounded like a Gary Cooper Western, which may have been intentional, but it was more World War stuff and a brazen copy of *Lilac Time*. The man from Wyoming was another soldier believed dead by his beloved, but merely wounded. The minor variation was that the heroine was no French girl but an American beauty in the ambulance corps . . . and in France, and gathering lilacs! The girl was June Collyer, a minor Paramount ingenue and Anderson Lawler's sometime date before she married Stuart Erwin. She was pretty enough, but no Colleen Moore for personality. The Cooper portrayal was now considered standard by reviewers, who dismissed the picture generally. *A Man from Wyoming* was by no means inept, but thematically it proved the law of diminishing returns.

Then came not a Western but its near cousin, the horseless "northwestern," with a few sled dogs. With the talkies stabilized, it seemed appropriate to have another go at *The Spoilers*, to capture the sound of fists crashing into skulls. Rex Beach's chest-pounding Alaska yarn had already been thrice filmed in silence. The second version in 1917 contained "the fight to end all screen fights" when William Farnum and Tom Santschi almost killed each other, lacking the advantage of trick photography. Viewers rated the 1923 effort as rather too tame with Milton Sills and Noah Beery slugging it out, so unprecedented gore became the quest of later editions. In a 1942 picture shaped around Marlene Dietrich, the principal brawlers were John Wayne and Randolph

Scott; and in 1955 the blood oozed from Jeff Chandler and Rory Calhoun.

The 1930 opus was designed as a Gary Cooper star vehicle but not even the ten-minute fight scene was properly conceived. The fight was titanic, but it looked like a mismatch. Cooper's foe was William Boyd—not the blond fellow who later silvered into Hopalong Cassidy, but an identically named older man. To be distinguished from the Boyd who had preceded him in films, the one that fought Cooper was customarily billed awkwardly as William (Stage) Boyd because he had been on the stage; but so had the other William Boyd, who would have been a more reasonable challenger. The lean Cooper fought a mean-looking but paunchy middle-aged man. Still, Boyd managed to hurt him.

The Spoilers was shot mainly in Oregon. The fight sequence, however, was an event for the first sound stage built in the studio —which meant that little microphones concealed on the players' bodies were almost things of the past. Bill Farnum and Tom Santschi were honored guests watching the mauling, as was Noah Beery; and Milton Sills had also been invited but had just committed suicide. Every maneuver for the Cooper-Boyd bout was carefully worked out prior to shooting so there would be no retakes. But there were many camera setups, and the combatants grew woefully sore as the sequence took several days to film. There were no broken bones, but Cooper wrenched his back and was in pain for weeks afterward. He also tore a hamstring and was bruised purple after the ordeal.

He moaned, "And I got into the movies because I thought it was easier than punching cattle!"

His wounds would have been more easily healed by a better picture. *The Spoilers* was commercially volatile but humdrum, although Cooper was acquiring a commanding physical presence that was evident long before the climactic fight. He derived little enjoyment from the production, which had an unhappy leading lady. She was Kay Johnson, an able stage actress called to the talkies for a pair of De Mille exercises that flopped. If only to himself, Cooper was beginning to fret about his career becoming a routine. He was a commodity in routine pictures. But aside from the fortuitous *Lilac Time*, he had not been allowed to film away from Paramount, and his services were increasingly requested by other companies. Raoul Walsh had tried to borrow him for *The Big Trail*, a Fox super Western filmed in a new wide-screen process. Paramount refused to lend him, and Cooper continued to sulk after *The Big Trail* was counted a failure . . . along with the unknown young man who got the part, and whose name was John Wayne. At about the same time, the Columbia company that was beginning to transcend its Poverty Row origin put in a bid for Cooper to play the old Barthelmess role in a remake of *Tol'able David*. At twenty-nine he was probably already too old for the role; but he liked the story and reasoned that it would be a better picture, say, than *A Man from Wyoming*. Paramount rejected the bid because it would be demeaning to send a star player to small-potatoes Columbia. It would be a different story with *Mr. Deeds Goes to Town* some years later, but in 1930 Cooper felt cheated when *Tol'able David* emerged a well-liked little talkie, with the twenty-year-old Richard Cromwell in his first screen role.

Cooper poured out his thoughts to a new friend—a bright fellow named David Selznick, younger than himself, who had become Schulberg's executive assistant and was exercising a subtle influence in casting decisions. Selznick was himself displeased that another carbon copy was planned for Cooper—it was called *The Californian*—and would have welcomed any excuse to get it scrapped. Selznick scanned the roster of major projects being readied and found only one plum role unassigned. It was the John Barrymore take-off in *The Royal Family of Broadway*, for which Cooper was definitely not right, as he agreed. Selznick was despairing of the studio using Buddy Rogers or Phillips Holmes in the part, which he knew called for the fast-rising Fredric March—who, however, was more or less set for the Foreign Legion thing on Sternberg's schedule. Cooper reminded Selznick that he'd played *Beau Sabreur* . . .

So Fredric March joined *The Royal Family* and Cooper went to *Morocco*—a trade, as they say, that helped both teams.

When the talkies came, it was something to sing and dance about. The photographed stage play came first, but then the musicals took over. At the peak of the novelty, the moviemakers were inspired that theatrical films could serve as their own elaborate publicity releases, with their stars all dancing and singing for the studio, in the studio, and most definitely *about* the studio. Metro-Goldwyn-Mayer lit the first firecracker with *The Hollywood Revue of 1929* and threw in Norma Shearer, Marion Davies, Joan Crawford, John Gilbert, Buster Keaton and did it matter that they couldn't all sing and dance? Then Fox reeled off *Happy Days* and there were Will Rogers, Janet Gaynor, Charles Farrell, Warner Baxter and it hardly mattered that not all of them could sing or dance. Warner Brothers, grown into a giant by its talkie pioneering and having absorbed the huge First National in a capitulative merger, brought 1929 to a close with *The Show of Shows*: John Barrymore, Dolores Costello, Richard Barthelmess, a barking Rin-Tin-Tin . . . and it mattered just a little that all couldn't sing or dance. The pictures all were blockbusters before the word existed. They introduced standard popular hits—"Singin' in the Rain"; "Whispering"; "You Were Meant for Me." They all offered sequences in the new, experimental Technicolor process. At bottom they were preening exaggerations of their producing companies' own importance.

Paramount was beaten to the punch: Paramount, the first major company, still the most illustrious for its accrued prestige but challenged now, no longer omnipotent, perhaps soon to be surpassed by M-G-M and even by Warner . . .

At about the same time that Gary Cooper was being posed in costume for Norman Rockwell, he was whisked into the Hollywood studio to be a song-and-dance man for a project being shot all over the lot by a multitude of directors, and in the New York studio as well. Adolph Zukor, the jealous patriarch, would show his competitors that Famous Players-Lasky still reigned supreme. He would put *Paramount on Parade*. This picture would have *more* songs, *more* dances, *more* Technicolor, and many more stars than any of those other pictures. It would be bigger in every way, even though it might not be longer.

But it would *seem* longer. Robert Benchley remarked that "It ran less than two hours but I came out of the theater several years older." It could not possibly be the worst movie ever made, but possibly it was the most vulgar, the most ludicrous. Ruth Chatterton was a Parisian chanteuse like no other. Evelyn Brent, who couldn't dance, proved it. Most of the songs were dreadful or were only poorly served, and the nearest thing to a hit number was

Clara Bow's "I'm True to the Navy Now" . . . which was reprised in her next picture, called *True to the Navy*. Every Paramount star and featured player was aboard, but only Chevalier was entertaining. One of the poorest numbers, and with the most lurid Technicolor, was "Let Us Drink to the Girl of My Dreams," by the composer of the *Lilac Time* theme song; and while Gary Cooper, Richard Arlen, and James Hall sort of sang, Fay Wray, Jean Arthur, and Mary Brian sort of danced.

It was released in mid-1930 when the talkies had lost their novelty, the musicals had vanished from overkill, and the nation was acknowledging the Great Depression in the aftermath of the stock market crash. *Paramount on Parade* was the only major film to have its company name in the title, even if Sam made *The Goldwyn Follies*. Well, it didn't lose money but it lost prestige. Paramount no longer was number one. Made to salute a new era, the picture signaled the end of an old one—of the glory days of Paramount. It was also a catharsis, the last echo of the birth cry of the talkies.

Gary Cooper became the eighth star on the 1930 roster. Jack Oakie, certified months later, made it nine. Twenty-one held featured player contracts, with many others employed for support. A few of the ones merely featured—Fredric March, Miriam Hopkins, Kay Francis—soon would be Paramount stars. More often the featured players were on their way out—the James Halls and Stanley Smiths, even the Mary Brians and Evelyn Brents.

The stars besides Cooper and Oakie were Clara Bow, Nancy Carroll, Ruth Chatterton; and George Bancroft, Maurice Chevalier, William Powell, and Charles (Buddy) Rogers. Powell and Clara Bow would make their last Paramount pictures the next year. Rogers would be cut adrift in 1932, and Miss Chatterton would follow Powell to Warner Brothers. Chevalier, Bancroft, and Nancy Carroll would leave in 1933, and Jack Oakie would stay awhile but lose his stardom.

Gary Cooper, in the fold only four years, very soon would be the studio's veteran star. He was also destined to lead in prestige; but that would take a while longer.

5

☆ ☆ ☆
_____
☆ ☆ ☆

BEHIND THE
HEADLINES

A SURE WAY to get Gary Cooper started talking, according to Adela Rogers St. Johns, was to introduce the subject of horses. Jim Tully found that any mention of guns would do the trick.

Guns and horses; or Cooper retired into a peculiar characteristic silence. He seemed neither bored nor distracted, and an appealing thought was that he was contemplating some deeper mystery. His social behavior indicated that he was probably exceptionally intelligent, or just pretty dumb.

Miss St. Johns, the remarkably durable author and journalist, was the superstar among writers for the fan magazines when the talkies came in and for some years afterward. She was the most persistent chronicler of Cooper's romantic escapades, and shaded her accounts in a way that would not alienate him but would strengthen their friendship. She found in Cooper a subtle intelligence and innate wisdom. Jim Tully, who called Cooper "the most benign person I've met out here," became friendly with the rising star and wrote nice things about him, while privately holding the view that Cooper was not very bright. Tully, a former hobo who became a popular author of slice-of-life novels and then found he could get richer writing about the stars in Hollywood, once called Cooper's head "a gorgeous room with no furniture in it."

More people probably agreed with Tully. Louis D. Lighton, who wrote or produced several Cooper films, said "Coop is never as quiet as you hear. He talks a good deal but isn't clever, and nobody ever remembers anything he's said. That doesn't matter so much, because he's a nice fellow and everyone likes to have him around."

He was certainly around, and not just in the endless run of parties where he was a fixture, usually with Lupe. He began receiving invitations to functions whose small scale implied their exclusiveness. This move upward in filmland society was commensurate with his rise in professional standing but motivated not only by that. In his own way he courted the favor of the Hollywood bluebloods, and Jack Oakie remembered Cooper's exultation upon receiving his first invitation to Pickfair. He soon became a familiar presence there.

Douglas Fairbanks personified an ideal for Cooper, both before and after they became intimate friends. An uncredited source says that watching Fairbanks on the screen in *The Mark of Zorro* made Cooper decide to become a movie actor. Cooper might have seen that picture in Montana, probably in very early 1921, at least two years before he gave even a hint of having Hollywood in mind, although it could have been a notion he kept entirely to himself. Before they met in Hollywood, Cooper followed Doug's activities with the impulses of a fan, even keeping clippings about him. He may have been impressed by Doug's ability to derive so much enjoyment from being in the public eye. In any event, Fairbanks had attained and for a long time had retained the two things Cooper most wanted—he was at the top of his profession, and he was universally well liked.

It is possible, even likely, that Lupe Velez initiated their friendship. Lupe's screen bow in Fairbanks' *The Gaucho* preceded the beginning of her affair with Cooper by little more than a year, and Fairbanks retained a fondness for her. Mary Pickford may not have shared that fondness, for Lupe was rarely if ever a Pickfair guest; and Cooper began attending small functions there alone, during a period when he and Lupe were going full blaze. Doug's friendship with Cooper was quickly affirmed and was in no way patronizing. He was genuinely interested in the kind of life Cooper had known in Montana, and as a child had regretted being torn from the Colorado of his birth and taken to the East. Fairbanks was Hollywood's ultimate world traveler and had done some big-game hunting. Cooper wanted to indulge in both, and Fairbanks was influential in Cooper's growing assertion of independence in his dealings with Paramount. He said, "They can't afford to be tough with you. They need you more than you need them, Gair." Fairbanks never called him Coop.

The Pickfair scene that assimilated Cooper was clouded by the erosion of the Pickford-Fairbanks marriage at that time. Yet Cooper also developed a personal relationship with Mary that existed apart from his friendship with Doug. He said that "being able to introduce my father to Mary Pickford was the nicest thing I could do for him." Even when the separation of Mary and Doug became a fact, Cooper returned to Pickfair only as Mary's guest. When *Secrets* was being prepared for her, without anyone suspecting it would be her last picture, she wanted Cooper as her leading man even though he was more than a foot taller than she. He was agreeable to the assignment but Paramount wasn't, so Miss Pickford chose Leslie Howard as her unlikely American frontiersman.

At the beginning, though, Doug and Mary were both in royal residence at Pickfair, where Cooper became really acquainted with Samuel Goldwyn for the first time. The early loss of Cooper had become a matter of personal injury to Goldwyn, who was already talking of getting Cooper back when he became free. Cooper also met the fading D. W. Griffith at Pickfair; and also Charlie Chaplin, who with Griffith, Fairbanks, and Miss Pickford had formed the original United Artists about a decade earlier. He also met the junior Douglas Fairbanks and his wife of the moment—the Joan Crawford who gave every indication of being one of the biggest stars of the talkies. The younger Fairbanks was also finding success in establishing his own identity, and was approximately at Cooper's own level of establishment, although eight years younger. Adela Rogers St. Johns said Cooper became almost as much a son to the senior Fairbanks as was the junior Doug, and seemed even more so, because the two Douglas Fairbankses were more like good pals than like father and son.

At Pickfair he also renewed friendship with his *Lilac Time* patron, Colleen Moore, who had temporarily retired from pictures after two talkies which had not been considered especially disastrous; certainly not so disastrous as the two talkies that finished off the career of Norma Talmadge, another acquaintance he made at Pickfair. Constance Talmadge simply quit without making a talkie, and four was the limit for Mary Pickford.

Toward the end of the 1930 summer, Cooper was asked to attend a small reception at Pickfair in honor of Mary's latest titled house guests. He was filming *Morocco* near Palmdale on the rim of the Mojave desert, but made an early departure from the set to make the long drive to Hollywood and get into his dinner clothes, which were no longer rented. He endeavored to get every formal effect just right for the occasion in the heights of Beverly Hills, since Mary had hinted that the count and countess had expressed a desire to meet Gary Cooper.

Count Carlo di Frasso was a courtly, middle-aged Italian. His wife Dorothy was an American and somewhat younger than he, but already past forty. They were prominent in the new international set and traveled the world, living mainly in their huge villa near Rome. Mary and Doug had visited them there.

Before her first polite meeting with Gary Cooper was over, the countess was telling him that he ought to see Italy, too.

Josef von Sternberg was not born into the aristocracy. He was Jonas Sternberg in the Vienna of his birth, and for a time in New York during his youth was plain Joe Stern. The accomplishments of Erich von Stroheim may have prodded him to add his own "von" during his early pursuit of cinematic grandeur. It was a frustrating pursuit as he toured the Hollywood studios as an assistant director during the early twenties without apparent progress. But in 1924, when he was thirty, he took a small cast and only a three-man crew down to the Los Angeles waterfront at San Pedro; and for less than $20,000 made a grim picture called *The Salvation Hunters* from his own original scenario. Its sordidness prevented it from getting much exposure in theaters, but it attracted enough serious attention to invite the thought that Sternberg might be a genuis.

He really was a genius—perhaps the foremost pictorial stylist of the American cinema, wherein he was firmly in the Germanic tradition of the fluid camera. He did not make his way easily, however. In the aftermath of his first prestige success he was hired to direct pictures, then fired because he was overbearingly arrogant and generally impossible to work with. He was again an assistant director, coaching Gary Cooper's only scene in *It* at Paramount in 1927; but later that year the visually exciting *Underworld* fortified his claim to genius, and his next films just about proved it. Emil Jannings, whom he had directed in *The Last Command*, had returned to Germany, a refugee of the talkies; but in 1930 Jannings summoned Sternberg back to Europe to direct *The Blue Angel*, from a Heinrich Mann novel about a professor degraded by sex.

Sternberg fashioned a masterpiece, accented by the perverse eroticism that would inhabit many of his works. *The Blue Angel* was a big international success, and in America was shown both in the original German and in a dubbed English edition. It made a world figure of the woman who played the heartless Lola Lola and sang Frederick Hollander's "Falling in Love Again." At twenty-nine, Marlene Dietrich had been in German films for almost a decade and had flashed her legs in the music halls without making a solid name. But now Paramount, as U.S. distributor for the profitable *Blue Angel*, put her under contract even though foreign-accented players were the least desirable commodity in Hollywood just then. No doubt Sternberg urged the company to take Dietrich on and to let him shape her American debut vehicle. They were already lovers before coming to Hollywood together in mid-1930.

Morocco was prepared from a German story especially for Fräulein Dietrich, but the plan was to showcase her opposite a leading American star for insurance at the box office. An effort was made to borrow John Gilbert from M-G-M, but this was refused. Then, as Gilbert's failure in the talkies became more apparent, M-G-M tried to beg Paramount to take Gilbert and they wouldn't, although Sternberg still wanted him. The first decision was to go with Fredric March as Tom Brown, the American in the French Foreign Legion who becomes involved with the world-weary cabaret singer Amy Jolly. When David Selznick pulled the casting switch that gave Gary Cooper the part, there was widespread surprise if not astonishment. Any Sternberg picture of that period smacked of major importance, and Cooper was fixed in the collective mind as a formula player for formula pictures. Furthermore, Sternberg didn't like the idea of using Cooper.

During their careers it often seemed that Cooper wanted nothing so much as to be liked, while Sternberg wanted only to be hated. Sternberg succeeded where Cooper didn't when they made *Morocco*. He did not warm to Cooper, who found it only too easy to despise Sternberg.

Although few of his pictures had courted high artistry, Cooper most often was their central exhibit, from the distinctly small *Arizona Bound* to the more robustly scaled *The Spoilers*. He was not accustomed to being ignored. Sternberg paid no attention to him during the first days of shooting, in the Hollywood studio. Every camera setup was undertaken for Dietrich's obvious advantage; and in directing scenes between the two principals, Sternberg's attitude indicated there was only *one* principal. Cooper was clearly vexed but kept himself under control, until Sternberg started giving direction in German. Jules Furthman was on the *Morocco* set, writing changes for each scene before it was shot, and reported the Cooper-Sternberg confrontation.

"I understood German pretty well, and Lee Garmes (the cameraman) seemed to know what Joe wanted in any language. Coop, though, couldn't make anything of what Joe was saying, in German *or* English. He may not even have cared, but he must have thought Joe barking in German was the height of arrogance. Well, Coop is sitting in the café where Marlene is singing, and Joe is hollering something, and Coop gets up and takes a few steps over toward Joe.

"I think Joe may have told him to sit back down, and said it in English, but Coop went right toward him and then picked him up, just grabbed him around the neck by the coat and lifted him. Joe's no more than about five-four. Coop is strangling him. Then he puts him down on his feet but keeps the hold on his shoulders and starts to shake Joe back and forth, really jostling him. All the color has gone from Joe's face—he's in shock, the only time I ever saw him that way. Coop is still holding him when he says, 'You god-damned kraut, if you expect to work in this country you'd better get on to the language we use here.' Then he turns loose of Joe and goes back to the café table and sits as if he thinks the camera is about to roll.

"Joe just stands there for what was probably a very long minute, and everyone is absolutely still and quiet, and Marlene has a kind of Mona Lisa smile. Then Joe just walks off the set and isn't seen again that day, and doesn't come back the next day—or so I'm told, I wasn't there. I wish I had been there when Joe came back, acting as if nothing had happened but being very reserved toward Coop, and you can bet he was talking in English."

Possibly Sternberg went screaming to the front office to have Cooper replaced, but that might have been difficult with substantial footage already shot. If Cooper was reprimanded, no one seemed to know of it. *Morocco* was completed well past schedule, but that was typical of Sternberg. He and Cooper barely spoke throughout the production grind, although they discussed Cooper's scenes with a strained formality before filming them. Cooper became aware of Sternberg's luxuriating in his responsibility toward Dietrich. All of her scenes were shot repeatedly, from different angles, the camera moving all around her. If Cooper had a scene without Dietrich, it was over and done with quickly, usually in a single take.

There is easy agreement among observers during that general era that Dietrich worshiped Sternberg, who was her personal Svengali for several years. Yet she and Cooper became friends, slowly at first, but much less guardedly as shooting progressed. It is unlikely that either of them sensed how well their scenes together were playing, and possibly not even Sternberg knew. *Morocco* is a film throbbing with sexual tension, not all of which can be attributed to Sternberg's remarkable use of light and shadow. It was the picture that thoroughly and permanently defined the Dietrich mystique: her Amy Jolly is cynical, a fatalist, compulsively erotic. It was so effective a showcase for her, and so sensationally received as such, that Cooper's own contribution did not obtain its deserved recognition.

It was by far his most impressive "performance" to that time although difficult to measure as conscious performance. Sternberg made Cooper angry, and while he was seething an undeniable contemptuousness took hold of him and it was just the right shading for Legionnaire Tom Brown's hold on Amy Jolly. For all the claims that would be made over three subsequent decades that Gary Cooper was an innately sexy man, no other Cooper screen portrayal would reveal the sensual substance of his taciturn *Morocco* soldier.

The picture would be a big hit—deservingly so, for it is a timeless classic—and its most famous scene is the last one, in which Cooper does not appear. Abandoning the wealth and stability that a kindly older man (played by Adolphe Menjou) can provide, Amy impulsively kicks off her heeled slippers, barefootedly to follow her Legionnaire over the desert sands to his new outpost. For the scene to work, the Legionnaire had to be firmly fixed in the mind of the audience, and this was Cooper's first triumph of overpowering, sheer personality.

Excitement over Dietrich gripped Paramount well before the picture was released for confirmation as a critical and commercial hit. A rough cut of the film was screened at the studio, and publicist Arch Reeve was directed to mount an unprecedented campaign on behalf of Paramount's stunning and mysterious imported star. At last there was another star who might seriously rival Garbo. Reeve got to work and did his job. All of this was going on without Cooper's awareness, for with *Morocco* having gone past schedule, he was already at work on another picture, off on location, when the rough cut was screened. When Cooper returned to the studio there were reminders of Dietrich everywhere. Contrasting poses of her were in framed photos lining the walls in the administrative offices. He certainly didn't object. But he did object when he saw the poster art that was being prepared in the advertising department, with Marlene Dietrich as the solo star billed above the title. He was featured below, with Adolphe Menjou. Cooper's contract did not exactly guarantee star billing, or even stipulate *first* billing, but he let David Selznick know he didn't think he was being dealt with properly. Sternberg, it seems, had insinuated himself into every phase of the *Morocco* activity and had urged the Dietrich emphasis. That emphasis held in the visual sense, every promotional display dominated by the Dietrich glamor. But Cooper won his point on the billing. There was no above-the-title star, and Cooper was billed first among the three featured principals. He did not rate it much of a personal victory. Almost every aspect of *Morocco* was unpleasant for him, and he took little satisfaction in the picture's success; or, probably, in being ignored when both Dietrich and Sternberg received Academy Award nominations (her only one), as did cinematographer Lee Garmes.

However, when *Morocco* had its triumphant New York opening in mid-November of 1930, it would have been almost impossible for him to find pleasure even in his own recognition. This was a trying time for him, both emotionally and physically, and it was about to get worse instead of better. The assignment immediately following *Morocco* was another Zane Grey Western, *Fighting Caravans*, shot mostly on location at Sonoma, California. But after leaving Sonoma he returned to the Hollywood studio along with Lili Damita and Ernest Torrence, the other principals, for a week of shooting interior scenes. In that same week Rouben Mamoulian put *City Streets* into production, shooting entirely at night. Cooper was doing double duty after having already shot seven pictures during the year.

He was physically exhausted, and it began to tell on him. Furthermore, he and Lupe were having trouble in their relationship, for which the strain of *Morocco* was not the best ointment. Based on Cooper's imitation of the German star, Lupe offered *her* Dietrich impression at a party and brought the house down, but did not enhance Cooper's relationship with Marlene. The primary difficulty was over Lupe's clash with his mother, finally out in the open with no more diplomatic niceties. It was a battle neither Lupe nor Alice could hope to win. Lupe begged Cooper to renounce his parents to prove his love for her. She really meant renounce "the mama who gets seek every time a girl try to take away her Garree"; but Cooper was still living with both his parents, and in any event would renounce neither of them.

He did, however, move out of their house on Franklin Avenue, in a break that caused tears and hard feeling. It would heal, but he never again shared a residence with his parents. That failed to appease Lupe, who wanted Cooper to stay at her house; what she really wanted was marriage. Instead, he rented a house at 1919 Argyle Avenue; and after he got settled in, Anderson Lawler would often spend his nights there.

Nor could Cooper easily jettison Lupe as his mother implored him. Even when they were "through" in the collective mind of their observers, and even after Lupe made slurring remarks about Garree as well as the mama, he would return to Lupe's house time and again. It was evident that to some extent she was still irresistible to him.

At this very time, his mad fling with Clara Bow came back to haunt him. He was embarrassed if not humiliated by revelations of their affair that were made in a courtroom. Clara brought suit against her former secretary, Daisy deVoe, who had tried to blackmail her and had embezzled $16,000 of Clara's money. Miss DeVoe was convicted on only one of thirty-seven charges, and although she served a brief jail term, the real loser was Clara herself. On the stand, Daisy accomplished a thorough character assassination of Clara and the newspapers made capital of it. The star's carnal activity was exposed comprehensively; and although many prominent names emerged in Daisy's inventory—Victor Fleming and Gilbert Roland rated brief mention—the ones cited most explicitly were Gary Cooper and Clara's more recent lover, Harry Richman. (He had flipped over Clara when he went to Hollywood for the *Puttin' on the Ritz* picture that echoed his theme song.) There were other disclosures: Clara's romp with the football team was reprised; Daisy said that Clara occasionally hired male prostitutes; and she hinted that America's favorite redhead was heavily into drugs.

In the public mind it was "the Clara Bow trial" and it occurred in January of 1931. It would force her to report late for *City Streets*, which was to reunite her with Cooper in a co-starring venture, a rare thing at Paramount then. Cooper was cast in *City Streets* only because he refused absolutely to do *Dishonored* with Marlene Dietrich for her *Morocco* encore. He did not object to filming with Dietrich for any director other than Sternberg—who, however, was in charge of *Dishonored*. He was cast in *City Streets* after Clara was; and it was actually conceived as a remake of one of her more successful silent pictures, *Ladies of the Mob*— although it was only a distant cousin to the original after Dashiell Hammett adapted it. Cooper lately had seen little of Clara, perfunctorily when their paths crossed in the Hollywood studio. They were still friends, however awkwardly; or they were friends until Clara brought Daisy deVoe to trial. Cooper, at least, had welcomed the *City Streets* assignment in the interest of his career. With the brilliant young Rouben Mamoulian directing, it figured to approach the production quality level of *Morocco*—more so, certainly, than the *Fighting Caravans* Western potboiler he'd just finished. Clara Bow, too, was still Paramount's most reliable star for selling the tickets—again, she was that until the trial.

By coincidence, a new Bow picture was getting released while the lurid trial was exploited in the headlines, and the more mercenary Paramount executives figured its box-office revenue would be increased by the current events. Lloyd Sheldon, who supervised production of many Paramount features, including some of Cooper's, said the Bow-Cooper casting for *City Streets* now was unbeatable. Instead, there was sudden and mounting public pressure against Clara's new picture, which was called *No Limit* and was no great shakes, but surely no worse than some of her big moneymakers. But women's clubs and other righteous elements boycotted the picture, and in some cases caused it to be withdrawn. It failed bewilderingly at the box office. So did her other new film—*Kick In*, completed just before the trial—when put into theaters a few months later.

With stunning suddenness, Clara Bow was washed up, commercially comatose. Paramount, though, would honor her contract, hoping for a change in the public disposition toward her. There was slimy curiosity around the studio over how Clara and Gary would act toward one another when brought together on the *City Streets* set in the wake of the trial, but the answer was never given. Clara failed to report. The trial itself, and then the swell of national anti-Bow sentiment, shook her into a nervous breakdown. She was replaced in *City Streets* by Sylvia Sidney, a demure New York actress whose only previous film had been for Fox in a minor role. A few months later Clara was reported fully recovered, although compulsive eating had caused her chins to multiply. Paramount was still willing to sponsor a new Bow film, although the one offered—*The Secret Call*—was distinctly minor. A pallid newcomer named Peggy Shannon replaced Clara on the eve of her reporting, when she suffered withdrawal tendencies and defaulted on her contract.

She never returned to Paramount, and a later two-picture effort by Fox failed to resuscitate her stardom. She did, however, marry cowboy actor Rex Bell in 1932, and then have two sons by him—the same Clara who didn't think she could have babies, back when Gary Cooper might have married her.

Whether Paramount was worried over possible public censure of Gary Cooper, *he* was clearly worried—indeed, agonizing once more over whether he still had a future in pictures. In that regard he may have been fortunate that the display advertising for *Morocco* primarily emphasized Marlene Dietrich. That picture was still in the theater traffic and holding nicely. *Fighting Caravans* was released quietly, and while its commercial performance was inconclusive, there was no evidence of organized anti-Cooper sentiment among patrons.

In Cooper's own mind, he was on professional probation. He figured his career could sink or swim with *City Streets*. Nor did Daisy deVoe's explosive disclosures unnerve him only for their possible effect on his career. He could not face his mother, who seemed to discount the possibility that her son had done anything wrong because she did not accept Daisy deVoe's testimony as even possibly true. Cooper avoided his father altogether.

Lupe had seldom introduced the name of Clara Bow in her conversation with Cooper, but now she taunted him and shattered the last fragment of their bond. It was probably with considerable relief that Cooper went to New York for partial filming of *City Streets*—the first time he worked in the Astoria studio, which Paramount would close the following year.

City Streets was only Mamoulian's second film, following a sensational debut as director of Helen Morgan's backstage picture, *Applause*. In the urban gangster melodrama, Cooper played a young man who unknowingly is working for the mob. Sylvia Sidney played an innocent girl jailed for one of the mob's murders. *City Streets* has been downgraded historically for its self-consciously cinematic technique but it was a wow in its day, and one of the most highly praised films of 1931. It was not the hoped-for box-office sensation, but did good business in the face of generally declining theater receipts as the Depression burrowed in. The picture started Sylvia Sidney off impressively and Paramount made her a star before the year's end. Not even Cooper was given star billing in *City Streets*, as a precaution against a possible boycotting of the film by sanctimonious elements. He and Miss Sidney led a solid featured cast that included Paul Lukas, Wynne Gibson, and Guy Kibbee. The most praised member, however, was Cooper. Critics continued to express amazement that he really could *act*. In a trenchant dramatic situation he was a natural human substance, not really actorly at all. The picture proved effectively that the Clara Bow scandal had absolutely no influence on the public's acceptance of him.

Yet he had little cause to smile. He had been a marathon runner of a movie actor over almost a two-year period; and that, along with his considerable emotional turmoil, had drained him. It actually had shriveled him. From the time of his arrival in Hollywood, his weight had fluctuated only between 170 and 175 pounds, until 1930. Then, from the time he filmed the fight scene for *The Spoilers* until he completed *City Streets* half a year later, he lost nearly 30 pounds. At only 148 he was a zombie for his height.

He needed a rest but accepted a new assignment with no argument. *I Take This Woman* didn't sound like a Gary Cooper picture but the script, at least, appealed to him—the society girl falling for the shy cowboy and vice versa, with predictable complications. The woman he took was Carole Lombard, who had been at Paramount less than a year and was just being nudged into leading roles. She was an arresting blonde with a zestful personality and a salty vocabulary. She might have inspired Cooper toward complete physical recovery, but for the fact that she was the bride of the star recently departed from Paramount, William Powell.

In his weakened condition, Cooper contracted hepatitis but continued to work on the picture, anxious to wrap it up and pursue the rest-and-rehabilitation scheme that was forming in his mind. He lost a few more pounds and threatened to dip below 140. In his haggard state he also lost any lightness that might have aided a supposed romantic comedy. *I Take This Woman* was turgid, both while it was being shot and when it played in the theaters. By then, Cooper was out of the country.

It was just as well that he should take a faraway vacation before he killed somebody, if not himself. In the first three months of 1931 he was ticketed four times for speeding, once for going sixty in a fifteen-miles-per-hour zone on Wilshire Boulevard. The government got on his back with an income tax lien of almost $600, which feasibly could have been avoided by sound business management. But two bogus "business managers" hauled him into court wanting a cut of his income although they had accomplished nothing for him; and they won a settlement because he wanted to be rid of them.

It was time for a vacation, and he knew he had earned one. They told him to take four weeks—possibly even six, if a new picture was not ready for him before then.

He sailed for Europe.

Had a visit to Italy been in the back of his mind all along? It was April 1931. Before leaving from New York on an Italian steamship, he spoke only of going to Venice, where he had reserved a hotel for two weeks. He had not booked his return passage. Wasn't it odd, some asked, that he was traveling alone?

Cooper was a big enough movie star to have his shipboard activities covered in the press—dining at the captain's table, playing shuffleboard with an aide to Benito Mussolini, remaining on deck just to experience a mild storm that sent all the other passengers scurrying below. In the ship's ballroom a photographer tried to get Cooper to dance with the Austrian-born Vicki Baum, whose *Grand Hotel* was the international best seller of the moment. Cooper, who wanted to avoid publicity, refused to dance with the novelist even after he was offered three dollars. Then it seemed more newsworthy that he had refused.

If he took a camera to Venice, any pictures he may have taken were not seen afterward. He went there to satisfy a powerful whim to ride in a gondola, and he may not have stayed two full weeks. He met an American couple who were motoring to Rome, and became their passenger. He did no sight-seeing in the Eternal City, and after making a telephone call took a taxi to the sprawling Villa Madama outside Rome, where resided the Count and Countess di Frasso.

He had brought letters of introduction from some of the titled couple's Hollywood friends, in case they did not recall meeting him at Pickfair; but both the Count and the Countess di Frasso recalled meeting Gary Cooper.

Within only a few days, pictures began appearing in newspapers and then in magazines around the world. They showed the American film star Gary Cooper in the company of a woman clearly older than himself. Cooper and the Countess di Frasso were on the beach at Viareggio in their swimwear; they were appraising silk scarves in the Florentine market; the countess was his tour guide through the ruins of Pompeii; in Bologna she gave him a cake on his thirtieth birthday.

Where was the count?

She was never a poor little rich girl, for she always gleefully exploited every advantage.

She was Dorothy Taylor and her family had long been accustomed to wealth and position. Her maternal grandfather, Roswell P. Flower, was governor of New York State after Dorothy was born in 1888. Her father, the first Bertrand Taylor, was an early Wall Street shark who amassed a fortune of fifty million dollars. In 1912 Dorothy Taylor married Claude Graham White, the first great English aviator, who landed a plane on the White House lawn during his courtship of her. They were divorced in 1916, shortly after Dorothy came into an inheritance that was variously estimated from ten to fifteen million dollars. Her brother Bert got an even better shake, and also became a power on the New York Stock Exchange.

That was an age when a woman seeking a title could acquire one by marrying an impoverished nobleman. Count Carlo di Frasso was charming and courtly, and he was broke. They married in 1923 and Dorothy poured a million dollars into restoring the count's enormous villa, actually a sixteenth-century palace. She made it into an international showplace. The Di Frassos also maintained town houses in London and New York. Elsa Maxwell, the high priestess of café society, was Dorothy's closest friend, and Dorothy called her "Fatty."

The Di Frassos were a devoted couple, and remained congenial after each began taking other lovers. That was some time before Gary Cooper showed up at the Villa Madama.

The countess was not annoyed that Cooper arrived during her preparations for a sit-down dinner for two hundred invited guests. By all means he must join them; the roll call had just about everything except an American movie star . . .

The standard version later milled by the Paramount publicity department and echoed by the writings of Adela Rogers St. Johns and other magazine chroniclers was that a seriously ill Gary Cooper was nursed back to health and vitality by his dear friends, the Count and Countess di Frasso. Yet the most authoritative reporter was undoubtedly Elsa Maxwell, who had the advantage of close observation and was sometimes a third participant in Dorothy and Gary's shenanigans. Elsa Maxwell offered a quite different interpretation of the events—both on the spot and as she recalled them a quarter-century later, following Dorothy's death. It is basically her version that is encapsulated here.

Dorothy Taylor White di Frasso, in the instant of meeting Gary Cooper on her own turf, fell in love as she had never fallen before. For the next three months they were always together; she would hardly let him out of her sight, lest the wind or some younger charmer blow him away.

She saw how he was dressed and concluded he was just not "smart"; but she would make him smart. He wore an old-fashioned dangling watch chain that extended from his waistcoat button with a locket. She removed it immediately.

"Big boy, you're coming with me. There's a very good men's tailor in Rome."

She took him to Rome and bought "dozens" of new suits, all tailor-made in the newest styles. Although he protested, she paid for everything. She was pleased that he knew so little about the ways of living really well, for it would give her particular delight to teach him. To Elsa, though, she confided that there was one important department in which her new young man required absolutely no instruction.

She taught him to read menus in French, Italian, and German. She schooled him in wines—both the preferred labels and the vintage years. She coached him in social protocol.

Socially he was no ignoramus, nor had he ever been one. During his childhood in Montana he was made acutely aware of the social graces and mastered them as they existed, there and then. In Hollywood Louella Parsons might say that Gary Cooper had *once been* a loud, loud dresser, but only to emphasize a more recent acquisition of good taste. Alice Cooper acknowledged especial gratitude to Evelyn Brent for turning her son into a polished gentleman. Dorothy di Frasso surely exaggerated Cooper's social awkwardness as a means of making him more dependent on her.

He called her Dorothy or just Do in private, but she was the countess in every third-person reference to her. She called him Gary, Big Boy, and G.C. Yet she never referred to him as Mr. Cooper to the press or to anyone; she called him Gary Cooper because she wanted everyone to know he was the movie star.

She told him there were only two reasons that one should live in Italy—the weather and the art treasures. So they visited all of the major art galleries and private museums, not only in Rome and Florence but Genoa, Turin, Milan, and back to Venice. She had a stable of cars from limousines to racing models, and Cooper was free to use any or all of them. He was bowled over by Dorothy's generosity, and by Dorothy herself: she was dynamic, authoritative, smothering him in a way he found exciting, while initiating him into a way of life that a certain part of him must always have craved. Elsa Maxwell knew he was more than just a grateful but passive recipient of Dorothy's favors. He was in love with her, at least in the beginning of their liaison.

For a while he was uneasy over the count's disposition toward his and Dorothy's sexual union that everyone presumed existed. The time did not come when Cooper was *not* uneasy about this. But Dorothy and others assured him that the count was an experienced and agreeable cuckold, who also did all right for himself on the side—but perhaps never so openly.

The second party Cooper attended at the Villa Madama was a reception in his honor, and the guests included His Royal Highness, Prince Umberto, Crown Prince of Italy, and eighty others, among whom the titled folk outnumbered those without titles. The count was the toastmaster, introducing *his* very good friend . . .

Count di Frasso arranged to have the well-known horseman of the American screen ride with the Italian cavalry's premier riders in a grueling and treacherous steeplechase event. Some even suspected the count of a diabolical motivation, but Cooper met the challenge impressively, finishing the course that vanquished most of the Italian riders. The countess was ecstatic over his riding display. She was entirely serious when she told Cooper he should train for the international polo matches. She talked as if he were in Italy to stay.

"The studio, the studio—it's all I hear! I ought to just *buy* the studio . . . I wonder if I could?"

Dorothy scolded the Big Boy for allowing the studio to push him around. When he increasingly cited his obligation to Paramount, she shrieked, "Your obligation should be to yourself!" She seemed confident that she alone could give him everything he really wanted.

Cooper indeed was behaving as though he might never return to Hollywood. He had arrived at the Villa Madama not expecting to stay more than a week, and his visit stretched to ten weeks. He received two wires ordering him to return to the studio, and ignored both of them. Nor did he make any effort to get in touch with B. P. Schulberg when the production chief was in Rome, trying to get in touch with *him*. Schulberg, on a European sight-seeing junket of his own, telephoned the Villa Madama hoping to talk with his errant star, but Cooper was off somewhere looking at Old Masters with Dorothy. Schulberg left a number where he could be reached, and a message to the effect that Cooper had been taken off salary.

In June, Cooper received a letter from David Selznick, who was running production at Paramount during Schulberg's absence. Selznick sought to interest Cooper in *Girls About Town*, a comedy being prepared for Kay Francis. The male role could be built up, the script already was first-rate, and he felt it would benefit Cooper to work with George Cukor, a talented new director. Cooper had learned to rely on Selznick's judgment and had about decided to return to Hollywood over Dorothy's protests; then a wire came from Selznick, telling Cooper of Selznick's own resignation from Paramount—he would soon be in charge of production at RKO. Cooper took the wire as a sign that he should not go to Hollywood for *Girls About Town*. That he almost did, however, brought his dilemma into the open.

The countess wanted him to give up the movies.

She was fighting to hold on to him, and would marry him if she had to.

Cooper may have been having the time of his life, but guilt was eating at him. In early July, he received a terse wire signed only by "Paramount Publix Corp." ordering him to return to work for a picture called *Sal of Singapore*. He knew nothing about the picture, whose title suggested he would not have the focal role, but he thought it wise to make a show of co-operativeness. He packed his suitcases and prepared to head for home.

Dorothy begged him to stay. He said he could make the picture in a couple of months and come right back. She stormed about, furious that he was letting the studio push him around. When she yelled, "You've got to be your own man!" he came right back at her: "If I become your gigolo, will people say I'm my own man?"

It had often been said that Gary Cooper was easily ruled by women, as a dog on a leash. But Dorothy di Frasso was the strongest and most willful woman he'd met, and he was not giving in to her. He wanted to get back on salary for income that was really his own, and he did not want to stop being a movie star.

Yet apparently he wavered. On July 11, only a few days after Cooper received the Paramount telegram, the headlines were bolder and in larger print: The Countess di Frasso would divorce her husband and relinquish her title, and would marry Gary Cooper.

Soon afterward and in years to come, he would deny that either of them had any thought of marriage. Elsa Maxwell as a personal confidante knew better. And if the countess decided on divorce and then changed her mind, it may only have meant that Gary Cooper had changed *his* mind.

Finally, Dorothy conceded that she could not hold him in Italy, and gave assistance for his departure. The Di Frassos, having issued jointly a denial of recent and unsettling rumors, gave Cooper a farewell party that was attended by the Duke of York (later to become George VI) and Prince Christopher of Greece, as well as Barbara Hutton and her prince Girolamo Rospigliosi. Dorothy also arranged a London stopover for Cooper during his return voyage to the United States, and booked him as house guest to her friends, the Earl and Countess of Port Arlington.

She was devastated by Cooper's departure. She went into seclusion and for several weeks there were no more parties at the Villa Madama. Other than its legion of servants, the villa was occupied only by the count and countess. Then Elsa Maxwell came for an extended visit. She found Dorothy vague and emotionally distracted, unalert to other people's conversation.

The countess paced the large rooms and hallways audibly muttering, "I've lost him, I've lost him . . . I've got to get him back!"

Assaulted by reporters on his arrival in New York, Cooper said, "The countess is a very dear personal friend. So is the count." He was relieved that he did not immediately have to face the Hollywood press. He would shoot *Sal of Singapore* right there in the Long Island studio, and in the waters of the Sound.

Almost half a year had passed since he had worked before the movie cameras. *City Streets* had been playing the theaters when he left for Europe, and *I Take This Woman* had also completed its bookings. For the first time in several years, Paramount did not have a Gary Cooper picture among those stockpiled for forthcoming release, so there was anxiety to get a new Cooper project in motion.

He was sufficiently experienced to recognize formula junk. He supposed, though, that a yarn about a taciturn sailor and a shady lady should make money, and it seemed advisable to return to the screen in a commercially sure thing. He did persuade the producers to discard the title in favor of one emphasizing the leading players about equally; so *Sal of Singapore* became *His Woman*. And his woman was Claudette Colbert, who was becoming a personage of some consequence to the studio. She rode into the talkies on Broadway's first wave and gained secure footing, although her important stardom lay in the future. Her opinion of *His Woman* may have been no higher than his. In years to come, Gary would call it the least favorite among his Paramount talking pictures.

His Woman was filmed in September and October in the Astoria studio's last burst of energy. That large complex, the world's first to have built-in sound stages, was closed by Paramount as an economy move early the next year. When Cooper reported for work, Anderson Lawler was there winding up the *Girls About Town* picture that Cooper had declined. Tallulah Bankhead was making a picture with Fredric March, and it was then that Cooper introduced Lawler to the irrepressible Tallulah, who was also a close friend of the Countess di Frasso's.

The countess kept tabs on Cooper. After a brief period of being out of touch with him, she began peppering him with notes and telegrams, supervising his New York movements from a distance of several thousand miles. Gary Cooper joined Manhattan's café society and found he had many friends there because they were Dorothy's friends. She sent Cooper a telegram that urged him to get in touch with Jerry Preston at the Plaza Hotel; she was certain that Preston would have a proposition that would appeal to him.

Jerome Preston was a wealthy horse breeder in the Kenya colony of British East Africa. He and his wife were about to take a small team on safari in the game-rich Tanganyika region. Why didn't Cooper come with them and hunt some big game?

Of course he wanted to go, but thought it was out of the question. He had learned that Paramount had bought a new Dashiell Hammett crime novel, *The Glass Key*, for Cooper to play the Ned Beaumont role, and that he would be expected on the Coast very shortly to begin filming it. He said no; then the lure of safari conquered him, and he telephoned the Prestons just before they left New York to see if he could still tag along. He decided not to ask the studio for another leave of absence; he would simply tell them he was going. He did, and again he was taken off salary.

Once more he was gone six months; and once again his activities were sure fodder for the newspapers.

The Prestons' party of five sailed from New York to Naples in early November. In the group with the Prestons and Cooper were the playboy brothers, William and James Donahue. From Naples they took another boat to Alexandria, then went by train to Cairo. They chartered an airplane for the long journey over the Nile down to Nairobi, south of the Equator. The flight consumed three days, with nightly stops in primitive villages. Native drivers were waiting in Nairobi to take them to the Prestons' ranch at the edge of the big-game country. The party remained there two weeks, making comprehensive preparations for their ten-week safari. Cooper waited for his countess.

Dorothy di Frasso joined him four days after he arrived. The count did not accompany her.

This was towering adventure for him.

Their caravan consisted of five light trucks loaded with supplies and their native carriers, and two passenger cars.

Recounting it later, Cooper said, "Don't get the idea this was dude hunting. It's just sensible. Real safari only came into its own with the motor car. There are no horses down there because they can't stand up under the heat, and a hunter is lost without a car for any lengthy jaunt. You drive where you can, then when the end of the car's possibilities is reached, you get out and walk."

Twenty natives supported them as gun bearers, porters, guards, and camp servants. Before leaving the Preston ranch for the bush country, Cooper was thoroughly schooled in the art of taxidermy by Jerry Preston. Treating the animal coats and hides made for busy camp activity, for the group took more than three hundred specimens. Cooper alone had eighty-two kills, although he was the only novice on safari among the white hunters.

He got his lion, and tigers of different species. A majority of his prizes were antelopes—impala, gazelles, others more rare. Tanganyika teemed with zebra and water bucks, and Cooper saw herds of great elephants. Every night he heard the bizarre laughter of jackals and hyenas. He was officially credited with a rhino that surprised him in the bush and put him to chase. Downing the beast was a collaborative effort. Cooper's own favorite kill was very nearly his first: an oryx, a huge buck with two graceful horns —an exotic and fleet-footed relative of the deer.

There was a large camp tent. The sleeping tents accommodated two persons, and it can only be imagined how they were assigned. They were in splendid isolation, yet Jerry Preston kept in touch with the outside world by radio; and the outside world, perhaps relying on invention, kept a running account of the jungle odyssey of the countess and the film star. When Gary Cooper bought a chimpanzee at a village on the rim of the Nubia desert, the world knew about it. He named his pet Tolucca, and Tolucca was a sensation here and there—first in Rome.

In February of 1932 a supremely bronzed Gary Cooper emerged from darkest Africa to accompany the countess back to Rome. At the Villa Madama he was greeted by Count Carlo as if he were a long-lost brother. There were more parties, and it seemed that Dorothy di Frasso had succeeded in making Gary Cooper forget all about his responsibility toward the world of motion pictures. He was pointedly, brazenly, out of touch with his employers, and his calculation was that his continued absence would only make their hearts grow fonder toward him.

He carefully packed and crated the prizes of his safari for shipment to Hollywood, then relaxed to enjoy the countess's latest brainstorm. If Cooper really had to get home eventually as he insisted, they could have fun getting him there: nothing less than a Mediterranean cruise touching all the bright spots along the Italian and French Rivieras, and on to Monte Carlo.

Cooper was gratified that the lady was paying, for he had financed his safari and faced steadily dwindling reserves with no salary coming in. He also appeared to derive perverse satisfaction in his dealings with newspapermen, giving them the just-good-friends line while gossip merchants in Hollywood and around the world continued to speculate on a possible marriage between the cowboy star and the presumed-to-be-ex-countess. Yet the count accompanied them on the cruise that kept the papers supplied with a new splash of pictures. Oh, how they reveled! Until, in Monte Carlo, Cooper heard over a gaming table that an industrial crisis gripped Paramount Pictures.

The economic foundation of the old company had collapsed and it was going into receivership for a wholesale reorganization.

The pioneer Jesse Lasky, who often seemed the sanest of the moguls, had been dumped. Famous Players-Lasky, the organization for which Paramount once had only been the name of its distribution arm, now ceased to exist entirely. Paramount would go on, of course, for most of its pictures still earned profits as individual items of commerce; but the company was too vast, too complicated, and would undergo immediate and radical streamlining.

The Long Island studio was closing its doors. All production would be concentrated in Hollywood but there would be less of it —considerably fewer pictures than in past years. B. P. Schulberg had already been relieved as production chief and now was only one of the subordinate producers. His successor in Hollywood would be Emanuel Cohen from the New York office. The shakeup of personnel affected every creative department. Victor Fleming, one of the more reliable directors, had gone over to M-G-M. Both Ruth Chatterton and Kay Francis had defected to Warner-First National. The studio already had dropped Jean Arthur, Buddy Rogers, Mary Brian . . .

At different times Gary Cooper had been given reason to believe he could move to any of several rival studios and probably improve himself financially. He had not considered a move because he trusted Paramount for an insurance that was professional as well as economic. Now he learned the crisis did not begin and end with Paramount. There was industry-wide panic. Partly it was the Depression, but it also related in no small extent to radio. More and more people were buying radios and staying away from the movies, whose attendance figures were now declining sharply, after having leaped during the novelty of the talkies. Salary cuts were being made in all the studios, sometimes as high as 50 per cent.

Then he read a gossip column story that said if Gary Cooper was thinking of returning to Paramount, he might not find the welcome mat out. The studio was breaking in a new actor from Broadway, where he had been known as Archie Leach but who would become Cary Grant for the movies. Lose a Gary, catch a Cary: to Cooper it suggested a pretty low tactic.

It was time for Cooper to see if he still had a movie career. He had no idea what kind of business *His Woman* had done. The studio's "curtailed" activity could mean that he was out on the street; and if that were the case, he might have nowhere else to go.

The pleasure cruise ended hectically and abruptly in Monte Carlo. Cooper booked passage to New York, and the Di Frassos accompanied him on the voyage. At the very least, he was still hot copy. On one evening the ship's movie fare was a piece of Paramount fluff called *This Is the Night* and Cooper decided to watch it because his new rival was in the cast. When asked what he thought of Cary Grant, Cooper said, "I say he's a crack comedian, and isn't competition for me at all." Which didn't mean he wasn't worried.

Their arrival in New York was covered sensationally, but even the figures in the strange romantic triangle were brazenly upstaged by the chimp, Tolucca, who was put on a train to California. The Di Frassos remained in New York when Cooper flew to Hollywood. He was working into a nervous state and had no patience for the long train ride, so he reserved a transcontinental flight. He was practically broke, so Dorothy paid for his ticket.

As usual, he had worried unnecessarily. He was welcome at the studio and there were no recriminations. They even had a picture ready for him—not *The Glass Key*, which had been put on the shelf. He was handed a script for a submarine melodrama called *The Devil and the Deep*. A quick reading failed to excite him, but the important thing was that he was restored to the salary roll, with nothing said about a salary cut.

He also heard that there was only desperate press agentry behind the selling of the new Cary Grant as Cooper's "replacement." If that kept Gary Cooper on his toes, so much the better. Cooper met Cary Grant the day he returned to the studio, and learned that even the Cary-Gary business was entirely coincidental, as were the transposed initials. His employers initially were only going to purge the Leach surname for the obvious reason, and make him Archie Grant. Then they frowned on Archie. The fellow who had been Archie Leach had most recently played on Broadway a character named Cary Lockwood in a play called *Nikki*, by Cooper's friend John Monk Saunders; so Cary had been his own idea. Furthermore, Cary Grant was going to be supporting Cooper in *The Devil and the Deep*.

Cooper had been back on the Coast only a few days when he was approached by Myron Selznick, David's older brother, to join his client list. Myron was flexing a lot of muscle as a talent agent; indeed, he had become the bane of the studios. His clients included many of the screen's solid star names. Myron Selznick had engineered the sneaky maneuver that sent first William Powell from Paramount to Warner at a huge gain in salary, then the Misses Chatterton and Francis for payoffs even handsomer than Powell's.

Selznick said the so-called panic was a lot of crap and that Cooper had a golden opportunity with his Paramount contract about to expire. He could join the Selznick list and have a wide choice of studios. The money, too, would be awesome; it was Myron's job to make the money awesome.

Cooper was tempted but he hardly knew Myron Selznick. By keeping his wise-owl silence and carefully digesting everything he heard, he also suspected that Myron's character was not of the highest order. Yet Cooper basically trusted his younger brother, so he telephoned him at RKO where David Selznick now was running the whole show.

David Selznick urged Cooper to sit tight. Whether or not Cooper realized it, Paramount valued him above any other star contracted to them; of that David was certain. Cooper's absence really had made the heart grow fonder.

"Gary, if they know you're thinking of leaving, they may be surprisingly generous about getting you to stay on. You have healthy options. You can renegotiate your contract—propose your own deal, and see if they'll go for it. If they don't, you can tie in with Myron any time."

Cooper huddled with Emanuel Cohen and Albert Kaufman at the Paramount office. The great Ernst Lubitsch came in and audited the discussion—silently, but signaling with his eyes that Cooper should be catered to. Cooper was not represented by agent, manager, or counsel, but had been thoroughly advised in every aspect of negotiation and knew what he wanted. From a very low point, his confidence had risen almost to its zenith.

First, he didn't want to make *The Devil and the Deep*. He'd read the script, and submarine or no submarine, it struck him as a woman's picture. Furthermore, he had the poorest of the three leading roles, one that would surely be overshadowed by the woman's sadistic husband, who commanded the sub. More importantly, though, he did not want and would not accept a contract that allowed him to be worked to death. He did not specify what he might consider a reasonable limitation. He expected them to suggest five pictures a year or maybe only four, and was going to hold out for three. When Cohen suggested an annual obligation of three pictures, Cooper said let's make it two. They offered two thousand a week and Cooper, who secretly wanted three thousand a week and would have settled for it, said he wanted five.

They kicked it around and agreed on four thousand a week. He would be paid every week for making only two pictures a year, and if he made more than that for Paramount, he would receive extra pay. He would be free to accept work for other companies but no more than one picture annually, for which he would be paid his regular pro-rated salary with Paramount taking a lender's fee. He could not be made to accept outside work unless Paramount loaned him for one of his own commitments—which they couldn't do anyway without his approval, for he had extracted another important concession. He had both director approval and script approval; he really wouldn't have to make any picture he didn't want to make.

They capitulated to his demands when he agreed to make *The Devil and the Deep* to close out his old contract. He wondered why it was so important, and they explained. They were trying to save Tallulah Bankhead, who was a dud at the box office, and maybe only Gary Cooper could save her.

When Tallulah Bankhead signed her Paramount star contract in the New York home office, she met the press with her characteristic frankness. She said she was looking forward to going out to Hollywood so she could lay Gary Cooper.

The remark didn't get printed right away but it got around, and Cooper was wary of her—first when he was filming *City Streets* in New York, then when he was at the Astoria studio between his European and African episodes. He had heard all the talk about Tallulah the man-crusher. He already had more of that type than he could manage, so he went to great lengths to avoid meeting her at the studio, and even rejected party invitations in fear of her being there. When he attended the end-of-shooting party for *Girls About Town* because Anderson Lawler was in the cast, he couldn't have suspected that Tallulah would show up and greet him like an old friend or a destined lover, with a "Dahling!" oozed in her unique affectation.

That was when Cooper introduced the illustrious Tallulah to the star-struck Lawler, who nevertheless kept his stability and matched wits with her. Miss Bankhead must have been impressed, for now she and Lawler were living together—living, in fact, in Cooper's rented house on Argyle Avenue. Cooper had given Lawler the keys when he dashed off on safari, but he had not kept in touch and was startled by this new development. He told them to stay there, though; he had to find a larger place anyway, one that was suitable for displaying mounted souvenirs of his safari adventure. But until he found a place—well, they would just have to watch after Tolucca.

Lawler had not worked in pictures since *Girls About Town* almost a year earlier, and his only stage role had been in a flop that quickly closed. Yet Tallulah consoled him with the thought that her career was in poorer shape than his, because Andy's reputation wasn't getting any *worse*. She had made four pictures for Paramount, every one a turkey. *The Devil and the Deep* would be her fifth—and as matters would have it, also her last. She hated the script. She and Cooper were the nominal co-stars, but she agreed with him that neither had the picture's best role.

Not until shooting commenced did Cooper meet Charles Laughton, who was assigned the role of the possessive and jealous husband just before the cameras rolled. Already celebrated as a character actor in his native England, the thirty-three-year-old Laughton had been brought to America to play H. G. Wells's Dr. Moreau in *Island of Lost Souls*, then was loaned around when that picture got delayed. Due to logistical peculiarities at the various studios, *The Devil and the Deep* would be his third American film but the first one released, and his performance as the loathsome commander would make him a star.

Not that it could make *The Devil and the Deep* any great shakes as a picture, despite the historical interest it would command for its illustrious cast—Miss Bankhead, Cooper, Laughton, and the tyro Cary Grant. Anderson Lawler even got into sailor costume and appeared uncredited in a couple of scenes. With nowhere else to go, Lawler was an everyday presence on the set, sneering at director Marion Gering behind his back. Earlier the Russian Gering had directed Cooper in *I Take This Woman* and neither, apparently, had faith in the other. At one point Gering despaired of Cooper's reticence in a scene with Miss Bankhead and took him to task.

"Mr. Cooper, will you now begin to act?"

Gering's shrill impatience provoked an unexpected response from the sidelines.

"He *is* acting, you idiot," thundered Charles Laughton, "only *you* don't see it. But the cam-ar-rah does!"

Charles Laughton continued to express appreciation of Gary Cooper's subtle art, although it was the only film in which they would work together. While *The Devil and the Deep* was still in production, he said, "I knew in a flash Gary had something I should never have. It is something pure and he doesn't know it's there. In truth, that boy hasn't the least idea how well he acts."

Once when they were between takes, Tallulah chided Cooper

for appearing more interested in how a submarine works than in perfecting his dialogue.

"What the hell does it have to do with acting?" she wanted to know.

"Well, Talloo, I think it's pretty important. I figure that if I get to know what all of these things are, all I have to do is just push levers and turn wheels and not have to think about acting at all."

Still, Laughton got all the reviews, such as they were. For Cooper, the picture did next to nothing, other than assure his fans that he had returned from his international fling with personality unaltered and intact.

As for Tallulah Bankhead, she finally had a picture that was not a commercial failure. Even so, it was only marginally profitable, and that was attributed to Cooper's drawing power. Paramount decided to settle her unique contract—six pictures at $100,000 each—by lending her to M-G-M for the final commitment. It was called *Faithless*, a title that could have served any of her thirties films; but still the public wasn't buying her. Where the movie cameras brought out something in Gary Cooper that could never have been revealed on a stage, they somehow stifled the incandescence that was Tallulah's in life.

So she went back to Broadway where she belonged, and got into a fashionable play called *Forsaking All Others*. She saw to it that her young man, Anderson Lawler, played one of the leading roles—the playboy enacted by Robert Montgomery in the subsequent Joan Crawford screen vehicle that also had Clark Gable. For about two years Tallulah and Lawler were seen everywhere together, then only sometimes, and finally he faded from her life. Perhaps he tired of being only a prop for the busy production that was Tallulah.

Miss Bankhead was then married briefly to actor John Emery. During World War II she returned to pictures as the sophisticated heroine of Steinbeck and Hitchcock's *Lifeboat*. She was a sensation, finally much appreciated on film. In her later years she became outspoken about her bisexuality, and was an often pitiful caricature of herself. Over the years she saw Gary Cooper often, mostly in New York, and they were considered good friends.

Whenever she was reminded of why she said she went to Hollywood in the first place, Tallulah was adamant that she had accomplished her stated objective.

Until Gary Cooper returned to Hollywood, his parents had not seen him for fourteen months. They had been filled with wonder and alarm, following newspaper accounts of his escapades that were rather at odds with the letters he wrote. His presence reassured them; he was in marvelous condition and high spirits. Arthur brought his own family from Montana for a reunion and some Hollywood sight-seeing. Alice, becoming more exuberant and fluttery with age, was easily captivated by the descriptions of Count di Frasso's villa, and of the very scenic Mediterranean cruise. Charles, growing ever more silently distant, might occasionally mutter that he wished his son would get married and begin to act his age.

Judge Cooper was permanently vexed that he had advised his son to invest in land around Palm Springs when it could be bought for forty dollars an acre, only to be rebuffed because Gary said it would just be throwing away good money. His father had been quietly efficient nevertheless, and now Gary was realizing handsome returns from capital he had asked his father to invest. Despite his recent profligacy, Gary Cooper was in splendid financial shape after all, and buoyed by his new contract that called for escalations to seventy-five hundred dollars per week before its expiration in 1937. He calculated that he would earn almost two million dollars by then, and felt secure enough to begin spending it.

He took rooms in the Roosevelt Hotel until he could find the house he wanted. He settled on a low-slung Spanish ranch-style house that had once belonged to Greta Garbo, on Chevy Chase in Beverly Hills. Compared to the other places he'd lived in around Hollywood it was vast, with a living room that could advertise many of the prizes of his hunting adventure.

He retrieved his well-stuffed menagerie from storage and mounted the heads himself, in the workshop that was another feature of the new house with particular appeal for him. A decorator transformed the huge living room and other chambers into a veritable jungle. Even the rugs were reminders of Cooper's hunting prowess. Nevertheless, the chimp Tolucca was not at ease in the simulated habitat and became a nuisance, eventually dispatched to a zoo.

Even before the house was ready according to his specifications, Elsa Maxwell was a live-in guest, sent there by the Countess di Frasso to keep watch on Cooper. Miss Maxwell briefly was employed as a consultant to one of the studios on matters of high society. While she was living in Cooper's house she also hunted for a place worthy of the Di Frassos . . . and found one, within easy walking distance.

The return of count and countess to the filmland touched off a new round of parties. They were also hosts for affairs that lured the Hollywood nobility. As the count became increasingly involved with "business" that kept him from the scene of revelry, the countess and Cooper formed a regular threesome with Elsa Maxwell. Cole Porter came to Hollywood and made it a foursome.

Dorothy was trying desperately to hold on to Cooper, and while she still appeared to be leading him on an invisible leash, he was looking for an out. Whether they were photographed as an Indian brave and squaw, or as circus clowns in whiteface at some other gala, Cooper's countenance betrayed his mounting unease. Speculation that they might marry ended well before their romance appeared to. They had planned another safari, for which Cooper had bought special guns and elaborate camping equipment. Then Cooper backed out, after it had been all he could talk about. Jack Moss said Cooper had had such a good time getting ready, he just didn't have to go. The real reason, though, was that he was trying to disentangle himself from the countess.

Cooper was now Hollywood's "most eligible bachelor." He dated Lupe Velez again on a couple of occasions, but their old fire was doused by Lupe's teasing reference to the *abuela*—her pet name for the countess, as "the grandmother." Nor was Lupe desperate: her new boy friend was the Olympic swimming champion Johnny Weissmuller, who was also the new Tarzan at M-G-M.

Cooper was trying to break free gently, not wanting to hurt Dorothy's feelings. Elsa Maxwell later reported, however, that as

Cooper and the Countess di Frasso began really to become "just good friends," Dorothy truly was deeply hurt.

"I haven't read six books in my entire life," Gary Cooper once told Jim Tully in an interview.

One book he apparently did read was Charles Dickens's A *Tale of Two Cities*. He made loud hints that he would like it to be the picture to inaugurate his new contract. Emanuel Cohen, the studio boss, protested that a re-creation of the French Revolution would require a larger budget than Paramount could then afford. Nevertheless, Cohen put first Garrett Fort and then the team of Gene Towne and Graham Baker on an adaptation, and for two years the studio advertised A *Tale of Two Cities* as a production vaguely for the future.

John Engstead tells of a Paramount party some time earlier, when the studio players attended in the costumes of the characters they most wanted to play—Jack Oakie as Merton of the movies, Kay Francis as Cleopatra, Claudette Colbert as Juliet, and Jean Arthur as Peter Pan. Eventually Miss Arthur played Peter Pan with great success but on Broadway, not in a film; and Colbert, not Francis, was De Mille's *Cleopatra*. Gary Cooper came as Sydney Carton, and made an earnest bid for the role a few years later, when David Selznick made A *Tale of Two Cities* after moving from RKO to M-G-M to serve his father-in-law, Louis B. Mayer. Selznick explained that Gary Cooper could never be his idea of an Englishman, and tentatively set the new Brian Aherne for the part. Then Ronald Colman revealed his own interest, and went on to play Carton with great success.

Cooper, though, began to evidence a proprietary interest in his career from an increasingly literary perspective. He had not read Ernest Hemingway's A *Farewell to Arms* but knew its reputation, and reasoned that the ambulance-driving Frederic Henry was especially "right" for him, as earlier similar roles in *Lilac Time* and *Shopworn Angel* had also been right, and important in his progress. When Paramount obtained the screen rights, Cooper put in an early bid to be cast. He received no encouragement, and began hearing that the front office did not consider him sufficiently actorish for the part. A high level of drama was the objective for A *Farewell to Arms*, and when the studio borrowed Helen Hayes from M-G-M to play nurse Catherine Barkley, it seemed to rule out Cooper altogether. Miss Hayes had just won the Academy Award as best actress; and Paramount's Fredric March had been recognized as best actor for Dr. *Jekyll and Mr. Hyde*. March had also become rather quickly certified as the studio's best and most versatile actor, so the inspiration was to get him in the Hemingway story opposite Miss Hayes.

Fredric March had become one of Cooper's good friends, and Cooper regularly sought his advice on scripts he was considering. One was *Hot Saturday*, from a novel by Harvey Fergusson, whose earlier *Wolf Song* had brought Cooper and Lupe Velez together. *Hot Saturday* was proposed as a co-starring venture for Cooper and Nancy Carroll, but Fredric March said, "Don't do it, Coop. Never take a straight lead when there's another part that's better written and sure to take the play away from you." March indicated a secondary role that was actually ideal for Cooper, less conventional and more "westernly." Cooper rejected *Hot Saturday* as his contract entitled him, and Cary Grant was cast opposite Miss Carroll. The other male role went to the young Randolph Scott, who had taken over in the studio's Zane Grey Westerns and was getting promoted as "another Gary Cooper." *Hot Saturday* marked Cary Grant's first leading role but Scott stole the notices, such as they were.

Next Cooper was offered the Pinkerton role in a nonsinging *Madame Butterfly* with Sylvia Sidney as Cio-Cio San. Fredric March didn't even have to read the script.

"Even if the picture turns out all right, it could hurt you, Coop. It's a dreadful part, and Pinkerton's a cad."

So Cooper rejected *Madame Butterfly*, which emerged anything but all right on film. It was a flop, poorly serving Cary Grant, who of course became Lieutenant Pinkerton.

Then Charles Laughton tipped Cooper to go after the role of the Roman Centurion hero in *The Sign of the Cross*, the promised spectacle that was bringing Cecil B. De Mille back to Paramount. The plan was to borrow Charles Farrell from Fox; but Laughton, who was already set to play the Emperor Nero, sensed that De Mille was wavering because Farrell had recently slipped at the box office. Cooper did not see himself as anybody's Roman, but he planned to talk to De Mille. Then Fredric March decided to talk to De Mille because March was upset that John Cromwell was being relieved as director for *A Farewell to Arms*, and wanted to get out of the assignment. So March became a De Mille hero and Cooper talked his way into *A Farewell to Arms*, although the announcement of his casting was received with skepticism throughout Hollywood. Cooper, they said, was an effective player of a type, for certain roles; but playing with Helen Hayes he'd be getting in over his head.

A Farewell to Arms gave every promise of being a "big" picture, more so than *The Virginian* or *City Streets* or anything Cooper had done; even *Morocco* assumed an artistic importance only after its release. Those who conceded that Cooper had replaced a less suitable Fredric March in *Morocco* felt that *A Farewell to Arms* carried a dramatic requirement beyond his capability. Yet Frank Borzage, brought in to replace Cromwell as director, said he expected Cooper would be perfect.

Before shooting began, Cooper agreed to take a part in the episodic *If I Had a Million* and not charge it as a contract assignment. This would become one of the screen's all-time curiosities: a picture filmed in one week, by seven directors each working with a full crew, spread all over the studio and all over town. It was a fairy tale of the Great Depression, each episode focusing on someone receiving a million dollars as a gift from an eccentric tycoon who thinks he's dying. (Many years later the theme was appropriated for a popular TV series.) Vignettes featuring George Raft as a hood on the lam and Gene Raymond going to the electric chair were melodramatic if not tragic, but most of the episodes were sentimental or comical. Such wily performers as May Robson, W. C. Fields, and the team of Charlie Ruggles and Mary Boland were well served; and the best-remembered sequence was the briefest one, directed by Lubitsch—Charles Laughton blowing a razzberry at his boss. Just about everyone agreed the weakest component was Cooper's. He received his gift check in the guardhouse he shared with fellow soldiers Jack Oakie and Roscoe Karns, then gave it to a waitress, thinking it was only a joke. *If I Had a Million* is one of those pictures that become more famous and cherished with age; and despite Cooper's minimal contribution, he led the billing among the fourteen "stars."

It was certainly a strange warm-up exercise for *A Farewell to*

Arms. Cooper went to work facing his sternest dramatic challenge to date, yet not knowing how the story or even his character would be resolved. The script would depart from the novel by necessity, for the Hays Office could not condone the illicit sexual union between Frederic Henry and Catherine Barkley. The screen translators would endeavor to emulate Hemingway's vision of tragedy and destructiveness in the World War, while laundering the affair between the principals.

Frank Borzage said he gave no direction to Cooper because it wasn't necessary; Miss Hayes established a level of authoritative underplaying that Cooper followed effectively. Borzage also believed that Adolphe Menjou, who would win praise for the Rinaldi role, subdued himself as if on cue from Cooper. Borzage, surely the confirmed romantic among all American film directors, elevated the story's emotional content while carefully shaping the film in a sentimental design that was ludicrously opposed to the spirit of the Hemingway novel. The picture worked, but as some other story. It threatened to become *Lilac Time* with a sad ending, until that also was changed. Borzage filmed a just-in-case alternate ending, with Catherine not dying and the lovers facing the future together. That was the version that went into release as Paramount's Christmas offering for 1932.

When shooting finished, Cooper gave a party for the company —the first one in his Africa-scented manor, and the only one in which he had Dorothy di Frasso's assistance as hostess. Mary Philips, who had a good supporting role in *A Farewell to Arms,* urged Cooper to talk her discouraged actor-husband into remaining in Hollywood. Cooper seldom was inclined to talk anyone into or out of anything; so he merely listened as the fellow blasphemed the movie business. After two years in Hollywood and a handful of rotten pictures, the man with the unlikely marquee name of Humphrey Bogart was going back to New York, and was saying he'd never return. Cooper made no effort to change the actor's mind, because he did not expect the movies would ever have a particular need of him.

A Farewell to Arms collected eloquent reviews. If it wasn't Hemingway, it was a beautifully composed lachrymose love story. Charles Lang's delicate cinematography won the Academy Award, and the film itself took a nomination. It also made money. If the reviewers gave the edge, expectedly, to Helen Hayes, they also gave Cooper's performance a solid endorsement that startled his detractors and excited his employers. A fair assessment was that Cooper did not match Miss Hayes in depth, but unmistakably revealed a sensitivity that was wholly unexpected of him. Even Ernest Hemingway liked Cooper's delineation, although he hated the picture.

It was only Helen Hayes's fourth talking screen appearance, but she had enormous prestige. She went back to M-G-M for another batch of films that failed to stimulate her, and a few years later forsook Hollywood for steadily mounting reputation in the theater that had bred her. A *Farewell to Arms* was a nice embellishment to her screen career, but in no way crucial to it. Yet it was enormously vital to Cooper, and really the first picture to suggest that major stardom was a prospect for him.

Because he had fought for the role, the experience persuaded him that he knew what was best for Gary Cooper.

Left,
The Winning of Barbara Worth
(1926).
*The Cooper breakthrough,
here in a scene with Vilma Banky
and Charles Lane.*

Below,
Lilac Time (1928).
*A silent picture
saved by a theme song,
and a smash hit;
with Colleen Moore,
a top star of the era.*

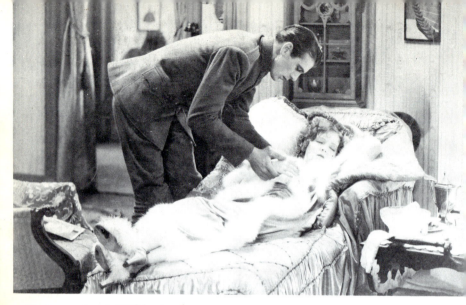

Shopworn Angel (1929). *Cooper passes his vocal audition in a fondly remembered part-talkie with Nancy Carroll.*

The Virginian (1929). *An important film in formulating the standard Cooper screen character; with Mary Brian as Molly and Cooper's good friend Richard Arlen as Steve.*

Seven Days Leave (1930). *Sentimental Barrie whimsy with Beryl Mercer, and Cooper's first star-billed appearance.*

Morocco (1930). *Josef von Sternberg directing Marlene Dietrich's first American film, and Cooper's first undisputed classic.*

Right,
City Streets (1931).
*An arty gangster picture
directed by Rouben Mamoulian,
with the new Sylvia Sidney in
the role intended for Clara Bow.*

Below,
A Farewell to Arms (1932)
*An important one for Cooper,
as Frederic Henry opposite
the Catherine Barkley
of Miss Helen Hayes.*

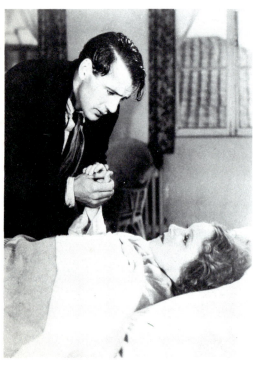

One Sunday Afternoon (1933). *Nostalgic charm was the substance of the best of the four films that teamed Cooper with Fay Wray.*

Design for Living (1933). *Fredric March, Miriam Hopkins, and a "miscast" Cooper in the Noel Coward business now rated a Lubitsch classic.*

Above,
Lives of a Bengal Lancer *(1935).*
Rousing adventure with
a mustachioed Cooper,
Richard Cromwell, and
Franchot Tone.

Right,
Peter Ibbetson *(1935).*
A strange film containing Cooper's
most atypical performance,
with Ann Harding.

Above,
Mr. Deeds Goes to Town (1936).
*Frank Capra's populist
bell-ringer, here in the famous
park scene with the
enchanting Jean Arthur.*

Right,
The General Died at Dawn (1936).
*Clifford Odets provided the script
for an oriental melodrama with
the alluring Madeleine Carroll.*

Above,
The Plainsman (1936)
*Again with Jean Arthur in the best
of Cooper's four DeMille pictures.*

Right,
Souls at Sea (1937).
*Nautical costume melodrama
and George Raft.*

6

THE COWBOY
AND THE LADY

GARY COOPER AND Clark Gable first met in 1925, when Cooper was an extra for a Ken Maynard Western in which Gable played a small role. Discouraged by his failure to progress in films, Gable tried the stage and became an employable actor, first in stock and eventually on Broadway, without acquiring real fame. When Gable returned to Hollywood in 1930 for another crack at movie acting, Cooper was solidly established in the talkies. Before long, however, Gable's movie fame eclipsed Cooper's and also threatened to surpass just about everyone else's. He exploded on the screen in a dozen 1931 releases, in small parts at first, but was an established star by the end of the year.

Gable and Cooper were often described as close personal friends in the wishful literature of the fan magazines. They did become congenially acquainted, even going on a few hunting trips together. If they attended the same Hollywood party, they might seek an obscure corner to pursue talk that was inevitably about guns. If they wished, they could also have compared the advantages and disadvantages of involvement with older women. Gable's recent past was as a stage gigolo, performing stud service for such actresses as Pauline Frederick and Laura Hope Crews, who were considerably older than he. He had once been married to a much older woman who was his first acting coach and who also paid for his new false teeth. Now he was married again, to a woman seventeen years his senior, the Texas heiress Rhea Langham, who had underwritten his successful assault on movieland—and who already had become one of Dorothy di Frasso's close friends in Hollywood.

But if they were only casually friendly, Cooper and Gable had a deeper commitment as rivals. Over the years each would build an impressive gun collection, apparently not to be outdone by the other. Both men were also car-crazy and courted the friendship of the film colony's high-powered dealers in international automobiles. In 1932 Dick Hadley delivered to Cooper a custom-built Duesenberg. Gable saw the car at the Riviera Country Club and accepted Cooper's invitation to take it for a spin in the Pacific Palisades. Right after that he got his friend Al Menasco to order a Duesenberg built especially for himself, but with additional silver trim and the guarantee that it would be one foot longer than Cooper's model.

At about that same time, Cooper was growing jealous of Gable's affiliation with Metro-Goldwyn-Mayer, the studio that boasted "more stars than there are in heaven." Coming under the influence of Jack Moss, whom he hired upon finally deciding he needed a business manager, Cooper began to feel that staying with Paramount was a mistake of his own making. During a period in which only *City Streets* and *A Farewell to Arms* pleased Cooper among his pictures, Gable at M-G-M had been prestigiously teamed with both Greta Garbo and Norma Shearer, and with Jean Harlow in *Red Dust* had scorched the screen for a financial windfall. Cooper was a he-man star but Gable, he thought, was more so on the basis of shrewd promotion by the studio. The young and portly Jack Moss insinuated that Cooper couldn't really test his star potential fully until he worked for M-G-M. Then Cooper's jealousy of Gable helped bring that about.

Gable was something of a problem at M-G-M for his carousing activities although he ostensibly was properly married. The problem magnified when he fell in love with Joan Crawford, and she with him, while she was married to the younger Douglas Fairbanks. In an effort to keep them apart, Louis B. Mayer personally removed Gable from the co-starring spot in a forthcoming Crawford picture. Mayer offered Gable to Paramount for one picture, in exchange for Gary Cooper as Crawford's leading man.

Cooper had hoped to follow *A Farewell to Arms* with *Secrets*, as Mary Pickford's husband in a pioneer saga. Frank Borzage was set as Miss Pickford's director, and Cooper liked the working atmosphere of a Borzage picture. But Louis B. Mayer, with whom Cooper had not previously been acquainted, called on him personally to rhapsodize over *Today We Live*, the Crawford vehicle. Cooper felt he shouldn't forsake an opportunity to work at M-G-M, so he sent his regrets to Miss Pickford. Then he was amused that Paramount put Gable in a picture they had prepared for Gary Cooper before he turned it down. Nevertheless, by playing in Paramount's *No Man of Her Own*, Clark Gable became acquainted with Carole Lombard.

Anita Loos has said that Gable was "even duller than Gary Cooper in his conversation," and that the M-G-M star actually had few friends among his fellow screen actors who were generally brighter than he. Cooper, however, began to acquire many close friendships that were both personal and professional, without ever indicating a desperate need of them His closest friend at Paramount during much of his tenure there undoubtedly was Richard Arlen, but in 1932 Cooper was at least indirectly responsible for bringing into the Paramount fold a great friend who would also become one of the great stars, possibly even the greatest in the long Paramount history.

Cooper met Bing Crosby even before Bing had started to conquer radio, or had married Dixie Lee—when, as a minor Fox player, she was still considered "bigger" than Crosby. Lupe Velez, who seemed to know all the boys, introduced Cooper to Bing when he was vocalist with Gus Arnheim's band at the Cocoanut Grove, venturing out on his own after his stint as one of the "Rhythm Boys" with Paul Whiteman. Crosby sometimes joined Cooper, Arlen, and the gang for the stag parties that remained popular for a time, and often took Cooper sailing. When Crosby's phenomenal success on radio as a solo act came almost instantly, he let Cooper know that pictures were definitely an objective for him. Yet Bing apparently flunked the kind of "screen test" in the form of an interview that Cooper had once passed at Paramount, and he got his start in pictures by reprising his popular hits in a series of musical shorts produced by Mack Sennett for Educational. Soon it was evident that Bing's two-reelers helped sell the features they supported, and at the same time Bing was cited as one of the radio stars who were keeping people at home and causing movie receipts to dwindle. All at once every film company wanted to get Crosby under contract.

After Crosby signed with Paramount, it was revealed that both Fox and Warner had offered him more front money, although Bing's pact had several "riders" that would spell a handsome financial pay-off if he succeeded in pictures, as succeed he would. Crosby, though, said he decided to go with Paramount because Gary Cooper was there, and he wanted to be around friends he could trust. When the Crosbys' first son was born in 1933, he was named Gary; and Cooper became his godfather.

Bing Crosby's arrival at Paramount in 1932 relieved some of the tension that had coalesced during the company's financial difficulty. The studio acquired something akin to school spirit, for which Bing and Carole Lombard were the acknowledged cheerleaders. Yet Cooper's dressing room was the center of gravity for the stars' spirited socializing at the studio. Paramount accommodated its stars with dressing bungalows all in a row—a dozen of them, with a hinted pecking order. (Mae West, at her insistence, had number one; and Cary Grant, insecure in his early Paramount stardom, occupied number twelve.) Cooper's bungalow was smack in the middle, but Bing Crosby said the reason it became their headquarters was that Coop was the only one among them whom everyone else liked.

Getting together in Cooper's bungalow became a ritual to solemnize the end of the day's shooting. It was a period when most movie stars, upon completing one picture, went into another one almost immediately. Mae West and Marlene Dietrich did not film with the frequency of the other players, and there was also a steady transition as George Bancroft yielded his chambers to Cary Grant, or Nancy Carroll hers to so brief a tenant as Kate Smith. Yet a Paramount nucleus was forming whose lady members were no match collectively for M-G-M's, and whose men were overshadowed by their counterparts at Warner, but who on balance could define a nice studio "look": Mae West, Claudette Colbert, Marlene Dietrich, Sylvia Sidney, Miriam Hopkins, and Carole Lombard; and Gary Cooper, Fredric March, Bing Crosby, George Raft, Cary Grant, and the illustrious Charles Laughton.

Carole Lombard called Paramount the fun house among the studios, and said the happy hour at the end of the day was the best of all, when they did a little drinking and a lot of singing and also plotted role-swapping because they knew better than the studio bosses what they should be playing. In the closed company of known friends, Gary Cooper was a talker and not a bad singer, amusing and amused.

Still, everyone talked about what it was like over in Culver City, at M-G-M . . .

The M-G-M press releases said Joan Crawford had insisted on having Gary Cooper as her co-star for *Today We Live*. Miss Crawford later adopted that line in her own autobiographical writings. At the time she probably regarded Cooper as a satisfactory replacement for Gable, but was not pleased that Gable had to be replaced. Later, when it became apparent that she had fallen in love with Franchot Tone (soon to be her second husband), the studio revived the Crawford-Gable co-starring team time and again. The studio gossip had held that Joan would almost certainly fall very hard for Cooper once they were in a clinch for the camera. Instead she was swept off her feet by Tone, recently of New York's Group Theater, and making his movie debut as Joan's brother.

Today We Live would be scarcely remembered, despite some literary curiosity value as William Faulkner's first writing credit for the movies. Joan Crawford was mistakenly cast as an aristocratic English girl, and it was wartime stuff with some planes, which may have explained why Howard Hawks was brought in to direct. It was his only M-G-M picture, and he tangled with Mayer and others at the studio.

The outdoorsman Howard Hawks was by then already one of Cooper's boon companions. Hawks said it was his own pitch for Cooper that caused Mayer to lure the Paramount star for the Crawford picture. There may have been a deeper intrigue, for Irving Thalberg was believed to have cast covetous glances toward Cooper as an M-G-M star for the future; and Hawks was Thalberg's brother-in-law at the time. Mayer and Thalberg had fallen out, and this had divided M-G-M into two political camps although a high diplomacy was exercised. Mayer rated himself the premier star-maker, and usually resisted or did not support Thalberg's candidates for the M-G-M firmament. It is well known now that Mayer thought Thalberg was making a mistake going after "someone who can never be a star" when Thalberg engineered the "steal" of Spencer Tracy from Fox. If there was any thought of trying to steal Gary Cooper from Paramount, the thought died when *Today We Live* disappointed at the box office. The indication was that Gary Cooper had been overrated as a box-office draw; he was weaker than either Gable or Robert Montgomery in co-starring chores for Crawford pictures that were probably no better than *Today We Live*. Even before the commercial fate of *Today We Live* was known, Cooper was back at Paramount telling his chums that M-G-M wasn't paradise after all. But he knew he wanted to make more pictures with Howard Hawks.

He rejected Paramount's offer of a proletarian drama called *Pick Up*, so George Raft took the part opposite Sylvia Sidney, and Cooper got a role he really wanted. He had even prodded Paramount to purchase the property, after getting a tip from Fredric March. It was a daily ritual for March to check in at the story department to see what new novels, stories, or plays were under consideration for purchase. March read the script of an unproduced play called *One Sunday Afternoon* and thought the principal role of a shy young dentist at the turn of the century was the sort of thing Cooper should be doing. Cooper thought so, too, and he lobbied with Bud Lighton to have Paramount buy it. Although the James Hagan play was undoubtedly acquired with Cooper in mind, there was little enthusiasm for it at the studio, and both Cooper and Lighton had to do some heavy lobbying to get a production commitment. Then Frank Tuttle, the director originally assigned, quit the picture before filming a scene, recommending its cancellation.

It wasn't scrapped, but it proceeded on a reduced budget and with one of the second-rank directors, Stephen Roberts. Then, while the first scenes were being shot, the play opened on Broadway with young Lloyd Nolan in the role of the dentist Biff Grimes, and it was a surprise major hit. Suddenly more importance was attached to *One Sunday Afternoon* and there was even talk of assigning yet another director. Cooper stood behind Roberts, however, and the picture was completed on its streamlined schedule.

Perhaps more than any other picture, *One Sunday Afternoon* offered the quintessential illumination of the young Gary Cooper. His Biff Grimes was selfless, inarticulate, and thoroughly good. As an actor he appeared to understand the dentist completely, and subtly expressed his frustration in both love and professional life. He played well with both of his leading ladies—Fay Wray for his last occasion with her; and the demure Frances Fuller, in pictures briefly from the stage. One of the story's nice appointments was the friendly yet antagonistic relationship between Biff and his go-getter friend Hugo, played by Neil Hamilton. Oddly enough, the property in which Paramount at first exercised so little faith would become a Hollywood staple. Warner later purchased it from Paramount to give James Cagney a turn as Biff Grimes, and as *Strawberry Blonde* it also offered Olivia de Havilland, Rita Hayworth, and Jack Carson. Less successful was the eventual Warner musical version reverting to the original title, with Dennis Morgan as Biff.

As a nostalgia piece it was fondly saluted by the reviewers, yet *One Sunday Afternoon* did only ordinary business. It didn't quite transcend the aura of the "little" picture although, like most consciously made period pieces, it would become less dated than the general run of photoplays.

Cooper was shooting *One Sunday Afternoon* in the spring of 1933 when the Countess di Frasso was photographed boarding the train that would take her to the East, where she would then book passage for Europe. Her statement was that Gary Cooper would join her at her Italian villa when his picture was finished. Instead, he stayed in Hollywood most of the year, and canceled himself from another big-game expedition that had been set for India. The heart had its reasons.

They met for the first time in New York, where he caught a glimpse of her at a social function he attended shortly after his return from African safari.

She was a stunning beauty: dark hair, creamy visage, and gray-green eyes as luminous as Gary Cooper's baby blues. She was also slender and almost tall, and had the stately bearing of unmistakable aristocracy.

Veronica Balfe was born to privilege and in Gary Cooper's eyes she was privilege's best advertisement. And she was just twenty years old.

He introduced himself, and was impressed that while Veronica Balfe certainly knew who he was, she did not appear to have lost her composure in meeting him. They made small talk; he actually resorted to telling her she ought to be in pictures. She even hinted that might be a possibility, for she knew some people in Hollywood and expected to visit there soon.

He learned more about her. Her father was the millionaire Harry Balfe, chairman of the board of Austin Nichols & Co. Her parents were divorced, and Veronica's mother was remarried to an even wealthier man—Paul Shields, a governor of the New York Stock Exchange. Veronica Balfe lived on Park Avenue in winter, at Southampton on Long Island in the summer. She was presented to society as a debutante, and had attended the exclusive Bennett School for girls in Millbrook, New York. She had been romantically thrilled when, with some of her classmates, she watched Cooper play the sensuous Foreign Legionnaire in *Morocco*.

They were introduced again in 1933, but in Hollywood; and she was not Veronica Balfe any longer, but Sandra Shaw. She was the niece of Cedric Gibbons, the M-G-M art director who was also one of the social dictators of the movie colony, and married at that time to Dolores Del Rio. Gibbons had made friendly acquaintance with Cooper during the *Today We Live* filming, and invited Cooper to a party he was giving for his niece, who had just arrived from the East to undertake a career in pictures. Cooper did not know that the invitation was given at Gibbons's niece's own instigation.

Cooper was smitten by this newcomer to the filmland, and began to extricate himself from the demands of his "friendship" with the countess, who was more than twice Veronica's age. He began asking her on dates and she was responsive, but sufficiently reserved so that Cooper was anything but confident of their budding relationship. Bing Crosby observed a Gary Cooper who "was so frightened of losing this new girl that he lost his balance and started bumping into things and breaking them."

Veronica simply would not be rushed, and although Cooper suspected that she was perhaps equally attracted to him, he saw that his mere presence in her life did not prevent Veronica Balfe from dating other new acquaintances—most of whom were probably younger than he.

Even after he declined to join the countess for another Roman holiday because he was fixed on his pursuit of Veronica, Cooper also had other dates. Indeed, he was more visible in the company of a young German actress named Wera Engels than on the arm of the beautiful new Sandra Shaw. Cooper also dated a minor Paramount actress, Judith Allen, and was later embarrassed when newspaper stories exploited a triangle composed of Cooper, Miss Allen, and her husband, the wrestler Gus Sonnenberg. Cooper had not known Miss Allen was married, and had failed to ask.

His romance with Veronica/Sandra was managed much more discreetly, so that they were not in the probing public eye. To settle the matter of her name, he began calling her "Rocky," enhancing the popularity of a nickname that had been attached to her only tentatively. Cooper's friends believed that the little scandal growing out of his mild flirtation with Judith Allen had been the last straw; he had grown weary of his wild playboy image, and sought to escape the headlines for the relative novelty of a quiet, essentially secret relationship. He may also have begun to regret the rather public sowing of his wild oats; for when he reached the stage of serious talk with Rocky, she let him know that her mother and stepfather would not put their stamp of approval on him as a marriage prospect for her. That marriage was something he could only attain with a struggle seemed to make it more desirable for Cooper. He endeavored to change his image, purging the Hollywood hell-raiser in favor of a sedate, proper fellow who moved in the best industrial circles.

Finally he stopped squiring other girls altogether, yet his percolating romance with Rocky remained something of which only Cooper's closest friends were aware. Even the redoubtable Louella Parsons caught on only belatedly that Cooper had a serious interest in Sandra Shaw, and the fan magazines were even tardier in their cognizance. As the romance began to reach its peak, one magazine story depicted Gary Cooper as heartbroken, sitting alone in his Beverly Hills house lamenting the loss of Lupe Velez, who had just married Johnny Weissmuller.

Cooper, in fact, was no longer living in Greta Garbo's old house when the story appeared. After having been there as a renter for barely a year, he vacated the place, packed up his mounted antelope heads and other trappings, and bought a ten-acre "ranch" just over the Hollywood hills in Van Nuys. Obviously he was seeking a residence more suitable for Rocky. The house on Chevy Chase Drive had become garishly masculine.

Shortly after he moved out in July of 1933, he was sued for breakage and other extensive damages by Eliza Albertson, the landlady, who won a nice out-of-court settlement. Jack Oakie remembered that the last party Cooper gave in his Beverly Hills place was strictly a stag affair that sort of marked the end of an era, not only for Gary Cooper.

In August of 1933, right after moving to Van Nuys, Cooper went to court to have his name changed legally to Gary. He was also investing in oil leases. He was a man getting his house in order, with the expectation that the house would soon contain a woman.

Indeed, after Rocky had given tentative acceptance of his proposal, it was confirmed that her mother and stepfather did not approve. They had read of his escapades in recent years; but so, surely, had Rocky herself. She had the situation well calibrated, and could prevail on Cedric Gibbons and perhaps some other friends to influence her parents on Gary Cooper's behalf. Meanwhile, Rocky met Charles and Alice Cooper and they liked her immediately, and perhaps with a sense of relief. Finally there was no obstacle to their getting married, and it was only a matter of choosing the time and the place.

Their romance bloomed in the summer of 1933. They traveled together while Cooper indulged himself in a long vacation after filming *One Sunday Afternoon*, and their deepening relationship became generally suspected in the film colony only after Cooper returned to work in *Design for Living*. Then suddenly all the journalists were scurrying to get information on "starlet" Sandra Shaw, who had obtained a player contract with RKO studios. She had not appeared in any RKO films, but was loaned to independent producer-director Rowland Brown for *Blood Money*, a melodrama with George Bancroft and Frances Dee, and in which Judith Anderson made her screen debut. Sandra Shaw had a good little part, and the reviewers who mentioned her thought they detected some dramatic promise as well as the obvious beauty. But if Rocky's later depositions accurately reflected her attitude, she never had real enthusiasm for a movie career and was pursuing one only as a lark. Sometimes she denied having actually made even walk-on appearances. Her scenes for *Blood Money* were shot while Cooper was occupied with *Design for Living*; and after he wrapped up that one, they took off for some hunting in Arizona's Kaibab Forest, north of the Grand Canyon.

A rumor took hold in Hollywood that Gary Cooper and Sandra Shaw were about to elope. In early November a missing Cooper was traced to the Kaibab, and the Associated Press report said that rumors were completely unfounded that Gary Cooper was about to marry Sandra Shaw, nor was Miss Shaw even in his hunting party, which consisted of actor John Gilbert, his wife Virginia Bruce, and a Miss Veronica Balfe.

Noel Coward wrote *Design for Living* as an acting piece for himself and the illustrious husband-and-wife team of Alfred Lunt and Lynn Fontanne. It was a play about "three people who love each other very much"—two men and a woman, all free spirits. It was a witty thing played in fine high style by its disarming principals, and expectedly achieved a smart Broadway success. The *ménage à trois* was something with which the movies simply could not cope in view of thematic restrictions then enforced by the Hays Office. Yet Paramount bought the screen rights, for if anyone could suggest the unsuggestible, it was Ernst Lubitsch; and Lubitsch was enchanted by the play.

Lubitsch particularly wanted to shape a *Design for Living* film for Miriam Hopkins, his favorite actress in Hollywood. She had sparkled in his own productions of *Trouble in Paradise* and *The Smiling Lieutenant* (opposite Chevalier in the latter) and had performed smoothly in other pictures, yet had not captivated the general fandom, which caused Paramount to become uneasy about her. Lubitsch believed that elegant exposure opposite two polished leading men would seal the Hopkins stardom, and he sought Ronald Colman and Leslie Howard. Colman had freed himself from his long contract with Samuel Goldwyn but was ruled too expensive for the Paramount project, and Leslie Howard said he wouldn't take either role, not wanting to invite comparison with either Lunt or Coward. Other British actors were ruled out as box-office liabilities for the American market, so Lubitsch decided that while the settings of Paris, London, and New York would be retained in that sequence for the film, the three principals would all be Americans. Ben Hecht was therefore engaged to rewrite the script with a line-by-line paraphrasing of the Coward dialogue into convincing Americanese.

Fredric March, whose harrowing Mr. Hyde had been played against Miss Hopkins' tormented Ivy, was set for the playwright. All other actors at the home studio, even Cary Grant, were scratched as possibilities for his painter friend. The free-lancing Douglas Fairbanks, Jr., was then invited; but because he became ill as reported, or because he was rumored "through" at the box office, Paramount dropped him. Lubitsch then asked Gary Cooper to play the role, and most Hollywood folk thought that even the genius Lubitsch had finally gone too far. Gary Cooper play smart drawing room comedy? Cooper himself thought it was a strange notion, and doubted that Lubitsch could talk him into playing it. But Lubitsch surely did.

"The critics will not like our picture," Lubitsch told the *Design for Living* company. "They will say we have ruined Noel Coward's play and it is true that our picture will be quite different. But the people who do not read reviews or care about them will love it, and Noel Coward means nothing to most of them. Gary Cooper means something to them, and they will be happy to see that he is an accomplished light comedian."

Lubitsch was right and wrong. The critics generally carped that both Cooper and March were badly miscast. They were more generous toward Miriam Hopkins and Edward Everett Horton, who played the fourth leading role of the kindly older man that Miss Hopkins actually marries, before she jilts him for *both* of her unconventional male friends. Lubitsch defended the work of both Cooper and March as highly professional and true to their own personalities, which could not have been easily reconciled to the spirit of Noel Coward. Lubitsch was wrong, though, in believing

that America's movie-goers were ready for a picture with so curious a romantic resolution. They wanted Miss Hopkins to "get"
somebody in the end, and a majority seemed in favor of Cooper,
even though March was the more prestigious player at the time
and consequently was top-billed. *Design for Living* was a major
disappointment for Paramount in the commercial sense, and that
probably hastened Miriam Hopkins' departure from the studio
about a year later. But there was still high optimism over the picture when the edited print was previewed at the studio, and
Lubitsch was rhapsodic about Gary Cooper.

The director equated him with Greta Garbo: "They are both
essentially photogenic creatures, who are bland and almost dull,
except when the cameras are on them. Then they are magic. Gary
Cooper is like wax you could mold in front of a camera."

Lubitsch later told Garson Kanin that he believed Cooper and
Garbo were really the same person. "After all, we've never seen
them in a picture together."

Lulled by Lubitsch's encouragement, Cooper agreed to attend
the Hollywood première of *Design for Living*, in November only a
few days after his engagement to Sandra Shaw became official. Because of the experience, he would never attend another one. Leaving the theater with Rocky and without adequate police protection, Cooper was accosted by a horde of squealing fans who
proceeded to rip his dress suit to shreds, leaving him in a state of
partial undress when he was finally rescued. He later said, "If only
the critics had been that enthusiastic about my performance."

The judgment of history is that the critics were wrong. *Design
for Living* is a delightful picture, brilliantly informed by the
"Lubitsch touch." Fredric March continued to earn recognition as
an actor of dramatic power over four subsequent decades, and
Design for Living is one of the films that document his exceptional ability as a light comedian. Miss Hopkins, whose undoubted ability was often compromised by an essential coldness,
gave perhaps her most effervescent account. Edward Everett Horton was fine, as he most always was. The revelation, though, is
Cooper; and the wonder is that contemporary movie-goers and
critics alike failed to appreciate it. In his sharpest departure from
type, playing his first really sophisticated role, he revealed a consistent light touch. It was apparent that he understood shading for

comedic effect, and that he was either practiced in the all-important skill of timing or came by it naturally.

Still, it was a setback for him. *Design for Living* followed the generally beguiling *One Sunday Afternoon*, which in turn had followed *Today We Live*, a high-gloss production at the very least. Yet none of Cooper's 1933 releases rang the bell commercially, and that included *Alice in Wonderland*, Paramount's "miracle picture" released simultaneously with *Design for Living*.

Cooper took a few days off from shooting the Lubitsch film to play his one scene, wonderfully made up as the aged White Knight continually falling off his horse. In fact, his chore was often singled out for praise, but various appealing parts failed to add up to a whole that could please either children or adults. This *Alice in Wonderland* was incredibly fey and surely too "literal" an adaptation of Lewis Carroll, its humors finally elusive despite actors donning masks for a production that remarkably duplicated the Tenniel drawings. W. C. Fields was Humpty Dumpty, Cary Grant was the Mock Turtle, and Jack Oakie couldn't remember if he was Tweedledum or Tweedledee. Stirred into the broth were such enjoyable performers as Edna May Oliver (Red Queen), May Robson (Queen of Hearts), Alison Skipworth (Duchess), Edward Everett Horton (Mad Hatter), Charlie Ruggles (March Hare), and Sterling Holloway (White Rabbit). Richard Arlen was unrecognizable, but those were presumably his eyes inside the stuffed Cheshire Cat. The blond, adolescent Charlotte Henry was a quite enchanting Alice, and the picture was recognized as an important technical achievement. Yet it was quickly conceded a flop, and it was a difficult time for theaters as the Depression kept its cruel hold. Released at about the same time as *Alice in Wonderland*, the Marx Brothers' incomparably zany *Duck Soup* was even more commercially disastrous; and the boys left Paramount, thenceforth to dispense their surrealistic comedy for M-G-M, and without Zeppo.

Cooper, at least, had no regrets about his five-minute scene in *Alice in Wonderland*. Playing in it had been his own idea when he saw how much fun everyone was having, and it was not charged as one of his contractual commitments. He was being adventurous after all, testing himself in new directions. It had been a long time since he had appeared in a Western.

All of the newspaper stories leading up to the nuptials nevertheless emphasized the romantic incongruity of the serene Park Avenue lady and the rough-sketch Montana cowboy.

The engagement was announced to the press in Los Angeles on November 13. Rocky displayed her large diamond and hinted that the career was already over for Sandra Shaw, whose first credited screen appearance could be assessed in local theaters. The *Hollywood Reporter* implied that Cooper's fiancée was giving up her career reluctantly and RKO's Pandro S. Berman expressed regret that his company was losing "a likely future star." In his own interviews Cooper uttered such striking homilies as "A woman's place is in the home" and "One career is enough for a family." Yes, they both hoped there would be children.

After the traumatic *Design for Living* première on November 17, the betrothed couple went to New York to observe Thanksgiving with Rocky's mother and stepfather, who artfully concealed any objections toward Cooper that they may still have had. A few days later the Shieldses hosted a large dinner party in their apartment at 778 Park Avenue to announce the engagement formally. It became one of the more talked-about social events of the winter season, and was a smashing fashion show. Cooper was himself in white tie and tails, acquitting himself admirably in mixing with the bluebloods. Most of the guests were friends of Rocky's and the Shieldses', with some token representation from Paramount's home office in New York City. A few theater personages also attended, including one of Gary Cooper's leading ladies—Helen Hayes. And Elsa Maxwell was present with Cole Porter, conveying to the engaged couple the best wishes of the Count and Countess di Frasso.

At the time of the engagement party, no date had been set and the wedding was off there somewhere in a vague future, probably in early 1934. But as Cooper himself explained, "One evening I said we might just as well get it over with. I didn't say it quite like that, of course, but it meant the same thing. We called the minister the next day."

In contrast to the celebration of the engagement, the wedding on December 15—also in the Park Avenue apartment—was about as small as one could be. Rocky's bridesmaid was her sister, Barbara Shields. Cooper was attended only by his rotund business manager, Jack Moss. The only observers were Mr. and Mrs. Shields. The Episcopalian ceremony was performed by the Reverend George Trowbridge, who, at the couple's behest, omitted the word "obey" from the ceremony. The bride, not yet twenty-one, wore gray satin with sables. Cooper, renouncing his status as movieland's Most Eligible Bachelor at age thirty-two, was married in a brown checkered business suit.

The honeymoon wasn't a public event, but neither was it very private. The newlyweds decided upon Arizona where the Shieldses had a winter place. They all took the train to Arizona together— Gary, Rocky, and Rocky's parents. Charles and Alice Cooper drove from Hollywood to Phoenix to join them, in time for the Christmas holiday. Cooper and his bride drove back to Hollywood with his parents; and he said, "That's how we got by the professional train-meeters."

The newlywed Coopers occupied his ranch on the near rim of the San Fernando Valley. Its ten acres were mostly in citrus and walnut groves. It was more agreeable to Rocky than Cooper's jungle scene might have been, but it wasn't ideal for her and they began making plans to build a new home of their own. Emanuel Cohen gave the Coopers an elaborate dinner party as a means of introducing Rocky to Paramount's front rank of Hollywood executives. Cooper and his bride achieved instant success as a couple, and were the prettiest pair in town.

Bing Crosby said he never doubted that Cooper had found the right girl at last. But Jack Oakie said, "Most of us gave it a year at the most, and thought six months was probably closer."

Cooper's return to movie work was delayed by his inability to reach accord with Emanuel Cohen on his next assignment. Cooper soon accepted credit for turning Bing Crosby into an agreeable light comedian, for two projects rejected by Cooper were refashioned with songs for Bing, who proceeded to have mildly successful pictures back-to-back. Cooper backed away from *Here Is My Heart* because he remained unpersuaded that sophisticated comedy was his forte. It was a remake of a well-liked silent called *The Grand Duchess and the Waiter*, and Paramount's hope had been that Cooper's presence could retrieve a sinking star—Elissa

Landi, one of the more interesting failures of the era. When Crosby became a singing waiter, however, the grand duchess became the operatic Kitty Carlisle in her screen debut.

Cooper shunned *She Loves Me Not*, from a popular play by Howard Lindsay about a movie queen on a college campus, because he thought Miriam Hopkins would have the better role. Instead Crosby, beginning to refine his assured, easygoing style, almost took the show away from Miss Hopkins, whose Paramount tenure ended with the picture.

Soon afterward Cooper acknowledged that either picture would have been more advisable for him than the one he finally made. When Paramount had nothing to please him, he agreed to pay a second visit to M-G-M for one of his contractual commitments. It was another one-picture, actor-for-actor swap, a Cooper for a Cooper. Eleven-year-old Jackie became Paramount's *Lone Cowboy*; and Gary, feeling he couldn't refuse her, joined Marion Davies for the Civil War melodrama of *Operator 13*.

For half a dozen years William Randolph Hearst's Cosmopolitan unit had been an autonomous production component of M-G-M, concerned almost exclusively with vehicles for Hearst's favorite movie star, his mistress Miss Davies. Her palatial "bungalow" on the Culver City lot had come to rival even Pickfair as the obligatory scene for dignitaries visiting the filmland. M-G-M and Louis B. Mayer in particular sought to indulge Hearst, who as an early backer helped make the company solid. For that, plus the fringe benefit of social eminence they brought the company, the Hearst-Davies pictures were politely tolerated by M-G-M. The pictures were never terrible but they were seldom very good; nor did they lose money, but they were consistently the studio's least successful entries commercially.

Yet in lists or visual displays of the studio's fabulous array of stars, Marion always came first—ahead, in 1933, of Shearer, Garbo, Dressler, Crawford, Hayes, Gable, Beery, Harlow, Montgomery, Novarro, Gilbert, Lionel Barrymore, and the late-blooming Myrna Loy, in that order. The comparative shortage of leading men made it mandatory to borrow them from other companies—for the Davies pictures, at any rate. Other than one appearance each by Gable and Montgomery in Davies talkies, M-G-M refused to sacrifice its male stars to Marion's lackluster pictures. This led gradually to Hearst's falling out with the M-G-M hierarchy, which was further provoked by the Mayer-Thalberg schism. When the company bought first the successful play *The Barretts of Wimpole Street,* then the celebrated Stefan Zweig biographical novel of *Marie Antoinette,* Hearst got the notion that Marion should enact both Elizabeth Barrett and France's doomed queen, even though Thalberg rather obviously planned both as vehicles for his wife, Norma Shearer.

Knowing that he risked alienating Hearst, Mayer reluctantly sided with Thalberg, being unable to see Miss Davies—a comedienne with a stuttering problem—as either an invalid poet or a French historical figure. The decision was given while *Operator 13* was in production, and it infuriated Hearst. He vowed to cancel his agreement with M-G-M and take Marion and Cosmopolitan elsewhere; and indeed, he made a deal with Warner soon afterward, and Marion's bungalow was dismantled by sections and carted off to the Warner studio where it was reassembled. *Operator 13* was Marion's last M-G-M picture, and its production scene was no less melodramatic than its story line, which found Miss Davies as a Union spy, falling in love with Confederate soldier Cooper.

Hearst was always on the set and in a dreadful mood. He was also unreasonably jealous, and was hostile to director Richard Boleslavsky throughout the production, convinced that Boleslavsky was out to seduce Miss Davies. Cooper had the benefit of established friendship with both Marion and her overseer, yet believed that Hearst was suspicious even of Marion's leading man, who was only recently a bridegroom. The experience of filming *Operator 13* at M-G-M was even less enjoyable for Cooper than *Today We Live* had been, for there was none of the relaxed atmosphere that could make filming enjoyable for him. He also was bewildered trying to take direction from Boleslavsky, who was a graduate of Stanislavsky's Moscow Art Theater and had notions about character motivation that were seldom a concern with Cooper.

He left M-G-M saying it was his worst experience as an actor since his legs shook through the silent *Children of Divorce.* He was also convinced he'd made a flop. Oddly enough, *Operator 13* was an efficient, frequently exciting movie, even though Miss

Davies was rather obviously too old to be vamping Cooper. It holds up fairly well, as the only one of Marion's M-G-M pictures granted an occasional airing on TV. Yet it was not a success when released in mid-1934. With no further political obligation to its star or to Hearst, M-G-M released it without especial fanfare, although the Hearst newspapers pounded the drum as usual. The disappointing returns only pointed up that Cooper again had failed to rescue a lady star of dubious commercial rating.

The picture he made on returning to Paramount was a snappy box-office success, yet little credit would go to Cooper although he and Carole Lombard were the nominal stars. They were merely caught in the swirling Shirley Temple tornado. The seductive charms of the ringleted charmer had been showcased in the "Baby Burlesk" one-reelers produced by Educational, and Fox Films signed her for small roles in features. When Paramount sought to borrow her to play *Little Miss Marker,* Fox said fine, but take her for two pictures, not just one. Then Shirley Temple and the Damon Runyon yarn spelled a box-office sensation in 1934, and Fox had the unexpected dividend of a phenomenal star. Indeed, the people at Fox were chagrined that Paramount insisted on cashing in on the stipulated second picture, which became *Now and Forever.* It was also foreseen as a steppingstone to stardom for Dorothy Dell, a zestful blonde who had also been in *Little Miss Marker.* Then Carole Lombard stepped in when Dorothy Dell was killed in an automobile accident. Gary Cooper came aboard during the studio's steady upgrading of the project.

Cooper and Lombard played jewel thieves reformed by the adorable waif—formula stuff but unbeatable for the cash register. The real thief, of course, was Shirley Temple; Cooper had never before been so thoroughly upstaged. For him, *Now and Forever* was notable only as his first picture signed by his close friend Henry Hathaway, who would become the most frequent director of Gary Cooper pictures.

For one who had so thoroughly "gone Hollywood" several years earlier and had been reliable as fodder for the gossip columns, Gary Cooper did an astonishing turnabout after his marriage and appeared to become one of the more retiring members of the film community, certainly among those who were stars. He and Rocky did not become reclusive at all, and were often hosts for small gatherings of only one or two other couples. They also made the rounds on the same basis, popular as guests but on a private basis, out of the public eye. Their appearances at the splashier filmland parties became few and selective, possibly because awkwardness could not always be avoided.

For instance, in August of 1934 the Coopers emerged from seclusion, still beheld as newlyweds, and attended a formal dinner dance of the Little Club, a short-lived social organization of the movie elite, conceived along country-club lines as an alternative to the rigidly structured Los Angeles society, which still excluded most movie folk. At the Little Club affair the Coopers were confronted by the Johnny Weissmullers. Lupe Velez and the movies' Tarzan had married only shortly before the Coopers, but already their union was stormy and believed shaky. An enterprising photographer got the Weissmullers and Coopers together and posed a group picture, then attempted to get a two-shot of Gary and Lupe. Cooper was amenable, but the Mexican Spitfire was not; she said she was highly insulted. For the Coopers such experiences were bound to recur, and would always be slightly embarrassing.

Rocky, at least, extended an offer of friendship to Lupe Velez. Her disposition toward Dorothy di Frasso is less certain, and a provocative account by Elsa Maxwell of one of their meetings, reported many years later, did not have the ring of truth. The countess accepted an invitation from Rocky for lunch at the Mocambo, and described the date as "a real frame-up" to Miss Maxwell. Rocky, the countess said, took out some emerald studs and cufflinks that were one of Dorothy's gifts to Cooper and "threw them across the table," explaining that "Gary wanted you to have these back. He has no use for them now." According to the countess, Lupe Velez was also at the luncheon, collaborating with Rocky Cooper in an apparent effort to humiliate her.

Miss Maxwell's highly prejudiced relating of the incident is easily suspected by such a word as "threw." The jewelry was doubtless handed over discreetly, and there could also have been such pleasant small talk as never reached Elsa Maxwell's ears. As a self-promoted hostess and society journalist, Miss Maxwell was an altogether unaccountable phenomenon of American life, and Dorothy di Frasso was her dearest friend. Furthermore, the countess was devastated when Cooper married a girl from the Social Register, and Elsa waged a marathon of bitchiness at Rocky's expense, on behalf of her titled friend. Miss Maxwell continued to exploit her own friendship with Cooper and kept flattering him in print, but as late as 1944 she wrote a magazine article that subtly invited readers to view Rocky critically, by the technique of the backhanded compliment:

"Rocky, although as lovely as any film star and as beautifully dressed, is in every other respect completely un-Hollywood. There are those who find her cold. There are those who feel she is pretentious and a snob. Those people do not know her. Few do, actually."

Indeed, Rocky appeared determined not to become a known commodity. Most who observed the Coopers during the early period of their marriage expressed only admiration for Rocky's graceful bearing upon undertaking the often thankless role of the Star's Wife. She gave up her career but not her identity. She was not content to be the wife as professional secretary, or to exist benignly in the shadow of another's fame. From the beginning of their romance and continuing into their marriage, she never fawned on Cooper as had his earlier succession of romantic objects. She would not be taken for granted, and elected not to accompany him on location shooting trips, saying, "Gary and I should not be cemented to each other."

Her most difficult adjustment was in realizing that her husband would always be number one—that other people and especially other women would always look first at him, not at her. She resigned herself to being "the little wheel." She concluded that marriage with Cooper was good even with its special trials and tribulations: "If I'd married a nice young man in a business suit, none of this would have happened. But he never bores me, and to be bored with the life you lead is the deadliest boredom."

She was driving and energetic; he was quiet and lackadaisical. She pumped him up; he quieted her down.

Their friends believed this had much to do with Cooper's being so obviously smitten with Rocky. Those who had been his pals through all his amours believed this was the first time Cooper was completely in love.

Robert Taylor once remarked that of every man he knew in Hollywood, Gary Cooper had the most friends. "Everybody likes Coop because there's no pose. He accepts you as you are, and asks only that you accept him in the same spirit. He isn't temperamental, and just being around him is relaxing because of that."

Taylor became a special friend of what might be called Cooper's "middle period," following the early Paramount camaraderie and before Cooper's deepening friendship with James Stewart served a later period. The more famous the friend, the more publicized was Cooper's association with him. His most durable friendships, however, were with his directors; and his longest, strongest, and closest association was with Henry Hathaway.

They met at Paramount even before Cooper was under contract there, when Hathaway was in charge of logistics as assistant director on location work that employed Cooper as a horseman. Hathaway, only three years older than Cooper but an authentic pioneer, had been a child actor in early movies before enduring the assistant director's drudgery for fully a dozen years. He became a fully accredited director only after the talkies were securely established.

He was assistant director for many of Cooper's formative pictures, including *Shopworn Angel*, *The Virginian*, and *The Texan*. Perhaps he learned vitality from Victor Fleming, charm from Richard Wallace, subtlety from John Cromwell, and the traits of various other directors. At any rate, his was a fully assimilated talent when he started directing Paramount's Zane Grey Westerns in 1932. That figured to be another treadmill for him, until about a dozen pictures later he seized the melodramatic opportunity of *The Witching Hour* and came through with a "sleeper" owing its unexpected success to sheer direction. His next assignment, carrying his first substantial budget, was the *Now and Forever* opus built around Shirley Temple, and Cooper agreed to play in it only because Hathaway was directing.

Hathaway was still comparatively unknown, but his next picture was destined to place him permanently in the front rank of directors, besides being a welcome and much-needed major hit for

Gary Cooper. And *Lives of a Bengal Lancer* is one of the most fondly recalled films of the thirties.

Francis Yeats-Brown's novel was a 1930 best seller and Paramount bought it then, projecting it with Fredric March in the role Cooper would eventually play, although Cooper was also set for the original cast, along with Clive Brook and Richard Arlen. The project got delayed for reasons of logistics, then abandoned altogether during Paramount's economic retrenchment. The novel, too, was quickly forgotten after its vogue passed.

Henry Hathaway had accompanied documentary director Ernest B. Schoedsack on a movie-making tour of India, and returned with an abundance of random but impressively atmospheric footage around which a story film might be built. It was primarily the inspiration of the indefatigable Bud Lighton to resurrect the dormant *Bengal Lancer* project. It began as a routine feature, then kept getting reconceptualized on a larger scale, with several writers working on the script not together, but individually by turns.

Gary Cooper was cast as Captain "Mother" McGregor when it was still reckoned a relatively small picture. M-G-M loaned Franchot Tone to play Lieutenant Fortesque, while the cowardly but sympathetic Lieutenant Stone was Richard Cromwell's specialty. Paramount bought half of Cromwell's contract from Columbia, and filled out the assembly with distinguished British regimental types—predictably, C. Aubrey Smith and Sir Guy Standing. There was Kiplingesque derring-do and barracks comedy, somewhat forecasting the later, rollicking *Gunga Din* that George Stevens made for RKO, utilizing the same American locations. *Lives of a Bengal Lancer* was more serious stuff, however, and was also imbued with the mystical philosophy that was an unusual aspect of the novel. But for striking an agreeable balance between humor and sobriety, all the while seething with sinister intrigue and good popping action, *Lives of a Bengal Lancer* was saluted as the ultimate adventure film. It made Henry Hathaway's reputation while earning him an Academy nomination, in addition to several others, including best picture. In the *Film Daily*'s annual poll, only *David Copperfield* collected more votes among pictures exhibited in 1935. Although *Lives of a Bengal Lancer* probably would have been a smash hit anyway, it did amass super-lative reviews. There was general agreement that Franchot Tone's relatively polished account took the show completely away from Cooper, which may have made the ending more tolerable for viewers: Tone survived; Cooper was mortally wounded.

Cooper, though, was almost solely credited with pushing the picture to its extraordinary success, which had not been taken for granted. Paramount, in fact, was tempted to change the title when many early viewers said they didn't understand it. The venture either proved or reaffirmed that given a strong picture along the line that had once been expected of him, Cooper was a power-ful draw. It hardly mattered that he was nobody's Englishman; at least he had the good sense not to imitate one. His performance was also informed by a fatalism that recalled his brief but memo-rable scene from the silent *Wings*.

Cooper's experimental mustache was less favorably received. Clark Gable had adopted a mustache in 1934 with the effect of enhancing his already considerable popularity, and other actors were giving it a try. For *Lancer* it was entirely Cooper's own idea, and not abandoned immediately.

His stint as Mother McGregor was also his most heroic projec-tion probably to that time. It was not an overstated quality, nor mythic in the way that *The Virginian* perhaps was heroic in a mythic sense. Henry Hathaway said it was a case of the role merely coming to Cooper, rather than of an actor coming to a role. His McGregor, despite foibles of personality that his adver-sary friend Fortesque may ridicule, is innately strong, instinctively resourceful. It is acceptable that Cooper and Tone, in one of the more memorable sequences, can withstand the torture of bamboo slivers under their nails although Richard Cromwell's lieutenant cannot.

Because of its successful result, a return by Cooper to films primarily of action substance might have been expected, but *Lancer* actually appeared to have little effect on the peculiar pattern of his roles and films in the mid-thirties. Still, it was a much-needed lift not only for rescuing him from a declining quality curve, but for sustaining him over the failures that would follow it: honorable, interesting failures, but failures nevertheless.

Above,
Bluebeard's Eighth Wife (1938).
*Claudette Colbert and
a seven-times-wed Cooper
in a Lubitsch comedy.*

Left,
The Cowboy and the Lady (1938).
*Twenty-seven writers worked on a
script for Cooper and Goldwyn's
hard-sold Merle Oberon.*

Beau Geste (1939). Cooper's brothers are Robert Preston and Ray Milland; their Foreign Legion pals are Broderick Crawford and Charles Barton.

The Westerner (1940). Cooper upstaged by Walter Brennan as Judge Roy Bean with William Wyler directing.

Right,
Meet John Doe *(1941).*
A rather grim Capra comedy
with Cooper as the pawn
of evil Edward Arnold.

Below,
Sergeant York *(1941).*
His first Academy Award;
here as the young Alvin.

Left,
Ball of Fire *(1941).*
A successful Goldwyn farce about a
professor and a burlesque queen—
Barbara Stanwyck as
Sugarpuss O'Shea.

Below,
The Pride of the Yankees *(1942).*
As baseball's tragic Lou Gehrig,
here in the dramatic farewell
to the Yankees.

Above,
For Whom the Bell Tolls *(1943).*
The Hollywood inflation of
Hemingway's Spanish Civil War
novel, with Ingrid Bergman
and Katina Paxinou.

Right,
Saratoga Trunk *(1945).*
An Edna Ferber costume commotion,
again with Miss Bergman.

Left,
The Fountainhead *(1949).*
When he really needed a good
picture, this one was at least a
big one; with Patricia Neal
and Raymond Massey.

Below,
High Noon *(1952).*
An epochal comeback
and a second Oscar;
here with Grace Kelly
at the picture's end.

Vera Cruz (1954). A violent yet engaging Western with Burt Lancaster.

Friendly Persuasion (1956). Quakers confront the Civil War; with Dorothy McGuire and Anthony Perkins in a Wyler gem.

Love in the Afternoon (1957). *Billy Wilder's May-December romance filmed in Paris with glorious Audrey Hepburn.*

The Naked Edge (1961). *The melodramatic Cooper farewell, with Deborah Kerr.*

For as soon as he completed *Lancer*, Cooper got himself involved in the strange, bewildering case of Anna Sten.

From the moment that Greta Garbo said, "Gimme a viskey, baby, and don't be stingy" in *Anna Christie* to prove that she would endure and be glorified as a foreign-accented talking actress, every film company dispatched scouts to search for a "second Garbo." Marlene Dietrich, although she became Garbo's rival, was fortunate to have transcended that distinction even before she had made an American film. But others came and then they just kept coming—Tala Birell, Lili Damita, Sari Maritza, Gwili Andre, Lilian Harvey, Lil Dagover, Ketti Gallian, *ad infinitum, ad nauseum*. The collective impression of the European imports only enhanced Garbo's singularity.

Samuel Goldwyn, though, was obsessed by a mission to find not a second Garbo, but someone greater than Garbo. He never became reconciled to the sacrifice of Vilma Banky on the altar of sound, and said his only comparable disappointment during that period was letting the young Gary Cooper slip away from him. He said it was always in the back of his mind to get Cooper back. But in 1932 Anna Sten, Russian and blond, entered the front of Sam Goldwyn's mind quite by accident.

He hired a writer to develop a script from Dostoevsky's *The Brothers Karamazov*, hoping that the prospect might persuade Ronald Colman, whose contract was about to expire, to accept an extension. Goldwyn learned that there was an excellent German *Karamazov* and asked to see it, and then was astonished by the beauty and the dramatic ability of its Grushenka. Anna Sten was then twenty-two, but had acted with Stanislavsky as a teen-ager before emerging as a splendid young heroine in several Soviet films. *Karamazov* was her first German picture, and she married Eugene Frenke, its director.

Goldwyn screened all of her Russian films and approved of everything he saw. He arranged to meet Anna Sten, and brought both her and her husband to America. He would not be impatient: he would have her thoroughly schooled in English before planning her first Goldwyn picture. Meanwhile, he would mount the largest and shrillest publicity campaign that ever anticipated the advent of a major star. He planned eventually to use her as

Grushenka in his own *Karamazov*, but not for a while because, anyway, he no longer had Ronald Colman.

He finally selected Emile Zola's *Nana* as her debut vehicle. It was his first mistake and possibly the only one, but it was fatal and irretrievable. After all the reams of publicity, the public finally could meet Anna Sten on the screen as *Nana* in 1934, and wonder what the fuss was about. She was sufficiently gorgeous, and a passable actress in an unpassable role. There was a clear suggestion of star quality. But *Nana*, encumbered by the Hays Office criteria, was a silly and ridiculous film, pretentious and inflated, and it might have brought even Garbo down. Critics were respectful toward Miss Sten, but America's movie-goers turned their backs on her vehicle and made it the flop of the year.

Disappointed but not dismayed, Goldwyn prepared Tolstoy's *Resurrection* for her, retitled it *We Live Again*, hired the very cinematic Rouben Mamoulian to direct, and conceded the need of an established male star to play opposite her. Fredric March was hired because he was the top-rated actor of the moment, and could be secretly auditioned as Dmitri Karamazov. *We Live Again* was previewed to an enthusiastic response and was the beneficiary of generally splendid reviews upon its release in the autumn of 1934. Goldwyn believed he was on the verge of accomplishing everything he'd intended, for and with Anna Sten. But *We Live Again* died at the box office, cursed by *Nana*. Now Goldwyn was worried. He reasoned that only a male star of emphatic and reliable popularity could salvage Miss Sten's career. Fredric March, after all, was a solid star actor yet not regarded as a *name* capable of carrying any picture. Sam made a diplomatic overture to Ronald Colman, who wanted no part of the proposition. In the eyes of the community, Anna Sten was already jinxed.

So Samuel Goldwyn invited Gary Cooper to dine with him and Anna Sten. *We Live Again* was playing its bleak first-run engagements, and Cooper was shooting *Lives of a Bengal Lancer*, which Goldwyn could not then have foreseen as the huge hit it became. No matter; Sam was aware that Cooper could make a deal for himself apart from his obligations to Paramount, and he would offer Cooper $100,000 to make a picture with Anna Sten. Cooper was actor enough not to reveal that he was flabbergasted. He said yes, he'd be happy to film *The Wedding Night* with Miss Sten; but he insisted on having top billing as Fredric March hadn't. So Abe Lee had come home to Uncle Sam.

The Wedding Night was carefully produced, and could perhaps serve as a textbook for the ways of film craft. King Vidor, the director, considers it one of his strongest pictures. Cooper and Miss Sten had a nice personal rapport while filming it, and that relationship could easily be sensed in their close shots together. Cooper's performance, in fact, revealed a perhaps surprising depth, especially as he subtly conveyed the guilt feelings of a man falling in love against his better judgment, or at least against social convention. He played a married author, seeking retreat on a Connecticut farm to write, only to come under the spell of a pure and lovely Polish girl living nearby. The title referred not to their wedding, but the girl's to fellow Pole Ralph Bellamy—the obligatory "other man" of the era—just before the tragic climax. The tragedy of the girl's death from a fall down a flight of stairs was the most artificial element in a film often characterized by simple eloquence. But the fact that the picture was conceived as a tragedy in the first place probably sealed the issue for Anna Sten. The American audience in 1935 simply wanted a happy ending. Lacking one, *The Wedding Night* collected unfavorable word of mouth. The reviews were good, but not good enough. The audiences were larger for *The Wedding Night* than for *Nana* and *We Live Again*, but not very.

After all was said and done, it was a flop. It did no real harm to Cooper, for *Lives of a Bengal Lancer*, which had preceded it only by a few weeks, had a history of held-over engagements and was still playing second runs when *The Wedding Night* disappeared, spent and soon to be forgotten. Anna Sten, though, was finished as a star or as the prospect of one. Goldwyn settled her contract, and said it was all very friendly. Miss Sten, at least, had the character and stability to adjust to her failure. She continued to live in Hollywood, still happily married to Eugene Frenke, and became one of the best-liked citizens of the community, taking only occasional and nonstellar work in pictures. The Frenkes and the Coopers remained good friends. And for the record, Samuel Goldwyn never got around to making *The Brothers Karamazov*.

In 1935 rumors infiltrated the film community that the Coopers, wed less than two years, were about to separate. Asked by a reporter to confirm or deny the rumor, Gary Cooper got so angry that his response was taken as confirmation. Cooper said, "There's no such thing as people 'about to separate.' Either you're separated or you're not, and my wife and I haven't even thought about it." After that, Hazel Flynn in the Hollywood *Citizen-News* theorized that the Coopers *had* separated and just weren't talking about it.

At the studio, Cooper was generally accessible to members of the press who had scheduled their appointments properly, and he could be disarmingly vocal at times. He made it an early rule, though, not to receive reporters at his home, enforcing the rule particularly after his marriage. Writers and photographers who had been given access to his rented Beverly Hills diggings with their African motif were not welcome in Van Nuys, or in Hollywood, where the Coopers lived briefly before occupying their "permanent" Brentwood home; and especially not there. The fan magazines would have to illustrate their Gary Cooper stories with portraits of the star made at his studio, and with photographs of him with Rocky that were obtained from the news agencies.

The Brentwood house that the fans could only imagine was sleek white in the Bermuda style, with gleaming red doors, emulating the mansions of their favorite vacation spot. The estate covered almost four acres, and its lush vegetation included every variety of citrus tree. From the living room bay window, the vista of lawn extended to a huge willow, hanging like a mist over an aquamarine pool. Above a hedge, a tower of the distant Marymount school for Catholic girls revealed a crucifix against the sky. The view also encompassed the new UCLA campus.

The sunken living room revealed a distinctly Chinese influence. The walls were an avocado shade, the floors a deeper green. A grand piano dominated, and there was a huge fireplace. The wood-paneled library with its gilded leather volumes would become a guideline to the Coopers' tastes in art, eventually to display a Pierre Bonnard landscape above the fireplace. Canvases by Georgia O'Keeffe and Max Weber, their favorite American painters, would hang in other rooms. The house would become a genuine home and retreat with capricious additions over the years —particularly Cooper's "paradise playroom," a separate building completely hidden by trees. It began as a billiards room but came to resemble an old curiosity shop, with a dusty cowboy hat, spurs, some bullets, various artifacts, and everything subdued by a mounted eagle with a seven-foot wingspread. It was Cooper's own Idaho trophy: "I had to stalk on my belly for several hours before I finally got that eagle."

From the start, Rocky refused to kill an animal and never changed her policy. She said, "I do not hunt. I just go along." So she became a good skeet shot. And she went along often, but no more than Cooper subordinated himself to his wife's primary interests. They were seldom in southern California if Cooper was not making a picture. They would be at a place of his choosing, or hers, or theirs. Rumors that all was not well with the Coopers would start up inevitably, it seemed, whenever they dropped out of sight for a while.

Rocky apparently coveted privacy such as Cooper had seldom experienced since becoming a movie personality. Whether it was entirely her influence or some natural evolution within himself, he now appeared to crave privacy almost to the point of mania. The Coopers' public appearances became even more rare, and even in private social congress they were increasingly selective.

The Hollywood community itself simply did not satisfy all their drives. Until he became a continent-hopper in the custody of the Countess di Frasso, Cooper had been very much the Hollywood homebody, leaving the community only for occasional hunting trips. Rocky, though, had long been accustomed to travel, and it would be increasingly pursued as their common interest.

Besides Bermuda, their home away from home was Rocky's Southampton, where Cooper spent most of his time fishing on Paul Shields's ample yacht. If he could see a substantial break between picture-making assignments, the Coopers would plan a trip to Europe almost every year. The visits to New York became commonplace. There Rocky reveled in high fashion; yet she could get dudded up in dungarees to go off into the western wilds with Cooper, and it only accented her glamor. She also liked to ski, and Cooper took up the sport and found it exhilarating. He also began playing tennis, after having long resisted it, because Rocky was hooked on the game. A tennis court was an eventual appointment of the Brentwood estate. Both Coopers also played golf, but all of these were things Rocky did first, and Gary later.

In their doing and going they were often alone together. With no one to see them, it just caused talk.

The regular hands at the Hollywood studio agreed that he was a decidedly changed Gary Cooper. An assistant director who said Cooper had been "Paramount's paramount skirt-chaser" observed that the script girls and secretaries had to adjust to duller lives with Cooper no longer priming them with attention for whatever came afterward. At the end of a day's shooting or of other activities at the studio, he was anxious to make an early break for home.

Once again Mary Pickford's house guest on an extended visit to Hollywood, Dorothy di Frasso evidently was still willing to have whatever share of Gary Cooper she might manage. It was believed that he handled her adroitly and with diplomacy. As a favor to the countess, Cooper even consented to act with Jean Howard in her screen test for RKO. Miss Howard was the blond Texan who briefly disrupted the private life of none other than Louis B. Mayer, but who never made much headway in pictures despite having the staunch support of the countess, and Gary Cooper to test with.

If Cooper was still a threat to all his leading ladies, he was certainly discreet in a way that had not formerly been characteristic of him. His friend Roger Offitt said, "Coop got awfully smart awfully quick. Rarely can you see that marriage has changed a person so much. The difference with Coop was not in his character or personality. In those respects he never really changed, thank heaven. But no one had thought of him as mature, I'll say that. And all of a sudden, he just seemed to have control of himself and his life."

For six months he did not appear before a movie camera. He said that was the way it was going to be: he would work only half of the time, and would spend the other half doing the things he enjoyed. The demands of a motion picture required about three months of a star performer's time, sometimes more than that, but seldom more than ten weeks of actual shooting in the production rhythm of the thirties. In 1935 he took a half-year vacation all at once, and traveled with Rocky. When he returned he got involved in possibly his least characteristic movie project.

The Last Outpost would have been characteristic. Just as *Lives of a Bengal Lancer* had been initiated because of some leftover footage from an expedition to India, *The Last Outpost* was the outgrowth of footage left over from *Lancer*. Cooper planned to return to work in *The Last Outpost* because it was a picture everyone believed he should do. Then he had a capricious change of mind and insinuated himself into a film and role that no one thought he should do; and inevitably, Cary Grant replaced him in *The Last Outpost*. Undoubtedly Cooper's friendship with Henry Hathaway was part of the lure, but he was genuinely intrigued by Hathaway's new project—George du Maurier's *Peter Ibbetson*.

It was one of the most romantic titles in all literature, and had been a fussed-over novel before the century's turn. Paramount became interested in it in 1931 when Deems Taylor made an opera of it, with Lucrezia Bori scoring a great personal success at the Met. Paramount bought film rights to both opera and novel, briefly with the notion of producing a musical hybrid for Jeanette MacDonald. Grace Moore's operatic success in *One Night of Love* rekindled Paramount's interest in *Peter Ibbetson* as some kind of operatic film. Yet such a project seemed to require either Grace Moore or Jeanette MacDonald and neither could be obtained; Miss MacDonald had become an M-G-M star and Miss Moore was committed to Columbia. So *Peter Ibbetson* evolved into a straight romantic drama, if anything so fantastic could be termed "straight." The story was of two lovers who meet first as children, then only briefly as adults, but come together in dreams many years afterward, while Peter spends most of his life in prison irons as the convicted murderer of his beloved's cruel husband, the Duke of Towers.

It became an especially pampered project at Paramount, and was assigned to Hathaway because of the cinematic essence of *The Witching Hour* and the popular success of *Lives of a Bengal Lancer*. Fredric March was initially figured for the title role, but then March rejected a contract renewal to become the first successful free-lance actor. Carole Lombard wanted to play the Duchess of Towers but the studio was aghast over the commedienne's whim. Miriam Hopkins registered a personal success as

Becky Sharp in the newly refined Technicolor process for RKO, and Paramount invited her back to be the duchess, but she said no—her Paramount memories were unpleasant except for her Lubitsch pictures. It was announced that Robert Donat, who had been Hollywood's Count of Monte Cristo, would play Peter. Then the popular Irene Dunne appeared set as the duchess, and Donat withdrew rather than yield first billing. Brian Aherne was tentatively assigned but there was another production delay and Irene Dunne went into another picture. Aherne suggested Ann Harding, his co-star in a recent romantic film for RKO, *The Fountain*. Miss Harding, an important star of early talkies whose career had slipped badly, was happy to sign a contract to play the duchess. Aherne withdrew because Katharine Hepburn wanted him for *Sylvia Scarlett*. At that point *Peter Ibbetson* almost got canceled altogether; then Gary Cooper suddenly wanted the title role. His explanation was that he just happened to read the script and was intrigued; and with Hathaway directing . . .

It was one of those pictures that get more attention before they are made than afterward. After it was filmed, edited, and test-screened, Paramount remained uncertain if it had a great picture or a dreadful one. The audience would be about equally divided, reacting to *Peter Ibbetson* only in extremes. Finally, though, the audience was never quite large enough, and the picture was regarded as a failure although it managed a profit and was a hit in its English screenings. It almost revived Ann Harding's career but was, instead, her last major starring film. At the time she and Cooper certainly resembled an odd combination for a marquee, for her career had just about washed away in a torrent of suds, and viewers didn't know whether to expect a "woman's picture" or the sort usually delivered by Cooper. Women, in fact, tended to adore the picture, although they could not be convinced it had a "happy" ending. Can a story about a man who spends most of his life in prison and dies there be happy? *Peter Ibbetson* is very nearly a unique American film, still cherished by a minority; and despite its apparent failure it had the immediate effect of enhancing Henry Hathaway's reputation rather than damaging it. A more recent opinion by Andrew Sarris, however, is that "the legendary romanticism of *Peter Ibbetson* can now be clearly traced to Lee Garmes's camera."

If the opinion of contemporary critics is to be honored, then playing Peter was indeed Gary Cooper's own mistake. He was well liked in the romantic melodrama that carried to about the first half, and he and the blond Ann Harding were a stunningly elegant pair; even Cooper's mustache seemed appropriate. Reviewers felt that Cooper nevertheless lacked conviction in the ethereal scenes as the aging Peter, when only a powerful conviction could make the ultraromantic thesis work. His performance, which was not without ambition, had few defenders; but one of them was Ernst Lubitsch, who could have prevented Cooper's casting but encouraged it.

In yet another Paramount upheaval, Emanuel Cohen was deposed as production chief and Adolph Zukor placed the esteemed Lubitsch in charge. Lubitsch abdicated his throne as director and attempted to become a catalyst for upgrading all of Paramount's productions. He didn't succeed, and held his supervisory position only briefly. In the near future he would begin to direct some more classics. In late 1935, however, he turned over to Frank Borzage a project he had thoroughly planned, based on an obscure (to Americans) European play such as he was forever digging up. It was called *Desire*, an arbitrary title that sounded less like a sparkling comedy than a tempestuous drama, especially with Marlene Dietrich on display.

Lubitsch still argued that Cooper's truest talent was for light comedy, and he was determined to reunite the stars of *Morocco* in a romping exercise. Cooper had to be talked into it. He had become friendly with Marlene Dietrich over the years and had no objection to his proposed co-star—although Dietrich, like Ann Harding, was believed in 1935 to be washed up commercially if only slightly tarnished in prestige. Surely Cooper would welcome reunion with his director for *A Farewell to Arms*. Yet he was insecurely disposed toward sophisticated comedy, mainly because of reviews he received for Lubitsch's *Design for Living*. He told Lubitsch he just didn't want to act in *Desire*, because he didn't believe he could handle Edwin Justus Mayer's dialogue, which was so clever.

Lubitsch said, "Very well, Gary, do not try to be clever. Just say the lines straight and give them your own sweet personality, and they will be excellent comedy lines."

Of course Lubitsch persuaded Gary Cooper to film *Desire*, and of course Cooper played it knowingly—even deliciously—as comedy; and of course Cooper was quite wonderful. So was Dietrich. She was an exotic jewel thief, he an automobile designer, and it was a bubbly trifle. Lubitsch was nominally the producer, Borzage the credited director, but one could only imagine how the master's personality must have dominated every creative aspect. It *seemed* like a Lubitsch picture. That it fared poorly in the financial returns could only suggest that Dietrich really *was* box-office poison, and that Cooper could help her no more than he could help Ann Harding or poor Anna Sten. Each of Dietrich's Sternberg pictures had been less commercially vital than its predecessor, and *Desire* initiated her post-Sternberg career. The next Dietrich vehicle would be the enchanting *Angel*, personally directed by Lubitsch but another box-office dud, and the Dietrich swan song at Paramount. Perhaps they should have done something about the title . . .

Desire was also a significant transitional film for Cooper. As a young man being conned by a voluptuary, he was working into his own element, which might be called the comedy of innocence. He was, in fact, collecting different things from each of his pictures, and they were becoming facets of a screen persona that was more splendored than he may have realized. Some people were already beginning to say, with lazy reasoning, what is said of all actors with distinctive star personalities—that Gary Cooper always played himself. Actually he had lately tackled a wide range of roles. The soldier of *A Farewell to Arms* could hardly be more different from the car designer of *Desire*; and the shy, earthbound dentist of *One Sunday Afternoon* was a stunning contrast to the haunted Peter Ibbetson, who was transported to nightly heaven by love. The painter of *Design for Living* and the novelist of *The Wedding Night* were two quite different persons, although each was unmistakably Gary Cooper.

All of these facets were about to come together.

One of the reasons Cooper resisted *Desire* was that he didn't want to miss out on an opportunity that had come his way, even though it would mean working at Columbia. Lubitsch also felt that Cooper shouldn't let the Columbia prospect slip by; then Cooper consented to *Desire* when it appeared there would be no real conflict.

Frank Capra said he'd be willing to wait.

7

FROM DEEDS TO DOE

GARY COOPER REMEMBERED Poverty Row.

He didn't believe he had done any riding for Columbia in his days as an extra, for Columbia didn't make Westerns in those days. Harry Cohn said he couldn't afford the horses.

The ragtag production companies that were collectively labeled Poverty Row began to die out in the late twenties. If the talkies didn't kill them, the early exigencies of the Great Depression did. In 1935 Republic represented a merger of several bankrupt Poverty Row outfits, and Monogram was similarly conceived. Tiffany, built along lines similar to Columbia, had started the talkie era with promise but went bankrupt in 1931, leaving Columbia in a class by itself among American producing companies.

Of all the little companies that had defined Poverty Row, only Columbia endured to grow and prosper. It wasn't a "major" but it had outgrown every vestige of Poverty Row except the stigma. When double features became the phenomenon of 1932 as an antidote for declining receipts, Columbia assumed a strategic importance to the major companies as a provider of features for the bottom half of the bill. Columbia could make pictures cheaper than any other company because Harry Cohn always ran a tight ship.

Harry, his brother Jack, and Joe Brandt formed CBC Film Sales in 1921 and got into production with virtually no capital. By 1923 it was Harry's one-man show and he renamed it Columbia. Other Poverty Row companies could make pictures as cheaply, but the Columbia product was rather better because Harry Cohn had pride and a knack for hiring people who had the taste he lacked. In 1928 he hired Frank Capra, who had first gained a reputation directing some screamingly funny Harry Langdon comedies. Capra made good pictures for Cohn, and as Capra became better known so did Columbia.

Yet Columbia lacked the resources for building stars. Among its handful of contract players, only the middle-ranking Jack Holt was any kind of name. If Cohn wanted to give one of his pictures the embellishment of even a moderately established personality, he had to go begging to M-G-M or Warner or Paramount. On at least two occasions he made pitches for Gary Cooper—for *Tol'able David* in 1930 and for something called *Hollywood Speaks* in 1932, wherein Pat O'Brien acted the role Cooper might have played. Players at the big studios called it slumming when they reported to the modest Columbia studio on Gower Street, often sent there to do penance for some kind of misbehavior. The only star to emerge at Columbia in the early talkie years was Barbara Stanwyck, almost exclusively in the Capra pictures; and she was hardly "developed" but simply exploded, a vivid star personality.

In 1933 Frank Capra made two Columbia pictures that brought exceptional recognition: the dazzlingly erotic *The Bitter Tea of General Yen* with Stanwyck; and the Damon Runyon *Lady for a Day* that gave old May Robson her famous characterization of Apple Annie and became a runaway smash hit. Capra was regarded as such a sure thing that M-G-M and Paramount sent Clark Gable and Claudette Colbert into the well-known slum for *It Happened One Night*, with historic results. That was 1934 and it was Columbia's year of emergence. Howard Hawks came in with *Twentieth Century*, a John Barrymore vehicle that was also the comedic turning point in Carole Lombard's career. Lewis Milestone made an adroit shipboard comedy, *The Captain Hates the Sea*. Grace Moore, an early talkie failure, returned for unexpected but emphatic success as a prima donna in *One Night of*

Love; and Capra sealed the Columbia phenomenon with another winner, the racetrack yarn *Broadway Bill,* for which he had no difficulty borrowing Fox's Warner Baxter and M-G-M's Myrna Loy.

No longer would players object to being farmed out to Columbia. From about that time, Columbia would continue to mine its efficient B product but could also be counted on for six or eight major features annually, of a standard comparable to any large studio's. Hollywood's biggest stars now were especially alert to any overtures that Frank Capra might make. In 1935 he made an overture to Gary Cooper.

Capra, for whom movie-making was becoming an increasingly personal adventure, had purchased a country-boy-outwits-city-slickers story typical of journeyman author Clarence Budington Kelland, who was best known for the Scattergood Baines stories. Robert Riskin adapted it as *Mr. Deeds Goes to Town,* and it told of a young fellow living in a small town called Mandrake Falls and writing verses for greeting cards . . . until an obscure relative leaves him a fortune of twenty million dollars. So Longfellow Deeds goes to the Big City and is exploited as the "Cinderella Man" in the papers, then is taken for a raving eccentric as he starts giving all his money away. It's still the Depression, see?

Frank Capra said, "As soon as I thought of Gary Cooper, it wasn't possible to conceive anyone else in the role. He could not have been any closer to my idea of Longfellow Deeds, and as soon as he could think in terms of Cooper, Bob Riskin found it easier to develop the Deeds character in terms of dialogue. So it just had to be Cooper. Every line in his face spelled honesty. Our Mr. Deeds had to symbolize uncorruptibility, and in my mind Gary Cooper already was that symbol."

Cooper read an early draft of the Riskin script and said he'd like to do it. He would work for his Paramount salary scale, and would make a point of being available when Capra needed him. Meanwhile Capra, as one inspired, kept building the *Deeds* project, enriching the theme and necessitating a production on a much larger scale than, say, *It Happened One Night.* The Gable-Colbert picture also had said some things about integrity and irresponsible wealth, and an earlier Capra picture called *American Madness* had been clearly addressed to the Depression, with the enlightened "little people" saving a bank from failing. *Deeds* was being even more consciously themed to the little people, with Gary Cooper materializing as the tall little man. But Capra was taking his time, so Cooper made *Peter Ibbetson* and *Desire* before making his ironic return to Poverty Row.

Then, while Capra was waiting for Cooper, he turned his attention to the matter of who should play the girl. The role was of a size and importance to command the enlistment of an established female star, and there were some alluring and interested candidates—Barbara Stanwyck perhaps, and definitely Carole Lombard and Loretta Young. A comeback for Nancy Carroll was hinted. Then Capra found the actress where he least expected to, right in the Columbia studio. Jean Arthur, thirtyish but a veteran, was the studio's best all-purpose actress. A few years earlier she had been terminated by Paramount after having almost become a star there. She had returned to pictures only recently after some Broadway stage work, and had contributed a particular sparkle to *The Whole Town's Talking*, a well-liked comedy John Ford made for Columbia in 1935. Edward G. Robinson played the dual role of a timid clerk and a self-parodied gangster boss, and as the clerk's fellow worker Jean Arthur suggested new possibilities for the working girl as film heroine. If she was not outstandingly pretty, she at least looked distinctive, and was already accruing renown for her voice. Oddly enough, it was a voice Paramount considered a liability when talkies came in, squeaky-hoarse yet appealing. First it was the voice that seduced Frank Capra, but in time Jean Arthur became his favorite actress. He was certain that *Mr. Deeds Goes to Town* would make her a major star, and he was right. While the picture was destined to become historic in various ways, it was also historic for the teaming of its principal players.

Cooper remembered Jean Arthur from her Paramount days but was not prepared for what she had become. Her insecurity on the set would become legend, but as Frank Capra said, "Turn the camera on her and she became magical." In *Deeds* it surely helped that the star was not easily intimidated by his leading lady's foibles. Cooper simply did not become involved in Miss Arthur's tantrums, and when they played scenes together there was an extraordinary quality of interplay and mutual sympathy.

Here Miss Arthur's working girl was a newspaperwoman and she was conning the Cinderella Man to get her story, but conning him only to a point; she was also falling in love with him, and would assert her own integrity to become his staunchest champion. Deeds needed one, for he was confronted with various human symbols of social corruption.

Capra said, "Cooper was easy to direct. In fact, he was hardly directed at all. The story was really just a simple parable, and the Deeds role did not require an actor of intellectual resources. Cooper's basic intelligence was all he needed—that, and his instinct, which was remarkable. Especially his bodily instinct. Most people probably do not think to consider that directing an actor often isn't so much getting him to say his lines the right way as getting him to use his body believably. Cooper was a very physical actor. He did wonderful things with that long body. He was actually very sparing of gestures but they were all sharp, definite. I don't think it was practiced. It was just natural. All of the best of Gary Cooper was natural."

As Longfellow Deeds, Cooper emerged as something more than merely Capra's spokesman for the little man. He was the prototypical populist hero of the American film, saluted by the New York *Times* as the movies' "uncorruptible Galahad." A later Cooper director, Sam Wood, observed that "Writers working on a Cooper picture had an easy time of it, because they didn't have to put in business and exposition to show that he was good. Coop's natural goodness spoke for itself."

Capra trusted Cooper's essence and left him alone. Although Capra often conceptualized his film projects from a literary viewpoint, he was not a literary directorial stylist. As a graduate of the sight-gag school of silent screen comedy, he concentrated on the visual frame rather than on the actor as its center of interest. He established a rhythm for the *Deeds* picture, and Cooper caught the beat. Cooper himself would call his *Deeds* chore "just about the easiest acting I ever did . . . some roles that didn't turn out nearly as well were certainly harder."

Right away he sensed he was on to something; and in the small Hollywood studio where much of *Deeds* was shot, he got into a habit he'd pointedly avoided at Paramount—he watched the "rushes," the day's scenes projected without sound. Cooper suspected he was riding a winning horse long before the picture was finished, and Capra was exuberantly confident.

Deeds was anticipated, even hailed, as an Event before it opened. It came in with the 1936 spring and made Frank Capra the most important moviemaker in the country in the opinion of most critics, and almost the only director whose name would be valued by the average movie-goer. The *New Republic's* Otis Ferguson set the tone: "Everywhere the picture goes, from the endearing to the absurd, the accompanying business is carried through with perfect zip and relish. It is a humdinger and a beauty, but—like anything so conceived and expressed in terms of motion—literally too much for words, more to be seen than heard about." Of the actors, Ferguson noted that "Gary Cooper is not the I-swan stooge of tradition but a solid character, shrewd and not to be trifled with, sincere, gay, charming, the girls will want to muss his hair. And Jean Arthur is well set off, smart, a little husky, with good emotions in reserve. Everywhere you go in this picture there is someone who is a natural in the part . . ."

Writing from a feminist perspective for the New York *Times* in 1977, Nora Sayre could take issue provocatively: "In Frank Capra's films, Gary Cooper and James Stewart were terribly dependent on being coached and propped up by women like Jean Arthur whose brainpower outran the simpletons'. In many of his movies, Cooper's mind works so sluggishly . . ."

There were almost no naysayers in 1936, however, and despite its many timeless traits, *Mr. Deeds Goes to Town* was a picture for its time. It was the favorite to win the Best Picture award in the Academy reckoning, but M-G-M had more voters than any other studio and with some powerful internal lobbying pushed the nod to *The Great Ziegfeld*, a movie monstrosity. Capra, though, was cited for the second of three times as best director. Commercially *Deeds* was a bonanza.

Cooper did not win the Oscar, nor was he expected to. There was powerful competition in the more exacting characterizations of Walter Huston's *Dodsworth* and Paul Muni's *Pasteur*, and Muni won. Cooper's first nomination, though, brought him to a new plateau in his profession. He had actually been getting nice reviews consistently throughout his career, but without inviting the suggestion that he might be an artist. His good work too often had been acknowledged in the spirit of *surprise*. Some of his friendly notices no doubt had been patronizing because he was an appealing personality if not a finished actor. He was complimented for apprentice work. *Deeds* took him out of every other classification, made him no longer tentative: Gary Cooper was a major star.

One of the primary fallacies of movie legend is that the coming of the talkies ruined many star careers because the players lacked adequate voices. Almost anyone can talk, and remarkably deficient voices are rare. Vilma Banky and Emil Jannings were rather special cases, yet Greta Garbo faced the same problem they did, and became an even greater star in talkies than she had been in a silent phase of no small glory. The foreign accent was almost irrelevant, except as it defined a range of roles for Garbo to play. What mattered was that her throaty, somber voice perfectly matched the personality that had been established in silence, and enhanced that personality in the era of sound.

There were few actual "casualties" of the talkies. Mary Pickford, Gloria Swanson, and Lillian Gish would all appear to have made the transition successfully, but were phasing themselves out with voluntarily reduced activities. Douglas Fairbanks was not intimidated by the talkies, but in any event was too old to continue for very long in his standard athletic exercise. Thomas Meighan was even older. Constance and Norma Talmadge had had their day, too. It can be seen historically that even before the talkie revolution began, the hierarchy of screen stardom had undergone a radical transformation.

Many who today are most easily classified as "silent stars" and are therefore assumed talkie failures were actually very effectively showcased in early talkies. The only clear vocal failures were the gratingly nasal Corinne Griffith and the tragic John Gilbert, whose voice has been misrepresented by legend and was really quite nice after M-G-M had refined its sound recording. But Gilbert's voice did not emulate the personality that had made him a great silent star.

Marion Davies, Colleen Moore, and Bebe Daniels all made the grade in talkies, as did Richard Barthelmess, Richard Dix, and Ramon Novarro. So did Charles Farrell, despite a strident voice.

The public anticipated a nauseatingly vocal Clara Bow but she surprised them, and the talkies had nothing to do with the collapse of her career. Yet actors such as Barthelmess and Dix, and such an actress as Miss Daniels, could not keep pace with the new stars despite high praise accorded their early talking appearances. It was partly because their screen personalities as modified by their voices simply were not strong enough for permanent stardom. And it was because acting for the movies with speech introduced criteria altogether different from the silent era. So eventually they fell by the wayside—the Farrells and Novarros and the Colleen Moores. The roster of sovereign stars was in steady flux during the first talking decade, changing almost imperceptibly but always changing. John Barrymore's sudden, pathetic professional collapse, though, left Ronald Colman entirely alone among male silent stars who were durable talkie stars as well. William Powell and Warner Baxter, veteran silent players, only became stars with the crash of sound, just ahead of Gary Cooper. The only women from the earlier era who still qualified were the M-G-M triumvirate of Garbo, Shearer, and Crawford, plus Fox's Janet Gaynor, who only came in with the last hush of silence. They were assimilated into a new cycle of stardom much richer in its mythology than the silent era ever was. Collectively they evolved into an authentic Establishment.

When Gary Cooper joined the top class in 1936, he shared a pedestal with Clark Gable and Cagney, personality stars despite acknowledged skills; Paul Muni, Leslie Howard, and Fredric March, essentially prestige stars for their dramatic credentials; and Ronald Colman and William Powell, the hybrids. At the next rung, the one just vacated by Cooper, were such players as the soon-to-fade Warner Baxter, the steady Robert Montgomery, and a few others, not to exclude Wallace Beery. After long apprenticeships, Spencer Tracy and then Cary Grant were on the threshold of their majorities. Bing Crosby was still only a commodity star, who like Fred Astaire would become more than that, if Nelson Eddy perhaps would not. The near future would mark the emergence of James Stewart, Errol Flynn, Henry Fonda, Robert Taylor, Tyrone Power . . .

The major female stars included Irene Dunne, Claudette Colbert, Barbara Stanwyck, Jeanette MacDonald, Myrna Loy, the soon-to-retire Janet Gaynor, and the soon-to-die Jean Harlow . . . and Katharine Hepburn, whose incandescence was just beginning to be challenged by Miss Bette Davis. They all held steady while the Ann Hardings and Constance Bennetts faded. Then Kay Francis, Sylvia Sidney, and Miriam Hopkins also faded; yet the "fading" Marlene Dietrich could never be excluded from the select circle. Jean Arthur and Carole Lombard were just moving into celestial orbit, as was Ginger Rogers, with or without her dancing partner. Margaret Sullavan, it was agreed, would be a major star if she would only put her mind to it. The likely prospects for Olivia de Havilland and Rosalind Russell were still off in the distance, and Ingrid Bergman was just beginning in Swedish films. Not a "major" star exactly but rather in a class by herself was Shirley Temple, inevitably of limited tenure.

This was the great studio era. It is also saluted now as the Golden Age of the Movies—golden for movies still treasured in memory though the decades roll by, and golden mainly because everybody went to the movies then, and most went regularly. Movies were America's unifying passion, and the national opiate during first a depression and then a war. In such an atmosphere there could be no bogus stardom; the pretenders would be found out. The Elissa Landis, Gene Raymonds, Anna Stens, Francis Lederers, Jean Muirs, and Phillips Holmeses could not be hard-sold. The real stars of that era were "bigger" than those before or after, because they met exacting requirements imposed by the movie-going public. The great stars were all highly individual—formulated, but each to a unique formula.

Deeds synthesized the essential Gary Cooper, defining his formula indelibly. To the extent that he would "always play Gary Cooper," thenceforth he would always play Longfellow Deeds, whether in a business suit or cowboy togs, in sober films and inebriated ones. He would not again be mistaken for Peter Ibbetson even briefly. Some would regret that the sensuous Legionnaire Tom Brown of *Morocco* would be purged from the Cooper mystique. Gary Cooper, though, was finally defined for the screen by a democratic vote of the American people, and the result would have a world-wide endorsement.

Of all the stars, Cooper was the one most clearly circumscribed as the Hero. The very idea of Cooper playing an unsympathetic role was unseemly. All of the other male stars would occasionally do screen villainy, or play downright bad guys, if colorfully. Even James Stewart could be unmasked as the surprise villain at the climax. John Wayne, emerging later but supplanting even Cooper as a mythic screen figure, could be mean and function thematically as the antagonist, and the public didn't mind. But the public often made capricious demands. Gable should not be allowed to die; Cagney almost had to. The public would allow Cooper to die on film from time to time but only heroically, after having accomplished his splendid mission. The primary public insistence was that Gary Cooper had to be *good*.

The public undoubtedly was right, for he had been good and noble and pure from *The Winning of Barbara Worth* onward, until it was difficult to imagine him otherwise.

Deeds also made Gary Cooper a household word. In 1936 he made the *Motion Picture Herald*'s closely watched "top ten" list of box-office draws for the first time. But not for the last time.

Joel McCrea told of attending a Hollywood Bowl concert in a foursome including his wife, Frances Dee, and the Gary Coopers.

"In the middle of a splendid symphony an autograph seeker popped up in the box behind us and kept hissing, 'Mr. Cooper, Mr. Cooper!' Well, Coop must have heard the fellow, but gave no sign, just sat there listening to the music. A moment later the fellow tried again, louder this time, 'Mr. Cooper, can I have your autograph?' Coop never budged. I couldn't stand it, and turned around and ordered the guy to be quiet. After the concert was over, Coop rose and rubbed his hands together that way he has when he is pleased, and said, 'Fine program, wasn't it?' Sure, he meant it. As far as he was concerned, nothing had happened to mar his evening. I had to laugh when we were making our way out of the Bowl and I heard the autograph seeker say, 'Why, Gary Cooper must be deaf.' But Coop just never would hear what he didn't want to hear."

There are a few such charming stories about the benign Gary Cooper. There is a fund of production anecdotes in which Gary Cooper inevitably falls asleep during camera setups. The same stories often got replayed with slight modifications. At a time when he was entering his maximum fame, it was a challenge for Hollywood journalists to find something to write about him. After having been the screen's most-written-about bachelor, he became its least-written-about married man. How often could you say Gary Cooper likes to hunt?

They said he liked to cook. It was something he did only rarely, and then enjoyed because he didn't *have* to do it. Rocky also could enjoy cooking things because the kitchen had novelty value for her. They had servants—a live-in Scandinavian couple—to cook and keep the house in order, and they were also well trained to discourage the more enterprising tourists from trying to get a peek at the star and his wife.

Cooper's enormous appetite was old news but still a part of him. He liked a huge breakfast, and his reported self-prepared specialty was truly awesome: wild duck blanketed with bacon strips, four eggs on the side, garnished by a small beefsteak.

He had a small studio in the new house and began painting again, actually more often and more thoughtfully than he ever had. Western scenes remained his specialty, and he decided his paintings were good enough to be distributed as gifts among his friends.

He bought a lot of phonograph records and collected Hawaiian music while it was a fad. It was said that he bought and sold cars like a man changing his neckties. The slow-talking Cooper was also described as the town's fastest driver, who seemed always in quest of speed.

Shortly after the Coopers moved into their Bermuda-Georgian mansion, they joined the court crowd at the Beverly Hills Tennis Club. Rocky was the better player, but Cooper found some people he could beat, such as Sam Goldwyn and Harry Cohn. Charlie Chaplin, though, could always take him. Cooper was about evenly matched against Clark Gable, who joined the tennis scene as Carole Lombard's new swain. Gable and Lombard went hunting in the wilds and it made all the papers, and it was well publicized that Carole became a skeet champion. So did Rocky Cooper, but anonymously; and the Coopers made hunting trips about as often as Clark and Carole, over basically the same terrain, but it was not newspaper fodder. Their hunting grounds were mostly in Colorado, Wyoming, and Idaho, but sometimes they roamed the hills of nearby Malibu after coyotes and bobcats, when assured that no reporters suspected their forays.

After *Deeds* was released, Cooper took Rocky to Montana, returning to Helena as a conquering hero after nearly a dozen years. There was a parade and an official ceremony. His parents and brother were also there. Cooper saw Jim Galen, Hugh Potter, Jim Calloway, Harvey Markham; they all called him Frank. He appeared to be the only one among his old Montana gang who hadn't stayed there or eventually returned. He also visited the old ranch and it looked the same, although the house itself seemed much smaller to him.

At about that time Rocky and Gary virtually were charter members of the Sun Valley set. The Union Pacific Railroad developed the Idaho resort and opened it in 1936. It would become a regular retreat for the Coopers, scenically arresting the year round, a paradise for hunting, fishing, and hiking in the summertime, and for winter skiing. Ernest Hemingway paid a visit the first year to appraise the resort, and met Gary Cooper for the first time— only casually, for their real friendship would flower a few years ahead. But Cooper made a distinct impression on Hemingway, who was planning a new novel . . .

For the Gary Coopers to get their names in the paper somewhere other than in Louella's column, they just about had to report a robbery. There were two break-ins on occasions when the servants were away from the house—once when the Coopers were in New York seeing the plays, and later when Gary and a pregnant Rocky were visiting friends more locally. Rocky's jewelry was the primary loss both times, and it was insured; but the burglaries only intensified Cooper's quest for privacy, and he tightened his security.

Samuel Goldwyn had his detractors. He was also an object of ridicule for mangling the English language with such "Goldwynisms" as "include me out," which were sometimes the inventions of other imaginations. He was hated and envied. In a Hollywood where everyone in power was some kind of con man, Sam was thought to be actually quite honest but in a tough, shrewd way. He enjoyed dealing with other people who were tough and shrewd if they would also level with him, and Gary Cooper filled the bill.

Cooper knew he had been outfoxed in some of his early negotiations, and became more cunning in making his own deals. One of his friends said, "Coop is a hard businessman. He doesn't like to be reminded of his shrewdness, but his success by no means was pure luck."

In June of 1936 Gary and Rocky Cooper got together with Sam and Frances Goldwyn to play some bridge. Sam maneuvered Cooper aside to talk about his future, as they had done intermittently, with Goldwyn often hinting that he'd like to get Cooper under personal contract.

While they were winding *The Wedding Night*, Goldwyn made a bid to have Cooper stay with him for an encore in *Barbary Coast*. Miriam Hopkins had joined Goldwyn's contract list and it was to be her first picture for him. Cooper read the script and saw that the gold-seeking frontiersman hero conformed to every notion of Gary Cooper, but he thought the character actor role of the heroine's possessive employer in a waterfront pleasure house would steal the show, and said so to Goldwyn. Eventually Sam got a good picture by building the heavy into a star role for Edward G. Robinson, and for "the Gary Cooper part" he got the nearest facsimile, Joel McCrea, whom he also placed under personal contract. But Sam didn't lose interest in Gary Cooper, or vice versa.

Cooper was about to begin *The General Died at Dawn*, after which the final escalation on his Paramount contract would put his weekly salary at $8,000, for its final annual commitment of two pictures. Goldwyn knew all of this, and also knew that Cooper had been in discussions about a new Paramount contract. Cooper said yes, there had been a kind of agreement reached; but nothing had been signed. Sam said any offer they make, mine will be much better.

So Cooper and Jack Moss met with Goldwyn in his office and worked out an agreement that for its time was quite extraordinary: six pictures in a six-year period, each carrying a $150,000 guarantee with various bonus clauses attached. Goldwyn confided he'd had to go higher than expected; yes, Cooper could be tough and shrewd.

Goldwyn, however, was delighted, the cat savoring its canary, and he released an announcement to the press. Gary Cooper had signed an exclusive contract with Samuel Goldwyn Productions, to begin immediately upon expiration of his current Paramount contract. The "exclusive" part was not exactly true, for Cooper had made provision to take outside work, including possible Goldwyn assignments beyond the specified six; he certainly expected to make more than one picture per year.

It hardly mattered how accurately Sam's publicists had reported the Cooper acquisition. The news took Paramount completely by surprise. Adolph Zukor, who had resumed a more active role in running the studio, was furious—especially so because it was Goldwyn. William LeBaron, nominally the production superintendent in the wake of Ernst Lubitsch's brief tenure, confronted Cooper demanding to know what had prompted him to betray them. Cooper said he wasn't betraying anybody; why, he loved Paramount and everyone connected with it, but Sam Goldwyn had made an offer that really couldn't be refused. Besides, he still owed Paramount three pictures, counting the one still shooting.

And while *The General Died at Dawn* was still in production, Paramount's lawyers decided they had a case. The studio brought suit against Goldwyn and Cooper, ostensibly seeking payment for damages, but more accurately aimed at invalidating the Goldwyn contract and retaining Cooper as a Paramount star. Cooper appeared quite surprised by the revelation that his existing contract contained a clause giving Paramount priority for subsequent negotiations, which implied that Cooper was not free to accept an offer from Goldwyn or anyone until he had rejected one from Paramount. This was a nonstandard provision, similar to the controversial "reserve clause" in contracts for organized baseball, or to the publisher's option clause for contracted authors.

Goldwyn, of course, had lawyers of his own, whose conciliatory strategy was to share the actor in question. Technically Goldwyn "lost" the suit or was convicted of whatever charge was made against him; yet he lost nothing. He still had Gary Cooper for six pictures in six years. The court ruling was that since the contract afforded Cooper plenty of extra time, he would still be under obligation to Paramount when not working on a Goldwyn commitment.

Cooper wasn't disappointed and had every reason to be ecstatic. He was being "forced" to sign with a studio where he felt entirely at home, but the studio was being legally forced to match Goldwyn's $150,000 salary offer to Cooper. He was really in the big money now. Inwardly he believed he owed Paramount something, and soon was gratified to know he had given them a hit.

Clifford Odets was the sensational new American playwright of the thirties, politically committed to the left, an exciting prose poet of lower middle-class American life. He left Broadway for a couple of years, lured by the lucre of film writing, and in the Kaufman-Ferber *Stage Door* play was the model for a playwright character who had "sold out" to Hollywood.

The General Died at Dawn was one of those occasional pictures for which primary attention was paid to the writing. It was "the Odets picture," and would represent his only screen credit for the thirties although he was fitfully engaged on other projects. Its protagonist was an American mercenary in the Orient, and *Chinese Gold* was the title throughout the shooting schedule. Odets found opportunities to insert some Marxist platitudes, but most of his dialogue worked for melodramatic effect. Indeed, *The General Died at Dawn* was pure melodrama, only hinting at aspects of an adventure film, and it was nothing if not cinematic. Shot almost entirely inside the Paramount studio, it was exotic as opium, most of the story delivered in one long night sequence, with the title giving away the ending. Its fogbound set gave Victor Milner an unusual opportunity for which his cinematography was Oscar-nominated. As directed by Lewis Milestone, the picture was unusually slow but rather more spellbinding than sluggish— brooding, muted, somber, all of it shaped in a way that seemed to point to tragedy. Graham Greene thought the happy ending was a cop-out but raved about the picture on general terms, as many critics did. It had pronounced intellectual appeal but was also a popular success. One reason was that Gary Cooper and Madeleine Carroll were the season's handsomest movie team.

Madeleine Carroll was an English actress of spectacular blond beauty and aristocratic demeanor, and was considered the foremost star of British films. *The General Died at Dawn* was only her third Hollywood assignment, and first positive exposure.

She was not accompanied by her husband, and participants on the set kept sly watch to see if Cooper, who in bachelor days would never miss a good bet, might still be up to his old tricks. He and Miss Carroll gave the gossipers no ammunition, but they worked smoothly in their scenes together. He was the soldier of fortune who would summon up a heroic reserve to save himself, his ravishing blonde, and much of strife-torn China from the evil designs of the mortally wounded war lord played by Akim Tamiroff, who was coming into his own as Paramount's premium character actor.

Those who contend that Cooper is a monotonous actor perhaps should witness his big scene, shot in an extended take: a remarkably varied, beautifully sustained filibuster—his plea to the dying general. Nor was his effectiveness limited to scenes that were clearly "his." Akim Tamiroff was determined that Cooper would steal no scenes from *him*. And "For three days I acted rings around him. I've got him stopped. Against my acting he can do nothing. So I look at the rushes. On the screen I am there. Everybody else is there. But what do I see? Nothing! Nothing, that is, but Gary Cooper. He isn't doing anything at all, but he's taking the scenes away from me."

In *The General Died at Dawn*, Cooper spoke an Odets line that would be appropriated for other scripts so often as to become a catchphrase. Believing they are doomed, he tells Madeleine Carroll that "We could have made beautiful music together." They made box-office music, and Cooper would stay in the groove awhile longer. His next picture would be a huge moneymaker, and his first De Mille epic.

At least commercially, Cecil B. De Mille was in a groove of his own. After his return to biblical spectacle with *The Sign of the Cross*, he kept his attention on fairly remote history with *Cleopatra* and *The Crusades*. *The Plainsman* was his trumpeted return to the American West—a scene first celebrated in his pioneering *The Squaw Man* for Lasky and Goldwyn. *The Plainsman* was the story of Wild Bill Hickok; or that's what it was supposed to be. De Mille may have missed noting that the picture's point of view was more strongly Calamity Jane's.

She was Jean Arthur. Since *Deeds* she had made three pictures to Cooper's one, and her career was zooming. *The Plainsman* was their second picture together and their last one, although many people undoubtedly believe they made several more, so vivid is the memory of them as a team. The story of Wild Bill Hickok and Calamity Jane had been told on the screen before and would be reprised many times afterward, but the consensus undoubtedly is that when Cooper and Arthur played it, it stayed played. All the evidence suggests that De Mille, concentrating on an action spectacle, remained unaware of the alluring and somewhat Freudian drama that was created by the principal players, largely by innuendo.

The historical writer Harold Lamb, whose *The Crusades* had spawned the previous De Mille epic, was retained as a writer for *The Plainsman,* and many years later joked about having stocked its script with innuendo that not even Cooper and Arthur grasped, but came through in their playing nonetheless—"and all good stuff." Cooper is as reasonable as any other candidate for the screen's best representation of Hickok, but Jean Arthur is surely the definitive Calamity Jane, though just as surely softer and more intelligent than the woman of history. Her anguished love for a man who cannot articulate his own feelings gave *The Plainsman* an emotional texture that was extraordinary for a Western, and that allowed it to exist comfortably on two levels. As a cowboys-and-Indians spectacle it was unbeatable, and it initiated what can now be seen as De Mille's period of highest achievement as a screen entertainer. As Paramount's Christmas release for 1936, it swamped all competition. As Hickok, Cooper was a provocative, enigmatic figure, a screen image of deepening mythic substance, and so natural a presence that it was hard to believe that it was his first Western in almost six years.

Paramount's pleasure, though, would have been for Cooper to follow *The Plainsman* immediately with another Western. Studio hands were shaping *Wells Fargo* on an even more ambitious scale, and it was proposed as the vehicle to conclude Cooper's contract. His own inclination was to work with Henry Hathaway again, in a maritime period piece called *Souls at Sea.* He also said in an interview that while he wanted to make more Western films and felt he had absented himself from the genre too long, he preferred to vary his types of films and did not wish to make Westerns back to back. Still, not that many super-Westerns were projected in the thirties, and he sensed that he could make *Wells Fargo* and almost certainly cash another big winner.

Then Frank Lloyd acquired the functions of both producer and director for *Wells Fargo*. Lloyd had joined the Paramount fold only recently, not having worked there since going through his ordeal with the raw Gary Cooper in *Children of Divorce* a decade earlier. In the interim he had won a couple of Oscars for direction and had also made *Mutiny on the Bounty*; but Cooper held a grudge and to him Frank Lloyd was only an old tormentor. He hated to pass on *Wells Fargo*, but director approval was a feature of his contract; and he said he'd make the sea picture with Hathaway. Then Frank Lloyd made a personal plea to Cooper. The budget for *Wells Fargo* was a million dollars, almost unheard of in that era. There was no one at Paramount to lead the cast— Randolph Scott perhaps, but he wasn't really big enough, and they would need box-office protection or have to scrap the whole thing. Cooper told Lloyd he had no problem; all he had to do was call Sam Goldwyn and borrow Joel McCrea.

Cooper called *Souls at Sea* his "almost" picture.

"It was almost exciting, and almost interesting. And I was almost good. George Raft *was* good."

Souls at Sea was the first picture since *Design for Living* in which Cooper appeared with another actor who also held star rating, the *Lancer* business with Franchot Tone perhaps apart. George Raft had been at Paramount since 1932, a star there almost from the beginning although never held in high regard as an actor. He was the studio's gangster predecessor to Alan Ladd and played in the same cold, expressionless style. He was quite popular for a while, though no serious rival to Warner's mercurial Cagney; but his stock had been slipping steadily, and the talk was that Paramount wanted to settle his contract. Ironically, *Souls at Sea* would be rated a disappointment and a comedown for Gary Cooper, but would be an unofficial but definite comeback for George Raft and provide the best notices of his career.

The young George Raft had gangland connections, of which he was often remarkably candid. To his biographer, Lewis Yablonsky, he recalled an incident from his earliest Hollywood days involving Gary Cooper, whom he had not then even met.

"I got a phone call from a mob man in New York who wanted

me to handle an emergency job. One of the big men in the rackets had traced his missing girl friend to Hollywood. 'She's crazy about a young actor,' the guy told me. 'If you want to save his life, you'll find the girl and hustle her out of town. Otherwise this actor winds up on a slab.'"

The actor in question was Gary Cooper. Raft said he got on the phone to Wilson Mizner, who knew everyone in Hollywood, and who got the girl's address. "So I went to her apartment, got her packed in a hurry, took her to the station, and got her on the first train east. I never told Gary Cooper what I had done, even after we became good friends."

In *Souls at Sea* Cooper and Raft were sailor companions in mid-nineteenth century, first on a slave ship, then on a passenger vessel destined to sink spectacularly. The story was based rather loosely on an actual historical incident. As "Nuggin" Taylor, Cooper had the God-playing function of determining who would occupy the sole, inadequate lifeboat, as scores of passengers thrash about in the ocean water struggling for survival. For preventing additional passengers from entering the boat after it becomes overloaded, he is court-martialed as a murderer. The George Raft character meanwhile has gone down with the ship.

Cooper said, "Parts of *Souls at Sea* were pretty terrific, and if it had followed some of my weaker pictures it would have looked like a good thing for me. But I'd had a nice run of hits and everything is relative, in pictures as in other things. *Souls at Sea* was nothing to be ashamed of, and it had an audience. But I thought the love story with George Raft and the little French girl was more arresting than my more conventional one with Frances. Then, too, George played part of the picture with a ring in his ear, and people thought that made him a better actor."

The little French girl was Olympe Bradna, an ingenue who never made the grade, but not for lack of effort on Paramount's part. Frances was Frances Dee, the film's third star and the beautiful wife of Cooper's alter ego Joel McCrea, who was also becoming his best friend. And not everyone thought the earring necessarily made Raft a better actor. One critic noted that "In a scene with Gary Cooper and George Raft, the cigar-store Indian appears to be over-acting."

George Raft, trusting his memory, tells of shooting the *Souls at*

Sea drunk scene. "Coop and I are drinking rum together. Both of us were quiet actors, you know, we didn't like a lot of dialogue. Mainly we looked at each other. Finally he said to me, 'You know I love you.' The script had 'look at him, pause, and then say, "I know I love you too." ' The director yells 'Print!' Coop jokingly told Hathaway, 'You can't put that in the movie. People are going to think Cooper and Raft are a couple of fags.' I guess he figured we were right because he cut it."

Raft is wrong. The scene is still in the picture, its dialogue intact. Nor could the suggestion of faggishness have arisen in any event, certainly not in Hollywood. Compared with George Raft, even Cooper was a novice as a movieland Lothario. When once asked who was Hollywood's greatest lover, Carole Lombard quickly replied "George Raft . . . or did you just mean on the screen?"

Maria Cooper was born on September 15, 1937. It is expected of new fathers to be foolish about their infant children, and perhaps especially of little girls. Cooper's friends believed nonetheless that *no one* was quite so foolish over a child as was Gary Cooper toward his daughter.

Bing Crosby said in 1943 that "If Gary had four of them like I do, he might be more reasonable about it. But he only tells me one girl is worth four boys."

Cooper couldn't resist talking about Maria, and people would exclaim that he absolutely adored her; but they would be shown no pictures of his daughter. From the beginning the Coopers provided a very sheltered existence for Maria, whose father was believed to have an obsessive fear that she might be kidnapped. Maria would have a "normal" if rather privileged childhood in that she would have a lot of time for play and enjoy many friends; but it would be in a custom-made world, supervised with affection but with caution, and with maximum security protection. Special precautions were taken whenever the three Coopers went on a trip or a junket to the mountains. When the four-year-old Maria's picture appeared in newspapers and magazines, showing her romping in the snow at Sun Valley, Cooper was angrily distressed.

A new gossip columnist, the former actress Hedda Hopper, said Maria Cooper had become the number two woman in her father's life. A contrary opinion held by some in the community was that she had supplanted Rocky as number one.

Maria's birth undoubtedly was the most important event in Gary Cooper's life in 1937. It might be frivolously suggested that the second most important event, toward the end of the year, was Cooper's appearance on the Chase and Sanborn Hour, an immensely popular radio program starring Edgar Bergen and Charlie McCarthy. Cooper had been characterized in the fan magazines as a supremely silent fellow, so Bergen's writers worked on that thought for comic effect, devising dialogue that would have Bergen and McCarthy asking the movie star every kind of question, but getting only two kinds of answers. Every Cooper response was "Yup" until Charlie asked if he couldn't say something other than just yup, and Cooper said "Nope."

The yup-nope business would grow into its own legend, and Cooper often would resort to the monosyllables for comic effect in everyday conversation. A story would be invented that he had said "yup" repeatedly in *The Virginian*, which was not so. Anyway, it solved a problem for the impressionists, who could give their imitations of Cagney, Robinson, Gable, and Colman, but couldn't seem to "do" Gary Cooper. So they just said yup and nope.

In retrospect, 1936 is seen as a fantastic year for Gary Cooper. *Desire*, a supple comedy, was released during the waning winter. The virtuoso display of *Deeds* came with the spring and held on strongly through the summer. *The General Died at Dawn* was an autumn event, with *The Plainsman* coming at year's end. In sharp contrast, *Souls at Sea*, a midsummer release, was Cooper's only credit for 1937. Still, it was a better year for him than 1938, because one so-so picture is more to be desired than three variably disappointing ones. After two years in the box-office top ten, he slipped out of the select circle in 1938, not to return until 1941 with his second Frank Capra picture.

His 1938 films were *The Adventures of Marco Polo*, *Bluebeard's Eighth Wife*, and *The Cowboy and the Lady*. They could be compared unfavorably with pictures he might have made, but chose not to, and sometimes didn't get started because of his choosing.

Memo from David O. Selznick, Rudy Behlmer's collection of the producer's professional correspondence, makes it absolutely certain that Cooper could have played Rhett Butler in *Gone with the Wind*—that Cooper was Selznick's choice over Clark Gable and others who were in the reckoning, including Ronald Colman and Errol Flynn. Selznick's first mention of Cooper is in a memo to his story agent, Kay Brown, on May 26, 1936, when *Gone with the Wind* was still in the galleys stage and several weeks before Selznick bought the screen rights for $50,000. Cooper is a continuous reference throughout 1937 and into 1938, and materializes as the only logical alternative (in Selznick's view) to Clark Gable.

Aside from a matter of personal mutual dislike between Gable and Selznick, the independent producer did not wish to be forced into a distribution tie-in with Metro-Goldwyn-Mayer, which was the very steep demand made by Selznick's father-in-law, Louis B. Mayer, for the use of Gable. The public was clamoring for Gable in the part, for Rhett Butler had materialized as Clark Gable in their collective imagination while reading the book. Selznick believed, though, that the public could be easily reconciled to Gary Cooper in the role, and would eventually embrace him as Rhett Butler.

Selznick may have tried to arrange distribution through Paramount as a means of obtaining Cooper, as it was rumored, although the collected memos do not support that possibility. Carole Lombard, Gable's girl friend and future wife, wanted to play Scarlett O'Hara to Gable's Rhett and attempted a bizarre plot wherein Cooper would "accept" the Butler role, Paramount would get the distribution action, and then Cooper would cancel out—whereupon, she reckoned, M-G-M would spring Clark Gable to Paramount because finally they wouldn't miss the opportunity to have him play Rhett Butler. When Miss Lombard proposed the scheme to Cooper he would have no part of it, and gave her further assurance that under no circumstance would he play Rhett Butler. He wouldn't touch *Gone with the Wind* with a ten-foot pole.

But he kept Selznick guessing for two years. He wouldn't say yes and he wouldn't say no. The voluminously publicized, often comically embellished "search for Scarlett O'Hara" went on for two years simply because Selznick continued to resist the Gable casting as Rhett and the obligation to M-G-M. Hundreds of actresses, including many without any experience or otherwise completely unknown, were interviewed for Scarlett. Scores were tested, about ten of them quite seriously. No one was being "tested" for Rhett Butler. After Selznick rejected a Warner package that included Bette Davis and Errol Flynn (as well as both Leslie Howard and Olivia de Havilland, whom he finally borrowed anyway), it became a matter of either Clark Gable or Gary Cooper. If at any point Cooper had given a definite yes to Selznick, the decision on Scarlett O'Hara would have been made then and there and production would have begun much sooner, with Selznick releasing through United Artists as he customarily did, and as he much wanted to do.

The last mention of Cooper in the Selznick correspondence is in the August 25, 1938, memo informing United Artists boss George Schaefer of Selznick's capitulation to M-G-M. Selznick is regretful, explaining that "I cannot help but feel that the picture would have been made by now and would have been released through United Artists had we been able to secure the long-sought co-operation of Gary Cooper . . ."

Cooper vacillated while *Gone with the Wind* became the most popular American novel of the twentieth century, and while the preproduction drama of the movie version often assumed monstrous proportions. It mattered enormously that he was pitted against Clark Gable for the Butler role, but the fact that the public was screaming for Gable was probably not what prompted the definite no that Cooper finally gave Selznick. More likely it was the intense egoistic competition that existed between the Cooper-Gable friendship.

When Cooper reported to *Beau Geste* in mid-1939, *Gone with the Wind* was still shooting, with stories abounding of its production strife. Cooper told William Wellman, his *Beau Geste* director, that "*Gone with the Wind* is going to be the biggest flop in Hollywood history. I'm just glad it'll be Clark Gable who's falling flat on his face and not Gary Cooper."

At a time when he might have been making *Gone with the Wind*, Gary Cooper was falling flat on his face making *The Adventures of Marco Polo*. It initiated his contract with Samuel Goldwyn, who would have preferred to start Cooper in a pet project of his, a film biography of Hans Christian Andersen. Cooper was wary of trying to impersonate a nineteenth-century Dane, and may have felt that a thirteenth-century Venetian was more along his line. He was not particularly happy about the Marco Polo assignment, and was still lamenting having failed to get a part he really wanted.

The Frank Capra picture that followed *Mr. Deeds Goes to Town* was James Hilton's phenomenally successful novel, *Lost Horizon*. In the aftermath of the *Deeds* triumph, Cooper came to believe he would get another invitation from Columbia, to play Robert Conway in *Lost Horizon*. Newspaper columns hinted he was the likely choice. He heard that Harry Cohn, the studio boss, was mad for Gary Cooper to play the part. He wondered, though, why he wasn't hearing from Frank Capra.

Cohn did want Cooper, and so did Capra's writer and collaborator Bob Riskin. They both tried to persuade Capra, who had said that only Gary Cooper could play Longfellow Deeds, but who had other notions about Robert Conway.

"The Cooper business should never have been in the papers in the first place, because not once did I consider him," Frank Capra explained. "The part called for an Englishman, but that wasn't the main thing, people are skirting around that all the time. It was simply that Cooper didn't have the intellectual capacity for the part. Oh, he would agree with Shangri-La . . . but to *lead* it was far beyond his intellectual attainments."

Ronald Colman was cast as Conway, delivering a sensitive performance that proved to be exactly what Capra wanted. Then Cooper rejected the Paramount bid for *Swing High, Swing Low* in the belief that Carole Lombard had the better role; she did, and Fred MacMurray played opposite her, "replacing" Bing Crosby, who had "replaced" Cooper. Cooper chose *Souls at Sea* over *Wells Fargo*, completed his Paramount contract, and got into his Marco Polo costume for the Goldwyn company.

In a 1966 interview, a reflective Sam Goldwyn in retirement said, "The Marco Polo picture was the biggest flop I produced—yes, more than *Nana*." It was surely the most mismanaged. The eminent Robert E. Sherwood fashioned a rather spirited screenplay for, he supposed, Fredric March. John Cromwell was the original director who quit/was fired after one week. William

Wyler, Goldwyn's star contract director, refused to have anything to do with it, and John Ford came in for a few days' work, until journeyman director Archie Mayo was pulled off Sam's egoistic *Goldwyn Follies* project. Goldwyn's clash with Cromwell reportedly grew out of Sam's reasoning that with Gary Cooper as Polo, it would have to be an action picture, and Cromwell wasn't an action director. Throughout production no one really seemed to know what kind of picture it was supposed to be, or even who was in the cast. John Carradine and Verree Teasdale were yanked in favor of Basil Rathbone and Binnie Barnes—or was it vice versa? Goldwyn, still mesmerized by the Anna Sten syndrome, was "introducing" as his new discovery Sigrid Gurie. He had "personally discovered her in Norway," until a detective turned up the tidbit that she was a Brooklyn girl. An Idaho girl was briefly met in Kubla Khan's harem—the almost-new Lana Turner.

It was one of those pictures where the intentional comedy falls flat and the serious stuff gets laughed at. *The Adventures of Marco Polo* had no consistent style, or even inconsistent style, and Gary Cooper appeared quite bewildered over the whole thing. He got such reviews as never before had come his way. On a few occasions—*Design for Living; Peter Ibbetson*—they had said he was miscast; but there had never been a suggestion that he was inept.

Before *Marco Polo* was finished, Cooper knew that his next Goldwyn assignment would be *The Cowboy and the Lady*, but not for a while. So he returned to Paramount for the likely joy of a Lubitsch picture, *Bluebeard's Eighth Wife*. The prerelease attentions to *Marco Polo* dawdled, with the result that both *Marco Polo* and *Bluebeard* went into first-run engagements early in 1938. They were quite different kinds of failures.

The great Lubitsch may not have had a failure before, and most certainly had not made a poor picture during the talking period. Even the atypical, tragic *Broken Lullaby* was a prestige success, and critics generally admired Dietrich's *Angel*, which died at the box office. *Bluebeard's Eighth Wife*, at least, would be a mild financial success; as, indeed, was *Marco Polo*. Critics however, while admiring bits and pieces of the "Lubitsch touch," were generally appalled by what they beheld as poor taste uncharacteristic of its director. The sardonic, "adult" script was by the redoubtable team of Billy Wilder and Charles Brackett, but it relied perhaps too heavily on its stars to make the characters likable. The stars were Claudette Colbert and Gary Cooper—and in that order; it was the last time in Cooper's career that he received anything other than first billing—and they could not deliver sympathy for their roles.

Cooper was in no kind of *Marco Polo* fog; he clearly knew what he was doing and was even technically facile. "Miscast" was the operative word. He enacted an irresponsible millionaire with seven failed marriages, with an eighth wife determined to tame him. The scene in which Cooper and Colbert first meet over a pajama counter is nimbly comical and a fondly regarded set-piece, but it was downhill all the way from there. Delightful people were involved in the proceedings—Edward Everett Horton, Franklin Pangborn, the endearing Elizabeth Patterson. The fairly new David Niven showed unmistakable skill and would have been most suitable for the leading role.

Frank S. Nugent summed it up in the New York *Times:* "It all ends in an asylum with Bluebeard in a straitjacket, which proves they're always getting the wrong man: the one they should have grabbed was the chap who picked Mr. Cooper for the part."

Cooper had feared the worst for *Marco Polo* and was braced for the reviews; he had expected the best for *Bluebeard* and was rudely jolted. It was the first Paramount picture under his exorbitant new salary, so at least he was gratified that it made money. Lubitsch later said he may have misjudged the script but not his actors, reasserting his appreciation of Cooper as a romantic comedian. When Lubitsch was preparing *Ninotchka* and William Powell became ill, he made an overture to Cooper to get over to M-G-M and play opposite Garbo herself. Cooper probably feared it would be *Design for Living* and *Bluebeard* all over again. Despite the Lubitsch reputation and Cooper's friendship for him, Cooper was now convinced they were not compatible cinematically. He declined with thanks, for which admirers of Melvyn Douglas' polished performance opposite Garbo are surely grateful.

The Cowboy and the Lady was comedy too, but of a different order. It was an assignment for which no confidence was lacking on Cooper's part, and he never disparaged it even though *The Cowboy and the Lady* threatened to make *Marco Polo* resemble a masterpiece of management. Cooper's two-picture break-in as a Goldwyn star could hardly have been rockier.

The story survives in Hollywood table talk of how Leo McCarey conned Sam Goldwyn, with Garson Kanin's the most full-bodied account. This composite version can't be far off:

Not long after Samuel Goldwyn abandoned Anna Sten as an admission of star-building failure, he signed England's Merle Oberon, still trying to prove himself. His campaign for this rather unusual beauty was more softly modulated, and had a more encouraging initial response. Goldwyn reprised the silent Colman-Banky *The Dark Angel* as a talkie for Fredric March and Miss Oberon, who picked up an Oscar nomination. She gave good performances in two more Goldwyn efforts that were entirely presentable—*These Three* and *Beloved Enemy*; but the returns were mildly disappointing and it appeared that Miss Oberon was making no impact on the American scene. Leo McCarey, a top director who also did some writing, heard that Sam now was saying he needed to get Merle Oberon into a picture with Gary Cooper.

McCarey arranged a meeting with Goldwyn; and, when he sensed the opportunity, began telling Sam about his new idea for a picture he wanted to make—about an aristocratic girl with important connections, soon to be trapped into a mold and set up for a stuffy marriage, until she meets this rodeo rider . . .

He embellished the scene with arm gestures and exaggerated enthusiasm, while visions of Merle Oberon and Gary Cooper danced an adagio in Goldwyn's mind. Sam said what do you call the picture and Leo said he called it *The Cowboy and the Lady*. The Goldwyn orbs glistened. He said I'll buy your story and produce it, and you can direct; and he quickly closed a deal, purchasing McCarey's "story" for $50,000. McCarey had sold Hollywood's most illustrious producer on one of its more shopworn tales, for which not even a synopsis existed. Sam kept pleading for the script, Leo kept squirming off the hook. Eventually Sam realized he'd bought not a story but an idea, and not so much an idea as a mere title, which he then had to buy in a separate transaction. Not even McCarey had known that in 1922 there had been a Paramount picture called *The Cowboy and the Lady*, with Mary Miles Minter and Tom Moore; or that it had become the basis for an early talkie called *I Take This Woman*, with Carole Lombard and . . . Gary Cooper!

Goldwyn persevered, not dissuaded that it was a foolproof idea if only he could get a workable script. At one time or another, twenty-seven writers were known or believed to have had a hand in trying to produce a worth-while script for *The Cowboy and the Lady* from its banal premise. Among those involved were such solid literary names as Frederick Lonsdale, Richard Connell, Robert Ardrey, and Frank Capra's guy Bob Riskin; plus the husband-wife teams of Dorothy Parker and Alan Campbell, Anita Loos and John Emerson; and the eventually credited pair, the not-married S. N. Behrman and Sonya Levien.

Leo McCarey refused to direct the monster of his own making. William Wyler started the picture reluctantly, then proceeded so slowly that Goldwyn replaced him with the young H. C. Potter from Broadway and Yale, who had directed Miss Oberon in *Beloved Enemy*. Scenes were shot and thrown away as substitute scripts materialized. The picture had so many stops and starts that its in-joke shooting title became *The Old Cowboy and the Old Lady*. Thomas Mitchell completed his role as Miss Oberon's father but was working on another picture when new scenes were added, and his role was completely reshot with Henry Kolker. David Niven and Benita Hume had substantial roles that just disappeared in the final cut. Potter had to report to RKO for his previously contracted Vernon and Irene Castle project with Astaire and Rogers, so the final scenes were shot by Stuart Heisler, then only an editor.

One player who was in the proceedings from start to finish was Walter Brennan, an early acquaintance from days when he and Cooper were both extras. Brennan would become a fixture in Cooper pictures over several years, during which their friendship would deepen with admirable devotion.

The case history of *The Cowboy and the Lady* was entirely too well known. The critics were waiting for it. On its release in late 1938 they were civil, however—not pleased but not disrespectful. It was still a romantic cliché but the product of homogenized imaginations was slick. Cooper was generally regarded as its outstanding asset, and he credited Potter with salvaging a passable entertainment. The picture was not a flop; it even got its money back despite its blown budget. The title worked after all, because Cooper was the cowboy. His reliability at the cash register was credited with saving the day, while the feeling was that Merle

Oberon still hadn't caught on . . . but just around the corner, waiting as her "last chance," was *Wuthering Heights*.

Between his attentions to *Bluebeard's Eighth Wife* and *The Cowboy and the Lady*, Cooper took Rocky on a junket to England and the Continent, and was virtually the last American film star to visit Nazi Germany before the European outbreak of World War II.

Until that point he had been basically apolitical, professing an interest in history but reading little of it, lazily supporting a Republican partisan stance inherited from his father. To the extent he had considered the international scene, his own views had been isolationist, from opposition to Mr. Wilson's League of Nations until the fateful Munich Conference that immediately followed the Coopers' return to America. From that point he became increasingly active in the film community's pastime of playing national partisan politics. His allegiance to the right wing would be fairly consistent though never a sure thing, and in 1938 he ceased to be an isolationist.

On his return from Europe, he said of the Germans: "There's no question in my mind that those people want to have a war. They're determined to be a world power and seem to feel that's the only way to become one. Those storm troopers are awesome. The atmosphere in Berlin—well, I've never sensed such tension."

He said he believed the United States should become more involved diplomatically in world affairs, but felt it was no business of Hollywood's. He said pointedly that M-G-M's cautiously anti-Nazi *Three Comrades* with its Scott Fitzgerald screenplay should not have been made, and that thenceforth he would give more thoughtful attention to some of the film projects dangled for his attention. He believed there were some pictures he should have made and didn't, and perhaps some he shouldn't have made but did. In particular he was having second thoughts about *The General Died at Dawn*, which he earlier had referenced as one of his favorite assignments.

Walter Brennan said, "If you can't get Coop to talk about anything else, get him on the subject of Americanism . . ."

Cooper said once more that he did not wish to play cowboys in consecutive pictures, and that seems to have been his only reason for rejecting Cecil B. De Mille's invitation to ride the *Union Pacific*.

Had Cooper made it, he would have had a solid picture in the middle of what was a dry period for him. *Union Pacific* has aged better than almost any De Mille picture and is now a popular choice as his masterpiece. It may have been underrated in 1939, but it was a whopping moneymaker as most of De Mille's projects were. But Joel McCrea played the hero opposite Barbara Stanwyck.

It is surely unfair to label Joel McCrea historically as the poor man's Gary Cooper. McCrea had his own agreeably long run as a star of generally worth-while and quite varied pictures before settling into a late-career rut of minor Westerns that were nevertheless exemplary of their kind. In *The Great Movie Stars*, the perceptive David Shipman writes of McCrea: "Physically he was not unlike Gary Cooper, and they generally played the same sort of roles. Curiously, he was in as many good films as Cooper was, and was hardly less competent, but he hardly had the same allure; there was something just a little bit more forced about his playing."

Preston Sturges rated McCrea as the ideal protagonist for his comedies, and said he was better for *Sullivan's Travels* and *The Palm Beach Story* than Cooper, because "people are always aware they're watching Gary Cooper, and less aware of watching Joel, and that's better for the picture."

McCrea, however, was always the strategic Cooper substitute, a fortunate second choice. After *Barbary Coast* and *Wells Fargo*, there were similar instances. Hitchcock wanted Cooper for *Foreign Correspondent* but accepted McCrea, and it is inconceivable that the picture could have been any better with Cooper. Wellman wanted Cooper, but McCrea became *Buffalo Bill*; and McCrea starred in a remake of *The Virginian*.

At least as remarkable as any of this was the strong friendship that existed and endured between McCrea and Cooper. They were "best" friends in a way, except that they were never really thick. As McCrea explained, they would go long stretches without seeing one another: "Our paths often led in opposite directions, but when we got together again, we'd pick up where we left off."

Joel McCrea was a hometown boy, a graduate of Hollywood High School, who, with exceptional good looks and Cooperesque height, gravitated naturally to the movies. He was four years Cooper's junior, and played his first screen roles in 1929. Cooper thought they met about then but McCrea believed it was slightly later, at a Pickfair party. McCrea, always addressed playfully by Cooper as "McFee," recalled that "Each of us had heard about the other through mutual friends long before that. We weren't introduced. We simply encountered each other, shook hands and went over to a corner and sat down. We must have sat there an hour or so, talking some but not much, perfectly companionable all the while."

They were soon "separable best friends." McCrea married Frances Dee at about the same time the Coopers were married, and they were a sometime foursome.

McCrea recalled a long walk he took with Cooper after one of his trips to Europe. Cooper had a new gun he wanted to try out, and said he just wanted to walk.

"So we did. We walked for an hour or so, with never a word from him. Then, on the crest of a hill, over a beautiful vista, we stood for five or ten minutes perhaps, both of us silent. Finally Coop took a long breath and turned to me: 'You know, McFee, that European situation is a hell of a mess . . .'"

Then Cooper talked fluently for fifteen or twenty minutes. McCrea said Cooper was always likely to do that if he knew he had an interested listener. He just wouldn't waste words.

"He wouldn't say hello-how-are-you and never wait or care about your answer. If he asked how you were, you could be darn well certain he wanted to know. If he talked about the weather you could be sure he was interested in it."

Cooper, McCrea said, was no hypocrite. He couldn't pretend a regard he didn't feel, to save his life.

"He takes in stride whatever comes along. Maybe the actress he's working with is temperamental and keeps demanding this and that change in the script, action or what-have-you. Coop never says a word. He takes what he is given and does what he is supposed to do."

Joel McCrea, admitting to prejudice, said he thought Gary Cooper was the best there ever was.

The old Paramount gang was pretty well broken up long before Cooper became only a part-time presence at the studio. Richard

Arlen left Paramount in 1935, Jack Oakie the following year. Cooper continued to get together with them at times, but for meetings that were consciously reunions—most often at Pickfair, after Buddy Rogers married Mary Pickford and became squire of the manor.

Cooper's closest friendship at the studio in the late thirties was Fred MacMurray, who joined Paramount in 1935 and very quickly became its all-purpose leading man. The MacMurrays and Coopers began to form a "set" with two newlywed couples—Tyrone Power and Annabella, and Robert Taylor and Barbara Stanwyck, who for their combined rating were Hollywood's starriest marriage, if the equally newlywed Clark Gable and Carole Lombard were not that. The Gables joined the group just occasionally, with absolutely no dirty talk coming from the Lombard lips if Fred MacMurray's wife Lillian—whom Carole adored—was present.

It wasn't a rigid social thing. The Coopers might meet with the Taylors and McCreas, or the Powers and MacMurrays, and other possible combinations, or with all of them in even a larger group. On such occasions, when he knew his audience and the subject at hand, Cooper was likely to be the most verbal person on the spot.

The larger the crowd, the quieter he became. Raoul Walsh, a Cooper director much later but an early friend, said, "There came a time when Coop had to start playing Gary Cooper socially. His screen image was patterned after his own personality, but as it became slightly modified, he turned it around, until he was imitating his screen image. But all the stars do that. Look at Roz Russell: once she played Auntie Mame, she couldn't be anyone else. Or Kate Hepburn, who I think was the girl she played in *The Philadelphia Story* for a long time after that, until the old dame in *The African Queen* took over her. I know Coop had it in his mind that he was *Sergeant York* for a long time after that. That was why, I think, he got to liking being around other big stars after he became one—especially around other men. When they were just among themselves, nobody had to pretend."

In terms of quality, Cooper stayed in a professional rut for a while. His two 1939 pictures barely made the grade for merit, although each was successful financially—especially *Beau Geste*, very nearly a smash.

Critics, however, invariably compared the new *Beau Geste* unfavorably with the 1926 Paramount classic whose Beau was Ronald Colman. So did most older movie-goers who saw both versions. William Wellman's visual direction fell short of Herbert Brenon's earlier eloquence, and for an action picture the story plodded. Schoolboys generally cheered the Wellman edition, and gave no thought to Gary Cooper's supposed interpretation of a young Englishman.

He was as English as the new Robert Preston, who played brother Digby; but brother John was the Welsh-English Ray Milland, and they were an odd trio. They were also great pals, especially during the location shooting that was an entirely masculine event for both cast and crew.

Most of the picture was shot on the same Arizona desert where Brenon had made the original *Beau Geste*. Actors and crewmen numbered almost two hundred, and they had a seemingly unlimited supply of liquor. Ray Milland, who was on the brink of his own major stardom after a slow but steady ascent up the Paramount ladder, kept them all entertained with bawdy tales of his adventures as a Royal Grenadier. There were more contemporary bawdy goings-on at nearby Yuma, where several members of cast and crew spent some time in jail although Paramount effectively suppressed the news.

Cooper shared a location tent with Slim Talbot, his old Montana friend and now his stand-in. One night a sandstorm began to blow, and they rushed out to try to hold the tent down. Slim yelled, "Big blow, ain't it?" They battled the flapping canvas for more than an hour, until a violent gust tore it from their grip. As they ran for the nearest shelter, Cooper is said to have shouted, "Sure is!"

Sandstorms were a chronic problem during the *Beau Geste* filming. Rocky was also in Arizona at her parents' retreat near Phoenix; and Cooper received word that Maria, who was not yet two, had been taken ill. He fretted, growing increasingly anxious, and decided to telephone Rocky although the nearest phone was in Yuma, more than twenty miles away. A desert sandstorm was raging, rendering the dirt road to the location site impassable for a car. So Cooper, who said he had never been on a camel, rode one sidesaddle seventeen miles through the blowing sand to the paved state road, tied the camel to a billboard, and hitch-hiked into Yuma to make his telephone call and learn that Maria was recovered.

Beau Geste was the first of only two pictures Cooper made with Robert Preston but they formed a bond that became permanent. Cooper recognized Preston as more seriously dedicated than most beginning actors he worked with, and believed it was the first time he felt "fatherly" toward a co-worker. Preston had a strange, often frustrating career as a chronic almost-star, until his belated emergence as a powerful theatrical personality; and in 1957 Gary Cooper was there backstage to congratulate *The Music Man*.

Robert Preston called Cooper "probably the finest motion picture actor I ever worked with." He said, "I know Cooper doesn't have the reputation of a great actor except with us who knew him as an actor. But he was great. People used to comment on his little foibles, his idiosyncrasies. But Cooper never made a move that wasn't thoroughly thought out and planned."

Not all of Cooper's planning could prevent Brian Donlevy from stealing the picture from everyone in sight. As the crazed, bullying Legionnaire sergeant, Donlevy gave an astonishingly robust performance that nudged him into belated stardom after many years in support, usually in "heavy" roles. The desert scenes, at least, had a vitality that contrasted to the epilogue and prologue— scenes of classy English domesticity shot in the studio. Preston as Digby gave Cooper's Beau a Viking funeral and then died with him, leaving John alone to return home and get the girl.

The girl Ray Milland got was new and her inexperience showed, although she was believed one whose Scarlett O'Hara test had been seriously reckoned with. She was Susan Hayward, and it would take a while but she would make it big. Also of interest was that Beau Geste in the prologue was played by the thirteen-year-old Donald O'Connor.

Cooper's other 1939 film was even more emphatically an "action" picture of a kind seldom made by Samuel Goldwyn. *The Real Glory* was set in the Philippines but Sam Goldwyn called it a Western; he had also called the thirteenth-century, largely oriental *Marco Polo* a Western and had not been entirely incorrect. *The Real Glory*, some thought, represented propaganda for American militarism, as it focused on a small soldier band dealing with an uprising by a horde of Moro bandits. It was an unbelievably violent picture, to a degree not characteristic of its era. It was probably Cooper's idea to have Goldwyn import Henry Hathaway from Paramount to direct, and a wise choice. *The Real Glory* succeeded on its elementary action terms and collected favorable reviews. It was a commercial success despite being, rather curiously, the most expensive Goldwyn film to that time, its cost easily exceeding a million dollars. Very soon afterward it would be almost completely forgotten, because its dramatic content was negligible. It was made to order for Cooper, of whom the New York *Herald Tribune*'s Howard Barnes said, "He has had some fat parts before but not to equal this one, and he does a first-rate job, essentially in a cowboy-and-Indian show."

Cooper played a heroic army doctor. *The Real Glory* was a calculated *Bengal Lancer* Philippine paraphrase and Henry Hathaway made continuous reference to David Niven's part as "the Franchot Tone role." Niven was delightful, and also impressive was Goldwyn's other young contract player, the strikingly contrasted Broderick Crawford, who had also been one of the *Beau Geste* Legionnaires. Eventually both Niven and Crawford would win best actor Oscars.

The girl was Andrea Leeds, a fine young actress whose contract Goldwyn shared with Darryl Zanuck's 20th Century-Fox company, but who had been built mainly in Goldwyn projects. She followed *The Real Glory* with two leads for Zanuck, then got married and quit the movies—one of the few cases of an actress abandoning a career with fresh stardom within her grasp.

Cooper appeared unperturbed that his recent run of films had missed the mark of quality. If he sought only a prestige picture, he would not likely have rejected *Abe Lincoln in Illinois*, for which he was everyone's first choice. It was reported that he did not want to risk comparison with Raymond Massey's stage portrayal in the Robert Sherwood play, but Cooper privately confided that the comparison he sought to avoid was with Henry Fonda, who had recently been a splendid *Young Mr. Lincoln* for John Ford. Massey finally reprised his characterization for the film of *Abe Lincoln in Illinois* and it was a critical success but not the moneymaker it would have been with Cooper's participation.

To console himself for any disappointment, Cooper had only to check his bank account. It was revealed that in 1939 he made almost half a million dollars as a movie actor, making him the year's highest salaried employee in the United States of America.

In the summer of 1940 the Coopers vacationed in Sun Valley and took up famously with Ernest and Martha Hemingway. Their two or possibly three earlier meetings had been friendly but perfunctory. In their new closeness, Hemingway invited Cooper to read his new novel, which he had in galley proof. Cooper read *For Whom the Bell Tolls*, admired it immensely, and told Hemingway that if a movie should be made of it, he'd certainly like to have a go at the Robert Jordan role.

"That's good," Hemingway grinned, "because it was written for you."

A *Farewell to Arms* was one of three or four Cooper films of the thirties of which he was often audibly proud. Hemingway hated the film but liked Cooper, and liked him when they met in person, and he asked Cooper just to call him Papa. As much as the role of Rhett Butler in its novel text suggests Clark Gable, Robert Jordan suggests Gary Cooper, and possibly even more so; there was a consciousness of Cooper while Hemingway was writing *For Whom the Bell Tolls*, and Margaret Mitchell did not know of Clark Gable's existence when she wrote *Gone with the Wind*.

In the summer of 1940 a movie sale for the novel was off in the distance. It was not known then that *For Whom the Bell Tolls* would become a huge best seller and the year's literary event, although it could have been expected. It was Hemingway's interest in Cooper, though, that would cause him to nudge the property toward Paramount at the exclusion of other spirited studio interest; and it was Cooper's anxiety that nudged Paramount to buy it.

Meanwhile Cooper became a regular hunting companion to the author, who if not his "best" friend was the person whose friendship Cooper would most value, in his own star-struck way. They got together annually in Sun Valley, and occasionally would meet elsewhere. Hemingway chided Cooper for his shooting ability, jealous that Cooper was the better shot. He boasted, though, that he could take the measure of Cooper either wrestling or wearing boxing gloves, and it turned out he could.

The Coopers got together with the Hemingways again in 1941. The author's marriage was in trouble, and the Coopers' friendship would be sustained through Hemingway's change of wives. *For Whom the Bell Tolls* was by then a major topic of interest, not only in the literary world but in Hollywood, where various actresses were itching to play Maria, the heroine of Hemingway's novel about the Spanish Civil War. It was a foregone conclusion that Cooper would play Robert Jordan when the novel got filmed. That would only be two years later, but as early as 1941 Hemingway was asking Cooper what he thought about Ingrid Bergman as a possibility for Maria. Cooper said he'd only seen the girl a couple of times and hardly knew her, but he did know she was Swedish.

Historically Samuel Goldwyn has a reputation as a great producer of motion pictures, probably well-earned, but also owing much to William Wyler and perhaps to Gregg Toland as well. Eliminate from the Goldwyn inventory the eight pictures directed by Wyler and photographed by Toland, and it is not really so impressive a production record.

Goldwyn's search for a great director was almost as obsessive as his desire to create a great international star, and Wyler became the fulfillment of that particular dream. Goldwyn placed the modestly established Wyler under personal contract, and Wyler's first Goldwyn effort—the 1936 *Dodsworth* with Walter Huston and Ruth Chatterton—is an unquestioned masterpiece of the period. Wyler and Gregg Toland, who had been seeking a director sympathetic to boldly cinematographic innovation, immediately formed a remarkably harmonious collaborative association. After that Goldwyn wanted Wyler to direct everything under the sun. He replaced Howard Hawks with Wyler on *Come and Get It,* for which they are officially co-credited. Counting that one, Wyler made nine Goldwyn films, except that Wyler doesn't count it—but neither does Hawks, although it's a fine picture to do either or both of them proud. Every Goldwyn picture in a five-year period that Wyler *didn't* direct he seems only to have refused, excepting possibly *The Real Glory.* Eventually, though, Goldwyn became quite jealous of Wyler for the praise that was increasingly heaped upon him. When someone once referred to Wyler as the man who made *Wuthering Heights,* Sam bluntly corrected him: "No he didn't. I made *Wuthering Heights,* Wyler only directed it."

In 1940 Wyler was still very much Sam's fair-haired boy. The German-born, French-educated, thoroughly cosmopolitan Wyler was by then a director of literate and sophisticated dramas, yet he had started as a director of minor Universal Westerns, being the nephew of Universal's fabled relative-hirer, Uncle Carl Laemmle. Gary Cooper wasn't certain, but it figured that he had probably ridden in some Wyler pictures. And there was Wyler, and there was Cooper, both working for Goldwyn, who hadn't made a Western since the sort-of Western *Winning of Barbara Worth;* and they all thought it would be a good thing to get one going. Wyler had screamed bloody murder when Goldwyn tried to put him on the *Marco Polo* picture, and had worked only a few days on *The Cowboy and the Lady.* But now he would direct Cooper as *The Westerner.*

It was one of 1940's big hits—an impressively mounted frontier pageant in which the solo star-billed Gary Cooper played essentially the first supporting role of his talking screen career. He had the title role and had a slight edge in footage over Walter Brennan; but Brennan was the whole picture in the measure of interest, with a great character part as the ruthless yet curiously romantic Judge Roy Bean, an authentic historical figure inflated by legend. There was a conventional love story for Cooper, but Wyler was dissatisfied with the actress forced upon him—Doris Davenport, up from the Goldwyn Girls chorus, and destined to disappear almost immediately. So Wyler built up Brennan's part, altering the focus until what emerged was a kind of love story between the bad-good Judge Bean and the good-good laconic cowboy who could influence him, as played by Cooper.

Brennan was wonderful enough to pick up his third supporting Oscar in a five-year period—the first time the "secondary" award was given to someone playing a role as fat as it was juicy. Effective in a minor role was young Dana Andrews, in his debut under a Goldwyn contract. Andrews told Cooper that watching him in the silent *Legion of the Condemned* in 1928 was what shaped his decision to become a motion picture actor. Cooper, relaxed and effective to the maximum degree in his now-standard role, was nevertheless thoroughly upstaged and he didn't like it. He made light of it in his public pronouncements, saying he was tickled pink that it was Walter Brennan's picture. Only the fact that it was his now great friend Brennan rather than another actor may have prevented him from becoming hostile about the situation. Anyway, Sam Goldwyn was delighted over the only *real* Western he made. The critics were kind to *The Westerner* and it brought in a windfall, even though William Wyler does not give it a high rating among his own work.

It was a better picture by far than Cooper's other 1940 picture —which, however, was another huge grosser. *Northwest Mounted Police* was one of the sprawlier De Mille pictures, and it was an inflated but conventional Western, Canadian setting notwithstanding. Cooper reasoned he'd just have to abandon his rule about not making two Western films in a row. De Mille was in a blockbuster groove and it didn't seem wise to refuse the master twice running. Furthermore, there was a new emphasis on big-budget Westerns, which were a rare thing during the first decade of the talkies.

Stagecoach was the picture that changed everything. John Ford's photographic masterpiece was the prestige success among all Western films, bringing heightened attention to the genre. Walter Wanger, the independent producer whom Ford persuaded to sponsor *Stagecoach*, desperately wanted Gary Cooper and Marlene Dietrich for the outlaw-and-prostitute leads. Dietrich was believed thoroughly washed up and there was some doubt that she would ever make another film, but Wagner had a hunch that a showy Western role could resurrect her. When John Ford insisted that Claire Trevor had to play the whore, Wanger pushed the argument that it made Gary Cooper mandatory for the box office. It would be interesting to know if Cooper would have accepted or rejected the role of the Ringo Kid, but it was never offered. Ford was a stubborn man, and Wanger ultimately yielded to his capricious notion that the Ringo Kid had to be played by a fellow who'd been grinding out pulp Westerns for years on end: John Wayne.

Stagecoach opened the door for other Westerns. Cooper was offered, and did refuse, *Destry Rides Again*, a later 1939 picture. James Stewart, who was beginning to put together a string of gaudy hits and prestige successes, got the Destry part. Walter

Wanger had nothing to do with the picture, but it gave Marlene Dietrich her showy Western role and she registered a sensational comeback. Cooper soon admitted he regretted having turned down *Destry Rides Again.*

Northwest Mounted Police was his and De Mille's first Technicolor picture, and the studio grapevine hinted that Cooper took the bait because he was itching to get into another picture with the luscious Madeleine Carroll. They were the stars of a picture teeming with solid names. Paulette Goddard and Robert Preston had a tempestuous second-lead romance. As a character-comedy team, Akim Tamiroff and Lynne Overman had scored a hit in *Union Pacific,* so De Mille brought them back for an encore. And wonder of wonders, Gary Cooper didn't get the girl! That Madeleine Carroll should choose fellow Mountie Preston Foster over Cooper was about the only thing the picture delivered in the way of surprise. The public screamed about it, but the public had paid its money.

In 1940 Gary Cooper campaigned actively for Wendell Willkie as the Republican challenger to Franklin Roosevelt's quest for a third term. He believed Roosevelt was already too powerful and would become more so. He told Cecelia Ager, though, that he advocated most of the New Deal reforms and believed the GOP made a mistake by not emphasizing their intention of retaining most of them. He said, "There's no going back to the old ways of the Old Guard." Wendell Willkie, who was star-struck and also experienced as counsel to movie interests, was a well-known skirt-chaser; and he and Gary Cooper became great friends.

Off the screen Cooper was becoming ever more debonair. He was smoking filtered Parliament cigarettes and having a glass of dry sherry regularly before lunch. While making *The Westerner* he adopted "Howdy, partner" as a catchphrase he would retain, but he was less the cowboy. He said, in fact, that he would never again get on a horse unless it was called for in a script. He said his back hurt every time he got on a horse; and it was only while making *The Westerner,* at age thirty-nine, that he learned he had sustained a fractured hip in the automobile accident of his teen years.

There were no rumors that he and Rocky might separate; there hadn't been for years. They were written about blandly by fan-magazine journalists who never met them as "one of the screen-land's happiest married couples." There was talk among their friends that the Cooper marriage was stale, as dry as dust. As a couple they were seldom observed. There was talk, too, that Gary Cooper's mother was jealous of his wife; or that in any event, Alice and Rocky had not grown close to one another, but were more distant than before. Alice Cooper hinted that she would like to see more of her little granddaughter, of whom she saw really quite little. But then, the aged Charles Cooper said he almost *never* saw his son. He had become a permanently silent presence, vague and distant. He was struck by an automobile at Hollywood and Cahuenga and recovered nicely, but seemed to have just wandered into the street aimlessly.

Rocky had won the state skeet shooting championship, which gave Cooper something to gloat about when he saw Clark Gable. *Gone with the Wind* had made Gable, if possible, an even bigger star than before. For the moment it appeared that Gable—"The King"—was sharing his throne only with Spencer Tracy, and perhaps with two recent risers, Cooper's one time "successor" Cary Grant, and Cooper's new good friend James Stewart.

Very soon and for a while, Cooper himself would overtake them all.

Frank Capra followed *Deeds* and *Lost Horizon* with *You Can't Take It with You* and was honored by the Academy both as producer and director. Then in epochal 1939 he made what is perhaps his finest film of all, *Mr. Smith Goes to Washington*, an encore for his *You Can't Take It with You* stars, Mr. James Stewart and Miss Jean Arthur. That ended his twelve-year association with Columbia—which, when he left in 1940, was fully recognized as a major company primarily because of Capra's pictures.

The director and Robert Riskin formed a company of their own to produce through Warner Brothers. One of the reasons Capra affiliated with Warner was to have access to its strong roster of stars; but when Capra got the idea for his first Warner picture, again it was a case of having a story he believed had to be done by Gary Cooper or no one else.

So five years after he was Longfellow Deeds, he was Long John

Willoughby, who became a symbol for all the little people in Frank Capra's vision of the universe as plain John Doe. The one picture began his association with Capra, the other ended it; one made him a major star, the other made him *the* major star of the land. In the movies' well-known Tropic of Capra Corn, he bloomed as a symbol not of American humanity, but as that humanity eternally should be.

Meet John Doe is a strange film, only hesitantly regarded with favor by revisionist critics. Andrew Sarris notes that with the Doe adventure, Capra "crossed the thin line between populist sentimentality and populist demagoguery." Capra in his autobiography said *Meet John Doe* was an answer to Hitler's "strong-arm success against democracy," and that in their defense of democracy they would startle the public with a brutal picture presenting Cooper Doe as the antithesis of Cooper Deeds—a "drifting piece of human flotsam as devoid of ideals as he was of change in his pocket." But true to the substance of Gary Cooper, the man exploited by the forces of evil as a "John Doe" symbol for purposes of defrauding innocent people would finally rebel.

The trouble was that Capra and Riskin started only with an idea—a better one, surely, than Leo McCarey's idea of *The Cowboy and the Lady*, but still only an idea. Gary Cooper agreed to make the picture without seeing a script because one did not exist. So did the other leading players, as would anyone in 1940 for anything Frank Capra had in mind—as when, two decades later, Jack Lemmon would accept an assignment merely because Billy Wilder was directing.

They finally got a script going, of course, and it had great stuff. The volatile Barbara Stanwyck took "the Jean Arthur role" of the cunning exploiter-turned-sympathizer. Walter Brennan was John Doe's amiable hobo sidekick; Edward Arnold symbolized venal power. There was never any mistaking that it was a deadly serious picture thematically, but the script had a rich foundation of comedy; it was entertainment, an "audience picture"—for, Frank Capra believed, seven eighths of the distance. They didn't know how to end it. The bitterly disillusioned John Doe, resolved to make a suicide leap to his death, had to be inspired not to—but how? Four endings were shot, none satisfactory. Two different endings were test-released. Then Capra got an idea for a fifth ending, given in a letter from an early viewer who thought that only the real John Does of the world could talk the symbolic Doe out of jumping.

Capra recalled the prints, shot ending number five as the official ending, and it was the best one yet . . . but not good enough. Capra remains convinced that only the absence of an inspired ending prevented *Meet John Doe* from entering his pantheon of super hits.

Yet in 1941, it appeared to have made that class. Some critics called it Capra's best picture. Capra, possibly stretching a point, said it got the best reviews of any of his pictures, at least from "the intellectual crowd." It was box-office dynamite, and a National Event.

Some of the players may have been impeded by shooting a picture whose ending they didn't know, since it hadn't been resolved. That hardly mattered in Gary Cooper's case. His John Doe simply existed. If Cooper lacked the intellectual capacity for *Lost Horizon*, his lack of it made him approximately perfect for *Meet John Doe*. He is the simpleton as a device, crucially elevated to the simpleton as hero.

When *You Can't Take It with You* was released, Frank Capra's face was on the cover of *Time*. When *Meet John Doe* was released in March of 1941, the face on *Time*'s cover was Gary Cooper's. The accompanying article was a glorification, saluting "a personality that de-schmaltzes sentiment and de-rants rhetoric."

In early 1941 it was a foregone conclusion that Cooper's John Doe would receive an Academy nomination and possibly win the Oscar. That it was not a nominated performance was only a technicality: he was nominated for another 1941 performance that was better, in a picture that was bigger.

He was on top of the heap.

8

☆ ☆ ☆

☆ ☆ ☆

A PEAK AND A
VALLEY

ON OCTOBER 8, 1918, a thirty-year-old Tennessee back-woodsman named Alvin Cullum York managed a feat that made him the foremost popular hero of World War I. As an Infantry corporal taking part in the Argonne-Meuse offensive, he single-handedly crushed a German machine gun battalion, killing about two dozen and bringing in nearly 150 prisoners. France's Marshal Foch, the Allied commander-in-chief, called it "the greatest thing accomplished by any soldier in all the armies of Europe." York received the Congressional Medal of Honor, the Croix de Guerre, and promotion to sergeant.

Gary Cooper remembered hearing about York's extraordinary achievement when he was still a Montana schoolboy. Jesse Lasky had keener recall of the event, and remembered that York originally had been a conscientious objector, and had requested exemption from military service for his strong religious beliefs. He was opposed to killing, even in war.

In 1941 the United States faced the prospect of another war with Germany and the other Axis powers. Hitler had conquered most of Europe, but not gritty Britain. However belatedly, the American industrial complex and business community were preparing for war. Jesse Lasky sensed, however, that the American people were not preparing emotionally, psychologically; or they were not *being* prepared.

He conceived the idea of a movie about Alvin York that would inspire American patriotic commitment to a new world war.

Jesse L. Lasky is probably the most neglected major figure of American motion picture history, probably because he was no Goldwyn for color, no De Mille for theatricality, no Mayer for sanctimony, no Zukor for pompousness, no Harry Cohn for feistiness, no Carl Laemmle for eccentricity, and no person named Warner. He was simply a bland, genial fellow who once led a Hawaiian dance band but was also a true visionary of the movies. He was a pioneering success with his own company, merged with Zukor into the powerful Famous Players-Lasky that evolved into Paramount, and was eased out of the company in the 1932 realignment. Undismayed, he formed an independent producing unit and made pictures of consistent high quality, first for Fox and then in association with Mary Pickford for United Artists. Soon he appeared to be down and out again, but Lasky was a man who often got ideas. At the age of sixty he got the idea for *Sergeant York*.

He purchased screen rights for various biographical documents about York, got the old soldier's blessing, and tried marketing his idea. Mayer was interested but Lasky didn't like his terms. He refused to consider Paramount for the obvious reason, and had also had a falling out with 20th Century-Fox. He expected his early associate and former brother-in-law Sam Goldwyn would go for the idea but would make that only a last resort, for there was some bitterness there. He held Universal in low regard and didn't like Columbia's Harry Cohn, so that left only Warner Brothers. And they ate it up.

Lasky was made co-producer with the golden boy at Warner, Hal Wallis. From that point Wallis more or less took over, although Lasky approved of everything he observed. It was no sure thing that Alvin York had to be Gary Cooper. There was some thought that Cooper, nearing forty, was really too old, especially since much of the picture would explore Alvin's younger life before he went soldiering. James Stewart, for example, was very nearly perfect in age and every other way, and Henry Fonda was a logical possibility. For the splendid production the Warner folk envisioned, they supposed they could borrow almost anybody they really needed. Then Hal Wallis got the man he wanted to direct —Howard Hawks; and no question about it, Hawks wanted Gary Cooper to play Sergeant York.

It wasn't that easy. The problem wasn't over whether Cooper could be "borrowed," for Sam Goldwyn thought it was such a good bet for Cooper that he was willing to delay the *Ball of Fire* picture he'd scheduled. Cooper's next for Paramount was supposed to be another De Mille whopper, *Reap the Wild Wind*, but it was running into delays. So he was free; but Gary Cooper just didn't want to do it—didn't want to play Alvin York because the prospect scared him half to death. He gave Warner a definite, absolute no; but Howard Hawks said don't anybody worry, I'll talk Coop into this thing.

Only lately had Cooper begun playing historical figures and then in bizarrely fictionalized accounts—Wild Bill Hickok, Marco Polo, and even more remotely the sailor hero of *Souls at Sea*. He had certainly never played a *living* historical figure, and never expected to. The unexpected ace in the hole turned out to be Alvin York himself, who seldom ever went to the picture show but would every now and then, just to see what Gary Cooper was up to. He was really the only movie actor York knew or cared about. Alvin York was brought to Hollywood to meet Gary Cooper, and then Cooper went out to see York's Tennessee mountain country.

Of course Cooper agreed to do the picture, but he stayed scared. He felt challenged as he'd never expected to be. Then he seemed relieved when Sam Goldwyn appeared to change his mind about delaying *Ball of Fire*. Sam said he wouldn't release Cooper from his commitment. Oh, Sam was a wily one! He said he wouldn't let Warner have Gary Cooper unless Warner let him have Bette Davis for *The Little Foxes*.

The picture was put into production in February of 1941. It was undoubtedly an important "event" from the very beginning, but as work progressed acquired a more prestigious aura for all the talk about it. While it was shooting Gary Cooper was on *Time*'s cover as John Doe, and he was doing retakes on May 7—his fortieth birthday. The shooting schedule ran to four months, unusually long for that period. It had started with a solid script but the script kept growing as various writers—John Huston and Howard Koch among them—added new scenes and expanded old ones. The picture was previewed at a running length of over two and a half hours, then was trimmed by about twenty minutes.

Gary Cooper, that cool, relaxed individual, was nervously concerned throughout the production, and easily agitated. He was striving for a definite characterization, endeavoring toward an authentic hillbilly. He was never reconciled to his leading lady. He had nothing against Joan Leslie, the girl Warner was starting to push, but she was barely sixteen years old! Cooper said he felt like some kind of criminal whenever he embraced Joan Leslie for the camera.

About half of the scenes were shot in the Warner studio in Burbank, where Cooper had also been met as John Doe. Other scenes were filmed in various simulated backwoods locations, only a few actually in Tennessee. An unusually conscientious effort was made to give the picture an authentic look, and for adhering closely to the shape and facts of Alvin York's life it established a welcome trend in biographical films. But was it any good?

They certainly thought so in September when it was released. Cooper received the finest reviews of his career for the finest performance of his career. There was a magnificent performance by Margaret Wycherly as Alvin's mother. The inexperienced Joan Leslie was surprisingly effective. Such actors as Clem Bevans and Ward Bond were hill folk to the life, and Walter Brennan was on hand again as the preacher who was a primary influence on Alvin's life and thought.

Sergeant York was not by definition a war picture. Only the last third of the picture focused on his army service with the climactic heroic feat that some believe actually made the war end sooner. The first third revealed York the young hell-raiser, climaxing with his being struck by the fear and glory of God. The second third saw the more dedicated Alvin struggling to make a farm profitable, so he can marry his Gracie. Among films of its era, only *The Grapes of Wrath* surpassed *Sergeant York* as a group portrait of extreme poverty, and without the encumbrance of a sociological tract, *York* was also an eloquent picture of indomitability. The war scenes are well staged, but the strength of the picture is all before that, and there is where Cooper was revealed as an actor of color, range, and spiritual depth. His hillbilly accent was right on the mark, and never better than when he got all riled up and talked a rapid blue streak.

There is now an odd critical disposition toward *Sergeant York*. It is often dismissed as a flag-waving picture, but charges that it is propaganda may be inadmissible. No doubt it was a picture for its time, but its dramatic texture has barely dated. *Auteur* theorists and other Howard Hawks cultists dismiss *Sergeant York* as representing neither Hawks personally nor his best level of work, calling it a "produced" picture rather than a directed one. Jesse Lasky called it the most satisfying event of his movie experience, which spanned four decades; and surely most who remember seeing it would call it a classic.

Shortly after its release, the Veterans of Foreign Wars organization presented Cooper with its distinguished citizenship medal in a Hollywood ceremony that was also attended by the fifty-three-year-old Alvin York. He thought the picture was "perfect, just perfect." So did Charles Cooper, whose house guest the original Sergeant York was.

The VFW award was only the first of many from patriotic organizations, and that was only the beginning. At the year's end the New York Film Critics met to pick Gary Cooper as the year's best actor for *Sergeant York*. That professional body wastes no time, and makes its presentations only a few days after naming the winners. They couldn't find Gary Cooper. He was off hunting with Robert Taylor and no one could reach him. Not until he returned home did he find out he'd won.

America had gone to war by then. When the Japanese attacked Pearl Harbor on December 7, 1941, and the United States declared war on Japan and Germany the next day, *Sergeant York* was playing in theaters all over the country, accomplishing a purpose originally envisioned for it. Toward the end of January 1942, *Sergeant York* received twelve Academy nominations. Gary Cooper was favored to win as best actor, although the nominated competition included an even more historic title role, Orson Welles as *Citizen Kane*. There was a best picture nomination for the producers, one for director Hawks, and almost every creative department cited, including supporting players Margaret Wycherly and Walter Brennan. When the awards were presented in

February, *Sergeant York* earned just two wins, one for William Holmes's editing.

The other winner was Cooper. Since it was a time when he could do no wrong in the eyes of the American people, they would probably have disowned the Academy Awards if he hadn't won.

Cooper received his award, appropriately, from a man in uniform. James Stewart, the previous year's Oscar winner, was in the Army Air Corps, as the first movie player inducted into military service before the war commenced. Stewart wouldn't have been available to play York if Cooper had stuck to his refusal.

Stewart and Cooper embraced, then Cooper capped his brief acceptance speech with, "It was Sergeant Alvin York who won this award. Because to the best of my ability, I tried to be Sergeant York."

Charles Brackett and Billy Wilder, who had written *Bluebeard's Eighth Wife* three years earlier, served Cooper much better with *Ball of Fire*. Cooper returned to Sam Goldwyn's enterprise, accompanied by Howard Hawks, and they cranked up another winner, capping 1941 as Cooper's *annus mirabilis*.

The script grew out of a story Billy Wilder had written much earlier in Germany, about a professorial octet researching for a new dictionary. Cooper as Professor Bertram Potts was involved with the category of slang, and getting unexpected assistance from a burlesque queen. This was pretty mad stuff, bringing Cooper closer to pure farce than he'd ever been. The early war news was all bad, so *Ball of Fire* was welcome escapist fare for the holidays. If it wasn't in the same league with Hawks's earlier screwball classics *Bringing Up Baby* and *His Girl Friday*, it was near enough.

Ginger Rogers originally was set for the carny queen. Either because after winning her *Kitty Foyle* Oscar she thought the part beneath her (as reported) or because she was no longer available, the part was up for grabs. Cooper delivered his *Meet John Doe* co-star to Goldwyn, then later joked that it was a stupid thing for him to have done. As Sugarpuss O'Shea, Barbara Stanwyck took the show completely away from him. Cooper's absent-minded professor was a nice piece of light acting, but Stanwyck was sensational.

Cooper hated his tongue-twisting dialogue. It was "gibberish that doesn't make sense. I can't memorize it if it doesn't mean anything." A typical Billy Wilder sample: "The latest centrifugal research indicates that neanderthal bucolism performed by scientists has proved that syllogism is enigmatic to prolonged resistance, especially in the cavalry . . ."

Cooper charged into Sam Goldwyn's office making a rare demand for a story conference. He emerged muttering, "Two-dollar words okay, but not *ten*-dollar words!"

While *Ball of Fire* was filming, Goldwyn was preparing *The Pride of the Yankees* to follow it immediately. It would be the picture to close out Cooper's contract, although both he and Goldwyn supposed at the time they would renew the association. The Lou Gehrig story, however, would prove to be Cooper's last for Goldwyn, and a fine one for ending their association.

The great New York Yankee first baseman died in June of 1941, only two years after illness forced his retirement from baseball at age thirty-six. He was a victim of a rare paralysis that has a cumbersome medical name but today is commonly known simply as Gehrig's Disease. Within a few days of Gehrig's death, Sam decided to produce the Yankee slugger's story as a straightforward biographical film. Goldwyn contracted the venture through Gehrig's young widow, Eleanor. Paul Gallico did a story treatment that Herman Mankiewicz and Jo Swerling turned into a screenplay obeying Goldwyn's request for "plenty of baseball stuff." Sam even ordered a fat part for Babe Ruth to play himself, even though baseball themes had a jinxed box-office history.

When Goldwyn conceived the project, *Meet John Doe* was playing nationally while Cooper grappled for his characterization of Alvin York. Goldwyn never considered the possibility that Cooper would *not* play Lou Gehrig. The actor's initial reluctance astonished him. Cooper was eager for the De Mille sea spectacle of *Reap the Wild Wind*, which was set for shooting soon after he finished *Sergeant York*.

Sam said, "Forget about raping the wind, that will be the same old De Mille. The Gehrig thing is going to be a *great* picture! Gary, this will be my first production of something that started right in my own head."

He reaffirmed the Goldwyn "tradition of quality" and said he would assert his priority on Cooper's services that the court had given him, and Paramount was up the creek. Cooper could not have been terribly disappointed, even though Goldwyn's obstinacy deprived history of a Cooper-Wayne tandem. Ray Milland replaced Cooper in *Reap the Wild Wind,* and John Wayne was the other male star.

Cooper was fairly confident. If he could play the still-living Alvin York, he should be able to handle the role of the recently deceased Gehrig, who was closer to himself in age, background, and personality. Gehrig, in fact, had been a sort of Gary Cooper of baseball, a quiet hero much admired for his character. Cooper, though, had barely heard of Gehrig. When Goldwyn said, "Gary, this picture is about the *Yankees!*" Cooper was vague about what that might mean. He'd heard of Babe Ruth, of course, and was impressed that he would be working with him in a picture. He explained to Goldwyn that he knew very little about baseball, but he supposed he could learn.

Not know anything about baseball? Sam was incredulous. When little Sammy Goldfish arrived in America from Poland before the century's turn, learning to play baseball was one of the first obligations of adjustment. Sam supposed everyone followed the game. He often went to the local Gilmore Field to cheer the usually downtrodden Hollywood Stars in the minor Pacific Coast League. Cooper hadn't seen a game since old Joe McGinnity was serving 'em up in Montana.

Indeed, they were all shocked that Cooper had *never played* the game. How could he have been an American schoolboy and avoided it?

"Well, I think being in England for three years when I was a kid had a lot to do with it. But I'm not even sure how many bases there are—I know one's home."

They couldn't believe it.

"Well, goddammie, fellows . . . can't somebody teach me?"

Al Hicks, a one-time ballplayer, was hired to teach Cooper how to play the game and resemble one of its professionals. Cooper had to learn the defensive rudiments of first base, and how to run, throw, and slide. The important thing, though, was that he learn to swing a bat. Lou Gehrig played 2,130 consecutive major league games because he was an unbenchable slugger, one of the game's greatest, batting right behind Babe Ruth for a decade, then behind Joe DiMaggio for three more years.

The scouting report was that Cooper couldn't run, couldn't get the knack of fielding, and threw like a girl. That didn't matter; it could be faked, and doubles used in long shots. The good news was that Cooper took to hitting very well. He had a somewhat awkward stance but managed a smooth swing, and he could connect with real power.

Goldwyn had hired Sam Wood to direct because Wood had a specialty line of sports films. Wood was observing Gary Cooper in the batting cage, taking practice pitches at Wrigley Field in Los Angeles. Also watching were Bill Dickey, Bob Meusel, and Mark Koenig, who, like Babe Ruth, were all former Gehrig teammates set to impersonate themselves in the film.

"Coop's beginning to look like a real slugger, isn't he?" Sam Wood beamed.

"He looks all right," Mark Koenig said, "but he don't look much like Gehrig. Lou was a left-handed batter."

It was something that had not occurred to anybody. So it became a matter of Cooper having to learn to bat left-handed, or of making a baseball picture without showing Lou Gehrig at bat. Lefty O'Doul, a former two-time National League batting champion, was hired to attempt a left-handed conversion for Cooper, and soon gave assurance that it was an impossible task. Cooper was about as athletically graceful batting lefty as any other righty would be, and no more than that.

The problem was solved ingeniously. Cooper was photographed batting right-handed. The print, though, was reversed, giving him a left-handed stance with a semblance of normalcy. But it was tricky. The letters on Cooper's uniform, or on other uniforms or even on signs that were within the frame—all had to be reversed, so that in the film print they would be normal and readable. It all worked out for the batting sequences, and nothing was ever said of the fact that throughout the picture—in civilian clothing signing his Yankee contract, for instance—Cooper did everything else right-handed.

The Pride of the Yankees was a strong picture, and Gehrig was a fine role for Cooper. He now seemed to harbor new reserves for depth of feeling. Cooper-Gehrig is serious, genuinely shy, informed by capricious humor: one of his most appealing accounts.

The promise of "plenty of good baseball stuff" was delivered, but the emphasis was more toward the love story that was lachrymose but not cloying. Goldwyn's latest discovery was a sympathetic and quite good actress, although Teresa Wright seemed a shade too young for Cooper. For that matter, Cooper seemed a shade too old to be playing Lou Gehrig. *The Pride of the Yankees* required Cooper to impersonate Gehrig over nearly a two-decade span, from a teen-ager at Columbia University until his dramatic farewell as an active player. Some actors could get away with it, but people had already begun to note that Cooper was not aging well. He had lost none of his handsomeness but the youthfulness was gone; that had been apparent, too, in *Sergeant York*. His face was wrinkling early, and at forty-one he looked perhaps a few years older. So his playing was most effective as the mature Gehrig. In the younger scenes, the audience accepted him because—well, because he was Gary Cooper.

The Pride of the Yankees would become dated rather quickly for its sentimentality quotient, especially as embodied in Gehrig's relationship with his immigrant parents, and in some script hokum involving a hero-worshiping crippled boy. In 1942 it was a critically appreciated work, and a popular success that became the exception to the rule about baseball pictures. Cooper secured another Oscar nomination, although James Cagney's *Yankee Doodle Dandy* was as assured of victory as Cooper's *Sergeant York* had been the year before. Teresa Wright was also nominated for Eleanor Gehrig, as a lead role; but she also picked up a supporting nomination for *Mrs. Miniver* (as Greer Garson's daughter-in-law) and won the award. Walter Brennan played Gehrig's sportswriter friend—his sixth and last appearance with Cooper in a concentrated period. And no one could have played Babe Ruth nearly so well as Babe did.

The mortally ill Lou Gehrig's farewell speech at Yankee Stadium has entered into national legend. For many, it also provided Gary Cooper's finest moment of screen acting.

"Some people say I've had a bad break. But today I consider myself the luckiest man on the face of the earth . . ."

These were Gary Cooper's good days. He played at aw-shucks humility but was inhaling the glory. He gave just a hint of delight that he was stared at when he dined at Romanoff's. He was a glittering sartorial figure, dressed as one who knew he would be watched.

Now they were talking about his being a great actor. This truly embarrassed him, for he didn't know how to react. Still, he liked hearing it; and he was hearing it.

Cooper had entered the Sam Wood phase of his career. Wood was director for four of five Cooper films, broken only by one De Mille affair. While filming *The Pride of the Yankees*, Sam Wood said: "You're positive he's going to ruin your picture. I froze in my tracks the first time I directed him. I thought something was wrong with him, saw a million-dollar production go glimmering. I was amazed at the result on the screen. What I thought was underplaying turned out to be just the right approach. On the screen he's perfect, yet on the set you'd swear it's the worst job of acting in the history of motion pictures . . ."

Wood's statement, of course, had been paraphrased earlier and would be again. Directors and other actors championed him, but most often seemed on the defensive for Cooper when they praised him. The views of Cooper's co-workers were also echoed by some who *never* worked with him, such as the astute director George Cukor:

"He accomplishes really sincere acting with very few tricks. Someone like Gary is dismissed with, 'Oh, he is such a simple person, what he is playing is so simple.' Look at it right up close, and you see it is much more than that, sometimes rather complex, but always subtle."

Everybody wanted him now. It was generally known that his Goldwyn contract was ending and that he owed Paramount only two more pictures. Scripts were making a pile in his Brentwood den, and calls were being made about scripts that could be initiated if only Cooper indicated an interest. Projects were canceled when Cooper revealed no interest, or they sometimes became hits or prestige successes for other actors—*Sahara* for Humphrey Bogart, *The Ox-Bow Incident* for Henry Fonda, *Princess O'Rourke* for Robert Cummings, *Destination Tokyo* for Cary Grant . . .

People advised him, but Cooper picked his own parts. He trusted his instinct for what best accommodated Gary Cooper.

Yet by the end of the war in 1945, his career was finding a valley, perhaps inevitably. His first two screen biographies were his absolute peak.

The Coopers were usually in California when Gary was making a picture, and were usually elsewhere if he was at liberty. The war curtailed European travel, but Bermuda vacations had been regular for several years. Long Island was more than ever their home away from home. They were becoming "the Gary Coopers of Southampton."

Sun Valley was at least an annual thing, though, and the Idaho junkets became more intensified as *For Whom the Bell Tolls* took shape as a mammoth project for the screen.

Hemingway seemed to think he was writing the screenplay. He said he couldn't get Dudley Nichols out of his hair, although Nichols as adapter with no obligations to the novelist surely had a dandruff of Hemingway.

As a screenwriter Dudley Nichols had a distinguished record mainly in association with John Ford. Possibly Ford would have been interested in the *Bell* project were he not in military service, and possibly not. Frank Capra was also off to war, as were two other directors who might have been likely choices to direct the Hemingway special—William Wyler and George Stevens. Hemingway was most anxious about who would have the assignment, although all he seemed to know was that he didn't want it to be Frank Borzage, who had made *A Farewell to Arms*. Cooper was essentially empowered by Paramount to call all the shots, and was even urged to find a director who could also serve as producer. Cooper may have made a pitch for Henry Hathaway, who was no longer at Paramount. That was no problem; most directors were switching studios freely during the war years. Hathaway, though, was in a sluggish career phase—from which he would be resurgent. Cooper definitely felt Howard Hawks's pulse on the matter of directing *For Whom the Bell Tolls*, and Hawks wasn't interested; he hated the book.

Cooper then told Hemingway of how much pleasure he'd had working with Sam Wood on the Lou Gehrig picture, and what did Papa think about asking Wood? Hemingway said he would trust Cooper's judgment. Y. Frank Freeman, the latest production chief to enter Paramount's revolving door, thought Sam Wood was a splendid notion on the basis of his recent record—*Kitty Foyle; Kings Row*; the Gehrig picture. Sam Wood was most receptive to becoming producer-director for the likeliest "biggest" picture of 1943.

Cooper introduced Wood and Hemingway in Los Angeles in mid-1942. Wood, already impressed by the literary reputation, was sufficiently awed by Hemingway's commanding presence. But from the start, Hemingway hated Wood. Perhaps he would have had a jealous hatred of anyone directing a work of his, for it often seemed that writing the screenplay wasn't all that Hemingway wished he were doing. Anyway, he told Cooper that Sam Wood was an ignoramus, devoid of both intellect and charm. Cooper said, "Well, Sam's a lot like me." Hemingway replied, "No, Coop, you *do* have charm."

Hemingway hated most movie people, as he admitted, and especially the pretty-boy actors. The Robert Taylors went to Sun Valley to meet Cooper's famous friend; and Papa loved Barbara, loathed Bob. A Cooper pal Hemingway did like was Raoul Walsh; he thought Walsh had charm in abundance, and they all went trout-fishing together.

Cooper wouldn't bring Hemingway and Wood together any more than necessary. That Hemingway and Wood co-existed without open hostility was managed only by Cooper as intermediary. He said the preproduction work for *Bell* was about as easy as wrestling a mad bull. It may also have been that Sam Wood was telling Hemingway and Cooper one thing, and the people at Paramount something else, about the matter of whether Ingrid Bergman should play Maria, the heroine.

David Selznick had better luck than Sam Goldwyn when he chose a foreign beauty to groom for American stardom. He found Ingrid Bergman.

In 1937 Selznick screened two dramatic Swedish films that held the exquisite, twentyish Bergman in central focus: one that became Joan Crawford's *A Woman's Face* in an M-G-M domestic edition; and *Intermezzo*. Selznick got her under contract, drilled her in English, and prepared an American *Intermezzo* especially to showcase her. In 1939 it was a prestige success with the illustrious Leslie Howard, and she was hailed as a glorious "find." It was still the only American picture she had made when Selznick read an early copy of *For Whom the Bell Tolls* and thought it would be ideal for her, and she for it.

His correspondence reveals that he would have purchased the property but for his exhaustion from *Gone with the Wind,* and his reluctance to tackle a comparably big project so soon. So he lobbied on Bergman's behalf for Maria, and loaned her to other companies in hope that the right exposure would boost her candidacy. In 1941 she was in *Adam Had Four Sons* (their father was the veteran Warner Baxter), *Rage in Heaven* (over Robert Montgomery's psychosis) and *Dr. Jekyll and Mr. Hyde* (this time they were Spencer Tracy). She was good, they were all glossy, none was a solid success.

As early as January of 1941 Selznick knew that Hemingway's choice was Bergman, and Hemingway had queried Cooper on Bergman before that. Selznick believed he had talked everybody into wanting Bergman except the Paramount chiefs, who thought her wooden and dull; and it was Paramount's money. Meanwhile there was spirited competition for Maria. Some starry actresses and not-so-starry ones were lobbying, and Paramount had its own possibilities—most notably, perhaps, Paulette Goddard, who enjoyed some prominence there for several years. The casting of Maria became a running theme for the gossip and filmland "reportorial" columns—not to rival the Scarlett O'Hara ruckus, but to match anything since then. The role became even more a plum since the projected Robert Jordan—Gary Cooper—had risen to such heights.

When *Bell* was ready to go into production in the fall of 1942, Miss Bergman had been inactive a full year. Selznick tried to force Paramount's hand by saying he would lend Bergman to Warner for the possibly lackluster *Casablanca* project if they did not decide on her immediately as Maria. Paramount remained disinterested, and Selznick loaned Bergman for *Casablanca,* and that was that.

Paramount surprised everyone by giving the part to Vera Zorina, a German-born Norwegian ballerina, then married to ballet master George Balanchine. She, too, had been one of Sam's "discoveries," introduced in *The Goldwyn Follies* in 1938. Her screen career amounted to four pictures in which she had made little impact, sometimes billed only as Zorina. But Paramount had signed her for a build-up and had given her a nice specialty number in the *Star Spangled Rhythm* revue film. And she was Norwegian, after all: it seemed that any kind of foreigner could be Spanish in Hollywood, especially for *Bell*. Zorina cropped her hair—a specific demand of the Maria role—and they started shooting the picture in Nevada.

Cooper had been "thinking" Robert Jordan for two years, and must have also done some thinking about Maria. He knew from the start that assigning the Maria role to Vera Zorina was a dreadful mistake that could be fatal to the picture. He didn't convey this to Hemingway, for the author was ranting enough about it already; and if there was anything that anyone could do, there was nothing *he* could do. But the days ticked by, and Zorina continued to exhibit none of the authority that was mandatory for Maria, and Cooper asked Sam Wood if something couldn't still be done.

"Give her time, Coop, she'll be a sensation."

Cooper said no more about it. They worked a few more days, and Wood pulled Cooper aside.

"You were right, Coop. And I've already notified the studio that we're in trouble."

David Selznick said that Sam Wood insisted Zorina had been cast at Buddy de Sylva's insistence; but that De Sylva (Paramount executive producer) and Y. Frank Freeman (studio chief) said the insistence was Sam Wood's. Even so, when Wood sent an S.O.S. to the studio, they sent Sam an S.O.L. He was stuck with Zorina.

Then the recently completed *Casablanca* film was previewed, and word trickled out about Ingrid Bergman's magical showing in a Bogart film that was going to surprise a lot of people. It was all done very quickly: they sent Zorina home, and David Selznick packed Ingrid Bergman off to Nevada.

Zorina showed a lot of spunk, night-clubbing in Hollywood as soon as she was back, flaunting her close-cropped hair. Meanwhile, in Nevada, Ingrid Bergman was falling in love with Gary Cooper. Or if she was or wasn't, he was falling in love with her.

Her leading men generally did. Leslie Howard, cast against type off the screen as one of the great lechers, was believed either to have had a little "intermezzo" of his own, or to have sought one. Perturbations were rumored when she filmed with Robert Montgomery. Spencer Tracy, in the film exercise immediately preceding the one that brought him together with Katharine Hepburn, definitely fell very hard for Miss Bergman; but, as one of Tracy's M-G-M contemporaries said, "Spence knew this was one girl he couldn't have." Bogart, stormily married to alcoholic Mayo Methot when he made *Casablanca* with Bergman, insisted he'd made no advances but admitted he'd been smitten—all of that attested to some years later.

It was not an eroticism but a wholesome radiance that quivered them. She was incredibly beautiful without artifice, and had quick intelligence. She was twenty-six, had a four-year-old daughter, and was married to a doctor who had brought his practice to America and was said to be jealously possessive and dominant toward his wife. He probably knew nothing of Gary Cooper's reputation, else Ingrid Bergman might not have been permitted to go off on location.

There was frequent speculation if Cooper, after marrying, continued to have the same flavor of relationship with his leading ladies that had marked his premarital movie-making. The majority opinion seemed to be probably not. Yet Cooper had become ever more discreet. He knew much more about his deportment than anyone else, since no one knew anything. The same Paramount executive who said Cooper never stopped going after a good thing also said, however, that "affairs of the moment" were strictly that; he was certain that after Cooper married, he no longer *fell*—not as he had fallen for Clara, Evelyn, and Lupe.

That he had fallen for Ingrid Bergman was obvious to members of the *Bell* company because, apparently, he couldn't conceal it, it just showed. It also showed that she was powerfully attracted to him. (In 1968 Ingrid Bergman said, "Every woman who knew him fell in love with Gary.") No one knew what was going on, or *if* anything was going on, but there was speculation. No speculation crept into the Hollywood press, however. Both Hedda and Louella carried production tidbits but spoke only of a professional relationship, nor were there hints by the Sheilah Grahams and

Hazel Flynns, whose columns were sometimes written between the lines.

Sam Wood certainly sensed it. He also must have seen that the Cooper-Bergman love scenes would almost melt the celluloid. In mid-production with *Bell*, he got hold of Jack Warner and said Cooper and Bergman simply had to do the *Saratoga Trunk* thing; it was an Edna Ferber novel Warner had bought two years earlier, ostensibly for Bette Davis and Errol Flynn.

Indeed, Wood should have been grateful for his stars' love scenes. They provided a bonus of tension that was too often absent from the dawdling, 171-minute release print.

For Whom the Bell Tolls is a curiosity piece. When it opened its roadshow engagements in the 1943 midsummer, it looked like the most important event of the decade, with the classiest display advertisements. Its novel was already a "modern classic," it had the stars of *Casablanca* and the York and Gehrig biographies, and Technicolor, which wasn't then commonplace, and there was almost three hours of it. The public and critics alike were downright intimidated. The film received strange favorable reviews. It was a box-office smash about which no one raved. They talked about the love scenes, especially the one in the sleeping bag, lifted from the novel; but there was very little talk of a modern tragedy of sociopolitical substance. The picture brought Paramount ten Oscar nominations including best picture. The two stars were cited along with supporting players Akim Tamiroff and Katina Paxinou. The Academy revealed a shrewdness in not nominating the direction. The only award actually won was Katina Paxinou's, for one of the gaudiest jobs of overacting in the American cinema.

Yet within only a few years, critics would begin to reassess *Bell* and say it was sluggish and dull, and be unable to recall what the Spaniards were so impassioned about. Those Spaniards were actors of predominantly Russian origin, but also Swedish, Norwegian, Italian, Sicilian, and Hungarian. Paxinou was Greek; Joseph Calleia was Maltese. Not a Spaniard in the lot, although Arturo de Cordova was a Yucatán Mexican. In the later "international era" of films, Hollywood couldn't get away with a thing like that. The American Robert Jordan, at least, was played by an

American actor—who was very disappointed in his own performance.

Cooper, despite the consolation of an unexpected diversion or possibly because of it, could not get a hold on the character of Jordan, a man knowingly courting his own destruction. As he later conveyed to Hemingway, he was static, unable to stock his role with variation. "I couldn't show what I was feeling because I didn't know what I was feeling." He showed it when he felt it, but that was when he and Maria weren't thinking about the bridge they had to blow up.

Surely this was a time when Cooper, who often required no help, could have benefited from intelligent direction. Yet Sam Wood, who was not blameless, also could not be the scapegoat. The script was a monstrosity but so was the conception of the movie. Bewilderingly overproduced, it was done in finally by pretentiousness. So is the novel, in the consensus of revised literary criticism. *For Whom the Bell Tolls* now is rated clearly beneath Hemingway's *The Sun Also Rises*, *A Farewell to Arms*, and *The Old Man and the Sea*.

Whatever romantic actions took place between Cooper and Bergman may have had something to do with those magenta Spanish hills of old Nevada. They returned to the filmland from the shooting location and resumed their respective habits of living. Whether Dr Peter Lindstrom heard any of the talk, Rocky Cooper must have. Some months later, however, *Saratoga Trunk* went before the cameras in the Warner studio, with no sparks flying as Sam Wood directed Gary Cooper as Clint Maroon, and Ingrid Bergman as Clio Dulaine. They had a friendly relationship, warm but reserved and highly professional, filming another inflated subject in the fall of 1943. *Saratoga Trunk* was shot, edited, and put into cold storage for almost two years.

Warner elected not to put it into open competition with *For Whom the Bell Tolls*, which played only reserved-seat engagements through 1944, and was slated for national release at "popular prices" in early 1945. Warner expected the one picture to sell the other, hoping to exploit the together-again-by-popular-demand presence of the illustrious stars. Three more Cooper pictures would come and go before audiences would have opportunity to watch Ingrid Bergman outact Gary Cooper in *Saratoga Trunk*.

In May of 1943, Gary Cooper was in Washington, D.C., for a personal appearance promotion for *Bell*. He talked with a high government official about how actors could help the war effort "... and he said just by making pictures, pictures, pictures. They're what our soldiers and sailors in the distant parts of the world want more than anything else. The films bring them nearer their homes, and the more we can provide them with entertainment, good American entertainment, the more they'll be inspired to do what they have to do for us.

"So I say this isn't time to think of holding back and conserving for the sake of one's own box-office prestige or because of high taxes or anything like that. Why, the more taxes an actor can pay, the more he is helping to win the war."

Cooper was doing his part to help win the war. He was believed to have made *Saratoga Trunk* on a profit participation arrangement, with a guarantee of a quarter of a million dollars. So he was going to make pictures, pictures, pictures; but De Mille didn't have the *Wassell* project quite ready. Therefore he would do his part as many other movie stars and players were doing, and become a camp entertainer.

Most of the stars were touring military bases and other scenes of troop concentrations in the Pacific theater, some in Alaska, others in the Caribbean, only a few in the North Africa-Sicily-Italy zone. Many entertainers went right into the combat zones; and after the Normandy invasion they would also do their songs, dances, and skits in Europe.

Some of the players were doing the camp tours whenever they weren't occupied with filming. Others made only one tour, as Spencer Tracy said, "to get it off their conscience." Tracy had toured the northern bases in Alaska and the Aleutian Islands, and no longer felt guilty. He said, "Oh, hell, Coop, go on and do it, it's really sort of fun . . . but once is enough."

Cooper decided he would get it off his conscience. One thing, though: he wasn't going to sing. Tracy said, "Not sing! You have to sing—the worse you are the more they eat it up." Spencer

Tracy was tone deaf and could not carry a tune, and learned to sing his little song in *Captains Courageous* only after tortuous practice. But on his tour of the bases he sang "Pistol-Packin' Mama" with almost no melody but a bit of color, and was a big hit. He told Cooper not to worry, just sing "Pistol-Packin' Mama." It was a pseudo-Western nonsense song that swept the country in 1943.

Cooper signed on for an entertainment tour of army, navy, and marine bases in primitive New Guinea, for five weeks over November and December of 1943. His unit also included Una Merkel, an established and well-liked featured player; Phyllis Brooks, a personable lead in B pictures; and Andy Arcari, a young accordionist.

His conscience should have been thoroughly liberated. He toured camps and outposts in or near combat zones, and conditions seemed more primitive with each succeeding stop. He went a month without seeing a flush toilet. Reporting on his adventure after its completion, he said, "The boys don't have a thing, except good G.I. food—they do have that. And movies, yes, they have plenty of movies."

Most of the movies were new, including prints of some not yet released in the U.S. But old pictures were in traffic, too, and it had to happen: one picture making the New Guinea rounds was *The Adventures of Marco Polo*.

He regularly heard blasts of gunfire and mortar. One night he was awakened by a Japanese bombing attack that ruined some of the camp huts but cost no lives. On returning home, he said, "There's no coin in Hollywood, rich as it is, that can pay a fellow the way I've been paid for my little effort on behalf of the G.I.s out there. It was the greatest emotional experience of my life, meeting those soldiers in the mud, the rain, the jungle of New Guinea, and trying to reassure them that the folks back home are proud of them, and conscious to some extent of what they're doing for America.

"The boys are so appreciative of the slightest little thing you try to do for them, it's almost pitiful. You feel like bawling sometimes, and maybe you do a little, but you're happy at the same time. You're doing something really worth while, at least in the boys' opinions. Those kids'll be sitting out on a muddy hillside waiting for hours for the show to start. It can rain like hell, but they wouldn't think of moving an inch until it's over. Under those conditions, you rise above yourself and give it everything you've got."

Everything he had was "Pistol-Packin' Mama," just about. He craved some variation, but was a washout as an ad-libber, where Una Merkel particularly excelled; so he thought it best to strike a silent Gary Cooper pose and just smile. A G.I. asked him if he could do the Lou Gehrig farewell speech, and Cooper couldn't remember it . . . but another G.I. could, and wrote it all down on a piece of paper. It became a part of his standard repertoire and, he believed, always the best thing. It always brought a complete hush, regardless of the size of the gathering. And soon he was getting choked up every time he said it.

"Oh yes, and 'Mairzy Doats.' We sang that one together, and we'd sing it again and the boys would all join in. Andy on the accordion, he did a terrific 'Mairzy Doats' . . ."

He returned from New Guinea to join De Mille's *The Story of Dr. Wassell*, which was already "shooting around him." In an interview with Edwin Schallert of the Los Angeles *Times*, he said he wanted to quit biographies and do more comedies for a change.

"I'm honestly afraid that the biography business will catch up with me. I've been lucky so far but I can't stretch that luck. They want me to do the story of Eddie Rickenbacker but frankly I'm afraid it's going to become a habit. I think it best to stop right now on this high point of *Wassell*. Now, *Casanova Q. Brown* is a biography-sounding title, but it's not that kind of story . . ."

He really thought *The Story of Dr. Wassell* was "a high point" and so, perhaps, did many folks around the country. It was one of the top grossers of 1944, the best year ever for the movies' domestic revenue, on comparative terms. So he may not have sensed that his pictures were riding a steadily declining trajectory for quality and consequence. *Wassell* was a picture to make his recession visible, and *Casanova Brown*—they eliminated the Q.—continued the curve.

Like Sam Goldwyn with his Lou Gehrig picture, Cecil B. De Mille personally conceived the *Wassell* venture. The publicists' version is that he was listening to President Roosevelt on the radio, and became intrigued by FDR's reference to the remarkable heroism of a Dr. Corydon M. Wassell in the Pacific theater of operations, who saved a group of wounded marines from almost certain death at the hands of the Japanese. A script was produced that took place entirely in a Pacific jungle in a limited time frame, but with Dr. Wassell's biography conveyed episodically in flashbacks.

Gary Cooper was De Mille's first choice, and Cooper said yes. He went to Arkansas to meet the doctor and his wife, and found the Wassells rather more elderly than he expected, and quite retiring. Their life was not all that exciting, but in the fictional world of De Mille it could be made to seem as if it were.

At least it didn't dawdle, although it was plenty long. It was a lively action drama in color; there was much to watch and much to forget. The charming Laraine Day, nominally the leading lady and nicely billed, actually had only a bit part, entirely in the flashbacks. The most interesting character may have been Dennis O'Keefe as a wounded marine whose character was entirely fictional. Cooper was authoritative and the least artificial thing in the picture, with moments of eloquence.

Casanova Brown was a comedy, pleasant enough and efficiently done though bereft of style, but pitifully thin. No one seemed to know it was a remake except possibly Nunnally Johnson, who adapted *Little Accident,* a Broadway farce of the twenties written by Floyd Dell and Thomas Mitchell, for Mitchell to play. Under that title it was a minor early talkie with a twenty-one-year-old Douglas Fairbanks, Jr., in the lead. It was the same role a forty-three-year-old Cooper played as *Casanova Brown*—a man who learns his wife is pregnant while they're divorcing. That's all there was to it; yet Johnson, a top-rated writer who was also producer, wooed Cooper into the project, and Cooper brought in Sam Wood to direct and Teresa Wright to play the girl.

The significance of *Casanova Brown* was that it was the initial release for International Pictures, an independent company founded rather auspiciously by Nunnally Johnson, William Goetz, and former RKO boss Leo Spitz, who arranged International's distribution through RKO. They had no studio resources but had complete editorial control of their product and financial responsibility for it. Profitable pictures offset their shortage of capital, and *Casanova Brown* was profitable. International impersonated a major company by adopting an imposing global logo. Over the years about a dozen International pictures maintained a generally agreeable production standard. Then it was merged with Universal and for some years there was a hyphenated corporate name. ("Fly high with U-I.") Cooper became pleasurably acquainted with the International triumvirate while filming *Casanova Brown*, and reckoned he would like to be a producer with them. He had been saying for a number of years that he would like to try producing his own picture, and nobody believed him.

Actors were saying that all the time, except that more often they wanted to direct. That had no appeal for Cooper, who said, "If I had to work with actors as a director, I'd go crazy." Anyway, while the studio system stayed rigid through the forties, it was almost unheard of for an actor to produce his own pictures. Nunnally Johnson saw that Cooper was serious, and offered to write an International picture for Cooper to produce and star in.

If Cooper was determined to experiment, the time was right for it. He was free as the wind. *Wassell* was his last commitment to Paramount, eighteen years after he joined them, and he was not anxious to make a new studio tie-in immediately. He had awaited further starring bids from Sam Goldwyn, with whom he remained friendly; but Sam believed that comedy embellished by leggy Goldwyn Girls was the formula for wartime escapism. Between *The Pride of the Yankees* and the historic *The Best Years of Our Lives* four years later, six of Goldwyn's seven films were comedies spotlighting either Danny Kaye or Bob Hope. Even after *Best Years*, Goldwyn immediately remade the Cooper-Stanwyck *Ball of Fire* as *A Song Is Born* with Kaye and Virginia Mayo, and had a flop. Cooper secretly favored affiliating with Warner, having enjoyed his association there as John Doe, Alvin York, and Clint Maroon. Meanwhile he gave thought to a property for his producing venture, and thought Western.

He sighed, thinking about having to get back on a horse. His early riding experience had not left him sentimentally disposed toward horses, which to him had become only a sometime necessity of picture-making. He said, "I really wouldn't care if I never rode a horse again. Every time I mount one my back aches." Then he added that "On the other hand, they're safer than bicycles"; he still felt the effects of an injury sustained when he made *Casanova Brown*—a spill from a bicycle.

He almost got a production going on *American Cowboy*, conceived as a hoped-for epic to span thirty years of ranch life up to the twentieth century. That was "announced" by Cooper when he met the press in his new office with its pine desk, white walls, green chairs, tomato-red couch, and lemon-colored rug. Occasionally he would bring up the subject of *American Cowboy* over future years, but nothing came of it. He became attracted to a comical Western story about an inept itinerant cowpoke, and got Nunnally Johnson to write *Along Came Jones*. And Cooper produced it.

It was like the New Guinea camp tour: he got it out of his system and off his conscience. During production he said, "I've come to have more respect for producers than I ever would have. Not for their intelligence but their patience. It's the most mundane job imaginable, and most of it seems to have nothing to do with making a movie, although everything does. Now, I've got a second unit over in Arizona. They shot a lot of takes for a chase scene and I had to do the picking. I guess that's what David Selznick means when he talks about being a creative producer. But I wonder if David has to okay the purchase of some canned tomatoes, like I did."

A writer doing a story on Cooper the producer noted that the actor was easily annoyed by his new duties. Some sketches were brought in from the art and costume departments.

"What am I supposed to do with these?"

"Just initial them for approval, Mr. Cooper."

"Well, they look good to me."

He scratched his endorsement, but disapproved a cotton nightgown for Loretta Young as too frilly: "This is a Western, not a Paris salon."

He had observed production waste over the years and been bothered by it, and *Along Came Jones* was a model of economy. The novelty of Cooper's producing gave it an exceptionally attentive press, however, and it became one of the pictures to merit the "eagerly awaited" description. He got the Norman Rockwell treatment again, and Cooper as Melody Jones was on the *Post* cover just before the picture opened.

Along Came Jones was the most financially successful entry of International's brief history, so Cooper's flirtation with producing got him a passing score. It was an amiable picture but extremely minor—a simple-minded yarn about a simple-minded cowboy. Cooper said self-parody never once entered his mind, but it resembled that and some of his more literate champions took him to task for it. Gary Cooper, the most reliable screen figure for heroism, had not a touch of it as Melody Jones, and 'twas the leading lady that saved them all in the climax. Still, the Cooper personality was nicely illuminated and he was likable. Jones's "melody" was "Old Joe Clark," which Cooper warbled throughout the picture. Jones was a feller who couldn't shoot straight, couldn't shoot at all, but was taken for a fugitive killer who was really Dan Duryea, who had been in Cooper's last two pictures for Goldwyn. Cooper personally chose the entire *Jones* cast, always with stringent economy in mind. (He paid actor Gary Cooper his standard salary, however.)

The economic hiring also applied, oddly enough, to his leading lady. Loretta Young had been in pictures about as long as Cooper and had progressed to valid stardom, but then fell back and was at a career low point when given the *Jones* lead. It was one of the pictures that accomplished a rapid rehabilitation for her, and she reached her own career peak in the late forties.

Cooper hired Stuart Heisler to direct. He had shot a few scenes for *The Cowboy and the Lady*, then graduated from editing to directing minor features for Paramount, where he and Cooper were passing acquaintances. Cooper was fond of a little boy-and-dog picture called *The Biscuit Eater*, which grew into a sleeper for Heisler at Paramount, and he said Heisler was really the first director he thought of . . . after considering the likely salary demands of the Hawkses, Hathaways, and Woods.

Along Came Jones, at least mildly a hit in its spring 1945 release, is regarded more with contempt by the scholar-critics. Cooper seemed pleased with the picture, but said he'd never produce another one. Within a few years most stars would start becoming their own producers, and he would ride with the trend; but he would hire someone else to buy the tomatoes.

While he was becoming a producer in 1944, Cooper was also becoming a conspicuous party politician. It was a presidential election year, with the Democrats' Franklin Roosevelt following his unprecedented third term with a bid for a fourth one. The war news now was mostly good, and there was a general belief that victory was imminent. The Democrats said, "Don't change horses in the middle of the stream," and the Republicans claimed Roosevelt had been in the middle of the stream for eleven years.

"I've been for Roosevelt before . . . but not this time!" During the campaign, that statement, prominently attributed to Gary Cooper and displaying the actor's handsome face above it, was the basis of frequent full-page advertisements in major newspapers, paid for by the Republican National Committee. Cooper was himself extremely active on behalf of the Republican ticket led by New York's governor, Tom Dewey. Cooper gave speeches, did some entertaining for fund-raisers, was on a dais with Dewey in Los Angeles, and did some personal campaigning in the film community.

Whether Cooper had ever really been "for Roosevelt before" would have to be questioned. Possibly he voted for Roosevelt in 1936 during the second-term landslide. If so, it was not disclosed publicly. His visible voting pattern was straight Republican, with an element of heredity; Charles Cooper was an often vigorous partisan in Montana, and stuck to his beliefs in California retirement. Gary Cooper voted for Coolidge once and Hoover twice, including the 1932 election won by the challenger Roosevelt. He openly supported Wendell Willkie in 1940.

The liberals started going after him now. In 1943 Cooper was one of the founding members of the Motion Picture Alliance for the Preservation of Ideals, called merely "the Alliance" in the film colony, and increasingly illuminating Hollywood's extreme right wing. Its other early leaders included actors Robert Taylor and Adolphe Menjou; directors Sam Wood, Norman Taurog, and Clarence Brown; and producer Walt Disney. Clark Gable, thought of as one whose apolitical inclination was even more pronounced than Cooper's, was also a member. The Alliance's cheerleader was Lela Rogers, Ginger's feisty mother.

The film community was on the threshold of great internal strife and political turbulence. Within a few years it would, in fact, lose the unity that had made it a community, and become a war ground for two opposing camps. In 1947 the House Un-American Activities Committee, featuring a spectacularly aggressive freshman congressman named Richard Nixon, would undertake its investigation of Communist infiltration of the film industry. The picture people were especially vulnerable after a showdown between the Conference of Studio Unions and its individual components—but especially the Screen Actors Guild—on a plan to strike the industry. The conservative element finally prevailed in the Guild, led by the enterprising Ronald Reagan. But for many years to come, Hollywood was split wide open; and many would contend it was never again the happy place it had been for most of them.

It was typical of Gary Cooper that he could be firmly identified with one of the warring elements, yet keep the friendship and respect of most in the opposing group, as perhaps none of the other right-leaning actors could. Gradually he withdrew from the battle. Many believe that he had been sucked into it by Sam Wood, one of the more reactionary filmland politicians, and the most vocal leader—with Adolphe Menjou—of the Alliance.

Sam Wood is almost unique among movie directors who were once beheld as giants, merely for being virtually forgotten today. Most directors are somehow remembered, for the scholarly attention of the postwar "film generation" put their work under scrutiny, and the work has been written about and the directors' work formulated—especially as reflected in and by the *auteur* theory of film criticism. Yet Andrew Sarris's definitive *The American Cinema: Directors and Directions, 1929–1968* gives individual consideration to two hundred directors of the American talking screen, including many peripheral or extremely minor figures; and Sam Wood is not among them.

He was a journeyman director throughout the silent period and into the talkies, and became an M-G-M reliable. Supposedly he was the only man in town who wanted to direct a sports picture, so he made the silent *One Minute to Play* with the Galloping Ghost from the University of Illinois, Red Grange; and he made *Navy Blue and Gold* with James Stewart and Robert Young as football players at Annapolis. That was not his only qualification for directing the Lou Gehrig picture, however. Sam Goldwyn was obsessed with quality, and Sam Wood surfaced unexpectedly as a quality director in the immediate prewar years with *Goodbye Mr. Chips*, *Our Town*, *Kitty Foyle*, and *Kings Row*. When Capra, Ford, Wyler, and Stevens all went into military service, Wood appeared to have the major reputation among directors still working in Hollywood, and *The Pride of the Yankees* enforced that reputation and led to Wood's directing *For Whom the Bell Tolls* and *Saratoga Trunk*.

Then, no directorial reputation ever plummeted so quickly or thoroughly. After the inconsequential *Casanova Brown*, which was his last with Cooper, he had a string of rank failures broken only by the success of another baseball picture, James Stewart's *The Stratton Story*. Perhaps Wood should have made only baseball pictures.

To compare Cooper's performances in his Sam Wood pictures is intriguing. Cooper's Lou Gehrig is a remarkably complete performance, deeply felt, yet Cooper knew little of Gehrig before making the picture. Possibly Sam Wood had strong convictions about Gehrig and imparted them to Cooper, but had no similar convictions about Robert Jordan, Clint Maroon, and Casanova Q. Brown. Cooper is a strangely vacant actor in these roles that are partially redeemed only by his unmistakable presence. It would appear that when Sam Wood was toppled from the reputation he lacked the ability to retain, he brought Gary Cooper down with him.

Saratoga Trunk opened in November of 1945 on a reserved-seat basis in the well-known "key cities." It came at a time when Gary Cooper badly needed a good picture; or better, a strong one. Even the people who enjoyed *Casanova Brown* and *Along Came Jones* had begun to ask if such trifles now were all that was to be expected of him. The irony was that *Saratoga Trunk* appeared to be a whopping hit, at least at the outset, and despite a critical reaction that was lukewarm at best. Yet it did nothing for Cooper and he was almost lost in it. It was a big hit for Ingrid Bergman.

A further irony was that when *Saratoga Trunk* was filmed almost immediately following *For Whom the Bell Tolls*, Cooper was a much bigger star than Miss Bergman, but by the time the picture was released she was clearly a bigger star than he was. In fact, she was at that point bigger than any of them. Nevertheless, the cumulative effect of the ambiguous or otherwise disappointing Cooper films after *The Pride of the Yankees* could now be seen. They had all been financially successful, but in them he had stopped resembling a major screen actor. The belated release of *Saratoga Trunk* figured to restore him, but it only emphasized his downward trend.

After completing *Saratoga Trunk*, Ingrid Bergman was directed by George Cukor in *Gaslight* and was the Academy-honored best actress for 1944. Some thought it was a deferred Oscar for her near miss as Maria in *For Whom the Bell Tolls*, but it hardly mattered. *Gaslight* was a great success; and *Spellbound*, the Hitchcock piece that was her first credit for epochal 1945, was an even greater one. When Warner released *Saratoga Trunk*, RKO was also unveiling Leo McCarey's *The Bells of St. Mary's*, teaming Miss Bergman with the other incumbent Oscar winner, Bing Crosby. It would lead the year's pictures in the measure of ticket receipts. All of this had the effect of bringing Miss Bergman to a point of celebrity perhaps unpredecented in films. She would follow with yet another rousing success, for Hitchcock in *Notorious* with Cary Grant, before accomplishing an astonishing plummet of her own.

As a costume period piece set mainly in New Orleans, *Saratoga Trunk* came alive only occasionally, through Bergman's spirited and surprisingly colorful portrayal of a notorious Creole charmer named Clio Dulaine. She was the only worth-while thing in the picture. It was popularly believed that the distinguished Flora Robson was given a supporting Oscar nomination only out of sympathy for having been ludicrously made up as a mulatto. As for Gary Cooper—well, he had got by as Robert Jordan, but the critics wouldn't let him off the hook as the gambler Clint Maroon. He looked the part, and just kept on looking it, and the consensus was that he had seldom been so lacking in vitality. This clearly initiated a trend among critics to downgrade Cooper as an actor.

The trend was more discernible in 1946 when his only release was not even compensated by a nice financial return but was a failure on all counts, if not such a failure as to be regarded a flop. As a free-lance actor, he collected $300,000 to appear in *Cloak and Dagger* for Warner Brothers. It was what it sounded like—an espionage drama, stuff about the Office of Strategic Services (OSS—later the CIA) inside Germany. It was directed by the once-great Fritz Lang, with whom Cooper had strained relations throughout the filming. Cooper played an atomic scientist clearly modeled after Dr. J. Robert Oppenheimer. Critics generally said he was dull and lacked fire. Opposite him in her first American film was the thoroughly international actress Lilli Palmer.

She had come to Hollywood only to accompany her husband Rex Harrison, who in *Anna and the King of Siam* was the king to Irene Dunne's Anna, long before Rodgers and Hammerstein conceived one of their better musical ideas. As Lilli Palmer tells it, "I was just standing around in Hollywood and someone told me a German actress was needed for a Gary Cooper picture, and I thought what better way to begin my American career than in a Gary Cooper picture and decided to look into it. He was then the very biggest star in American films, which meant the biggest in the world, or at least that's what I thought. I knew I was lucky when they gave me the part. Then we made the picture and— well, it didn't turn out in a way to make anyone happy."

She enjoyed working with "adorable" Gary Cooper, and was astonished by his nonchalance when working. When she queried him about it, he said, "Kid, this is a cinch."

If he was complacent, the commercial report on *Cloak and Dagger* jarred him awake. The situation seemed to call for a blockbuster picture, so he accepted a call from De Mille and went back to Paramount for *Unconquered*.

It was a colonial yarn mounted on a huge scale but mounted on cardboard. *Unconquered* may have made money but not even the De Mille fans regarded it with affection. The critics who usually were rough on De Mille anyway tore this one to ribbons. Apparently that was what sent De Mille scurrying back to the biblical security of *Samson and Delilah*. It was Cooper's last De Mille picture, and his least. His performance remained in its recent rut, but he fared no worse than Paulette Goddard, Boris Karloff, or anyone else connected with *Unconquered*. Collectively, though, his reviews were the poorest he'd received since *The Adventures of Marco Polo*.

While he was with the Paramount studio, he got roped into one of those self-indulgent revue pieces, with film stars all playing themselves in vignettes wrapped around a thin story line featuring a studio "hopeful." The *Variety Girl* was Mary Hatcher, whose career very nearly ended where it began. It was an echo of the long-ago *Paramount on Parade* and was also the flop that finally killed the Paramount series. The wartime *Star Spangled Rhythm* had been a huge commercial success, the follow-up *Duffy's Tavern* much less so. The foremost achievement of *Variety Girl* seemed to be that it introduced a briefly popular song called "Tallahassee," which was sung by none other than Alan Ladd. Gary Cooper just stood around and said yup, and was almost the most uncomfortable person on the scene. The *most* uncomfortable was surely Barbara Stanwyck, forced to give a kind of commercial for the Variety Clubs in a conversation with Joan Caulfield.

An interesting appointment of the Paramount all-star pictures was that the studio avoided the "starring in alphabetical order" diplomacy and hit the issue head-on, telling people exactly how its stars were rated. Gary Cooper was the only one of the twenty billed stars not then actually working on Paramount contract, but people still associated him with the company. In mid-1947 he rated third billing, behind Bing Crosby and Bob Hope. The others in order were Ray Milland, Alan Ladd, Barbara Stanwyck, Paulette Goddard, Dorothy Lamour, Veronica Lake, Sonny Tufts, Joan Caulfield, William Holden, Lizabeth Scott, Burt Lancaster, Gail Russell, Diana Lynn, Robert Preston, William Bendix, Sterling Hayden, and Barry Fitzgerald.

Looking pained in *Variety Girl* and uncomfortable in *Cloak and Dagger* and *Unconquered* invited the thought that perhaps he wasn't comfortable at all. Cooper said he was "unhappy" while making *Unconquered*, but added that "it wasn't so much with the picture as with the way things were just going generally." The remark was taken to mean the way things were going in Hollywood in the first postwar years, with the mounting intramural political tension. It could have meant much more than that.

"Things" were certainly not going generally well with his career, and may not have been going well in his private life, and probably each element directly affected the other.

To all outward appearances, the Coopers appeared quite happy, or they appeared settled. They traveled everywhere together, and with the charming Maria made a splendid family picture. They also became a more visible public couple in the Hollywood of the mid-forties. Rocky had continued to bloom, and in her thirties was one of the more stunningly glamorous ladies of the filmland. She and Cooper rated as one of the colony's finest dancing couples, although he said, "I'm Charlie McCarthy and she's Edgar Bergen. Rocky just pulls the strings and it looks like I'm doing the dancing."

Yet Hedda Hopper would say a few years later that it was during this period that the Coopers "drifted." After the Ingrid Bergman speculation, there was no suspicion of Cooper being diverted, and no thought seemed ever given to how Rocky might have been spending time that was her own. The Coopers appeared friendly toward one another, perhaps rather formal for a married pair; yet daughter Maria appeared to have splendid individual relations with both her parents, and with them as a couple.

In 1946 Charles Cooper died in his eighty-first year. Not long afterward, Alice Cooper implied rather clearly that she disapproved of her granddaughter's being raised a Catholic. Alice in her widowhood became increasingly outspoken but was also taken less seriously by Hollywood folk, who were already aware of how she doted on Gary. Hedda Hopper made it a practice to telephone Alice regularly after Charles died, just to be friendly with her and ask no questions, but listening to everything Alice said. And Alice talked. Gary Cooper probably was never lax in paying dutiful attention to his mother, for whom he undoubtedly had a deep and special affection. Alice, though, said she didn't see nearly enough of him; and she expressed fear that Rocky was trying to turn him into a Catholic.

Meanwhile Gary Cooper continued to age harrowingly. For the Technicolored issue of *Unconquered* he presented a problem for the make-up experts, who were required to make a withering forty-six-year-old actor suggest a young frontier hero. When several "takes" of a scene were compared, the one selected might not be the best one dramatically, but the one showing Cooper to best advantage physically. He didn't look comfortable, but he also didn't look well. Perhaps he wasn't.

He believed he was overdue for a comedy, and found one he thought might restore some of the *Deeds* magic.

If Cooper reckoned that a Leo McCarey comedy would be more substantial than something like *Casanova Brown,* surely anyone would have agreed with him in 1948. McCarey had not made a picture since the sentimental Crosby tandem of *Going My Way* and *The Bells of St. Mary's* had made him a superstar among directors. Furthermore, champions of vintage McCarey were cheering a return to comedy for the man who once had made *Ruggles of Red Gap, The Awful Truth, Love Affair,* and even the Marx Brothers' deliriously anarchic *Duck Soup.*

When McCarey said, "This is going to be Coop's comeback," it was out in the open that Cooper's estate had fallen. So, recently, had the status of Ann Sheridan, who in the mid-forties had been Warner's glamor queen and a well-liked saucy actress. The new picture figured to help both stars, and some people felt they could hardly wait to see it.

But *Good Sam* was hardly any better than *Casanova Brown.* The picture, which was both produced and directed by McCarey from his own story, was very minor comedy in the Capra idiom about a man like Longfellow Deeds, who gives his money away and gets into trouble. McCarey had lately become obsessed or maybe possessed by ultraconservative political philosophy, and the fact that his character of Sam was rather obviously allegorical was only one indication that he was carping at the U.S. government and its own give-away tendency.

Still, it was a comedy that might have worked a few years earlier. The moviemakers were very slow to grasp how radically the war and the new postwar sophistication had altered the taste of the movie-going masses. Not even Capra himself could get with the new rhythm. Capra's marvelous *It's a Wonderful Life,* probably his definitive film, could not find a wide enough audience, even with a brilliant James Stewart performance; nor could Robert Riskin's piddlingly Capraesque *Magic Town,* also with Stewart. The criteria were changing, and now television was arriving, and everything was uncertain. *Good Sam* was a product that rather typified the dilemma.

It was cute, hokey, maudlin. To its benefit was a Gary Cooper who did not appear uncomfortable but relaxed and apparently enjoying himself. He and Ann Sheridan played charmingly. Possibly Cooper could not have been any better, but there could have been no surprise in performing a role that seemed bent on defining his limitations.

Good Sam was no comeback and Cooper knew it. He also knew it was time for him to obtain the security of a long-term contract, because maybe time was running out for him.

While he was still shooting his "comeback picture" he had his business manager I. H. Printzmetal and attorney Arnold Grant explore the various studio possibilities. The Cooper market value appeared to have declined only at M-G-M. Other studios, including Paramount, were ready to compete for him, but he could practically write his own ticket at Warner. So he did. On October 31, 1947, he signed a flexible contract for as few as six pictures or as many as ten, renegotiable in five years and carrying a bottom guarantee of three million dollars. His signing was big news in the film community, suggesting that Gary Cooper was still a superstar, if slightly tarnished.

Several projects were discussed as possibilities for his first Warner picture under contract. Some were things he could do merely as routine, such as *Silver River*, which was finally made with the fading Errol Flynn. Cooper was determined to get a property with a pre-established aura of importance.

He chose *The Fountainhead*. Ayn Rand's novel had been hysterically embraced by many readers, and was a huge best seller. It was foreseen as a prestige picture, and would enlist a young actress being groomed by Warner for major dramatic stardom.

She was Patricia Neal.

9

TROUBLE IN PARADISE

PATRICIA NEAL ADMITTED years later that she had been
warned about Gary Cooper.

Was she on her guard? No, she knew she could take care of herself. As a beautiful girl making her way in the legitimate theater,
she had always been able to before.

She was a Kentucky girl who had always wanted to act. She entered the highly respected theater arts department at Northwestern University for training she may not have needed. She was
a natural, with instinctive command and early evidence of technical discipline. When she arrived at Northwestern, the star actor
on campus was Charlton Heston. When she left, she was the star
campus actress.

On Broadway she became a replacement, several actresses removed, for Margaret Sullavan in the long-running *Voice of the
Turtle*. Pat Neal was only twenty then, but she already had a
commanding varnished voice and mature bearing. She would
never have to dwell in the ingenue purgatory. Lillian Hellman,
the playwright who would become her strong friend, saw what Patricia Neal had and then saw that she got a great part. For *Another Part of the Forest*, Miss Hellman brought back her charac-

ters from *The Little Foxes* but revealed them in their youth. Patricia Neal was the young Regina, whose mature self had given Tallulah Bankhead a great stage role and had also been a terrific showcase for Bette Davis in the splendid Goldwyn-Wyler film of it. *Another Part of the Forest* was not nearly as successful a play as *The Little Foxes*, but its reviewers put Miss Neal in the Bankhead-Davis league.

Every film company was interested, but Warner Brothers more so. They signed Patricia Neal, brought her to Hollywood, and undertook the most elaborate personality build-up in the studio's history, expecting to deliver a major star right from the post. The star build-up was not characteristic of Warner. Such actresses as Bette Davis and Olivia de Havilland were under contract there several years before proving themselves largely on the basis of their spunk and perseverance. Of course it helped to have powerful talent, but Warner was customarily slow to realize that women could have it. Men, yes: Robinson, Muni, Flynn, Cagney, and Garfield came along and were stars after their first vivid exposures. The Humphrey Bogart who drudged in second-lead heavies for half a dozen years was merely the exception that proved the rule. In any reckoning, the Warner faith in Patricia Neal was extraordinary. Obviously, everyone else thought, she couldn't miss.

That she eventually emerged as one of America's most respected actresses on both stage and screen and one of its most admired women may obscure the fact that she did miss, in the beginning, at Warner. It was not her fault. The build-up, more than anything else, harmed her, made her employers expect too much of her too soon—all at a time when the movie audience was diminishing and it was becoming ever more difficult to build a star. She missed; but that was not foreseen in 1948 when she met Gary Cooper.

They met at the Warner studio before either had been cast in *The Fountainhead*. Their first meeting was perfunctory, inconsequential. Warner had been a chummy studio in earlier days but its collective personality had changed. The Flynns, Sheridans, and Dennis Morgans were all playing out their contracts. The next Bette Davis picture would be her last for Warner, and there was mutual hostility between the star and the front office. Otherwise it would seem that Miss Davis would have been figured for

Dominique in *The Fountainhead*. But like Gary Cooper, she wasn't aging well, and the talk was of younger actresses. The early talk was of Barbara Stanwyck, actually months older than Davis; but Stanwyck had always been any age and ageless, displaying an early authority like Pat Neal's. Stanwyck was also never an ingenue. However, she was then no longer in the Dominique sweepstakes. Ida Lupino, whose employment generally had been in roles discarded by Bette Davis, was thought to be the front-runner. A younger, promising actress wanted the part—Eleanor Parker.

For the role of architect Howard Roark, only Humphrey Bogart's name was being mentioned, and he wasn't sure he even wanted the part. Bogart was slightly older than Gary Cooper but with his toupee didn't look it; and Warner wanted him in *The Fountainhead* because he was their most solid star, at the box office and every other way—more solid than the recently signed Gary Cooper, although such things were not discussed. They wanted Bogart in the picture to help make it a big hit and bring a large audience to see Patricia Neal. Even during all the talk about Ida Lupino and Eleanor Parker, they were planning to give her the part although Pat Neal didn't know that.

When she met Gary Cooper she was filming *John Loves Mary*, the comedy that would give her the "introducing" treatment, in the company of Ronald Reagan and Jack Carson. Although a light thing, it had been a big Broadway hit and Warner expected to duplicate the success commercially on film. They elected to defer selecting Miss Neal for *The Fountainhead* until the approximate moment that *John Loves Mary* finished shooting. The strategy, then, was to have her follow a comedy bull's-eye with a powerful drama, opposite a star of Bogart's magnitude.

Meanwhile, back in Brentwood, Rocky Cooper was reading *The Fountainhead* and being enthralled by it. She was a reader, Gary wasn't, and she kept him informed of what was going on in the world of books although she made it a point never to advise him on matters of his career. She had to be aware, though, that his star stock had fallen in the measure of prestige and that he needed a strong picture with an interesting role to play in it. So she broke her rule, and advised him to go after *The Fountainhead*. Cooper read the book and had a reaction similar to that of *For Whom the Bell Tolls*. It seemed ambitious. The leading role was more challenging than anything he'd had in years, if ever; but it was also a time when he should be courting challenge.

Cooper revealed his interest and everyone at Warner seemed delighted, especially in view of Bogart's dawdling reticence. King Vidor, the distinguished director assigned to the distinguished project for which Ayn Rand was doing her own adaptation, was especially pleased. The Cooper and Neal casting announcements were made almost simultaneously, and the picture was put into production late in 1948.

He was forty-seven; she was twenty-two.

And they made the picture that Rene Jordan calls "King Vidor's Wagnerian freak." It is a tempestuous dramatic exercise, spewing Ayn Rand's "objectivist" philosophy, which some people say espouses individual integrity and that others call foolish selfishness. Cooper as Howard Roark was Miss Rand's spokesman, as the artist—in this case an architect—who refuses to be compromised and corrupted by evil power and big business, is crucified, and remains the rebel. Miss Neal as Dominique is the classy, high-strung young lady who believes in him, and loves him passionately through their difficult, stormy, ultimately triumphant relationship. The picture has a high gloss; the production is overblown but in an impressively controlled way. It is now considered a credit to its director, even though counted a failure; and it was counted a failure in its 1949 release, though not a flop. It almost worked as a somewhat ludicrous American Gothic, and there were well-praised performances by Miss Neal and Raymond Massey. The critics gave careful attention to Gary Cooper's performance, sheathed their disappointment in diplomacy and euphemism, and still managed to convey the thought that he had ruined the picture, and a part for which he simply lacked the capability or the intellect, or both. The picture with which Cooper hoped to revive his reputation did it major harm that seemed irreparable.

But it was a star's performance, and Cooper tried very hard. It is one of his most consciously concentrating performances. His Howard Roark is not overdone but is unusually active; it isn't underplaying and it isn't just being Gary Cooper. It fails, but mainly in scenes of rhetoric where Roark is confronted by his tormentors. His scenes with Patricia Neal, which now are viewed with consciousness of their romance and its mythology, are quite arresting.

They did not immediately fall in love. Hollywood film production is an anthology of romances initiated with clashing cymbals on the first day of shooting, and ending with the cast party. Patricia Neal in her later interviews has said it was a gradual thing that only evolved in their heavy acting together.

The young Gary Cooper worked with some fine actresses— Marlene Dietrich, Sylvia Sidney, Helen Hayes, and Miriam Hopkins before his marriage, Ann Harding and the unfortunate but decidedly talented Anna Sten only shortly afterward. During his big-star period, however, he had worked with only four actresses who were strong in a professional sense—Jean Arthur, Claudette Colbert, Barbara Stanwyck, and Ingrid Bergman. Colbert and Stanwyck were Cooper's good friends, and their husbands were even closer friends to him. Arthur was also married, and the nature of her personality would also suggest that romance between her and Cooper might have been impossible. That left Ingrid Bergman, whose husband Cooper had only met formally, and who filmed with him in the wilds of nature.

Patricia Neal, too, was a strong actress and an intensely dedicated one. She was also unmarried and gloriously young, and classically beautiful. It was not in Gary Cooper's nature to be able to resist her, especially when they entered into zealous preparation for roles that cast them as tormented lovers. Cooper would not talk about their love affair during or after, but he implied that he had tried to resist as he had never tried to resist before, because of his genuine feeling, and because of his high regard for a young woman he didn't want to hurt. The problem was not just Gary Cooper. There would have been no problem if Pat Neal had really been able to take care of herself, but she fell in love instead.

"Ah, my love," Patricia Neal now says wistfully when someone brings up the subject of Gary Cooper. He might never have become her love had she been teamed with him in such a soufflé as *Casanova Brown*, or if he rather than Ronald Reagan had played John to her Mary. Their romance was born of dramatic dedication, and both supposed it might end with the picture; possibly both were hoping that. But it did not end, and even though it may have tapered off a bit, they were soon brought together in another picture.

Miss Neal might not even have been cast in *Bright Leaf* with

Cooper if the Warner people were aware of their involvement, or could have foreseen the imminent extent of it. But the romance was not generally known although logically it should have been suspected. King Vidor said it was near the end of shooting before he began to suspect anything. Apparently it meant too much to them to talk about with other people, and Gary Cooper was honestly ashamed that he was cheating.

Mutual friends of the Coopers have said that Rocky became aware of the affair early and was tolerant, figuring it would probably go away. After almost sixteen years of marriage, she probably thought she had her man pegged. But in all of Cooper's hinted postmarital romances, none had involved a girl who wanted to get married.

Patricia Neal has said that when she knew or began to feel that she wanted to marry Cooper, she was determined not to tell him. If it were to happen, it would have to be all of his own doing. She doubted it could happen. Cooper never disparaged his wife and only spoke highly of her, with admiration certainly, and also with affection. He was no forlorn man saying "my wife doesn't understand me"; if anything, Rocky understood him too well. Then, throughout the years of their marriage, Rocky had become an increasingly more devoted Roman Catholic. It was unlikely that she would consent to a divorce if Gary asked for one, but it was almost as unlikely that he would ask.

Then there was the matter of Maria Veronica Cooper, apple of her father's eye, eleven years old when he started filming with Patricia Neal. Surely above all else, Cooper did not want to hurt his daughter.

When *The Fountainhead* was getting clobbered by the critics and Cooper was filming *Bright Leaf* with Miss Neal, he made it unnecessary for her to tell him of her desire to get married, or to stop trying to hide it. He brought up the subject himself, and told her it was impossible. He and Rocky had too much of themselves invested in a long-term mutual commitment. He wished to be fair to Rocky in every way. He regretted having to hurt anyone, and knew he was hurting everyone including himself, but knew, too, that Pat would be the one most hurt.

Indeed, they tried to break it off; or they broke it off more than once. It was an affair of starts and stops, during which more and more people naturally came to know of it. Not while the Coopers continued to live together was the Pat Neal romance written about, unless readers were alert to extremely subtle hints in the gossip columns, or the guess-who type of tidbit that doesn't name names. The filmland establishment that thrives on gossip can occasionally show extraordinary respect, especially toward respected veteran stars. The Hollywood press did not acknowledge that there was a love affair between Katharine Hepburn and Spencer Tracy until almost twenty years after it began. The community showed similar respect for Cooper, whose May–December romance they probably expected to erode very soon.

Instead it was that cliché, the thing that became bigger than the two of them.

When Gary Cooper made pictures at Paramount in the thirties, it took only three months on the average between the time the cameras first rolled and the time the picture opened in theaters. A modest major feature would be shot in six to eight weeks. It could be edited in two weeks, and there were instances of important productions being test-previewed only ten days after shooting halted. The exploitation campaign—posters, display "wafers," billboards, press releases—was underway while the pictures were in production. Theaters had their schedules booked long in advance, often with firm dates for pictures still before the cameras.

That was the well-oiled studio system. It was the same at the other studios, although M-G-M customarily had a longer shooting schedule than Fox (later 20th Century-Fox) or Paramount, while pictures at Warner were shot with even greater dispatch, and years later look all the better for it. Columbia's rare major features, like those of such independents as Goldwyn and Selznick, generally were produced on scales as elaborate as M-G-M's, while even Universal's most ambitious efforts were shot very quickly.

This rhythm held through the prewar years, with some slight change. The subject that could be shot in eight weeks in 1933 required perhaps ten weeks in 1939. Nevertheless, the picture finished in May could be released in July. During and after the war, the complicated logistics of increasingly sophisticated production and the convoluted dogma of the labor unions made it ever more difficult and finally impossible to emulate the old rhythm. A film might go into production in January and finish in June, be edited and previewed in dissimilar versions, then might not be released for another six months. There was an evident trend to hold the likeliest major hits for December release to qualify them for the Academy Awards, whether the finished print was ready in February or October.

The *Saratoga Trunk* instance was by no means unique. In 1941 Frank Capra filmed *Arsenic and Old Lace*, which was a big hit of the Broadway season. In releasing the film rights, the producers of the play stipulated that the movie could not be shown until the play ran its course. *Arsenic and Old Lace* ran three years, and the movie was not seen until 1944—by which time it had the unusual aspect of the renowned Cary Grant playing opposite a girl—Priscilla Lane—who had washed out of pictures two years earlier. In 1946 Howard Hawks made *Red River* with the brilliant young Montgomery Clift but would not release his independent production until he had the kind of distribution arrangement he wanted; and when *Red River* was released more than two years later, the audience was already acquainted with Clift in *The Search*. Another Clift picture and a great one—*A Place in the Sun*—was shot in 1949 and not released until mid-1951, simply because director George Stevens spent more than a year editing it. Furthermore, it was a Paramount picture, and in the years 1947–52 there was often a full year's lag between a Paramount project's completion of shooting and its theatrical release.

The Fountainhead was filmed in 1948 and released in mid-1949. When Gary Cooper and Patricia Neal started work on *Bright Leaf*, audiences had become acquainted with Miss Neal in two pictures and she had completed a third one. Cooper, too, had started and finished another picture between *The Fountainhead* and *Bright Leaf*—a naval thing called *Task Force*. The Warner brass had not reached an opinion on whether Cooper's expensive contract was going to be a liability in the wake of the reception accorded *The Fountainhead*, but apparently they had already given up their hope of building Miss Neal into an important star. Such were the logistical curiosities of the lame-duck studio system as it closed the forties and limped into the fifties.

John Loves Mary had not been the hoped-for smash comedy. Neither a hit nor a flop, it was just there, it was cute, it came and

Above,
the gunsmith in the workshop
of his Brentwood home.

Left,
with Rocky at a Screen Actors Guild
gala in 1940.

The 1941 Oscar-winning players: stars Gary Cooper *(for* Sergeant York*) and* Joan Fontaine; *supporting players* Mary Astor *and* Donald Crisp.

Appraising a Louisville Slugger with Babe Ruth, who played himself in Cooper's The Pride of the Yankees.

Left,
Maria Cooper shows what a five-year-old
skier should wear in 1942.

Below,
camp entertainers Una Merkel,
Gary Cooper, and Phyllis Brooks
give autographs in Hawaii en route to
New Guinea in December 1943.

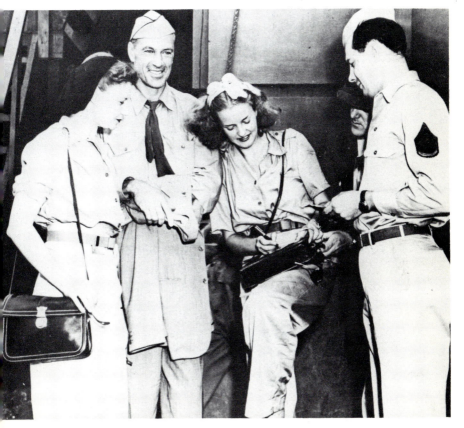

On the hunt with Ernest Hemingway and Taylor "Bear Track" Williams in 1943.

With Alice Cooper, his mother, and always his strongest booster, in 1946.

Cooper gives voluntary testimony to the House Un-American Activities Committee investigating communism in Hollywood in October 1947.

Patricia Neal and Cooper, when their romance was just starting.

Left, definitely one of the lighter moments during the often troubled filming of High Noon; with Grace Kelly. Right, recuperating in New Orleans from one of four hernia operations.

Down in Mexico in 1953, Cooper and supporting actor winner Anthony Quinn celebrate news of their Oscar victories with Ward Bond, Barbara Stanwyck, and Ruth Roman.

Left, with Greer Garson and Audrey Hepburn at the Friars' testimonial banquet for Cooper four months before his death. Right, Cooper usually had a sketch pad on the set; here he's drawing Barbara Stanwyck between takes for Ball of Fire.

Rocky, Gary, and Maria Cooper in Hawaii during the wonderful last years.

went and didn't lose money. Ronald Reagan perhaps had already begun to slip at the box office and Jack Carson was also on the downslide after a smart mid-forties display. More important to the Warner interests, Patricia Neal's comedy seemed the least bit forced, suggesting that heavier stuff should be her forte. They were banking on *The Fountainhead*. From what they had seen of the early rushes and then the rough cut, they were confident of a hit picture and less worried about Pat Neal. They assigned her to *The Hasty Heart*, which would probably be the best Warner picture of the year (December 1949 release) and easily the best she did for them; but they didn't know that yet in August while it was being edited. By that time they knew that *The Fountainhead* had failed and that Patricia Neal had not created a strong public reaction.

From that point, it is apparent that they just dropped her. The assignment to *Bright Leaf* is the first indication. It certainly looked like a big picture when it went into production, but Miss Neal was given only the second lead. Playing opposite Gary Cooper was Lauren Bacall. Miss Neal's next assignment—*Three Secrets*—was a showcase for three young actresses, but Eleanor Parker was in the primary focus while Ruth Roman had the showiest role. Miss Neal was star-billed in a good picture with John Garfield, *The Breaking Point*, but the "supporting" Phyllis Thaxter was functionally the female lead. Two more distinctly minor assignments completed her Warner contract, which was not renewed.

A player who isn't "making it," who is damaged goods, exists in a discouraging and hostile studio environment. Even if the romance between Pat Neal and Gary Cooper had been able to override the more easily seen complications, it would have been antagonized by professional tension—which was compounded by Cooper's career also adhering to a dismal trajectory. With the sausage-factory rhythm of the older studio system, *The Hasty Heart* might have saved her. But before it had rehabilitated her prospects, *Bright Leaf* probably killed them.

It brought together several veteran top hands at Warner, most notably director Michael Curtiz and cinematographer Karl Freund. Writer Ranald MacDougall had professional credentials. There were five billed stars to head a quite gaudy cast—Cooper,

Bacall, Neal, Jack Carson, and Donald Crisp, then revered as the dean of all Hollywood actors. The bright leaf was tobacco and Cooper was a "young" farmer rising to status as a cigarette-making tycoon. Patricia Neal was the bad woman who married him, Lauren Bacall the good woman who finally saved him from her. The actors were all competent, the project had the advantages of "production values," and it was dull, inspiring none of the affection that used to make people want to go to the movies.

The Cooper picture that preceded it, *Task Force*, offered surprisingly little action and much anguish of dubious motivation for something that ran two hours. The picture that followed *Bright Leaf* was a thoroughly undistinguished Western, lazily titled *Dallas*, with Ruth Roman. During this time Cooper was being glimpsed for a few seconds (as was Miss Neal) in an "at the studio" scene in *It's a Great Feeling*, built around the new Doris Day; and glimpsed for a few minutes in the unbelievably awful *Starlift*, appearing as himself and "singing" something called "Howdy, Stranger, I'm a Texas Ranger." *Dallas*, though, was the key. It indicated the Warner strategy of committing their expensive veteran star to bread-and-butter pictures that were sure to turn a small profit. They knew what he could do, and in *Dallas* he did it.

Before 1950 was over, Patricia Neal was gone from the Warner studio, her last contracted pictures to have release early in 1951: *Operation Pacific* with John Wayne, and *Raton Pass* with Dennis Morgan. Very soon afterward, she signed a star contract with 20th Century-Fox, which hardly made better use of her; but she was happier there—the tension was gone. Most close observers of the Cooper-Neal situation assumed there would be no "situation" with her gone from the Burbank studio. Instead, it was only after she left that the romance bloomed fully. They no longer saw one another at the studio, but they *had* to see one another; and thenceforth they met generally in more private atmospheres.

On October 23, 1947, Gary Cooper appeared in Washington before the House Un-American Activities Committee, not under subpoena but responding to invitation to give testimony on the status of Communist infiltration of the American motion picture industry. Before taking the stand, he joked with the congressmen that while he would endeavor to co-operate, perhaps they shouldn't trust him; after all, the Hollywood Women's Press Association had just voted him the least co-operative star (with Jennifer Jones his counterpart among the actresses).

The committee members just loved him. It was apparent throughout the sessions of the House Un-American Activities hearings that the congressmen had gone Hollywood in a big way; this was their show, and they loved meeting all the stars, whether they were crucifying Larry Parks or being regaled by a friendly witness like Gary Cooper. Other friendly witnesses appearing at the same session with Cooper were Robert Taylor, Robert Montgomery, George Murphy, Ronald Reagan, and the aging Adolphe Menjou. Montgomery had long been active in Republican national politics as a committeeman and later would be White House adviser in the Eisenhower administration. Murphy would serve as Republican senator from California, with a reactionary voting record. Reagan would become governor of California and the national champion of extreme conservatism. Taylor, Menjou, and Cooper would all retreat gradually from the political fracas that had splintered Hollywood, but only Cooper would eventually make a show of repudiating what he had done.

He never recanted his testimony, or said he regretted having been a friendly witness. He became conciliatory, however, during the subsequent, lamentable period of the blacklist. As an independent producer, he eventually hired players and technicians who had been blacklisted. He did say he had never wanted to see any actor lose the right to work, regardless of what he had done. Eventually he was under heavy pressure from the militant Hedda Hopper to renounce his professional association with Carl Foreman, but he stood by Foreman. He did believe that writers had gotten away with a lot in the way of propaganda, including two of the "Hollywood Ten" who went to jail for refusing to testify—Albert Maltz and Ring Lardner, Jr., authors of Cooper's *Cloak and Dagger* screenplay.

Shortly after the HUAC appearance, the films of Cooper, Taylor, Montgomery, Murphy, Reagan, and Menjou were banned first in Hungary, then in Czechoslovakia, and eventually in most of the Iron Curtain countries. So were those of Ginger Rogers and also, curiously, those of the tenor Allan Jones, seen usually in minor program features and also no militant.

On the witness stand Cooper himself had been nobody's militant. More than any of the witnesses, he made light of the Communists. Sure, they were in Hollywood just like they were everywhere but they were only a small fraction, giving the large patriotic body in the film community a bad name it didn't deserve. After his testimony, he received a standing ovation and vigorous applause. He later told Robert Taylor with a grin that "I got a much bigger hand than you did."

He got a bigger hand than any of them, and he must have loved that. He liked to be liked, hated to be hated, and hated to hate, and wished he could be friends with everyone.

He finally made the grade. Liberals who never forgave the other friendly witnesses generally made an exception of Gary Cooper. He had that kind of charm.

In 1950 Gary Cooper had an immense wardrobe for his dressing room, which was in itself an impressive size. His three double-door closets contained twenty-five suits. Fourteen drawers held his shirts and ties. They were mostly white shirts, a fetish with him; they were all expensive. One of his closest friends was Eddie Schmidt, his tailor. Cooper was not one to buy a clutch of clothing to tide him over a season and not go in a store until the next spring; Eddie Schmidt expected to see Gary Cooper every week.

He liked silk striped ties. The most prominent labels on his suits were Brooks Brothers and Peale of London. His sportswear was Kerr's. He loafed in moccasins by Farkas & Kovacs. He was elegant.

For a while his favorite car was a Lagonda, an English roadster with right-wheel drive. Then it was a Jaguar; but he always had a lot of cars and never lost his little boy's thrill with them. He gave Maria toys as presents often, and they were mostly cars and trains —little boy's things for someone he saw was sufficiently little girl anyway.

He knew all the wines, the best labels, the vintage years. He never stopped enjoying steaks but he acquired exotic gourmet tastes, and his favorite food was lobster. Joan Bennett said he was one of the two most sophisticated and well-dressed men in Hollywood, the other being Spencer Tracy.

The most sophisticated woman in Hollywood easily could have been Rocky Cooper. Despite their current triangular problem, the Coopers shared an aura of living that both adored. It was precious to Gary, and during the period of his back street romance he made a real effort to preserve it. There was a separation of sorts late in 1949 when Rocky took Maria to New York for Christmas without him, then took up residence at the River Club. That there was an official break was denied all around, however. Then, as a couple and as a threesome with Maria, the Coopers had extraordinary visibility in 1950 during what was most likely an uneasy reconciliation. They were seen surfboarding; they were swimming at Malibu and San Onofre; they were hunting in the Imperial Valley, or going after quail, duck, and dove north of Bishop. They were still doing Sun Valley. They skied and skied. The sport he took up late became his favorite pastime, and later he even tried scuba diving. At forty-nine, though looking strangely old and drawn, it was said that he had "the spring and reflexes of a college athlete."

Meanwhile the Coopers were glorified by their daughter. Maria was a blossoming beauty, resembling both parents but neither one too much. She was bright, cheerful, animated but poised, extremely sophisticated but ingenuous.

Cooper purchased seventeen acres and a large house in Aspen, Colorado, intending to develop it as a ski lodge. He was a major investor in the development of Aspen as a popular resort. He even went on a ski junket there with his old ego rival Clark Gable, just the two of them. He narrated and appeared in a two-reel featurette called *Snow Carnival* that Warner made at his urging, to help promote Aspen. He went to Aspen often with Rocky and Maria, and then less often; and finally, when they weren't going at all, he sold his interest there.

Toward the end of 1950, he was not being seen with his family anywhere. They were sometimes being seen without him; but there was no "news."

He made some more pictures.

Henry Hathaway was directing for 20th Century-Fox—had

been for a number of years, with consistent success that had given him reputation as one of the old reliables of the business. Old reliable Hathaway had a comedy that he thought old reliable Cooper would like, if he was amenable to an outside assignment.

Cooper was amenable when he read the script of *U.S.S. Teakettle,* which was loaded with good laugh lines; and perhaps he failed to see that few of the good lines were his. It was about inexperienced junior officers, all ninety-day wonders including Cooper, their decidedly mature commander on the *Teakettle.* It was an experimental craft equipped with steam turbine instead of the conventional diesel engines. The sailors, of course, were all incompetent to manage the craft, and that was the comedy. Actually it worked quite well, the fun yielding only now and then to the tedious obligatory scenes between Cooper and Jane Greer, co-starring as his wife and appearing none the happier for it. There were very engaging accounts by Eddie Albert, Jack Webb, and Millard Mitchell, and the harrowingly old-looking Cooper was at least amiable while being very thoroughly upstaged.

When *U.S.S. Teakettle* opened in New York in February of 1951, and in a few other eastern cities shortly afterward, the reviews were mostly complimentary and a few were quite enthusiastic. Its professionalism was appreciated. The first audiences really laughed, but they were small audiences. The subsequent audiences continued to laugh on cue but the audiences were getting smaller, not larger. The film was withdrawn, new titles were prepared, and it was called *You're in the Navy Now.* It played its first engagements on the West Coast under its new title, and didn't even get the good reviews. It was one of the brighter screen comedies in a season of too few of them, and it was a box-office disaster.

Now the word was out: Cooper's through. He couldn't even sell a *good* picture that was a sort-of sure-fire formula to begin with . . . or once had been.

Indeed, Cooper had just disappeared altogether from the *Motion Picture Herald*'s annual survey of the top ten box-office performers. He had been on the list nine successive years, moving up and down it but always being there, proof that he was still a guarantee if only as a commodity star. He had lost even that.

Another outside assignment required little of him. Dore Schary invited him to don his cowboy suit and be a kind of host and introducer of the vignettes, addressing himself to the theme that *It's a Big Country*. Schary had recently taken charge of production at M-G-M and this was his own pet project. It got fabulous press coverage while shooting under several directors, recalling Paramount's antic *If I Had a Million*. Then it opened in late 1951, played a few engagements, and was withdrawn out of embarrassment and hasn't been heard from since. It squandered a warehouse of first-rate talent: Fredric March, William Powell, Gene Kelly, Ethel Barrymore, Janet Leigh, Van Johnson, Keenan Wynn . . .

Back at the Warner studio Cooper finally got to make a picture with one of his favorite guys, Raoul Walsh. *Distant Drums* wasn't a Western exactly, but a historical "Eastern." There weren't any cowboys but there were plenty of Indians until army officer Cooper routed 'em, in pre-Civil War Florida. It was professional. It came and went.

Then he made *High Noon*.

There were also some he didn't make. He almost went to RKO for one called *Cowpoke* conceived especially for him. He said yes, but it went on the shelf and was never removed. He was also set at Warner with *Captain Dagger*, which sounded like more of the same junk, but also got canned.

He organized his own company once more, calling it Baroda and buying film rights to Alfred Hayes's best-selling novel *The Girl on the Via Flaminia*. He paid $40,000 for the rights, and $10,000 to Hayes for a screenplay. Bent on self-redemption, he wanted to appear in it with the young Montgomery Clift, the hottest actor in the business and also one of the best. Cooper could not arrange financing but broke even on his investment by selling the property to Leland Hayward and Anatole Litvak with the stipulation that Montgomery Clift would have to be in it. The film was never made. Litvak, however, eventually made a film of *The Chase* much later, with Marlon Brando in the sheriff role that was being talked of in 1950 as Gary Cooper's likely stage debut. John Hodiak took the role in Horton Foote's play when Cooper was unable to clear time with Warner Brothers, if indeed he tried.

He read a few other scripts. There weren't as many coming in as before, and the ones coming in weren't any good.

By the fall of 1950 nothing still was being written about Gary Cooper and Patricia Neal but everyone in the film community knew about them. It was widely assumed that the Coopers had arrived at an understanding, an "arrangement." All of his public appearances were with Rocky. He was living at home; but he was seen going to and coming from Miss Neal's apartment on Levering Drive in Westwood Village, more or less regularly.

Then Rocky and Maria went to Southampton. At Thanksgiving, Cooper was in Hollywood finishing *U.S.S. Teakettle* and telling friends he hoped to wrap it up in time to "patch up the rift" before Christmas. He made it to Southampton for the yuletide, and later the three Coopers came home together. In January, Louella Parsons reported that Gary was in Palm Beach with Rocky and Maria "and they seem to be ironing out their difficulties." No difficulties had been acknowledged, but that pried the lid and now all the column hints were not oblique, nor mere hints.

Surprised by a reporter who asked if she were in love with Cooper, Patricia Neal said, "Could be, maybe, but I'd be silly to advertise it, wouldn't I? After all, he's a married man."

He was also her delivery boy. Mildred Dunnock has amusingly related that when she was waiting in a New York hotel to receive a script Miss Neal was to send her, she was surprised to have the script delivered personally to her door by Gary Cooper.

Or were the Coopers really still living together? Rocky and Gary still occupied the same house but were seldom there at the same time. Without Rocky, he went on promotion tour for *U.S.S. Teakettle* before its rechristening and was gone several weeks. (The tour was not a roaring success: on the stage of New York's Roxy Theater, Cooper's personal appearance was said to be an embarrassment of stage fright.)

Cooper was photographed in the social company of Robert Taylor and his girl friend, Ursula Thiess. Taylor had asked Barbara Stanwyck for a divorce, and newspaper displays hinted that perhaps Cooper soon would follow Taylor's lead. At last it was revealed that Cooper had himself "taken hotel rooms."

Gary and Rocky Cooper separated in May of 1951. The news was played down, as if the "real" news was still to come. Hedda, Louella, and Sheilah were all saying of course, that the breakup was no surprise. Louella Parsons awaited the outcome somewhat guardedly and predicted that Gary and Rocky eventually would get back together.

Michael Rennie, who was then filming *The Day the Earth Stood Still* with Miss Neal at 20th Century-Fox, said the powerful gossip columnists were killing Pat's career with hostility when they should at least be giving her professional support and allowing people to lead their own private lives. It wasn't in lurid colors, but Pat Neal was being painted as a home-wrecker.

Cooper was gone awhile for location work in Florida on *Distant Drums*. When he returned, he and Miss Neal began to be seen together in public. Both appeared relaxed and "happy." But Cooper notified several Hollywood café owners rather formally that if they allowed pictures taken of himself and Patricia Neal in their establishments, he would sue them.

Through all of this Cooper gave steady evidence of poor health. In August he entered St. John's Hospital in Santa Monica, where Dr. Arnold Stevens performed a hernia operation. Before he was fully recovered from surgery, he drove south to the La Jolla Playhouse near San Diego to see Patricia Neal and Vincent Price in *The Cocktail Party*. He had made prior arrangements to assure that no photographers were present, but he chatted amiably with reporters. "Oh, I liked it very much. I had already seen the play in New York with Alec Guinness, and I thought it was awful. I've never been able to get with T. S. Eliot anyway. I called it *The Yakking Party* and didn't understand the yakking. But after I saw it I read the play, and then I knew what it was about. Hey, Pat's great, isn't she?"

He did not avoid the press but he avoided the subject. He would tell reporters that his four favorite pictures were *A Farewell to Arms, Mr. Deeds Goes to Town, Lives of a Bengal Lancer,* and *Sergeant York*. He would tell them about some interesting properties that his Girl Friday, Eve Ettinger, was researching for his Baroda company. He would tell them about the picture he was going to make for Stanley Kramer. He wouldn't tell them about Patricia Neal, and would sock them for any mention of her name.

Very soon Rocky was said to be dating "other men." For that matter, Cooper was dating other women. One was Kay Williams Spreckels Topping, who a few years later would become the fifth Mrs. Clark Gable. Another was Tyrone Power's former wife, Annabella.

It was reported that Graham Sterling, Rocky's attorney, was drafting her terms for a settlement. The Hollywood *Reporter* said, "When the Gary Coopers get around to making their property settlement, they'll have a cool three million to divide." Rocky had already issued a statement that "I am a Catholic and under no circumstances would I consider absolute divorce."

After finishing *High Noon*, Cooper was back in the hospital for the removal of a duodenal ulcer. Pat Neal was at bedside. Rocky sent flowers, as she had done when he had hernia surgery. In December Cooper was making no statements about his private affairs, but newspapers were quoting his "friends"—names not revealed—to the effect that Cooper was planning to marry Pat Neal and get a house. First he would move out of his bachelor hotel quarters and get a kitchen so he could cook.

Cooper took Pat Neal to Cuba to spend the Christmas holidays with Ernest and Mary Hemingway. They had all come over from Palm Beach after some midwinter pigeon shooting. Hemingway's biographers have indicated that Cooper was anguished, wrestling with a decision, and seeking counsel from Hemingway for a decision he would still have to make entirely by himself.

In January of 1952 the gossipy tidbit was that a millionaire businessman had flipped over Rocky Cooper and was desperate to marry her. Then it was revealed that Rocky was dating Bob Six, former husband of Ethel Merman, and an airlines executive who was definitely a millionaire businessman. By January 30, if she was quoted accurately, Rocky had completely changed her tune: "Any time Gary wants a divorce he can have one."

Patricia Neal, accosted by reporters, told them politely to go away. She was reported "cautiously elated."

In an official sense, nothing more seems to have been said. Very soon afterward, word spread in Hollywood and was picked up by the newspapers that Gary Cooper and Patricia Neal had decided to stop seeing one another, at Miss Neal's request. There was a report that Cooper had reached an apparently final decision not to seek a divorce, and that Miss Neal was not favorably disposed toward continuing their romance on the back street. However, a friend to both Cooper and Miss Neal said, "He solved the problem by doing nothing about it. Gary couldn't make up his mind because he's a mass of indecision, and Pat reached the point of having had enough."

They had tried to stop seeing one another before, but had always given in and responded to their hearts, not their heads. The wagering was that they would get together yet again.

Pat Neal fooled them. She saw no more of Gary Cooper, and began dating British author Roald Dahl. In 1953, when she was twenty-seven, she married Dahl and since then has lived with him primarily in England. The Dahls had five children, one of whom died tragically. There has been much drama in their lives, and their steadfastness has won them international admiration.

Patricia Neal did not fare well in her second studio contract. After five pictures she was let go by 20th Century-Fox. She did some impressive stage work, and Elia Kazan brought her back to the screen for A Face in the Crowd. She gave a great performance, and a few years later another one in Hud made her the Academy-honored best actress. She co-starred with John Wayne in In Harm's Way and at last was an authentic star. Then she had a massive stroke, and the world waited as her life hung in the balance. She recovered, for the exultant experience of The Subject Was Roses, and another Oscar nomination.

She is a great lady who still calls Gary Cooper "My love."

When it became apparent that Gary Cooper would not continue his romance with Patricia Neal, it was generally assumed that he would return to Rocky—no doubt almost immediately. Instead they continued to go their separate ways. Sometimes they would be together by design, with Maria; and at other times by accident, as when they met at parties and were friendly but not inclined to mix.

In mid-1952 the Cooper reconciliation-watch became almost a daily thing. Walter Winchell wrote: "The Gary Coopers apparently have made up. They are said to have leased a tepee in the new Carleton House on 62nd and Madison, soon to open."

Anticipating the back-together announcement, Louella Parsons noted that "The three Coopers look happy dining at Romanoff's."

Two weeks later Miss Parsons reported that the reconciliation, if there was to be one, apparently had been deferred. Gary Cooper had gone off to the Caribbean, alone, to do some fishing before starting work on *The Springfield Rifle*.

Also in the 1952 spring, Cooper went to New Orleans where Dr. Alton Ochsner, a renowned specialist, performed a second hernia operation. Next year Dr. Ochsner would fly twice to Europe for follow-up surgery, in Paris and Biarritz. Inevitably, rumor circulated that Gary Cooper was dying.

"If you made up a character like Coop, nobody would believe it. He's just too good to be true."

That was Ernest Hemingway speaking. If the evidence in all the Hemingway biographies were synthesized, it would probably reveal that Cooper was Hemingway's "best" friend when they were together. He was the one person in whom Hemingway apparently could find no fault. And that's curious.

Papa had a multitude of friends for he was a vibrant, exciting man who loved being in the vortex, and people were drawn to him. He was also thorny, arrogant, and difficult. He was intolerant of certain personal failings in people, and would have nothing to do with such people even though Gary Cooper had some of those same personal failings. As Hemingway grew older he became more spiteful, but even in his youth he eventually would fall out of friendship with most who were close to him. He continued to have fallings out with many people, but it is believed he never had any kind of strain in his relationship with Cooper, nor any grievance except those dealt with playfully.

He was a great tease, and was delighted that Cooper could be teased. He teased Cooper for his impeccable dress, and boasted that he himself was a champion slob. He teased Cooper for his illiteracy, although he despised other people for their lack of reading sophistication.

He told Cooper that "I like to be the best in everything I do. If I couldn't be the best writer I know, I wouldn't want to write. It goes with hunting, too. I only hunt with people who can't shoot in my league. You're the exception, Coop. You're a better shot, but I'm honored to challenge you."

Each admired the other's gun collection. Hemingway said, "Coop, if you die before I do, are you going to will me that Hornet?" Cooper had a .22 Hornet with a German telescopic sight, and Papa coveted it. Cooper said he would will it to him; he also said, "Hell, I might just decide to give it to you now so I can watch you enjoy it"; but it was his own favorite possession.

Hemingway was always vocal about hating the first version of *A Farewell to Arms* with Cooper and Helen Hayes, although he hated the second one with Rock Hudson and Jennifer Jones about equally; but he liked Cooper's Frederic Henry. He told Cooper that the character of Robert Jordan in *For Whom the Bell Tolls* was conceived in Gary Cooper's physical and spiritual image. Papa gave lip service to the overblown 1943 film version, said he liked it; privately he was disappointed, but never conveyed to Cooper any dissatisfaction he may have had with Cooper's portrayal. Indeed, he endeavored to withhold from Cooper Maxwell Perkins's displeasure with both the Cooper and Bergman accounts.

In an age of Freudian literary criticism, there has been much speculation in recent years over whether Ernest Hemingway may have had latent homosexual tendencies. There is easy agreement among Hemingway scholars and other critics that Papa was never actively homosexual, but the fact that he protested his masculinity so much in his books and in his life has aroused suspicion. Hemingway's tendency to beatify in Gary Cooper the qualities he found beastly in other persons is provocative.

A Hemingway scholar has maintained that Papa was profoundly impressed that Cooper was such a stud. He said, "I believe that in his mind he loved Gary sexually, but I believe furthermore that Gary Cooper never once suspected it. If I am correct, that proves the beauty of Gary's naïveté, which Papa always found so charming."

Cooper completed a Warner Brothers Western, *The Springfield Rifle*, in mid-1952 and departed almost immediately for the South Seas to film James A. Michener's *Return to Paradise*. He was accompanied by Roberta Haynes, a striking brunette.

She had made only one inconsequential film appearance, and would have no important credits afterward; but she was Cooper's leading lady in *Return to Paradise*. That was because she was his latest girl friend, and he told the director, Mark Robson, that he wanted her in the picture; and Robson said well, all right.

They made the movie in the Samoa archipelago. Cooper learned to play the bongo drums, but it was not sufficient to sustain the romance through the shooting schedule. They parted, after which Cooper spent most of the next two years outside the United States.

On the eve of his departure for Europe in 1953, Cooper dined privately with Dorothy di Frasso in New York. The aging countess, grown rather portly but still chic, had experienced and lost another "great love"—the gambler, mobster, and Las Vegas developer Bugsy Siegel, whose famous murder was later suggested by the *Godfather* film. Through the years Cooper and the countess had remained in close touch despite little direct contact. They had many friends in common among the international set, and one of Dorothy's frequent companions in New York was a theatrical producer named Anderson Lawler.

Cooper was in Europe the next year when Dorothy di Frasso died suddenly aboard a train, shortly after leaving Las Vegas with an illustrious entourage after partying with them there. She was sixty-six.

Cooper's plan was to spend eighteen months outside the United States in order to obtain tax reductions. He made three films in Mexico. When he wasn't filming, he was an international playboy, blazing through Paris, Rome, Madrid, Stockholm, Amsterdam, and various lascivious ports of call, inhaling the high life all the way. Sometimes he would be joined in his travels by Rocky and Maria.

Cooper was presented to Queen Elizabeth at the annual Royal Command Performance in London, the first since her coronation. The film was Walt Disney's live-action rendering of Sir Walter Scott's *Rob Roy* and Cooper did not find it rousing, nor did Richard Basehart, who also attended.

Cooper crash-landed in a plane in North Luffenham, England, but no one was seriously injured. In West Berlin he represented the Paris Office of the American Federation of Labor at an international conference, and remarked that the Soviet police reminded him of Berlin storm troopers in the same city fifteen years earlier.

There were news photos of Cooper attending the Jacques Fath show for summer fashions in Paris, accompanied by Mrs. Paul Nelson as his traveling secretary. Soon it was revealed that he had become involved with one of the models, the lithe Giselle Pascal, who had also appeared in a few French films. There was much talk and lively newspaper gossip that Cooper had taken Mlle. Pascal away from Europe's most eligible bachelor, Crown Prince Rainier of Monaco, who sent Cooper a caustic handwritten letter on the subject. Cooper and the French girl were photographed everywhere; then Giselle suddenly disappeared from his life, and Cooper was with another French girl—Lorraine Chanel, also a model. At different times it was rumored that he would marry one or the other, and both girls encouraged the speculation—especially Mlle. Chanel, who also accompanied Cooper to Mexico.

When queried about his intentions toward Giselle Pascal, Cooper told newsmen, "I'm afraid I can't talk about that. My wife might not appreciate it, and she's coming over here with our daughter next week."

Collier's produced a lavish display in a 1953 issue of Gary Cooper and his wife and daughter as world travelers. Nowhere in the article or captions was there a hint that the Coopers remained officially estranged, or even that they had ever been apart.

When the three Coopers toured Italy, they ventured off the main road to visit the village of Mignano Monte Lungo, near Cassino. There they had an emotional meeting with Raffaela Gravina, a fourteen-year-old Italian girl they had supported for several years through the Adopted Parents Plan for War Children. The primitive villagers were stupefied by the luxury of Cooper's brand-new Mercedes-Benz.

They did Rome, Florence, and Naples, and visited the Pompeii ruins. Rocky and Maria helped him select material for some custom-tailored suits. When his wife and daughter returned to America, Cooper stayed on in Europe, until his next film commitment in Mexico.

He was much in the news. Another *Collier's* spread, the photography dating to the production of *Return to Paradise*, offered a sequence of Cooper spearfishing in Samoa and impaling a rare kahala. He was doing a lot of spearfishing. He would also fly to Bermuda on a caprice, just to get in some skin-diving.

Everywhere he went he was cheered, sometimes mobbed. He cut a dazzling swath and flashed his famous grin. He seemed to be loving it all. One reason he was so apparently happy was also one of the reasons he was being cheered and mobbed: he was on top once more. In his time away from home, his career took an upward swing and he retrieved all of his lost prestige.

In the spring of 1954 he returned home. He went to Southampton and he and Rocky immediately enlivened the Long Island social set. Were they about to reconcile? Apparently not: he headed for California; Rocky stayed in Southampton.

In July, Rocky and Maria returned to California. The Coopers built a new house in a beauty spot of West Los Angeles called Holmby Hills, and it was largely of their own design.

Gary and Rocky Cooper moved into the new house and were happier together than they had ever been; and truly, they lived happily ever after.

10

☆ ☆ ☆
_____
☆ ☆ ☆

THE LAST HERO

WHEN *High Noon* went into production in the fall of 1951, it was just another new movie project, about which some pessimism might reasonably be expected.

The producer was a critics' darling whose "message" pictures didn't always make money. Later, as his own director of some potent commercial successes, he would be the critics' whipping boy. In the fall of 1951, Stanley Kramer had a recent credit record of six pictures. *So This Is New York,* derived from Ring Lardner's *The Big Town,* was a funny offbeat comedy and a thudding flop. A very different Ring Lardner story, *Champion,* was a smash hit that made a star of Kirk Douglas. *Home of the Brave,* about racial prejudice among soldiers in combat, was a prestige success that did only so-so business. Despite good reviews and a strong performance from a brand-new actor named Marlon Brando, *The Men* had been a cash-register disappointment. *Cyrano de Bergerac* had been an unexpected box-office hit and had given Jose Ferrer an Oscar. The sixth completed Kramer picture hadn't been put into release, but the grapevine report was that *Death of a Salesman* couldn't possibly make the grade, despite Fredric March's gaudy portrayal of Willy Loman.

One reason the critics favored Kramer in 1951, other than his obvious sincere quest for quality, was that he had started small and appeared to be staying small. In an age of rapidly escalating production costs, every Kramer picture had been held well below the million-dollar level, and some much lower than that. He did not overproduce (as eventually he would) and he relied on a small but talented and discriminating team. Perhaps the most vital member of Kramer's group was Carl Foreman, who had written five of the film scripts; he had not done the adaptation of Arthur Miller's play.

The Austrian-born Fred Zinnemann rated as a comer among directors. His only credit for Kramer was *The Men*, but he had been coming along nicely at M-G-M with such as *The Seventh Cross, The Search, Act of Violence*, and *Teresa*. The presence of Spencer Tracy in the wartime *Seventh Cross* notwithstanding, these too were all "little" pictures, revealing a conscientious and growing director.

So there was some cause for cautious optimism about the Western they were calling *High Noon*. That was offset, however, by the enlistment of a veteran star who had seen better days. In fact, all the talk was that Gary Cooper was through. He had been likable, successful, and mostly good over a long haul, but his talent seemed to have deserted him, he no longer made important pictures, and wasn't pulling his weight at the box office even in the sleazy ones. Even his marriage had broken up, after eighteen years. Furthermore, he was fifty now, and rumored to be in poor health.

Other than the highly respected Thomas Mitchell, none of the supporting cast could cause a ripple of excitement. There were two quasi-leading ladies, and both were completely unknown. A young Mexican actress, Katy Jurado, had appeared in only one film made by a U.S. company—*The Bullfighter and the Lady*, actually shot in Mexico. The Philadelphia aristocrat Grace Kelly had been limited to a bit part in Henry Hathaway's *Fourteen Hours*.

It went into production: the story of a marshal in a frontier town named Hadleyville, who learns on the day of his wedding that some outlaws are coming into town, sworn to kill him. He knows they mean business; he's scared. He goes all over town looking for help, but everyone in town is cowardly and wants to save his own neck. The outlaws come to town; there is a showdown; the marshal dispatches his tormentors without help except —crucially—from his bride, who is a Quaker, opposed to killing.

That was *High Noon*. It was produced independently, and production went smoothly enough. It was made carefully by conscientious craftsmen, and they thought they had done a good workmanlike job. They ran it off to see what they had and were not displeased. Then they previewed it and it was a disaster. Not just a disappointment but a drudge, a bore, commanding no fascination. Tedium. Probably a lost cause. This was not just the reaction of the preview audience. The makers of the picture knew they had heard the turkey's gobble.

Cooper, they thought, was really pretty good—nice things from him for a change, too bad it was going to be wasted. The girl—what's her name? Grace Kelly?—was just dreadful. She had what someone called definitive inexperience. Maybe in a few years she'd amount to a little more because she did have a certain something; but she wasn't ready. The Mexican girl, the one who had been the marshal's mistress—now there was a performance! At least it might help her get other parts.

What happens next must here be presented fairly, for there is disagreement among the creative hands of *High Noon* just what did happen, in terms of who ordered the changes, and who suggested which specific modifications. There is the Kramer version and the Zinnemann version, and to a lesser extent the Foreman version, and the irony is that the confusion over who turned *High Noon* into a miracle picture, and how, had the effect of estranging them, personally and creatively.

There is no Gary Cooper version. He simply smiled his smile and became the foremost beneficiary of the miracle. On one point, though, everyone agreed: such credit as applied to any individual should be shared with Elmo Williams.

Elmo Williams was the editor. Editors are the invisible men and women of the movie-making magic. They do not work on the set, but alone. No viewer really sees what it is that they have done. Great editing can become great directing in the mind's eye; and absence of good editing can damage if not destroy good direction, even good performances. *High Noon* was edited into a classic. It is a consensus classic: there is a school of film criticism whose least favorite well-known film *High Noon* seems to be. Its detractors are few but they are highly vocal and often highly literate. It is also highly feasible that one reason *High Noon* is despised by proponents of the *auteur* theory is that it seems effectively to demolish the theory. The *auteur* theory is that the director is the author, the creator of the film. By any deductive logic, however, Elmo Williams became the author of a picture that was produced by Kramer, directed by Zinnemann, and scripted by Carl Foreman from a story by John W. Cunningham called "The Tin Star."

Many who have seen *High Noon* once or many times might contend that its author is Gary Cooper.

After the disastrous preview, they got to talking about some things that might be done for the salvage attempt. The picture had no tension and it dragged. There was probably a lot that could be cut out, and a good place to start would be to cut out a lot of Grace Kelly. Another suggestion was that the tension could be heightened, or at least introduced, if there were a more conscious striving toward something they were calling "real time": *High Noon* was a concentrated story, everything occurring within the same day, actually within a part of the same day; and what might the effect be if it were all made to appear to be just happening minute by minute, second by second?

There seems to be disagreement over whether they had already shot all of the clocks or whether they had even shot any; or if perhaps they made some new shots of *the* clock, showing the progression of time. Anyway, Elmo Williams inserted quick glimpses of the clock, clock after clock after clock, throughout the picture. *High Noon* is a film you may set your watch by, except don't try it; the movie does fudge a bit, but it creates the illusion, the definite feel of real time.

The editor left a lot of Grace Kelly on the cutting room floor and tried to retain whatever the certain something was that she had in the scenes that weren't cut. Other machinations of editing were accomplished, and it began to appear that they were getting hold of some tension. Then another thought: Dimitri Tiomkin's score was helping things, it was in the right dramatic mood; but suppose there were a theme song, which could be delivered in the voice-over method, with a lyric content that suggested the marshal's dilemma. So Tiomkin devised a simple, Western-style melody and Ned Washington set words to it. Then Tex Ritter, that most mournful of all the cowboy balladeers, was hired to sing "Do Not Forsake Me, Oh My Darlin'."

And one more thing. Someone in mentioning the tentative effectiveness of Gary Cooper's performance had remarked about how ravaged his face appeared in certain scenes, and that he looked *really* worried about those outlaws. Were there any more worried looks in the out-takes?

Such shots existed by the score. The most unfortunate thing about *High Noon* during its shooting schedule was that Gary Cooper was in wretched health, often in considerable pain from his stomach ulcers. He had no business being in the picture in his condition, but he was making a game show of it and they respected him for that—so no one wanted to suggest he pull out, although in the early days of shooting some were wishing *he* would suggest it. Later on, of course, it was too late. But Stanley Kramer made what everyone knew was a logical point. If they lost Gary Cooper, they really had no picture. What they must count on was the movie audience's devotion to Cooper, their immediate recognition of him, their stored knowledge of his character, of everything he had represented in pictures.

In preparing the first cut, they had consciously eliminated many shots of Cooper obviously weary, sometimes clearly grimacing in pain. Even his walk appeared to be impaired, said to relate to an old hip injury that had recently flared up. The grimaces, the weary moist eyes, the painful walk—all of these things were put back in.

And Gary Cooper became a two-time Oscar winner.

The *High Noon* people had new hope when it was released with no special fanfare in April of 1952. But they were anything but certain, and the potential audience seemed anything but intrigued. From the ads and posters, from all that was available about it, it did not look like *The Plainsman* or even *The Westerner*; it looked a little like *Distant Drums*, more like *Dallas*.

What it really was, was *The Virginian*.

Cunningham's original story, or perhaps Foreman's treatment of it, could have been a conscious copy of Owen Wister's classic. The Virginian knows Trampas aims to kill him. The schoolmarm Molly Wood, his intended bride, has been urging the Virginian to lay down his guns, to get out of town, to be peaceful so she can marry him. But there is something about honor or cowardice and doing what's right that rules the Virginian's conscience, out there in Medicine Bow. And out there in Hadleyville, Marshal Will Kane knows that his Amy wants him to run away from his tormenters rather than risk a fight that is almost sure to kill him, but Will has a thing about duty. At the end of *The Virginian*, Molly Wood is clutching her vindicated young hero, who has killed Trampas; and at the end of *High Noon*, the bride Amy clings to Will after they have routed Frank Miller and his slimy companions.

High Noon opened to better reviews than anyone would have expected. Business was slow at first, then pretty good, and quite good, and started to build on a better curve, and just kept building. Its reputation has followed a similar curve over more than a quarter-century, and is building still.

High Noon did not win the 1952 Academy Award as best picture. It was no sure thing that it should have; a strong case could be made for John Ford's *The Quiet Man*, which also didn't win. The Academy voters, in one of their more sentimental gestures, decided to give the Oscar at long last to the aged Cecil B. De Mille for his penultimate directed film, the rather tacky circus spectacle of *The Greatest Show on Earth*. The secret of *High Noon* had gotten around, however, and the Academy honored Elmo Williams and his associate Harry Gerstad for the editing. Dimitri Tiomkin not only won for musical scoring, but took the best song award for the ballad that proved so strategic to the picture's mood, its success, and its everlasting fame.

The De Mille Oscar was controversial. Gary Cooper's award as best actor, equally sentimental, was universally applauded. It should be noted, too, that the New York Film Critics cited *High Noon* as the year's best picture, Fred Zinnemann as best director, and Gary Cooper as best actor.

The word "comeback" was seldom mentioned. So vivid, so immediate was his return to the major rank, so clearly did he belong there, that it was quickly forgotten he had ever been away. *High Noon* delivered him from a drought of pictures less deserving of him. It also sustained him through some subsequent ones not of a high order, until he had a respectable flurry toward the end. It didn't matter, really, if he ever made another movie, or even made only poor ones. It was his moment, and he had been solemnized.

The Springfield Rifle, his other film released in 1952, was standard minor Warner. *Return to Paradise,* the Michener piece, was an inert South Sea pastoral that was partially redeemed by Cooper's sheer pleasantness. That was a 1953 release, as was the first of the three he shot in Mexico, *Blowing Wild.* It also had a popular theme song, but was a lurid melodrama about some oil drillers that somehow worked—the kind of picture that could be enjoyable without having to be good. In an era of diminishing stars, there were veterans who even with tawdry subjects could show what real stardom truly is. They were Gary Cooper, Barbara Stanwyck, and Anthony Quinn. They were in Mexico making the picture when both Cooper and Quinn became Oscar winners— Cooper for *High Noon,* Quinn for his supporting role in *Viva Zapata.* Cooper's second Oscar was accepted for him at the Hollywood ceremony by John Wayne.

Making *Blowing Wild,* Cooper and Stanwyck almost got carried away. For a choking scene, Barbara warned him not to fake it: "I want my eyes to pop and the veins of my neck to swell. You've really got to choke me." She kept at Cooper until they both were seething. Cooper said, "The director yelled 'action' and I throttled. Her veins swelled, her mouth contorted. The director yelled 'Cut' and she slumped. It was two days before Barbara could talk, and three days before I could stop worrying."

The *Blowing Wild* director having the benefit of such brazen professionalism was Hugo Fregonese, an Argentinian who had a lackluster career but briefly was an intimate of Cooper's, and who actually had Cooper signed to play Don Quixote in a film, with J. Carrol Naish as Sancho Panza. Cooper had long been enamored of the knight of woeful countenance; and at the very least, such a project would have been interesting.

Cooper worked for the last time with his great friend and very likely his favorite director Henry Hathaway, but *Garden of Evil* was their least meritorious collaboration—a 1954 release, shot in Mexico and thoroughly predictable: Cooper was good, Richard Widmark was evil, and Susan Hayward was tempestuous. His other 1954 release was really great fun: *Vera Cruz*, now a cult film, a lively Mexican Western directed by Robert Aldrich. Good-guy Cooper and bad-guy Burt Lancaster were fellow adventurers. Cooper was an effective contrast, but it was Lancaster's picture. The actor so often rebuked for teeth-gnashing found a fine opportunity to do it all so it seemed just right. *Vera Cruz* was a triumph of sorts purely for its players' attitudes.

The cumulative experience of his Mexican-made films could have prompted Cooper to ask himself if making movies truly was easier than punching cattle. He was injured by dynamite explosions during all three projects, seriously in *Vera Cruz* when he was badly cut by blasted fragments from a bridge.

He had said long ago that he would make no more biographical films, but in 1955 he made *The Court-Martial of Billy Mitchell*. It was a poor Otto Preminger entry; even Billy Mitchell's widow expressed disappointment in Cooper's performance. No doubt the story appealed to Cooper on political grounds and Billy Mitchell may have been a hero to him: the general who accused the government of neglecting military needs. Cooper went on Ed Sullivan's TV show to promote the Mitchell film and home viewers were quite disappointed; David Shipman has referred to Cooper's "rather effeminate mannerisms in his TV interviews."

Then 1956 brought a rather wonderful picture—a fine one for Cooper, and he was fine in it. *Friendly Persuasion* was Jessamyn West's story of a Quaker family as the Civil War approached them. Cooper defined wonderful relationships with both his wife (beautifully played by Dorothy McGuire) and son (the new, brilliant Anthony Perkins). It was typical of the high polish and integrity that had come to be expected of a film directed by William Wyler. During the filming Cooper became quite sponsorial toward Anthony Perkins, giving him special help in preparing their scenes, and generally touting him as a rising actor in Hollywood. That was when Perkins was dating Maria Cooper. Later when the young actor was no longer seeing his daughter, Cooper was passing the word that Perkins was a callow boy who had plenty to learn.

Then there was Billy Wilder, with whom William Wyler is often confused at least nominally. Wyler's 1957 romantic comedy was called *Love in the Afternoon* and was a financial disappointment after receiving reviews that were also less favorable than might have been anticipated. It was a May–December romance between Cooper and the enchanting Audrey Hepburn. It also brought Maurice Chevalier back to U.S. screens after more than two decades, although *Love in the Afternoon* was filmed in Paris. Cooper's account was controversially received. Cary Grant had been sought for the role of the aging roué who is finally seduced by innocent charm. Some said Cooper was miscast; many imagined Grant and envisioned a better and funnier picture. Yet Cooper was essentially reprising his old role in *Bluebeard's Eighth Wife* almost two decades earlier and doing it better. At the very least, it was a performance with a star's authority. In the end, Cooper was taking roles Grant refused. Once it had often been the other way around.

Ten North Frederick, one of his two 1958 credits, was another big one, but a consensus failure. It had high gloss but Cooper was miscast. Spencer Tracy was set to play the politically ambitious Joe Chapin of John O'Hara's novel and would have been the better choice, but withdrew in poor health. There were weak performances by some inexperienced young players, while the well-seasoned Geraldine Fitzgerald outacted everyone in sight as Cooper's bitchy wife. Cooper was perhaps the most reasonable substitute in a role for which Tracy could not be adequately replaced; while not even Tracy, surely the greatest actor of the American screen, could have replaced Gary Cooper in *High Noon.*

Cooper got back in the saddle for *Man of the West,* which could also serve as a title for a Gary Cooper biography. Rated only a minor entry in 1958 and given scant attention, it is now well regarded by scholar-critics: standard Cooper, well framed by Anthony Mann's authoritative direction. *The Hanging Tree,* another Western, was also immeasurably better than the string he did for Warner before *High Noon.* It was set in Cooper's native Montana and could suggest the notorious tree that once stood outside of Helena. That was the first of three pictures showcasing Cooper in 1959. It also starred Maria Schell and Karl Malden—an odd combination all around.

The overt theme of Robert Rossen's pretentious *They Came to Cordura* was the nature of cowardice, with Cooper giving one of his most anguished and least heroic portrayals, at least until the climax. Rita Hayworth, Van Heflin, and some other well-known players were employed with varying results. An uncomfortable aspect of the film was that besides looking old, Cooper was looking so poorly, and actually filming against medical advice. *The Wreck of the Mary Deare* was a serviceable commodity film teaming Cooper with Charlton Heston, who in his wonderful *An Actor's Journal* notes that he sensed very early that it would be Cooper's picture but he didn't mind, because of all that the Cooper pictures and Cooper himself had meant to Heston, even as a child.

But Stanley Kauffmann minded in *New Republic:* "It is just painful to see a dignified man of almost sixty being dragged a hundred yards on his face by a runaway railroad handcar; socking and being socked; or diving in a frogman's suit and getting into an underwater fight. No matter that doubles are employed for the really rough stuff and that clever cutting helps the rest; it's the idea of the thing that's upsetting . . . Gentlemen of Hollywood, he is not a two-fisted brawler any more. It hurts—it actually hurts the viewer's joints and back—to see him pretend to his earlier admirable activity. In *They Came to Cordura* he had to do such feats again. They the producers are using this gentleman shamelessly . . . it ought to stop."

In 1960, for the first time since his first year in Hollywood, there were no new Gary Cooper pictures. There would be one in 1961—*The Naked Edge*, his last film.

The Coopers' new home was a stunningly modern accomplishment by architect Quincy Jones. Rocky was her own decorator. The house was a festival of button-pushing gimmicks, and many conveniences were designed with an eye to the comfort of a tall man. Cooper had a private bedroom with an unusually high basin in its adjoining bathroom, so he wouldn't have to lean.

In companionable Holmby Hills their neighbors included Bing and Kathryn Crosby, Judy Garland and Sid Luft, Claudette Colbert and her husband Joel Pressman, who was sometimes Cooper's physician, and also Humphrey Bogart and Lauren Bacall during Bogie's remaining time.

It was a great life for the Coopers when they were there, but that wasn't always. They spent an ever larger portion of their time in the East, where they rated as superior entertainers. Their beautiful-people friends included Aristotle Onassis, Jock Whitney, Lord Mountbatten, the Duke and Duchess of Windsor, the Duke and Duchess of Marlborough . . .

They were equally at home in Holmby Hills or Southampton, but no less so in Antibes, or in London or Paris or Rome.

Cooper, though, became more the homebody, paying more attention to bridge and backgammon . . . and to his dogs. He truly believed they were his best friends; they never disappointed him. He would recall his dogs through the years—the fine old boxer Arno; a white Scotty named Peter; and the comical mutt Biff Grimes, named for the Cooper character in *One Sunday Afternoon*. Now his taste had turned to Great Danes, Doberman pinschers, Sealyhams.

After decades of incomparable thinness, he began to have weight problems. He put on about fifteen pounds, pushing over 190, which on his frame was still slender. He knew the sedentary life was changing him—that, and getting plain old, even before his time.

The Coopers were always traveling somewhere. He said the reason he was selected the best-dressed screen actor in 1956 was because every time they went somewhere and he was in a fancy outfit, his picture got in the papers. They had a long European vacation and were in Moscow as official representatives for *Marty*, the first American film to play in the Soviet Union in many years. In Rome they were received in private audience with Pope Pius XII. It was also something of a vacation just to be in Paris for the long shooting schedule of *Love in the Afternoon*.

In 1958 he received embarrassing publicity over a face lift. He denied it, saying it was an operation to remove a cyst from his jaw. People thought his face looked quite different and the main opinion was that the operation just hadn't worked. He also had to have "another damned ulcer job and now I have to watch what I eat." The old hip injury now plagued him permanently, and finally he had to give up skiing.

He never talked of retiring, but when he wasn't actually filming he talked like a retired actor, with valedictory inflection; and talked *a lot*. He called the new school of actors "a bunch of goofballs" and could be caustic about "the method" advanced by the Actors Studio. Yet Lee Strasberg told everyone that Gary Cooper was a natural method actor, he just didn't know it. Cooper at least admired Marlon Brando's work, and even became a producing partner with his father, Marlon Brando, Sr.

He grew ever prouder of daughter Maria, who blossomed into a talented artist. Pablo Picasso said, "I like Maria's work, and I understand it." Cooper said, "That's fine, and I like your work, but I *don't* understand it." Great art abounded in the Holmby Hills abode, and Picasso was represented there, having exchanged a painting for a cowboy hat procured for him by Cooper. The dominant school on the Cooper walls nevertheless was French Impressionism, and an original Renoir was Cooper's personal pride.

He said all the business about his never saying anything was "a piece of crap" and he became gloriously vocal about his profession.

"You've got to have a fire under you, and when you're beginning, you've got one all the time. After you get established, you have to create your own fire, and it's never easy."

He said he'd never had an urge to be an actor on the stage— "Not since I was at Grinnell. When I gave them the story that I was trying to do a Broadway play, I must have been desperate for publicity. I figured it didn't matter what I said. I learned very early that nothing you ever say gets quoted verbatim by the press. So for many years I may have clammed up, but I guess I've reached an age where I don't particularly care. Anyway, I talk."

He talked about how Hollywood had changed: "I put in a call to Clark Gable to tell him about some deer I'd heard were running loose up in the Canadian Rockies. I was told he was on location . . . in Hong Kong. I called Robert Taylor. He was on location, too, in Italy, unless he had finished there and gone to England. Jimmy Stewart was in Africa. In the old days a company that went as far away as Texas was thought to be forsaking civilization for good. Today these countries are just part of the Hollywood scene and it's as Shakespeare said, all the world's a stage."

Citing *Mr. Deeds Goes to Town* as his personal revelation, he said, "Naturalness is hard to talk about, but I guess it boils down to this: You find out what people expect of your type of character and then you give them what they want. That way an actor never seems unnatural or affected no matter what role he plays."

Spencer Tracy knew that if he lived or died, *Guess Who's*

Coming to Dinner would be his last film. Fredric March's Harry Hope in *The Iceman Cometh* was a conscious valedictory. But Gary Cooper did not foresee *The Naked Edge*, which he produced with Marlon Brando's father, as his final film. Later he took Jerry Wald to meet Ernest Hemingway and they discussed *Adventures of a Young Man*, which Wald eventually made with Paul Newman.

Cooper filmed *The Naked Edge* with Deborah Kerr in London's Elstree Studios in the fall of 1960. His contract provided him with a bulletproof Rolls-Royce throughout the filming. Interviewed on the set, he said, "People hang on after they should quit, because the urge to act stays with you. Sometimes in the middle of a scene I find myself saying a piece of dialogue from fifteen years ago. I've thought of retiring lots of times, but then I think I would just go nuts, and probably spend all of my time searching for a really great Western script."

Toward the end, he fell in love with a Western script he hoped to do: *Ride the High Country*. He wanted to talk the new Sam Peckinpah into letting him do it with Joel McCrea; they'd never made a picture together. In 1962 it made a fine film with McCrea in the role Cooper had envisioned as his own, and old Paramount stablemate Randolph Scott in what he'd seen as the McCrea part.

Tracy and March were among the finest actors Cooper knew or knew of, but he said that actor or not, Gable was the greatest star —and Stanwyck, he thought, among the women. But the best actor he had worked with? It would surprise some people.

"I've been with some good ones, but maybe the best was Franchot Tone. I made two pictures with him and he stole both of them. Something went wrong with how he was handled; or who knows, maybe it was Joan Crawford. But he had everything— great at comedy and also at serious stuff if given the chance. Now *Lives of a Bengal Lancer* is one hell of a picture, but you could take me right out of it and it would still be one. But it couldn't be much without Tone."

His best friend? He was asked often, and playfully gave many answers, sometimes whimsically. More than once he cited that "new Gary Cooper of 1936," Mr. James Stewart.

Stewart was one of those who believed the last years of Cooper's life were his happiest. He thought it was only then that Cooper realized how much he loved his wife.

Another friend, a woman, said, "It's really strange. I've been a friend to both of them, but in the early time of their marriage, I didn't believe Coop and Rocky were right for each other. They didn't bring out the best in one another. Eventually I think they had to split to get reoriented. It was really a fine thing that Pat Neal accomplished, although she didn't know it. After they got back together Coop and Rocky found they had much to share. It was nice to see that while he had always adored Maria, in the end he adored Rocky just as much."

In 1959, Gary Cooper became a convert to Roman Catholicism.

He was in wretched health. Before he made *The Naked Edge* he had to bow out of a project he much wanted to do: *The Sundowners*, a fine picture that would have been an eloquent swan song for him. Early in 1960 he underwent a prostatectomy; later part of his colon was removed. He said, "I know some people don't get embarrassed about these things, but I get embarrassed."

His cancer had been diagnosed in the spring of 1960. Doctors did not tell him of his condition. Within a five-week period he underwent two major abdominal operations, and he may have suspected. But he went to England to film *The Naked Edge*, and returned later in the year to prepare a Project 20 documentary entitled *The Real West*. As host-narrator, he made his TV debut as something other than a star promoting a new film. He was passionately devoted to the project for its theme. He said few people ever saw any semblance of the *real* West, even in movies; he'd reached a point where he could recognize the same bushes in almost every Western picture.

On January 8, 1961, he was given a testimonial dinner in Hollywood by the Friars Club. It was a coincidental thing; his mortal illness was not generally suspected. The aged Carl Sandburg was there, calling Cooper "a tradition while he's living, something of a clean sport, the lack of a phony." The lovely Audrey Hepburn read a lovely poem called "What is a Gary Cooper?" Cooper accepted the cheers of his filmland friends and said, "The only achievement I am proud of is the friends I have made in this community . . . and if you asked me if I'm the luckiest guy in the world, all I can say is 'yup.' "

He didn't look well that night, but most observers thought he looked marvelous anyway. Then he began growing weaker, his condition worsening by days at an accelerated rate. Toward the end of February, Rocky informed him of his condition. She believed it would relieve the torture of uncertainty, and she believed he was strong enough inwardly for what lay ahead.

Cooper had grieved over Clark Gable's coronary death only a few months earlier; they were the same age. Now he was concerned about Ernest Hemingway, who was also knowingly fighting cancer. Hemingway telephoned and asked, "Which one of us will make it into the corral first?"

He continued to weaken, but entering April Cooper still hoped to attend the Academy Awards ceremony on April 17. Then it began to appear doubtful. He attended mass on Easter Sunday but it was his last outing. Scheduled to appear as a guest on Dinah Shore's variety show on April 9, he excused himself regretfully only a few days earlier. By then the Oscar ceremony was out of the question for him.

He watched the telecast, and knew that James Stewart's emotional collapse had tipped the world on his terminal status. Within the next few days, newspapers throughout the country began rushing serialized mini-biographies into print, side-barred by eloquent obituary tributes to a person still living.

Over the last slow days his visitors were carefully chosen: Sam and Frances Goldwyn; Fred MacMurray and June Haver; James and Gloria Stewart, Jack Benny, Danny Kaye . . .

Queen Elizabeth II sent a telegram of friendship, believed the first such gesture by any British ruler to a film star. President Kennedy telephoned and got the ashen Cooper laughing and smiling. Rocky said he never lost his humor.

At the Academy ceremony, someone asked how long Coop might last. Bing Crosby said, "He may see his sixtieth birthday."

Cooper was sixty on May 7. Six days later he lapsed into a coma and died the following afternoon, on May 14.

The Pope sent a message of condolence to Mrs. Gary Cooper. The Requiem Mass was held in the Roman Catholic Church of the Good Shepherd in Beverly Hills. Cooper's pallbearers were Jack Benny, William Goetz, Henry Hathaway, Charles Feldman, James Stewart, and Jerry Wald. With Veronica and Maria Cooper were the actor's eighty-eight-year old mother, Alice Cooper, and Arthur, his older brother. Burial was in the Grotto of Our Lady of Lourdes at Holy Cross Cemetery.

Ernest Hemingway never got Cooper's .22 Hornet but outlived his friend by a few weeks before taking his own life.

Alice Cooper said shortly after her son's burial that Gary had remained an Episcopalian at heart. She was certain that he had converted to Catholicism only as a favor to his wife. When the elder Mrs. Cooper died soon afterward, Rocky had the actor's remains transferred to a cemetery in Southampton. That rankled many citizens of the film community who believed Cooper should always be among them. But Rocky said, "Gary loved Southampton. He would want to be here."

The vivacious Maria Cooper married the renowned young concert pianist Byron Janis. She also continued to grow as a painter and has had several one-woman shows, most recently in New York in May of 1979.

Rocky also remarried, becoming Mrs. John Converse. Her husband is the plastic surgeon who performed a facial operation on Gary Cooper in 1958. The Converses have resided primarily in Southampton.

The Naked Edge, Cooper's last film, was released posthumously in June of 1961 and was not a success. Reminiscent of Alfred Hitchcock's *Suspicion*, it cast Cooper as a man believed to be up to villainy until very near the end of the picture.

He had remained a leading star throughout his final decade, when his annual income from acting never dipped below half a million dollars. He was believed to have earned more than nine million dollars as a screen actor.

He returned to the list of top ten money-making stars in 1952, the year of *High Noon*. In 1953 he occupied the number-one position. He stayed among the top ten box-office draws four more years.

John Wayne called him "the world's best man." He was universally beloved at the time of his death, and revered in Hollywood even by persons who had been opposed to him during the filmland's destructive intramural political melodrama.

A close friend said Cooper was loved because he was not deep, but had a simple view of life and the world. He never wanted to see anyone get hurt.

He had a few detractors still. One of them said, "The best of Gary Cooper is on film."

It is an estimable legacy. If motion pictures survive, he is an immortal.

It was long supposed that the peak of his career was marked by his biographical portrayals of Sergeant Alvin York and baseball's Lou Gehrig. That was the undoubted peak during his lifetime; and for many years after his resurgence in *High Noon* that phenomenal Western was thought of as an impressive comeback but not a comparable peak.

Historically, though, *High Noon* is vesting, and may now be seen as his high point.

Then he stood illuminated, the most mythological figure in world cinema—more so, in fact, than Chaplin's Little Fellow: the strong, uncorruptible, innately good man, the last American hero, the embodiment of all that had been wonderful in the human love affair with motion pictures.

GARY COOPER'S FILMS

(There can be no authoritative accounting of the innumerable motion pictures in which Gary Cooper appeared as an extra, usually but not always on horseback, in 1925 and 1926. This filmography lists every feature-length theatrical film in which he played an actual role, including guest appearances as himself, billed or unbilled.)

1.
TRICKS
(J. Charles Davis)
November 1925. Produced by J. Charles Davis; directed by Bruce Mitchell; original story by Mary C. Bruning (Marilyn Mills). 55 minutes.
With Marilyn Mills, Frank Glendon, Beverly (horse), Star (horse), Gladys Moore, William Lowery, Myles McCarthy, Henry Valeur; Gary Cooper unbilled.

2.
THREE PALS
(J. Charles Davis)
January 1926. Produced by J. Charles Davis; directed by Wilbur McGaugh; original story by L. V. Jefferson. 54 minutes.
With Marilyn Mills, Star (horse), Joseph Swickard, Martin Turner, James McLaughlin, William Emerson; Gary Cooper unbilled.

308 ☆ GARY COOPER'S FILMS

3.
A SIX-SHOOTIN' ROMANCE
(Universal)
March 1926. Produced by Orval Breese; directed by Clifford Smith and Alvin J. Neitz; scenario by Alvin J. Neitz, from the story "Dashing" by Ruth Mitchell. 53 minutes.
With Jack Hoxie, Olive Hasbrouck, William Steele, Carmen Phillips, Claude Corbett, Virginia Brandford; Gary Cooper unbilled.

4.
WATCH YOUR WIFE
(Universal)
April 1926. Produced by Victor Nordlinger; directed by Sven Gade; scenario by Sven Gade and Charles Whittaker, from a novel by Gosta Segercrantz. 71 minutes.
With Pat O'Malley, Virginia Valli, Albert Conti, Nat Carr, Nora Hayden, Helen Lee Worthing, Edward Humphrey, Aggie Herring; Gary Cooper unbilled.

5.
THE WINNING OF BARBARA WORTH
(Goldwyn/United Artists)
October 1926. Produced by Samuel Goldwyn; directed by Henry King; scenario by Frances Marion, adapted from a novel by Harold Bell Wright. 94 minutes.
With Ronald Colman, Vilma Banky, Charles Lane, Paul McAllister, Gary Cooper, Clyde Cook, E. J. Ratcliffe, Sam Blum, Erwin Connelly.

6.
IT
(Paramount)
February 1927. Produced by B. P. Schulberg; directed by Clarence Badger; scenario by Hope Loring and Louis D. Lighton, adapted from a novel by Elinor Glyn. 70 minutes.
With Clara Bow, Antonio Moreno, Julia Swayne Gordon, William Austin, Jacqueline Gadsdon, Priscilla Bonner, Gary Cooper, Rose Tapley.

7.
ARIZONA BOUND
(Paramount)
March 1927. Produced by Lloyd Sheldon; directed by John Waters; scenario by John Stone and Paul Gangelin with titles by Alfred Hustwick, from Marion Jackson's adaptation of a story by Richard Allen Gates. 53 minutes.
With Gary Cooper, El Brendel, Betty Jewel, Jack Dougherty, Christian Frank, Joe Butterworth, Charles Crockett, Flash (horse).

8.
CHILDREN OF DIVORCE
(Paramount)
April 1927. Produced by B. P. Schulberg and Louis D. Lighton; directed by Frank Lloyd; screenplay by Hope Loring and Louis D. Lighton, adapted from a novel by Owen Johnson. 74 minutes.
With Clara Bow, Esther Ralston, Gary Cooper, Norman Trevor, Einar Hanson, Julia Swayne Gordon, Hedda Hopper, Edward Martindel, Albert Gran.

9.
THE LAST OUTLAW
(Paramount)
June 1927. Produced by Lloyd Sheldon; directed by Arthur Rosson; screenplay by John Stone and J. Walter Ruben, from a story by Richard Allen Gates. 67 minutes.
With Gary Cooper, Betty Jewel, Jack Luden, Herbert Prior, Billy Butts, Jim Corey, Oswald Strickland, Flash (horse).

10.
NEVADA
(Paramount)
August 1927. Produced by Lloyd Sheldon; directed by John Waters; screenplay by John Stone, John Conway, and L. G. Rigby, from a novel by Zane Grey. 65 minutes.
With Gary Cooper, Thelma Todd, William Powell, Philip Strange, Ernie Adams, Christian Frank, Guy Oliver, Ivan Christy, Oswald Strickland.

11.
WINGS
(Paramount)
October 1927. Produced by Lucien Hubbard; directed by William Wellman; screenplay by Hope Loring, Louis D. Lighton, and Julian Johnson, from an original screen story by John Monk Saunders. 133 minutes.
With Clara Bow, Charles (Buddy) Rogers, Richard Arlen, Jobyna Ralston, Gary Cooper, El Brendel, Gunboat Smith, Henry B. Walthall, Arlette Marchal, Hedda Hopper, Julia Swayne Gordon, Nigel de Brulier, George Irving.

12.
BEAU SABREUR
(Paramount)
January 1928. Produced by B. P. Schulberg; directed by John Waters; screenplay by Tom Geraghty with titles by Julian Johnson, adapted from a novel by Percival Christopher Wren. 72 minutes.

With Gary Cooper, Evelyn Brent, William Powell, Noah Beery, Roscoe Karns, Frank Reicher, Joan Standing, Mitchell Lewis, Raoul Paoli.

13.
DOOMSDAY
(Paramount)
February 1928. Produced by Hector Turnbull; directed by Archie Mayo; screenplay by Donald W. Lee and Julian Johnson, from Doris Anderson's story adaptation of a novel by Warwick Deeping. 62 minutes.
With Florence Vidor, Gary Cooper, Lawrence Grant, James Renhult, Irene Falsetti, Charles A. Stevenson, Edgar Ormsby.

14.
LEGION OF THE CONDEMNED
(Paramount)
March 1928. Produced and directed by William Wellman; original screenplay by John Monk Saunders, Jean De Limur, and George Marion, Jr. 82 minutes.
With Gary Cooper, Fay Wray, Barry Norton, Lane Chandler, E. H. Calvert, Francis McDonald, Albert Conti, Voya George, Charlot Bird.

15.
HALF A BRIDE
(Paramount)
June 1928. Produced by Louis D. Lighton; directed by Gregory LaCava; screenplay by Doris Anderson and Percy Heath with titles by Julian Johnson, from the story "White Hands" by Arthur Stringer. 67 minutes.
With Esther Ralston, Gary Cooper, Freeman Wood, William Worthington, Mary Doran, Ray Gallagher, Irene Falsetti, Guy Oliver.

16.
THE FIRST KISS
(Paramount)
August 1928. Produced by B. P. Schulberg and Rowland V. Lee; directed by Rowland V. Lee; screenplay by John Farrow and Tom Reed, from the story "Four Brothers" by Tristam Tupper. 66 minutes.
With Fay Wray, Gary Cooper, Leslie Fenton, Monroe Owsley, Lane Chandler, Paul Fix, Malcolm Williams, Esther Robertson.

17.
LILAC TIME
(First National)
October 1928. Produced by John McCormick; directed by George

Fitzmaurice; screenplay by Carey Wilson and George Marion, Jr., from Willis Goldbeck's adaptation of a play by Jane Cowl and Jane Murfin. 101 minutes.
With Colleen Moore, Gary Cooper, Burr McIntosh, Kathryn McGuire, George Cooper, Cleve Moore, Eugenie Besserer, Edward Dillon, Harlan Hilton.

18.
SHOPWORN ANGEL
(Paramount)
January 1929. Produced by Hector Turnbull; directed by Richard Wallace; screenplay by Howard Estabrook, Albert Shelby LeVino, and Tom Miranda, from the story "Private Pettigrew's Girl" by Dana Burnet. 79 minutes.
With Nancy Carroll, Gary Cooper, Paul Lukas, Roscoe Karns, Pauline Garon, James Renhult, Finley Warmsden. (Gary Cooper's talkie debut)

19.
WOLF SONG
(Paramount)
April 1929. Produced by Lucien Hubbard; directed by Victor Fleming; screenplay by John Farrow, Julian Johnson, and Keene Thompson, from a novel by Harvey Fergusson. 69 minutes.
With Gary Cooper, Lupe Velez, Louis Wolheim, Russ Columbo, Ann Brody, Constantine Romanoff, Michael Vavitsch, Augustina Lopez, George Rigas.

20.
BETRAYAL
(Paramount)
May 1929. Produced and directed by Lewis Milestone; screenplay by Hans Kraly, Julian Johnson, and Victor Schertzinger, from an original story by Nicholas Soussanin. 70 minutes.
With Emil Jannings, Esther Ralston, Gary Cooper, Jada Weller, Douglas Haig, Bodil Rosing. (Gary Cooper's last silent film)

21.
THE VIRGINIAN
(Paramount)
November 1929. Produced by B. P. Schulberg and Louis D. Lighton; directed by Victor Fleming; screenplay by Edward E. Paramore, Jr., and Howard Estabrook, from the novel by Owen Wister. 90 minutes.
With Gary Cooper, Walter Huston, Richard Arlen, Mary Brian, Helen Ware, Chester Conklin, Eugene Pallette, E. H. Calvert, Tex Young, Victor Potel. (Gary Cooper's first all-talking film)

22.
SEVEN DAYS LEAVE
(Paramount)
January 1930. Produced and directed by Richard Wallace; screenplay by John Farrow and Dan Totheroh, from Sir James M. Barrie's play *The Old Lady Shows Her Medals*. 81 minutes.
With Gary Cooper, Beryl Mercer, Daisy Belmore, Nora Cecil, Arthur Hoyt, Tempe Piggott, Arthur Metcalfe.

23.
ONLY THE BRAVE
(Paramount)
March 1930. Produced by Hector Turnbull; directed by Frank Tuttle; screenplay by Edward E. Paramore, Jr., and Agnes Brand Leahy, from an original story by Keene Thompson. 67 minutes.
With Gary Cooper, Mary Brian, Phillips Holmes, Morgan Farley, James Neill, Guy Oliver, E. H. Calvert, Virginia Bruce, Freeman Wood.

24.
PARAMOUNT ON PARADE
(Paramount)
April 1930. Produced by Elsie Janis and B. P. Schulberg, with eleven directors and many uncredited writers. 102 minutes.
With Richard Arlen, Jean Arthur, George Bancroft, Clara Bow, Evelyn Brent, Mary Brian, Clive Brook, Nancy Carroll, Ruth Chatterton, Maurice Chevalier, Gary Cooper, Leon Errol, Stuart Erwin, Kay Francis, Skeets Gallagher, Harry Green, Mitzi Green, James Hall, Phillips Holmes, Helen Kane, Dennis King, Fredric March, Nino Martini, Jack Oakie, Warner Oland, William Powell, Charles (Buddy) Rogers, Lillian Roth, Stanley Smith, Fay Wray.

25.
THE TEXAN
(Paramount)
May 1930. Produced by Hector Turnbull; directed by John Cromwell; screenplay by Oliver H. P. Garrett, from the story *The Double-Dyed Deceiver* by O. Henry. 73 minutes.
With Gary Cooper, Fay Wray, Emma Dunn, Solidad Jimenez, Oscar Apfel, Donald Reed, James Marcus, Cesar Vanoni.

26.
A MAN FROM WYOMING
(Paramount)
July 1930. Produced by Lloyd Sheldon; directed by Rowland V. Lee; screenplay by John V. A. Weaver and Albert Shelby LeVino, from an

original screen story by Joseph Moncure March and Lew Lipston. 71 minutes.

With Gary Cooper, June Collyer, Regis Toomey, John Alois, Morgan Farley, E. H. Calvert, Mary Foy, Emile Chautard, Ed Deering, Ben Hall.

27.

THE SPOILERS

(Paramount)

September 1930. Produced by B. P. Schulberg and Lloyd Sheldon; directed by Edwin Carewe; screenplay by Agnes Brand Leahy, from Bartlett Cormack's adaptation of the novel by Rex Beach. 85 minutes.

With Gary Cooper, Kay Johnson, Betty Compson, William (Stage) Boyd, Harry Green, Slim Summerville, James Kirkwood, Jack Trent, Lloyd Ingraham, Edward Coxen, Edward Hearn, Hal David.

28.

MOROCCO

(Paramount)

November 1930. Produced by Louis D. Lighton; directed by Josef von Sternberg; screenplay by Jules Furthman, from Benno Vigny's play *Amy Jolly*. 91 minutes.

With Gary Cooper, Marlene Dietrich, Adolphe Menjou, Ullrich Haupt, Francis McDonald, Juliette Compton, Eve Southern, Albert Conti.

29.

FIGHTING CARAVANS

(Paramount)

January 1931. Produced by Otto Brower; directed by David Burton; screenplay by Agnes Brand Leahy, from a novel by Zane Grey. 67 minutes.

With Gary Cooper, Lili Damita, Ernest Torrence, William Austin, John Sainpolis, Paul Fix, Walter Hoskins.

30.

CITY STREETS

(Paramount)

April 1931. Produced by B. P. Schulberg and Rouben Mamoulian; directed by Rouben Mamoulian; screenplay by Oliver H. P. Garrett and Max Marcin, from Dashiell Hammett's adaptation of the story "Ladies of the Mob" by Ernest Booth. 86 minutes.

With Gary Cooper, Sylvia Sidney, Paul Lukas, Guy Kibbee, Wynne Gibson, Stanley Fields, William (Stage) Boyd, Paul Porcasi.

31.
I TAKE THIS WOMAN
(Paramount)
June 1931. Produced by Hector Turnbull; directed by Marion Gering; screenplay by Vincent Lawrence, from the novel *Lost Ecstasy* by Mary Roberts Rinehart. 74 minutes.
With Gary Cooper, Carole Lombard, Lester Vail, Helen Ware, Clara Blandick, Charles Trowbridge, Berton Churchill, Hepzibah Wooten.

32.
HIS WOMAN
(Paramount)
December 1931. Produced by Albert Kaufman; directed by Edward Sloman; screenplay by Edwin Justus Mayer and Elliott Clawson, from the novel *Sal of Singapore* by Dale Collins. 70 minutes.
With Gary Cooper, Claudette Colbert, Harry Davenport, Averill Harris, Douglas Dumbrille, Charles Trowbridge, Howard Phillips.

33.
THE DEVIL AND THE DEEP
(Paramount)
August 1932. Produced by Emanuel Cohen; directed by Marion Gering; screenplay by Benn W. Levey and Harry Hervey, from Hervey's original screen story. 74 minutes.
With Tallulah Bankhead, Gary Cooper, Charles Laughton, Cary Grant, Paul Porcasi, Juliette Compton, Henry Kolker, Dorothy Christy, Arthur Hoyt.

34.
MAKE ME A STAR
(Paramount)
September 1932. Produced by Lloyd Sheldon; directed by William Beaudine; screenplay by Sam Mintz, Walter DeLeon, and Arthur Kober, from the novel *Merton of the Movies* by Harry Leon Wilson. 70 minutes.
With Stuart Erwin, Joan Blondell, Zasu Pitts, Ben Turpin, Ruth Donnelly, Sam Hardy, Helen Jerome Eddy. (Gary Cooper appeared as himself in a scene depicting Paramount's Hollywood studio)

35.
IF I HAD A MILLION
(Paramount)
November 1932. Produced by Benjamin Glazer and Louis D. Lighton; directed by James Cruze, H. Bruce Humberstone, Ernst Lubitsch, Norman Z. McLeod, Stephen Roberts, William A Seiter, and Norman Taurog; screenplay by eighteen writers, from an original story by Robert D. Andrews. 89 minutes.

With Gary Cooper, W. C. Fields, Charles Laughton, George Raft, Jack Oakie, Charlie Ruggles, Mary Boland, May Robson, Richard Bennett, Alison Skipworth, Gene Raymond, Wynne Gibson, Roscoe Karns, Frances Dee, Lucien Littlefield, Joyce Compton, Gail Patrick.

36.
A FAREWELL TO ARMS
(Paramount)
December 1932. Produced and directed by Frank Borzage; screenplay by Oliver H. P. Garrett and Benjamin Glazer, from the novel by Ernest Hemingway. 80 minutes.
With Helen Hayes, Gary Cooper, Adolphe Menjou, Mary Philips, Henry Armetta, Blanche Frederici, Jack LaRue, Tom Ricketts, George Humphrey, Mary Forbes.

37.
TODAY WE LIVE
(Metro-Goldwyn-Mayer)
March 1933. Produced and directed by Howard Hawks; screenplay by William Faulkner, Dwight Taylor, and Edith Fitzgerald, from Faulkner's story, "Turnabout." 111 minutes.
With Joan Crawford, Gary Cooper, Franchot Tone, Robert Young, Roscoe Karns, Louise Closser Hale, Rollo Lloyd, Hilda Vaughn.

38.
ONE SUNDAY AFTERNOON
(Paramount)
July 1933. Produced by Louis D. Lighton; directed by Stephen Roberts; screenplay by Grover Jones and William Slavens McNutt, from the play by James Hagan. 71 minutes.
With Gary Cooper, Fay Wray, Neil Hamilton, Frances Fuller, Roscoe Karns, Jane Darwell, Sam Hardy, Clara Blandick, Jack Clifford.

39.
ALICE IN WONDERLAND
(Paramount)
December 1933. Produced by Louis D. Lighton; directed by Norman Z. McLeod; screenplay by Joseph L. Mankiewicz and William Cameron Menzies, from *Alice's Adventures in Wonderland* and *Through the Looking-Glass* by Lewis Carroll. 90 minutes.
With Charlotte Henry, Richard Arlen, Gary Cooper, Leon Errol, Louise Fazenda, W. C. Fields, Skeets Gallagher, Cary Grant, Sterling Holloway, Edward Everett Horton, Roscoe Karns, Mae Marsh, Polly Moran, Jack Oakie, Edna May Oliver, May Robson, Charlie Ruggles, Alison Skipworth, Ned Sparks.

40.
DESIGN FOR LIVING
(Paramount)
December 1933. Produced and directed by Ernst Lubitsch; screenplay
by Ben Hecht, from the play by Noel Coward. 88 minutes.
With Fredric March, Gary Cooper, Miriam Hopkins, Edward Everett
Horton, Franklin Pangborn, Isabel Jewell, Bosil Roding.

41.
OPERATOR 13
(Metro-Goldwyn-Mayer)
June 1934. Produced by Lucien Hubbard; directed by Richard
Boleslavsky; screenplay by Harvey Thew, Zelda Sears, and Eve
Greene, from a novel by Robert W. Chambers. 86 minutes.
With Marion Davies, Gary Cooper, Ned Sparks, Mae Clarke, Hattie
McDaniel, Douglas Dumbrille, Jean Parker, Ted Healy, Henry B.
Walthall, Sidney Toler, Katherine Alexander.

42.
NOW AND FOREVER
(Paramount)
October 1934. Produced by Louis D. Lighton; directed by Henry
Hathaway; screenplay by Vincent Lawrence and Sylvia Thalberg, from
an original screen story by Jack Kirkland and Melville Baker. 81 min-
utes.
With Gary Cooper, Carole Lombard, Shirley Temple, Sir Guy Stand-
ing, Charlotte Granville, Gilbert Emery, Henry Kolker, Jameson
Thomas.

43.
LIVES OF A BENGAL LANCER
(Paramount)
January 1935. Produced by Louis D. Lighton; directed by Henry
Hathaway; screenplay by Waldemar Young, John L. Balderston,
William Slavens McNutt, Grover Jones, and Achmed Abdulah, from
the novel by Francis Yeats-Brown. 116 minutes.
With Gary Cooper, Franchot Tone, Richard Cromwell, Sir Guy
Standing, C. Aubrey Smith, Douglas Dumbrille, Akim Tamiroff,
Kathleen Burke, Monte Blue, J. Carrol Naish, Mischa Auer, Colin
Tapley, Jameson Thomas.

44.
THE WEDDING NIGHT
(Goldwyn/United Artists)
March 1935. Produced by Samuel Goldwyn; directed by King Vidor;
screenplay by Edith Fitzgerald, from a story by Edwin H. Knopf. 83
minutes.

With Gary Cooper, Anna Sten, Ralph Bellamy, Helen Vinson, Sig Rumann, Esther Dale, Leonid Snegoff, Hilda Vaughn, Walter Brennan.

45.
PETER IBBETSON
(Paramount)
October 1935. Produced by Louis D. Lighton; directed by Henry Hathaway; screenplay by Vincent Lawrence, Waldemar Young, Constance Collier, John Meehan, and Edwin Justus Mayer, from the novel by George du Maurier, as dramatized by John Nathaniel Raphael. 89 minutes.
With Gary Cooper, Ann Harding, John Halliday, Ida Lupino, Dickie Moore, Virginia Weidler, Douglas Dumbrille, Donald Meek, Doris Lloyd.

46.
DESIRE
(Paramount)
February 1936. Produced by Ernst Lubitsch; directed by Frank Borzage; screenplay by Edwin Justus Mayer, Waldemar Young, and Samuel Hoffenstein, from a play by Hans Szekeley and R. A. Stemmle. 89 minutes.
With Marlene Dietrich, Gary Cooper, John Halliday, William Frawley, Ernest Cossart, Akim Tamiroff, Alan Mowbray, Zeffie Tilbury.

47.
MR. DEEDS GOES TO TOWN
(Columbia)
March 1936. Produced and directed by Frank Capra; screenplay by Robert Riskin, from the novel *Opera Hat* by Clarence Budington Kelland. 115 minutes.
With Gary Cooper, Jean Arthur, George Bancroft, Lionel Stander, Douglas Dumbrille, Raymond Walburn, H. B. Warner, Warren Hymer, Ruth Donnelly, Emma Dunn, Arthur Hoyt, Mayo Methot, Walter Catlett, Dennis O'Keefe.

48.
HOLLYWOOD BOULEVARD
(Paramount)
July 1936. Produced by A. M. Botsford; directed by Robert Florey; screenplay by Marguerite Roberts, from a story by Faith Thomas. 68 minutes.
With John Halliday, Robert Cummings, Marsha Hunt, Esther Ralston, Irving Bacon, C. Henry Gordon, Esther Dale, Frieda Inescourt, Alice Day. (Gary Cooper was among many former and present screen stars appearing as themselves)

49.
THE GENERAL DIED AT DAWN
(Paramount)
September 1936. Produced by William LeBaron; directed by Lewis Milestone; screenplay by Clifford Odets, from a story by Charles G. Booth. 97 minutes.
With Gary Cooper, Madeleine Carroll, Akim Tamiroff, Dudley Digges, Porter Hall, William Frawley, J. M. Kerrigan, Philip Ahn, Leonid Kinskey.

50.
THE PLAINSMAN
(Paramount)
December 1936. Produced and directed by Cecil B. De Mille; screenplay by Waldemar Young, Harold Lamb, and Lynn Riggs, from Frank Wilstach's biography *Wild Bill Hickok*. 114 minutes.
With Gary Cooper, Jean Arthur, Charles Bickford, James Ellison, Helen Burgess, Porter Hall, Victor Varconi, John Miljan, Johnny Downs.

51.
SOULS AT SEA
(Paramount)
August 1937. Produced and directed by Henry Hathaway; screenplay by Grover Jones and Dale Van Every, from a story by Ted Lesser. 94 minutes.
With Gary Cooper, George Raft, Frances Dee, Henry Wilcoxon, Harry Carey, Olympe Bradna, Robert Cummings, Virginia Weidler, Joseph Schildkraut, Porter Hall, George Zucco, Lucien Littlefield, Paul Fix, Tully Marshall.

52.
THE ADVENTURES OF MARCO POLO
(Goldwyn/United Artists)
February 1938. Produced by Samuel Goldwyn; directed by Archie Mayo; screenplay by Robert E. Sherwood, from a story by Norman A. Pogson. 101 minutes.
With Gary Cooper, Sigrid Gurie, Basil Rathbone, Binnie Barnes, George Barbier, Ernest Truex, H. B. Warner, Robert Grieg, Henry Kolker, Lana Turner, Ferdinand Gottschalk, Hale Hamilton, Stanley Fields, Harold Huber.

53.
BLUEBEARD'S EIGHTH WIFE
(Paramount)
March 1938. Produced and directed by Ernst Lubitsch; screenplay by Charles Brackett and Billy Wilder, from a story by Alfred Savoir. 80 minutes.

With Claudette Colbert, Gary Cooper, Edward Everett Horton, David Niven, Elizabeth Patterson, Herman Bing, Franklin Pangborn, Warren Hymer.

54.
THE COWBOY AND THE LADY
(Goldwyn/United Artists)
November 1938. Produced by Samuel Goldwyn; directed by H. C. Potter; screenplay by S. N. Behrman and Sonya Levien, from a story by Leo McCarey and Frank R. Adams. 91 minutes.
With Gary Cooper, Merle Oberon, Patsy Kelly, Walter Brennan, Fuzzy Knight, Mabel Todd, Henry Kolker, Harry Davenport, Emma Dunn, Walter Walker.

55.
BEAU GESTE
(Paramount)
September 1939. Produced and directed by William Wellman; screenplay by Robert Carson, from the novel by Percival Christopher Wren. 119 minutes.
With Gary Cooper, Ray Milland, Robert Preston, Brian Donlevy, Albert Dekker, Broderick Crawford, J. Carrol Naish, Susan Hayward, Heather Thatcher, James Stephenson, Charles Barton, Donald O'Connor, Billy Cook, Martin Spellman, David Holt, Harvey Stephens, G. P. Huntley, Jr., James Burke.

56.
THE REAL GLORY
(Goldwyn/United Artists)
October 1939. Produced by Samuel Goldwyn; directed by Henry Hathaway; screenplay by Jo Swerling and Robert Presnell, from the novel by Charles L. Clifford. 96 minutes.
With Gary Cooper, Andrea Leeds, David Niven, Broderick Crawford, Reginald Owen, Kay Johnson, Russell Hicks, Vladimir Sokoloff, Tetsu Komal.

57.
THE WESTERNER
(Goldwyn/United Artists)
September 1940. Produced by Samuel Goldwyn; directed by William Wyler; screenplay by Jo Swerling and Niven Busch, from a story by Stuart N. Lake. 98 minutes.
With Gary Cooper, Walter Brennan, Doris Davenport, Fred Stone, Chill Wills, Dana Andrews, Paul Hurst, Lilian Bond, Charles Halton, Trevor Bardette, Forrest Tucker, Charles Coleman, Tom Tyler.

58.
NORTHWEST MOUNTED POLICE
(Paramount)
November 1940. Produced and directed by Cecil B. De Mille; screenplay by Alan LeMay, Jesse Lasky, Jr., and C. Gardner Sullivan, from the book *Royal Canadian Mounted Police* by R. C. Fetherston-Haugh. 126 minutes.
With Gary Cooper, Madeleine Carroll, Paulette Goddard, Robert Preston, Preston Foster, George Bancroft, Akim Tamiroff, Lynne Overman, Walter Hampden, Regis Toomey, Lon Chaney, Jr., Montagu Love, George E. Stone.

59.
MEET JOHN DOE
(Warner Brothers)
March 1941. Produced and directed by Frank Capra; screenplay by Robert Riskin, from a story by Richard Connell and Robert Presnell. 122 minutes.
With Gary Cooper, Barbara Stanwyck, Edward Arnold, Walter Brennan, Spring Byington, James Gleason, Rod La Rocque, Irving Bacon, Regis Toomey, Warren Hymer, Sterling Holloway, Pierre Watkin.

60.
SERGEANT YORK
(Warner Brothers)
September 1941. Produced by Jesse L. Lasky and Hal B. Wallis; directed by Howard Hawks; screenplay by Aben Finkel, Harry Chandlee, Howard Koch, and John Huston, adapted from *The War Diary of Sergeant York* by Sam K. Cowan, *Sergeant York and His People*, also by Cowan, and *Sergeant York—Last of the Long Hunters* by Thomas Skeyhill. 134 minutes.
With Gary Cooper, Walter Brennan, Joan Leslie, George Tobias, Stanley Ridges, Margaret Wycherly, Ward Bond, Noah Beery, Jr., June Lockhart, Dickie Moore, Clem Bevans, Howard da Silva, Charles Trowbridge, David Bruce, Harvey Stephens, Joseph Sawyer.

61.
BALL OF FIRE
(Goldwyn/RKO)
December 1941. Produced by Samuel Goldwyn; directed by Howard Hawks; screenplay by Charles Brackett and Billy Wilder, from the story "From A to Z" by Billy Wilder and Thomas Monroe. 110 minutes.
With Gary Cooper, Barbara Stanwyck, Oscar Homolka, Dana Andrews, Dan Duryea, Henry Travers, S. Z. Sakall, Tully Marshall, Leonid Kinskey, Richard Haydn, Aubrey Mather, Allen Jenkins, Gene Krupa and his orchestra.

62.
THE PRIDE OF THE YANKEES
(Goldwyn/RKO)
July 1942. Produced by Samuel Goldwyn; directed by Sam Wood; screenplay by Jo Swerling and Herman J. Mankiewicz, from a story by Paul Gallico. 128 minutes.
With Gary Cooper, Teresa Wright, Babe Ruth, Walter Brennan, Dan Duryea, Elsa Janssen, Ludwig Stossel, Virginia Gilmore, Bill Dickey, Ernie Adams, Robert Meusel, Mark Koenig, Bill Stern, Addison Richards, Hardie Albright, Pierre Watkin, Veloz and Yolanda, Ray Noble and his orchestra.

63.
FOR WHOM THE BELL TOLLS
(Paramount)
July 1943. Produced and directed by Sam Wood; screenplay by Dudley Nichols, from the novel by Ernest Hemingway. 171 minutes.
With Gary Cooper, Ingrid Bergman, Akim Tamiroff, Arturo de Cordova, Joseph Calleia, Katina Paxinou, Vladimir Sokoloff, Fortunio Bonanova, Eric Feldary, Victor Varconi, George Coulouris, Frank Puglia, Alexander Granach, Leonid Snegoff, Leo Bulgakov.

64.
THE STORY OF DR. WASSELL
(Paramount)
April 1944. Produced and directed by Cecil B. De Mille; screenplay by Alan LeMay and Charles Bennett (original). 142 minutes.
With Gary Cooper, Laraine Day, Dennis O'Keefe, Signe Hasso, Paul Kelly, Carol Thurston, Carl Esmond, Philip Ahn, Elliot Reid, Stanley Ridges, Barbara Britton, Renny McEvoy.

65.
CASANOVA BROWN
(International/RKO)
August 1944. Produced by Nunnally Johnson; directed by Sam Wood; screenplay by Nunnally Johnson, based on the play *The Little Accident* by Floyd Dell and Thomas Mitchell. 94 minutes.
With Gary Cooper, Teresa Wright, Frank Morgan, Anita Louise, Patricia Collinge, Jill Esmond, Edmond Breon, Mary Treen, Emory Parnell, Isobel Elsom, Halliwell Hobbes.

66.
ALONG CAME JONES
(International/RKO)
June 1945. Produced by Gary Cooper; directed by Sam Wood; screenplay by Nunnally Johnson, from a story by Alan LeMay. 91 minutes.

With Gary Cooper, Loretta Young, William Demarest, Dan Duryea, Frank Sully, Russell Simpson, Arthur Loft, Willard Robertson, Chris-Pin Martin.

67.
SARATOGA TRUNK
(Warner Brothers)
November 1945. Produced by Hal B. Wallis; directed by Sam Wood; screenplay by Casey Robinson, from the novel by Edna Ferber. 136 minutes.
With Gary Cooper, Ingrid Bergman, Flora Robson, Jerry Austin, John Warburton, Florence Bates, Curt Bois, John Abbott, Ethel Griffies, Marla Shelton, Helen Freeman.

68.
CLOAK AND DAGGER
(Warner Brothers)
September 1946. Produced by Milton Sperling; directed by Fritz Lang; screenplay by Albert Maltz and Ring Lardner, Jr., from a story by John Larkin, Corey Ford, and Boris Ingster. 106 minutes.
With Gary Cooper, Lilli Palmer, Robert Alda, Vladimir Sokoloff, J. Edward Bromberg, Ludwig Stossel, Marc Lawrence, Dan Seymour, Marjorie Hosehle.

69.
VARIETY GIRL
(Paramount)
August 1947. Produced by Daniel Dare; directed by George Marshall; original story and screenplay by Edmund Hartmann, Frank Tashlin, Robert Welch, and Monte Brice. 84 minutes.
With Bing Crosby, Bob Hope, Gary Cooper, Ray Milland, Alan Ladd, Barbara Stanwyck, Paulette Goddard, Dorothy Lamour, Veronica Lake, Sonny Tufts, Joan Caulfield, William Holden, Lizabeth Scott, Burt Lancaster, Gail Russell, Diana Lynn, Robert Preston, William Bendix, Sterling Hayden, Barry Fitzgerald, Mary Hatcher, Olga San Juan, DeForest Kelley, William Demarest, Frank Faylen.

70.
UNCONQUERED
(Paramount)
September 1947. Produced and directed by Cecil B. De Mille; screenplay by Charles Bennett, Frederick M. Frank, and Jesse Lasky, Jr., from the novel by Neil H. Swanson. 147 minutes.
With Gary Cooper, Paulette Goddard, Howard da Silva, Boris Karloff, Cecil Kellaway, Ward Bond, Katherine De Mille, Henry Wilcoxon, Virginia Grey, C. Aubrey Smith, Victor Varconi, Porter Hall, Mike Mazurki, Marc Lawrence, Nan Sunderland, Alan Napier, Gavin Muir, Jane Nigh.

71.
GOOD SAM
(RKO)
July 1948. Produced and directed by Leo McCarey; screenplay by Ken Englund, from a story by Leo McCarey and John Klorer. 111 minutes.
With Gary Cooper, Ann Sheridan, Ray Collins, Joan Lorring, Edmund Lowe, Clinton Sundberg, Louise Beavers, Minerva Urecal, Irving Bacon, Ruth Roman, Todd Karns, Dick Ross.

72.
THE FOUNTAINHEAD
(Warner Brothers)
June 1949. Produced by Henry Blanke; directed by King Vidor; screenplay by Ayn Rand, from her novel. 114 minutes.
With Gary Cooper, Patricia Neal, Raymond Massey, Kent Smith, Henry Hull, Robert Douglas, Ray Collins, Moroni Olsen, Jerome Cowan, Paul Harvey.

73.
TASK FORCE
(Warner Brothers)
September 1949. Produced by Jerry Wald; directed by Delmer Daves; screenplay by Delmer Daves, from his story. 116 minutes.
With Gary Cooper, Jane Wyatt, Wayne Morris, Walter Brennan, Julie London, Bruce Bennett, Jack Holt, John Ridgely, Art Baker, Moroni Olsen.

74.
BRIGHT LEAF
(Warner Brothers)
June 1950. Produced by Henry Blanke; directed by Michael Curtiz; screenplay by Ranald MacDougall, from the novel by Robert Wilder. 110 minutes.
With Gary Cooper, Lauren Bacall, Patricia Neal, Jack Carson, Donald Crisp, Gladys George, Elizabeth Patterson, Jeff Corey, Taylor Holmes, Thurston Hall, Jimmy Griffith.

75.
DALLAS
(Warner Brothers)
November 1950. Produced by Anthony Veiller; directed by Stuart Heisler; original story and screenplay by John Twist. 94 minutes.
With Gary Cooper, Ruth Roman, Steve Cochran, Raymond Massey, Barbara Payton, Leif Erickson, Antonio Moreno, Jerome Cowan, Reed Hadley.

76.
YOU'RE IN THE NAVY NOW
(20th Century-Fox)
February 1951. Produced by Fred Kohlmar; directed by Henry Hatha-
way; screenplay by Richard Murphy, from a story by John W. Hazard.
93 minutes.
With Gary Cooper, Jane Greer, Millard Mitchell, Eddie Albert, Ray
Collins, Jack Webb, Richard Erdman, John McIntire, Harry Von
Zell, Harvey Lembeck, Ed Begley, Charles Bronson, Henry Slate, Jack
Warden. (originally released as *U.S.S. Teakettle*)

77.
IT'S A BIG COUNTRY
(Metro-Goldwyn-Mayer)
November 1951. Produced by Robert Sisk; directed by Charles Vidor,
Richard Thorpe, John Sturges, Don Hartman, Don Weis, Clarence
Brown, William Wellman; twelve writers. 89 minutes.
With Ethel Barrymore, Gary Cooper, Van Johnson, Gene Kelly,
Janet Leigh, Marjorie Main, Fredric March, George Murphy, William
Powell, James Whitmore, Keenan Wynn, Keefe Braselle, Nancy
Davis, S. Z. Sakall, Lewis Stone, Leon Ames, Bobby Hyatt, Sharon
McManus.

78.
STARLIFT
(Warner Brothers)
November 1951. Produced by Robert Arthur; directed by Roy Del
Ruth; screenplay by John Klorer and Karl Lamb, from Klorer's story.
103 minutes.
With Janice Rule, Dick Wesson, Don Hagerthy, Richard Webb,
Hayden Rorke, Howard St. John, Doris Day, Gordon MacRae, Vir-
ginia Mayo, Gene Nelson, Ruth Roman, James Cagney, Gary Cooper,
Virginia Gibson, Phil Harris, Frank Lovejoy, Lucille Norman, Louella
Parsons, Randolph Scott, Jane Wyman, Patrice Wymore.

79.
DISTANT DRUMS
(Warner Brothers)
December 1951. Produced by Milton Sperling; directed by Raoul
Walsh; screenplay by Niven Busch and Martin Rackin, from Busch's
story. 101 minutes.
With Gary Cooper, Mari Aldon, Richard Webb, Ray Teal, Arthur
Hunnicutt, Robert Barrat, Clancy Cooper.

80.
HIGH NOON
(Kramer/United Artists)
April 1952. Produced by Stanley Kramer; directed by Fred Zin-
nemann; screenplay by Carl Foreman, from the story "The Tin
Star" by John W. Cunningham. 85 minutes.
With Gary Cooper, Thomas Mitchell, Grace Kelly, Katy Jurado,
Lloyd Bridges, Otto Kruger, Lon Chaney, Jr., Harry Morgan, Ian Mac-
Donald, Eve McVeagh, Lee Van Cleef, Sheb Woolley.

81.
THE SPRINGFIELD RIFLE
(Warner Brothers)
September 1952. Produced by Louis F. Edelman; directed by Andre
de Toth; screenplay by Charles Marquis Warren and Frank Davis,
from a story by Sloan Nibley. 93 minutes.
With Gary Cooper, Phyllis Thaxter, David Brian, Paul Kelly, Philip
Carey, Lon Chaney, Jr., Alan Hale, Jr., James Millican, Gwinn
Williams, Richard Hale.

82.
RETURN TO PARADISE
(United Artists)
July 1953. Produced by Theron Warth; directed by Mark Robson;
screenplay by Charles Kaufman, from the book by James Michener.
100 minutes.
With Gary Cooper, Roberta Haynes, Barry Jones, John Hudson,
Vala, Moira McDonald, Ezra Williams.

83.
BLOWING WILD
(Warner Brothers)
October 1953. Produced by Milton Sperling; directed by Hugo
Fregonese; original story and screenplay by Philip Yordan. 90 min-
utes.
With Gary Cooper, Barbara Stanwyck, Anthony Quinn, Ruth
Roman, Ward Bond, Ian MacDonald, Richard Karlan, Juan Garcia.

84.
GARDEN OF EVIL
(20th Century-Fox)
July 1954. Produced by Charles Brackett; directed by Henry Hatha-
way; screenplay by Frank Fenton, from a story by Fred Freiberger and
William Tunberg. 100 minutes.
With Gary Cooper, Susan Hayward, Richard Widmark, Hugh Mar-

326 ☆ GARY COOPER'S FILMS

lowe, Cameron Mitchell, Rita Moreno, Victor Manuel Mendoza, Fernando Wagner.

85.
VERA CRUZ
(United Artists)
December 1954. Produced by James Hill; directed by Robert Aldrich; screenplay by James R. Webb and Roland Kibbee, from a story by Borden Chase. 94 minutes.
With Gary Cooper, Burt Lancaster, Denise Darcel, Cesar Romero, Sarita Montiel, George Macready, Ernest Borgnine, Morris Ankrum, Jack Elam.

86.
THE COURT-MARTIAL OF BILLY MITCHELL
(Warner Brothers)
December 1955. Produced by Milton Sperling; directed by Otto Preminger; original story and screenplay by Milton Sperling and Emmet Lavery. 100 minutes.
With Gary Cooper, Charles Bickford, Ralph Bellamy, Rod Steiger, Elizabeth Montgomery, Fred Clark, James Daly, Jack Lord, Peter Graves, Darren McGavin, Charles Dingle, Will Wright.

87.
FRIENDLY PERSUASION
(Allied Artists)
October 1956. Produced and directed by William Wyler; screenplay by Jessamyn West, from her novel. 140 minutes.
With Gary Cooper, Dorothy McGuire, Anthony Perkins, Marjorie Main, Richard Eyer, Phyllis Love, Robert Middleton, Mark Richman, Walter Catlett, Richard Hale, Mary Carr.

88.
LOVE IN THE AFTERNOON
(Allied Artists)
June 1957. Produced and directed by Billy Wilder. Screenplay by Billy Wilder and I. A. L. Diamond, from a story by Claude Anet. 129 minutes.
With Gary Cooper, Audrey Hepburn, Maurice Chevalier, John McGiver, Van Doude, Lise Bourdin, Olga Valery.

89.
TEN NORTH FREDERICK
(20th Century-Fox)
May 1958. Produced by Charles Brackett; directed by Philip Dunne; screenplay by Philip Dunne, from the novel by John O'Hara. 103 minutes.

With Gary Cooper, Diane Varsi, Suzy Parker, Geraldine Fitzgerald, Tom Tully, Ray Stricklyn, Philip Ober, Stuart Whitman, John Emery, Linda Watkins.

90.
MAN OF THE WEST
(Mirisch/United Artists)
October 1958. Produced by Walter Mirisch; directed by Anthony Mann; screenplay by Reginald Rose, from a story by Will C. Brown. 100 minutes.
With Gary Cooper, Lee J. Cobb, Julie London, Arthur O'Connell, Jack Lord, John Dehner, Royal Dano, Robert Wilke, Jack Williams, Frank Ferguson.

91.
THE HANGING TREE
(Warner Brothers)
January 1959. Produced and directed by Delmer Daves; screenplay by Halsted Welles and Delmer Daves, from the novel by Dorothy Johnson. 106 minutes.
With Gary Cooper, Maria Schell, Karl Malden, George C. Scott, Ben Piazza, Virginia Gregg, Karl Swenson, John Dierkes.

92.
ALIAS JESSE JAMES
(United Artists)
March 1959. Produced by Bob Hope; directed by Norman Z. McLeod; screenplay by William Bowers and Daniel D. Beauchamp, from an original story by Robert St. Aubrey and Bert Lawrence. 92 minutes.
With Bob Hope, Rhonda Fleming, Wendell Corey, Ward Bond, Iron Eyes Cody. (Gary Cooper was among several unbilled players appearing in a comical shoot-out climax)

93.
THEY CAME TO CORDURA
(Columbia)
September 1959. Produced and directed by Robert Rossen; screenplay by Ivan Moffatt and Robert Rossen, from the novel by Glendon Swarthout. 123 minutes.
With Gary Cooper, Rita Hayworth, Van Heflin, Tab Hunter, Richard Conte, Michael Callan, Dick York.

94.
THE WRECK OF THE MARY DEARE
(Metro-Goldwyn-Mayer)
November 1959. Produced by Julian Blaustein; directed by Michael

Anderson; screenplay by Eric Ambler, from the novel by Hammond Innes. 105 minutes.

With Gary Cooper, Charlton Heston, Michael Redgrave, Alexander Knox, Emlyn Williams, Virginia McKenna, Richard Harris, Cecil Parker.

95.
THE NAKED EDGE
(United Artists)
June 1961. Produced by Marlon Brando, Sr., George Glass, and Walter Seltzer; directed by Michael Anderson; screenplay by Joseph Stefano, from the novel *First Train to Babylon* by Max Ehrlich. 100 minutes.

With Gary Cooper, Deborah Kerr, Eric Portman, Diane Cilento, Hermione Gingold, Michael Wilding.

INDEX